REAL-TIME SOFTWARE

ROBERT L. GLASS

ASSISTANT PROFESSOR
SOFTWARE ENGINEERING PROGRAM
SEATTLE UNIVERSITY

PRENTICE-HALL, INC., Englewood Cliffs, New Jersey 07632

Library of Congress Cataloging in Publication Data
Main entry under title:

Real-time software.

Collection of papers on computer software.
Bibliography: p. 0000
Includes index.
1. Real-time data processing. 2. Electronic digital
computers--Programming I Glass, Robert L., 1932–
QA76.54.R425 1984   001.64¾2   83–3156
ISBN 0-13-767103-2

Editorial/production supervision
  and interior design: Karen Skrable
Manufacturing buyer: Anthony Caruso
Cover design: Edsal Enterprises

ROBERT L. GLASS books published by Prentice-Hall:

SOFTWARE RELIABILITY GUIDEBOOK
SOFTWARE MAINTENANCE GUIDEBOOK
MODERN PROGRAMMING PRACTICES: A REPORT FROM INDUSTRY

©1983 by Robert L. Glass

Printed in the United States of America

10 9 8 7 6 5 4 3 2 1

ISBN 0-13-767103-2

PRENTICE-HALL INTERNATIONAL, INC., LONDON
PRENTICE-HALL OF AUSTRALIA PTY. LIMITED, SYDNEY
EDITORA PRENTICE-HALL DO BRASIL, LTDA., RIO DE JANEIRO
PRENTICE-HALL CANADA INC., TORONTO
PRENTICE-HALL OF INDIA PRIVATE LIMITED, NEW DELHI
PRENTICE-HALL OF JAPAN, INC., TOKYO
PRENTICE-HALL OF SOUTHEAST ASIA PTE. LTD., SINGAPORE
WHITEHALL BOOKS LIMITED, WELLINGTON, NEW ZEALAND

CONTENTS

4

REAL–TIME TOOLS AND EXECUTIVES 249

5

REAL–TIME LANGUAGES 349

6

CONCLUSIONS 449

7

BIBLIOGRAPHY 451

PREFACE
AND
SUMMARY

Let me take you into the Software Development Laboratory of a major real-time project.

Over there, in the dominant position in the room, is the "target" minicomputer. It is the computer that will eventually control the real-time system for which the software is being built. (The software, of course, will control the computer that controls the system.) The computer is called a target because it does not contain the facilities—the compilers, assemblers, and linkers—that generate its code. A "host" computer, which is located in another part of the building and is a mainframe, does that job.

Sitting in front of the target computer console are a couple of programmers. They look perplexed. The computer's lights are not blinking; it has apparently stopped, and the programmers are attempting to determine why. From their conversation, we can tell that one programmer is trying to debug an application program; the other programmer evidently wrote the executive program that is being used by the application program, and there seems to be a difference of opinion as to who is to blame for the halt.

All around the programmers, occupying the rest of the Software Development Laboratory, are pieces of equipment. The equipment is a replication of devices that will actually talk to the target computer when the completed system is working. Cables connect the equipment to the target.

The Laboratory is not pretty. Instead, it looks . . . well . . . functional. Only when the Laboratory is transformed, after checkout, into an operational system will prettiness become a goal.

This is the world of the real-time software engineer. *Engineer* is the key word here, where it implies a certain amount of pragmatism and a dogged determination to make things work.

The programmers at the console have long since removed their coats, and one wearing a tie has loosened it. A stale cup of coffee sits on a table near the console, and an ashtray full of half-smoked cigarettes is next to it.

Here, in the Software Development Lab, is the grittiness—and the joy— of creating software for a real-time system.

The programmers are beginning to raise their voices. Apparently the fault is a complex one, and it really isn't obvious whose code went wrong. Let's tip-toe out.

The scene we have just viewed is characteristic of an environment that is becoming more and more pervasive. In this book we will see how real-time systems and real-time software are becoming commonplace. Although they service an amazing diversity of applications, the development process and the overall structure of real-time systems are surprisingly similar. The Lab is one of those similarities, as are the engineering emphasis and the team approach of the programmers. They will resolve their problem in the next ten minutes and move on to another.

The purpose of this book is to explore the world of the real-time programmer. We may not see things quite as graphically as stepping into that Laboratory—but there are many intangibles in the real-time software world, and most of us find them at least as interesting as viewing and touching the Laboratory hardware.

This book has five main chapters. Chapter 1 gives us an overview of real-time software. We take a look at some examples of real-time systems, where the problems lie in these systems, and what real-time software is all about.

In chapter 2 we move on to applications of real-time software. This chapter illustrates just how pervasive the world of real-time software actually is and explores some of the techniques of creating that software.

Chapter 3 is the real "how-to" chapter. There we dissect the process of software construction into some constituent phases and analyze how to perform each one. We look at a mix of practice and theory, perhaps best symbolized by a paper on the generation of a requirements specification that details the application of still fluid theory to an actual real-time project. We will despair at some of the obsolete practices in the field—there is a paper on "patching," for example—and yet cheer for the amazing success of real-timers who get these complex systems to work. They do so with a reliability track record that looks better for software, says another paper, than for other disciplines.

In chapter 4 we deal with some specifics. There is a collection of tools that a real-timer needs, and chapter 4 discusses not only what those tools are but what they should be like. The executive is one of them, and the language processor is another. A hard look is taken at some key aspects of those and other tools.

Finally, in chapter 5, we talk about languages for real-time software. Here the book places a heavy emphasis on pragmatism; some theoretic language advances are discussed, but the bulk of the material deals with the background and use of the more (potentially) mainstream languages, including a paper on Ada.

Before we move on into the material we have introduced, we must perform a few housekeeping functions. Think of this as the initialization routine for your real-time software system—it may not be very interesting, but nothing that follows will work well without it!

First of all, this book is a collection of papers. The papers were written by several real-time software experts. The papers were chosen to cover what your editor believes are the most important areas of real-time software and have been grouped into a readable structure.

Second, although these papers are a mix of tutorial and experiential works, the emphasis here is on the experienced real-time software practitioner and what will be useful to him or her. Certainly if you have had no previous exposure to software at all, and perhaps if you have had no previous exposure to real-time software, a tutorial text such as *Introduction to Real-Time Software Design,* written by S. T. Allworth (1981), might be a better starting place. Topics such as the relative efficiency of compiler- and assembler-generated codes, which are covered later in this book, may have limited value to the novice but are of critical value to the veteran.

Finally, no technical book is complete without a definition of its subject-matter terminology. For this book that means defining the term *real-time software.* This can be a surprisingly difficult task—some authors announce the decision to provide a definition, then cleverly write several pages but never provide one! However, an initialization routine cannot vacillate. Here we go:

> *Real-time software is that software that controls a computer that controls a real-time system. A real-time system is one that provides services or control to an ongoing physical process.*

That done, let us proceed to the material at hand.

ACKNOWLEDGMENT AND DEDICATION

Real-time software is a "doing" more than a "hypothesizing" kind of business. Because of that, and because of the well-known reluctance of "doers" to write about what they have done, I owe a deep debt of gratitude to the authors of the papers that form the substance of this book. Those papers—and this book—are the creation of doers who cared enough to share what they have done.

This book is dedicated to all the "doers" of real-time software.

ROBERT L. GLASS

AN OVERVIEW OF REAL-TIME SOFTWARE

The digital computer is becoming ever more present in the daily lives of all of us. Computers allow our watches to play games as well as tell time, optimize the gas mileage of our latest-generation cars, and sequence our appliances. Soon we may even have computers controlling the heating and lighting patterns in our homes.

All these computing interactions—be they helpful or intrusive—are examples of real-time computing. The computer is controlling something which interacts with reality on a timeable basis. In fact, timing is the essence of the interaction. Our game-playing wristwatch must respond within a few seconds or we will shake it to see if it is still working. Our car's optimized carburetor had better snap to instant attention when we depress the gas pedal. An unresponsive-real-time system may be worse than no system at all.

The computer in a real-time system may not be too different from the computer in a nonreal-time system. What is *really* "real" in a real-time system is the software. Here, in the intangible recesses of the computer's memory, is where the input is ingested, the decisions made, and the output sent—all in whatever quick-as-a-wink timing the real-time system requires.

Efficiency is always a goal in computer software, but in real-time software efficiency reigns supreme. Real-time systems often use marginal computer hardware—a little small, a little slow—to cut the cost of the total system. In those circumstances the real-time software person has to shoehorn too much software into the too-small machine in such a way that the system interacts with its external reality acceptably fast.

However, it is not simply efficiency that differentiates real-time software from other software. The papers which follow give an in-depth analysis of what characterizes this subject.

These papers take the form of a James Martin sandwich—two papers by Martin describe (1) what kinds of systems make up the spectrum of real-time systems, and (2) what difficulties characterize real-time software. In between, as a solid, meaty filling for the sandwich, is a survey paper on process control (that is, real-time) software by Janos Gertler and Jan Sedlak.

The Martin papers are taken from his book *Programming Real-Time*

1

Systems. In 1965 this book was *the* authoritative work on real-time software. In a field where most information becomes obsolete in well under ten years, what is amazing is that Martin's material is still clearly written, accurate, and insightful by today's standards. Only his example applications begin to feel a little dated.

In contrast with Martin's light writing style is the extremely thorough work of Gertler and Sedlak. Dealing on a level ranging from methodology to standardization, these two Europeans (Gertler is from Hungary and Sedlak from Czechoslovakia) have carefully sculpted a master overview of a difficult subject.

1-1 THE RANGE OF REAL-TIME SYSTEMS*

JAMES MARTIN

The real-time systems that have been installed to date vary from very small single computers with relatively simple programs, to the largest and most expensive multicomputer systems in the world. . . .

Fortunately, not all real-time systems have the same problems, and therefore it is important that the reader maintain a sense of perspective. It would be quite wrong, for example, to associate all the problems of a multi-programmed airline reservation system with a small real-time savings bank application.

When discussing the complexity, and hence the problems, of these systems, six aspects of the subject may be considered:

1. *The complexity of the equipment.* How many computers are used? How many communication lines and terminals? How many random-access files, and do they operate in parallel? Is back-up or standby equipment used to give added reliability?

2. *The response time.* That is the elapsed time between a transaction entering the computer system and the completion of its processing or the sending of a message in reply.

3. *The average interarrival time.* The average time between the arrival at the computer of separate transactions ready for processing.

4. *The total number of instructions* in the real-time Application Programs. Nonreal-time or off-line programs have not been included in this count because they do not substantially affect the complexity or problems of the real-time system. Supervisory or Control Programs have not been included either. A person with no knowledge of these can still assess the application of data-processing programs.

5. *The complexity of individual Application Programs.* How complex would the program be for processing one message by itself? On some large and complex systems, certain individual Application Programs can be quite small and uncomplicated. At the other extreme, on some small systems, such as a computer for optimizing the performance of a petroleum plant or job shop, the individual Application Programs may be relatively complex.

*From James Martin, *Programming Real-Time Computer Systems,* © 1965, pp. 25–34. Reprinted by permission of Prentice-Hall, Inc., Englewood Cliffs, N.J.

6. *The complexity of the Supervisory Programs.* This is the Control, or Executive, Program which schedules the work, organizes input and output operations, and so on. On small systems it can be a fairly simple program and may involve only a small addition to the standard program packages provided by the computer manufacturers. On large and complex systems it can be a very sophisticated and intricate group of programs. . . . Its complexity is determined by:

(a) The complexity of the equipment.

(b) The degree of multiprogramming, that is, the simultaneous processing of transactions.

(c) The complexity of the priority structure. On some systems all transactions have the same priority, but on others there are differences in priorities between different messages or different functions.

1-1-1 THE COMPLEXITY OF THE EQUIPMENT

The simplest form of a real-time system might have one device, such as a typewriter, which can send a message to the computer. The computer interrupts its processing, handles the message, perhaps sends a reply, and then continues its processing. The computer may have a random-access file attached, and the typewriter may update or interrogate this. Slightly more complicated would be a system with several terminals or typewriters. These may be attached to a buffer or they may be all on one communication line (Figure 1-1-1). Only one

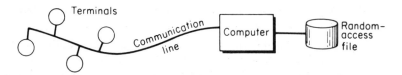

Figure 1-1-1 A system with one communication line.

terminal can send a message at one time. The next step up in complexity would be to have more than one communications line (Figure 1-1-2).

With two or more lines, message handling may or may not overlap in the computer. This depends upon the size and throughput of the system. Systems with a high throughput will process messages in parallel.

With some makes of equipment the communication line is able to go directly into the computer. The computer assembles the bits and characters from the line and compiles the messages under program control. With other systems the communication lines do not go into the computer but into a separate programmed *Multiplexor* or Line Control Computer. This is in effect a small special-purpose computer for controlling communication line input and

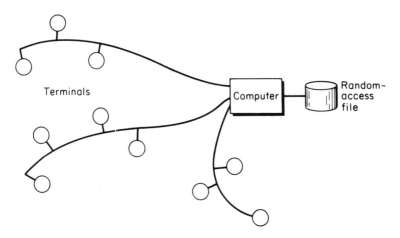

Figure 1-1-2   A system with several communication lines.

output. To it can be attached any general-purpose computer which reads data from it and sends data to it in the same way that it would to any input/output unit (Figure 1-1-3).

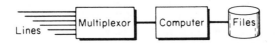

Figure 1-1-3   A system with a separate line control computer.

In some systems more than one computer has been used because one computer is not big enough or fast enough. In a two-computer system, one may handle the input and output to the Line Control device and files, while the other does the processing. A good reason for this could be that the processing computer is doing nonreal-time work, but is interrupted occasionally by the other which has assembled some real-time messages ready for processing (Figure 1-1-4).

Computer B in Figure 1-1-4 may be a much more powerful machine than A. Computer A may handle some simple real-time transactions itself, such as requests for interrogation of the files. When a transaction requires more complex processing it interrupts computer B. This prepares a reply for A to send and then continues its other work. Computer A may queue the messages so that it does not interrupt computer B very often. Computer B may have a program store on a disk file or drum so that it can load itself with the necessary real-time programs.

Because of the nature of the real-time work a very high degree of reliability may be needed in the system. This may be achieved by duplicating the components of the system. If one computer has a breakdown time of .2 percent, two

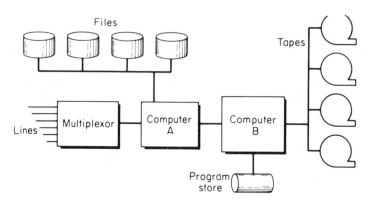

Figure 1-1-4 A multicomputer system.

similar machines backing each other up will have a breakdown time of approximately 0.04 percent. "Duplexing" in this manner increases the equipment complexity, especially if switchover on failure is to be automatic. A duplexed version of the system in Figure 1-1-3 is shown in Figure 1-1-5. Many systems of this type have been installed.

It will be seen here that if a Line Control Unit, computer, or file fails, the system can be switched so that the duplicate takes over.

The cost of this may not be as prohibitive as it seems at first sight if the standby computer can be doing other work while standing by. The complexity of the Supervisory Programs, however, is increased. Every time a file is updated, for example, it is necessary to update both files. If a file breaks down and is later returned to use, it must be quickly updated with all that it has missed, and this updating must not interfere with current work using the files.

Triplexing the equipment would, of course, give even higher reliability but would be even more expensive. On certain special systems, however, very high reliability is essential, whatever the cost. On the American [space] shots, for example, the monitoring computer [may even] be quadruplexed.

The configurations illustrated above are the types in common usage. It is possible to have systems that are much more complex than these, often with more than two interconnected computers. In systems where the interval between message arrivals is short and the file access time long, one computer can-

Figure 1-1-5 A duplexed system.

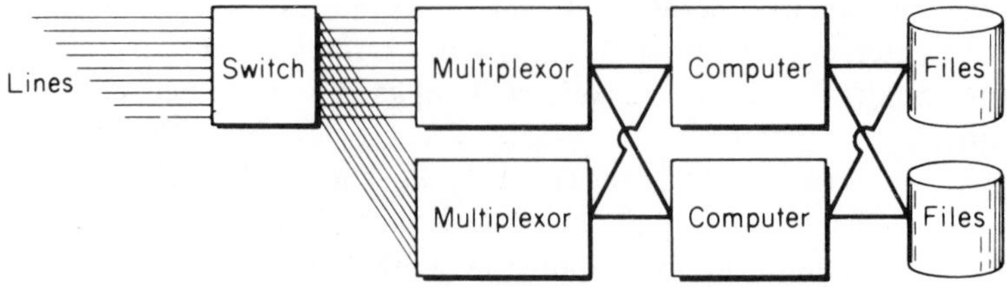

not cope without multiprogramming, that is, handling two or more transactions at once. In this case, it has been suggested that several small computers should be used instead and the work split between them. The programming techniques described . . . relate to systems such as those above. However, the principles and conclusions that emerge would be applicable to any configuration, not only to these more common ones.

1-1-2 THE RESPONSE TIME

The response time, in this discussion, is the total time a transaction remains in the computer system, that is, from the time at which it is completely received to the time at which a reply starts to be transmitted, or, if there is no reply, the time at which processing is completed.

In a simple case, then, the response time is the time the computer takes to interrupt what it was doing and to process the transaction. There may, however, be certain delays involved in the response time. First, there may be several transactions contending for the computer's time, so that the transaction may have to wait in various queues, like a customer going to the Motor Vehicle Licensing Office at a peak period. Second, the computer may, in some applications, be doing another job and the transaction will have to wait until it is convenient to process it.

In some types of systems a high-speed response time is necessary because of the nature of the work. The computer has to be programmed to react quickly. In others it does not matter—a response time of twenty seconds may be adequate.

The range of response times in some existing applications is shown in Figure 1-1-6. A bank teller or an airline reservation clerk may desire a response

Figure 1-1-6   Examples of required response times.

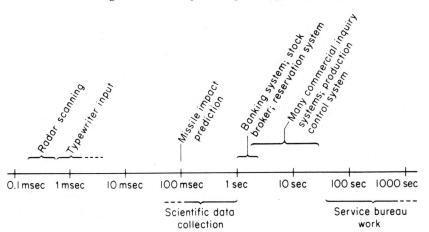

time of three seconds or less, so as to give customers or telephone enquirers the best possible service. A warehouseman making stock inquiries may be content with a reply in twenty seconds. For controlling a petroleum plant five minutes may be adequate, and for sending instructions to the shop floor of a factory perhaps a half-hour is soon enough. Some scientific control and data logging applications require . . . much shorter response times than these. Examples are data logging on a jet engine or rocket motor test bed, scanning radar readouts or tracking a missile to predict its impact point. The interval between events may be only a few milliseconds, and the response must be programmed not to exceed this brief period. A clock or similar device in a computer is used to prevent the computer from being tied up on one transaction so that it cannot provide this response time when required.

1-1-3 THE INTERVAL BETWEEN EVENTS

The interval between the arrival of transactions at the computer may be random and determined by external events such as a clerk pressing a key; or it may be cyclical and governed by a clock or scanning device in the computer.

As with the response time, it may vary from a fraction of a millisecond to a half-hour or more. The range of interarrival times is shown in Figure 1-1-7 for some existing applications.

An airline reservation system with a thousand terminals may have transactions pouring into it from all over a country at a rate that will be as high as twenty per second at peak periods. On the other hand, some inquiry systems may [have only] an occasional inquiry now and then. A savings bank with a steady stream of customers into each of its branches at lunchtime might average about one transaction every two seconds. In a European bank with a large

Figure 1-1-7 Examples of intervals between message arrivals.

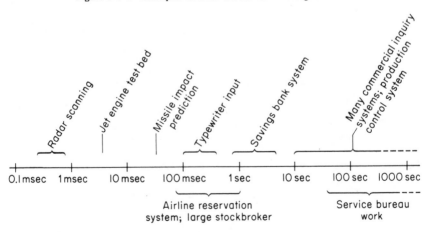

number of branches this could be much higher. A typist keying characters into an on-line terminal may send them at a rate of five to ten per second.

When considering transaction rates for random systems like these, it is necessary to examine the times of maximum traffic because the system must be built to handle these peaks. Indeed, it must in some way cater to the very rare circumstance of all the terminal operators pressing their buttons at the same instant. It will not attempt to process a flood of messages of this magnitude at once, but, on the other hand, if a momentary transaction peak reaches the computer, none of these messages must be lost.

In radar scanning or data logging applications the inputs are scanned with a fixed cycle time. This will probably be of the same order as the response time quoted above.

1-1-4 THE NUMBER OF INSTRUCTIONS IN THE APPLICATION PROGRAMS

The variation in the number of instructions in the real-time Application Programs gives a good indication of the range of complexity of these systems. Some small systems have less than a thousand instructions but the big ones exceed 200,000. Figure 1-1-8 illustrates this spread.

These figures are for the real-time programs only. In other words, this mass of coding is in the system ready for use at any one time. The programs must all fit together like cogs in a machine. Many nonreal-time systems have a

Figure 1-1-8 Number of instructions for on-line work.

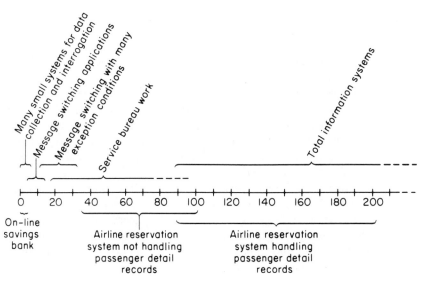

similar quantity of programming, but there it is not so significant because their work is done at different times, independently of one another. A new nonreal-time program can be written without any knowledge of those that already exist. A new real-time program must fit in with the others and conform to the rules they obey. Nonreal-time programs are soloists, doing their acts individually. Real-time programs are members of an orchestra and must work together, obeying the conductor.

There is, therefore, a big difference in system complexity between a system with a small number of program instructions and one with a large number. It is not merely a difference in quantity as it may be with nonreal-time programs. Much better *organization* is needed to put together the bigger system. A savings bank application with 2000 lines of code is like a sonata for a string quartet, and a reservation system with 200,000 lines of code is like an oratorio for full orchestra and massed choruses. The players in the string quartet may be as good as those in the oratorio or better, but the oratorio needs professional stage management.

In systems with a large amount of programming, only a portion of this will be in the core, or immediately accessible portion of the computer memory, at one time. The system with 200,000 instructions may have room for only 40,000 or less in [the] core. Indeed, even the system with only 2,000 instructions may keep those not frequently used in a backing file.

In some systems it will be necessary to continuously select and read segments of a program into the computer core. A large system may call these in at as high a rate as 20 or more per second, and an elaborate mechanism is needed to handle this. A small system will call in external programs only to handle an exceptional condition—perhaps once every half minute or less frequently than that.

1-1-5 THE COMPLEXITY OF THE PROGRAMS

The number of instructions is not directly related to the complexity of the programs. A large commercial system with many files to update for different purposes may have a large number of fairly simple programs. On the other hand, a system for tracking a missile and predicting its impact point, or for optimizing a chemical process, may have only one or two programs, but these are complex and involve elaborate mathematics.

The complexity of the Supervisory Programs will be more directly related to the size of the system. If there are multiple computers, or elaborate input/output devices, or a large number of random-access files, this will complicate the Supervisory Programs as the later chapters illustrate. If there are many Application Programs to be selected and called in from a backing file, an elaborate mechanism will be needed to organize this. The complexity of the priority structure will also have an effect. In some systems the transactions all have the same priority, like customers joining a cafeteria queue. Imagine how much more difficult it would be to organize a cafeteria queue if various customers had different priorities. This situation would be even worse if certain high-priority customers were in a raging hurry; so much so, that the actual serving of other customers had to be interrupted to serve them. In some real-time systems the messages to be processed have different priorities, and certain messages may be in a raging hurry. For example, in a system used for monitoring space flights from Cape Kennedy the priority structure is complex, and often the processing of one message is interrupted to process another more urgent one.

The Supervisory Program and the system testing will be more difficult if multiprogramming is involved, that is, the concurrent processing of more than one message. Where work on one message is stopped to work on another, either for reasons of timing or priority, sufficient details must be stored about the situation on the first message to ensure that work on it can be taken up again as though no interruption had occurred. Some Supervisory Programs have to control the situation where processing is constantly switching back and forth between one message and another.

One reason for this can be seen by inspecting Figures 1-1-6 and 1-1-7. In some systems the response time is less than the average time between the arrivals of messages, but in others new messages will arrive before the processing of the last one. In an airline reservation system during the peak period, the messages may flood in as fast as 20 per second or more, and it may take a second to process each message, including all the references to random-access files which take a relatively long time. While the file references are going on, the computer may have no more processing to complete on that message. It has to wait until its file request is satisfied. Therefore, it is quite practical for it to be working on another transaction. In fact, twenty or more transactions may be under way at the same time, but this considerably complicates the programming and particularly the testing of the system when the programs are fitted together.

It will be seen that the range of real-time systems is a wide one. There is a big difference in the effort required to implement a large, duplexed, multiprogrammed system and a small, single, real-time computer with serial processing. Some, but not all, of the techniques needed for the big system are also necessary for the small one.

It would be a mistake for potential users of a small system, such as a savings bank, to let themselves be influenced by reports of the problems and setbacks on some of the very large, complex systems. This, unfortunately, does tend to happen, and in some people's minds the mere term "real-time" conjures up horrific images of programming problems, regardless of system size. On the other hand, a firm that has successfully installed a small nonmultiprogrammed real-time system may be tempted to move upward to a more complex system without sufficient regard for the dangers that lie ahead.

The ocean of real-time systems is wide, and it is necessary to know where in these waters the systems discussed lie. . . .

1-2 SOFTWARE FOR PROCESS
CONTROL—A SURVEY*

JANOS GERTLER[1] AND JAN SEDLAK[2]

Software for Process Control Computers has been developing rapidly and attempts are being made to standardize the profusion of terminology, languages, and software packages.

The aim of this paper is to present a survey on Software for Process Control. Realizing the extreme extent of the field, the authors intended to concentrate on the most relevant subjects and adopted the following structure:

1-2-1. General properties of process control software
      1-2-1-1 Specialties of process control computer applications
      1-2-1-2 Structure of process control software
      1-2-1-3 Preparation of process control software projects
1-2-2. The present status of process control software
      1-2-2-1 Real-time executives
            —program, priority, data
            —core allocation
            —CPU allocation
            —peripheral handling
            —task states
            —event handling
            —time scheduling
            —executive calls

*Reprinted with permission from *Automatica,* Vol. II, No. 6, Janos Gertler and Jan Sedlak, *Software for Process Control—A Survey,* Copyright 1975, pp. 613-25. Pergamon Press, Ltd.

[1]Institute for Computing and Automation, Hungarian Academy of Sciences, Budapest, Hungary.

[2]Institute for Industrial Management Automation (INORGA), Prague, Czechoslovakia.

1-2-2-2 High-level general-purpose process control languages
—the Purdue Fortran
—other languages
1-2-2-3 Application packages and problem-oriented languages
—functional areas
—problem-oriented languages
1-2-2-4 Man-machine communication software
—man–machine communication in basic software
—communication software
—software for nonprogrammers
1-2-3. Servicing of process control software
—program preparation software
—debugging software
—testing software
—tuning software
1-2-4. Standardization

Work was shared according to the authors' experience and interest. Sections 1-2-1 (1-2-1-1 through 1-2-1-3), 1-2-2-4 and 1-2-3 were written by J. S. while 1-2-2-1, 1-2-2-2, 1-2-2-3 and 1-2-4 by J. G.

It should be noted here that process control software is a field where commercial interests are rather significant. The special position of the authors made it possible to take a most unbiased approach.

1-2-1 GENERAL PROPERTIES OF PROCESS CONTROL SOFTWARE

In this introductory section, some general properties of process control software will be dealt with, such as:

1. Specialties of process control computer applications.
2. Structure of process control software.
3. Preparation of process control software project.

1-2-1-1 Specialties of Process Control Computer Applications

Generally speaking, industrial control systems can be built on the following five levels:

1. Long-term planning and strategic management.
2. Management and data banks of industrial systems.
3. Order handling and production planning.
4. Operative production control.
5. Process control.

The development of industrial control systems shows the following main strides:

securing the computer–plant–computer feedback information flow;

formulating timing correctly in order to control the plant in real-time, that is to ensure the correct time-pace of control;

ensuring the required ordering of control programs by means of multiprogramming, based on dynamic priorities and time requirements;

processing possible interrupts in the control system caused outside the computer;

ensuring the continuous (twenty-four hour) performance of computer control;

enabling control optimization;

carrying out diagnostics and/or evaluation of another algorithm when the control algorithm does not use the computer.

1-2-1-2 Structure of Process Control Software

The algorithms of industrial process control in most cases are performed by four types of programs. These programs are controlled by a control program, the real-time executive. An idealized structure of such a system is illustrated in Figure 1-2-1. The lower modules (1,2) handle all the feedback information flows in real-time, that is, they control data exchange between man and machine and between plant and machine. For writing these program modules, symbolic-address languages and macroinstruction languages are mostly used. These modules usually work at the top priority levels in the multiprogramming system. Module 4 contains the mathematically formulated algorithms to process the measured plant data, and decision algorithms to produce qualitative and quantitative information to be flowed from the computer into the process. Management and construction of a data base for communication with the higher levels of the system are also included in the latter module.

Figure 1-2-1 Industrial process control program system.

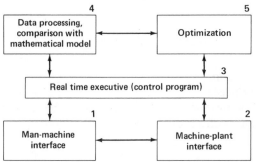

Algorithmic programming languages are used to write mathematical models. For writing the decision algorithms, however, it is necessary to choose a programming language which can easily describe logical conditions and ordering. These programs are mostly evaluated on lower priority levels. Module 5 contains the programs which modify, on the basis of current results, the control algorithm. These algorithms are often adaptive in nature; they are written in algorithmic languages. Module 5 can be evaluated either off-line or on-line, and mostly on a low-priority level, or sometimes its evaluation is called for by Module 3. Module 3 controls modules 1, 2, 4, 5. In many systems, Module 3 is the real-time executive as provided by the computer vendor. However, for some particular applications, the vendor's executive is too small, in terms of services, or too large, in terms of overhead. In such cases, special user executives, control programs, are written incorporating, if possible, [the whole vendor's system or parts of it].

Within process control programming, the following components can be discerned: executive systems, programming languages, application packages, and man–machine communication software. These components are accompanied by support software necessary for testing and tuning the complicated program systems.

Executive systems for these purposes have a rather unified function today. They coordinate the execution of the various programs and control the resources of the system, on the basis of time requirements and external events. The highly modular structure of executive systems permits them to do rather efficient process control even without peripheral memory. A more detailed description of the real-time executive systems is included in Section 1-2-2-1.

Process control programming languages have had a very hard road to standardization. The macroinstruction languages [E2], abandoned so early in other computer application areas, have rendered very useful service. It is these languages in which most process control programs and the basic software for process computers (for example executive systems and compilers) are written. Developments in industrial computer languages are quite varied, and can be classified into the following three categories [E3]: adaptations of general algorithmic languages, new industrial computer languages, and languages for the nonprogrammers, for example, form- or dialog-based.

The first two trends are quite natural. They were also observed in the data-processing area. The third trend is generally based on a macroinstruction system and a library of basic control algorithms, and leads to a programming technique that the user-technologist can employ without having any special programmer education.

To meet the needs of the different users of industrial computer systems, the vendors offer a wide range of application software. Among various application packages, we can find Linear Programming System Packages for on-line process optimization, Telemetry Application Packages, Gas Chromatography Packages, and Logic Sequencer for engineering logic sequence diagram manipulation. On the other hand, control computers are equipped with various peripheral control packages and drivers. A choice of them depends on the configuration of the control computer installed. Special application packages have been created for terminal communication systems which, beside the special hardware, require special software as well.

1-2-1-3 Preparation of Process Control Software Projects

Special aspects of industrial computer applications appear also in the procedures employed in designing these systems. The conventional and characteristic stages, namely pilot study, planning hardware implementation, developing application, installing hardware, and control of the real object and improving this control are well known from the development and realization of control systems. Managing real-time projects forms a special area of computer sciences today. [Aside from] correctly defining the objectives of control and determining the control algorithm, it is necessary to pay special attention to working team structures. Here the fundamental task is to ensure a mutually understandable interteam language. This necessity appears as early as during preparatory activities. Cooperation between the technologist, who defines the task, and the system analyst-programmer is a basic requirement. This cooperation starts at the early stage of formulating the control algorithm, that is, well before programming. Here we can mention two working phases, namely system specification and system analysis for programming.

The technologist should carefully prepare for the cooperation in system analysis by describing his requirements in the form of a *system specification*. From the methodological point of view, it is convenient to progress from a complete list of variables and plant parameters, through specifying their functional relations, to a specification of all the control components present in the system. Thus the following items are prepared:

a short description of the major control objectives and overall system, including its surroundings,

a detailed description of the controlled object, the plant,

a specification list of variables and plant parameters and, if necessary, a set of rules for data file ordering and management,

a set of rules for information flows between man–control computer, control computer–controlled plant, and . . . for direct man–plant communication,

a list of algorithms for data processing, for comparison with the mathematical model, and for decision-making based on this comparison—along with this, it is necessary to determine mutual links between algorithms and requirements for their processing in real-time,

a testing example for the whole system and for each of its sub-systems—the testing examples should be representative for both static and dynamic tests.

The details of the individual items of system specification are adjusted to the particular control project.

System analysis for programming begins with an algorithm written down in clear form. An internationally standardized algorithmic language, available for writing algorithms, is not yet in existence. Up to now, mathematical languages, technologist languages, flow-chart diagrams, decision tables, table layouts with various headings, and, for describing time relations, bar diagrams have been used.

Industrial control systems have mostly been specified without a deep knowledge of industrial computer technique. Therefore, it is very important to perform an analysis of the control algorithm from the point of view of implementation before starting to write a program.

This phase is completed with a mutually understandable formulation of the control algorithm in a form suitable for programming. No matter whether the process is discrete or continuous, system analysis consists of the following activities:

checking of the algorithm for consistency and completeness;

removal of unnecessary redundancies from the algorithm, that is, leaving only redundancies needed for testing;

implementation of some additions to the algorithm, found necessary in the course of the analysis;

clarification of variables, including their scope, range, and acceptable processing error;

clarification of the computer approximation of functions designed in the algorithm;

clarification of the control loops from functional and timing points of view, that is, defining the time pace of control;

incorporation of the interrelations between individual control loops revealed by system analysis, to be taken into account in timing;

clarification of the activity of the control algorithms during various phases of their operation, that is, starting, running state, alarm state, in relation to another, conventional, control contingent working simultaneously with computer control;

defining the computer configuration for a realization of the algorithm;

checking by means of a testing example supplied by the technologist in accordance with a predetermined plan, including input data and intermediate results varying with time;

checking the demands toward the man–process interface, that is, the possibility of affecting the process, messages on control states, and so on;

assignment of program priorities, also taking time into account, in accordance with the designed decomposition of the control algorithm.

A necessary conclusion of this system analysis is the approval by the technologist of a new version of the control algorithm. It is also necessary to determine regulations governing possible further changes by the technologist. It is desirable to limit the number of these changes because the volume of work needed to realize the algorithm on the computer, after the system analysis, is relatively great.

At the same time, a written formulation of the new version of control algorithm is concerned as a documentation for further teamwork during realization of the algorithm on the computer, and also for later acceptance of the tested program for normal exploitation in the controlled plant.

Experience has shown that system analysis improves the quality of the technologist's original algorithm contained in system specification. Such a course of activities detaches algorithm development from programming. Mixing of these two activities was one of the earlier erroneous courses of work on industrial control projects.

The timely and detailed preparation of the control algorithm thus speeds up system realization. Also, the necessary technical supplements to the computing system can thus be prepared with sufficient lead time. This proven course of control algorithm development will prevent us from getting into the unpleasant state of "never finished" industrial control systems.

1-2-2 THE PRESENT STATUS OF PROCESS CONTROL SOFTWARE

When surveying the present status of process control software, we will concentrate on four major areas:

1. Real-time executive systems.
2. High-level general-purpose control languages.
3. Application packages and problem-oriented languages.
4. Man–machine communication software.

Assembly level and macroprogramming will not be discussed because of its strictly machine-oriented nature. Note that the survey is restricted to the single stand-alone computer situation; the problems of interconnected computers will not be considered.

This part of our survey is mostly based upon a considerable amount of up-to-date written information, placed at the authors' disposal by the courtesy of several leading vendors of process control systems. The list of the manuals directly utilized for this work is found in the references. Also good use was made of an excellent survey by Herbert E. Pike [X 1].

1-2-2-1 Real-Time Executives

The operation of process computers is controlled by *time* and *events*. Some programs are due to execute at specific instants of time or after a certain delay or repeatedly at certain intervals. Other programs are initiated by *external events* originating from the process or operator. Programs just executing may also request some other programs. And *internal events,* like completion of an I/O operation, require some action of the computer as well.

The housekeeping of process computers is organized by the *real-time executive* software system which is named differently in some systems, for example, operating system, director, and so on. The fundamental functions of the real-time executive are allocating system resources, such as operative memory, central processor, and so on; handling peripheral operations; handling events; and time scheduling. While time- and event-controlled operation is characteristic of real-time applications, many of the techniques used in real-time executives, especially those of resource allocation, are common with other multiprogrammed systems.

PROGRAM, PRIORITY, DATA.   The system deals with [two types] of code: program and data. The program code describing the job to be done by the computer is broken into pieces. There are three major types of program units:

a. *Tasks (programs, core loads).* These are relatively large executable and generally relocatable program units. They are activated solely through the executive system and are usually scheduled on a priority basis.

b. *Routines.* These are relatively small program units for fast servicing of different events. They are activated by the executive system unconditionally.

c. *Subroutines.* These pieces of program are activated directly by the tasks and may be [A 5]:
   dedicated, that is, available for one task only;
   common, that is, available for several tasks but not interruptable;
   re-entrant, that is, available for several tasks and interruptable.

A mark of importance, its *priority,* is attached to each task. Priority may be either a permanent attribute of a task, or assigned to it when the task is activated.

In some systems, a limited number of *priority levels* exist, for example, seven levels [A 1], four levels [A 10], and each task is attached, statically or dynamically, to a certain level. In other systems, any natural number within relatively wide limits, for example 0–99 [A 5], 0–255 [A 3], may be assigned as the priority of a task.

The data units are either dedicated (that is, associated with a specific task) or common data units. The latter serve for data communication between the different tasks. A common data unit is accessible for any task, if declared so in the task. The access for a particular task may be of read-write or read-only type [A 7].

CORE ALLOCATION.   In very small systems with no background memory the whole code resides in core. In other systems which include bulk memory, disk, or drum, the core is divided into two major parts. One part accommodates the executive system, the whole or part of it, and may also contain core-resident routines, tasks, and common data areas. The other part serves as running area for the bulk-resident tasks. There are several approaches to handling this running core:

a. Only one bulk-resident task may stay in core at a time [A 5, A 9].
b. The running core for bulk-resident tasks is segmented at system generation time and each group of bulk-resident tasks is associated with a particular segment. However, only one task at a time may occupy a segment [A 3, A 7, A 8].
c. The whole running core for bulk-resident tasks is dynamically allocated at run time [A 1, A 2].

Bulk-resident tasks due to run for any reason need to be first transferred to core. They are placed on a core *waiting queue* (thread) and given access to core in the order of their priority. With respect to the bulk-resident task just staying in core, several solutions exist:

a. The newly activated task, even one of higher priority, has to wait until the task staying in the core running area or its assigned segment is completed [A 3].
b. Some previously specified tasks are interrupted and swapped by higher priority tasks [A 5, A 7, A 8].
c. Higher priority tasks always interrupt and replace lower priority ones [A 2].

CPU ALLOCATION.   Tasks which have been activated and stay in core, either as core-resident tasks or following a bulk-to-core transfer, compete for the use of the central processor unit. They are placed by the executive on the CPU waiting queue and are serviced in the order of their priority.

Whenever the executive starts operating, it takes over the central processor by interrupting the task just running. The outcome of the executive action as to the use of the central processor may be

a. Control is unconditionally returned to the interrupted task following a short executive computation, perhaps execution of some routines [A 7, A 8].

b. A priority-based selection is made from the CPU waiting queue to choose the task that will be allowed to run, which may or may not be the one just interrupted.

c. An unconditional transfer is done to another task.

If more tasks have the same priority, they are serviced either first-in first-out [A3] or in pure time-sharing [A1].

A special feature: under "crisis-time activation," the priority of the task is automatically increased if it is not executed within a specific time [A 1]. The executive investigates the CPU queue to make a selection following:

an external event (process or operator interrupt);
an internal event (I/O or bulk-memory interrupt);
a timer interrupt;
an executive call;
completion, termination, or suspension of the running task;
lapse of a given time [A 2].

Note that in each particular system, only different parts of this list are incorporated.

Following a lasting interruption of a task, type b or c above, return to the interrupted task may happen:

directly from the interrupting task—since the interrupting task can also be interrupted, this is a chained recursive organization of tasks [A 9, A 10];
through the CPU waiting queue according to priorities—that is, an independent organization of tasks [A 2-5, A 7].

In order to ensure its return, register contents are saved for the interrupted task.

PERIPHERAL HANDLING.   Input–output operations are handled by the executive system through specific calls from the requesting tasks. Core-to-bulk and bulk-to-core transfers in the course of execution of tasks are treated in a similar way.

Requests for peripheral operations are placed on the waiting queue of the respective peripheral device. The method of sequencing and servicing the requests is different in different systems.

a. The requests are sequenced first-in first-out [A 1].

b. There are two groups of requests, normal and priority, the priority requests preceding the normal ones. Within a group: first-in first-out [A 2, A 4].

c. The requests carry the priority of the requesting task [A 3, A 5].
d. The requests are assigned priority by the requesting task [A 7].

Some peripheral operations (some outputs) once requested, do not require return to the initiating task. Those which do are, in most systems, handled in two different ways:

a. After issuing a request, the task continues its execution. The completion of the peripheral operation is signalled as an internal event and is serviced (buffered) by a routine without affecting the scheduling of the tasks.
b. After issuing a request, the task suspends its execution. The completion of the peripheral operation is signalled and, in addition to being serviced by a routine, causes release of the initiating task. It then returns to execution through the CPU waiting queue.

Task States.   Summarizing the foregoing, we draw up a simplified scheme of task states as indicated in Figure 1-2-2. A task is always in one of the following states: running, ready, blocked, or inactive. The states *running* and *inactive* are self-explanatory. In state *ready* the tasks are waiting on the CPU queue. In state *blocked* the tasks are waiting on the core or some peripheral queue or being suspended, by themselves or by the operator, until an external event, a specific time or synchronization; actually, this state comprises several substates.

The possible state transitions are

inactive → blocked: an inactive bulk-resident task is activated;
inactive → ready: an inactive task residing or staying in core is activated;
blocked → ready: the blocking condition is lifted, that is, core found,

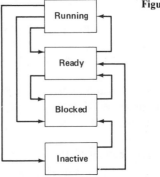

Figure 1-2-2 Task states.

	peripheral operation completed, event happened, time elapsed, synchronization done;
ready → running:	the task is of the highest priority among the ready tasks;
running → ready:	the task is interrupted by a higher priority one;
running → blocked:	the task is suspended waiting for the completion of a peripheral operation, the occurrence of an external event, specific time or synchronization with another task;
ready → blocked:	a ready bulk-resident task loses its running core;
running → inactive:	the task is completed or terminated.

Note that tasking is discussed here as implemented in most existing systems. Some new ideas will be introduced in connection with high-level languages in Section 1-2-2-2.

EVENT HANDLING.   Handling of external events, interrupts, is similar to that of internal events. If an event occurs, the executive takes over and locates the event. Then the response to an external event is either or both of the following actions:

a. An interrupt service routine is executed, without affecting the schedule of tasks.

b. A task is activated, generally by being placed on the core or CPU queue in accordance with its priority, or exceptionally by direct transfer of the control of the CPU [A 9]. Note that this activation may also be organized as an interrupt service routine.

Interrupt service routines are associated with events through tables and may be microprogrammed [A 3]. In most systems, interrupt service routines possess the highest priority with no priority sequencing among themselves. In some cases [A 9], they are arranged into different levels of priority and serviced accordingly.

External events are signalled to the system through special hardware facilities like "interrupt lines" [A 1], "event flags" [A 7], or "interrupt status words" [A 9].

TIME SCHEDULING.   Tasks that need to be executed at a specific instant or after a certain delay or at certain intervals of time, are placed on a time queue accordingly. The time queue is updated automatically at frequent times. Whenever a time-scheduled task becomes due, an internal event, an interrupt, is signalled and the task is placed on the CPU or core queue. Its priority is prespecified by the user.

EXECUTIVE CALLS. Executive calls, commands, and so on, serve for the communication of tasks with the executive. They are used to activate, time schedule, synchronize, suspend, or terminate a task; assign or change priority; request peripheral operations, including bulk transfer and file operations; obtain information [on] task states; obtain information [on] time.
Executive calls are serviced by special routines.

1-2-2-2 High-Level General-Purpose Process Control Languages

In this section, the high-level general-purpose process control languages will be discussed. These languages are especially meant for process control (or, generally, real-time) applications but are general purpose in the sense that they are not oriented toward any particular machine or application area within process control.

General-purpose process control languages are principally procedural languages. This means that most of their statements are executable, in the sense that they describe operations, and the sequence of execution of the operations is primarily determined by the order of these statements. In addition, these languages include some nonsequential specification type statements as well.

Process control applications possess two basic characteristics that programming languages should comply with:

a. Executive operations like tasking and I/O must be directly programmable.
b. Run-time efficiency of the programs, in terms of CPU time and corespace, is crucial.

The application of high-level languages to process control programming is unquestionably advantageous from [several] points of view, like the ease and quickness of program writing or transferability of programs. On the other hand, it inevitably introduces a certain degree of run-time inefficiency. This may be extremely critical in connection with some basic, very frequently executed functions, so these are advisable to program at lower levels even if high-level techniques are used otherwise. Also, high-level programming may make on-line program testing and, especially, program modifications more complicated.

High-level general-purpose process control languages are developed either by taking a general algorithmic language, such as ALGOL, FORTRAN, or PL/1, adding some features for executive operations and, perhaps, omitting . . . others, and imposing certain restrictions in order to improve run-time efficiency; or by defining a new language.

With the proliferation of languages and unification of language principles the difference between the two approaches is diminishing.

A considerable number of high-level general-purpose process control, or real-time, languages have been published in recent years. Some of them are real-time extensions of FORTRAN [B 3–B 7], while others are based on other general algorithmic languages or are new ones [B 8–B 16, B 18–B 20, B 22]. Most real-time Fortrans are implemented on a particular machine. The proliferation and acceptance of the other languages ranges from valuable academic exercises to relatively widely used national standards.

We are trying to avoid any classification or evaluation of the referenced languages and will restrict ourselves only to showing their basic characteristics. "Purdue Fortran" will be first discussed as a synthesis of several Fortran extensions. The real-time properties of some non-Fortran type languages will also be treated through the example of a few selected languages.

THE PURDUE FORTRAN [B 2].   "Purdue Fortran" has been developed by the Fortran Committee of the Purdue Workshop on Standardization of Industrial Programming Languages to unify the different process control extensions to Fortran. Part of the proposed language extension has already been adopted as an ISA standard, while the rest is being considered as discussed in Section 1-2-4.

The language extension takes ANSI Standard Fortran (X3.9–1966) as a basis and consists of a set of standard procedures. These realize different actions which are generally needed in a process computer control system but are not included in the Standard Fortran. Those procedures which have been adopted as an ISA standard [D 2] are: elementary tasking, process I/O, and bit string manipulations. A list of these procedures is given in Table 1-2-1.

The committee is currently revising that standard to also include bit manipulations and date and time information. These procedures are also shown in Table 1-2-1. The original standard allowed two variants of process I/O procedures, one causing suspension of the calling task and the other not. The revised standard allows only procedures which cause suspension as shown in Table 1-2-1. This change was necessary due to implementation difficulties with the nonsuspension procedures. Procedures for file handling are being considered for future standardization.

OTHER LANGUAGES.   Now the characteristics of some non-Fortran type high-level general-purpose process control languages will be described. As examples, four languages will be taken which are currently being investigated by the European Group of the Long-Term Procedural Language Committee of the Purdue Workshop. The languages are CORAL 66 [B 15], RTL/2 [B 20, B 21], PEARL [B 16, B 17], and PROCOL [B 22, B 23].

For one class of languages, like CORAL 66 and RTL/2, run-time efficiency has been the primary objective. These languages exhibit a straightforward structure and contain no explicit real-time features. Real-time operations like tasking and I/O are implemented by machine dependent procedures

TABLE 1-2-1 Procedures Adopted as ISA Standard

	Elementary Tasking
1. START	start a task after a specified delay
2. TRNON	start a task at a specified time
3. WAIT	delay continuation of a task for a given time
	Process I/O Procedures
1. AISQW	sequential analog inputs
2. AIRDW	random analog inputs
3. AOW	analog output
4. DIW	digital input
5. DOMW	momentary digital output
6. DOLW	latching digital output
	Bit String Manipulations
1. IOR	inclusive or
2. IAND	logical product
3. NOT	logical complement
4. IEOR	exclusive or
	Procedures Being Added in the Revised Standard: Bit Testing and Setting
1. IBTEST	bit test
2. IBSET	bit set
3. IBCLR	bit clear
	Date and Time Information
1. TIME	time of day
2. DATE	calendar date

and macros. Assembly or machine code sequences may be inserted into high-level program texts and also macroinstructions defined and used throughout the program. Note that both CORAL 66 and RTL/2 have been implemented on several machines and are used relatively widely.

In more sophisticated languages like PEARL and PROCOL, in addition to the more or less complete arithmetic features of the modern general languages, special language-level facilities are available for real-time operations. These real-time facilities fall into the following groups: system description, tasking, synchronization, and process I/O.

System description in these languages is necessitated by the fact that they deal with events (interrupts) and external variables (process or console points) through symbolic names. Symbolic names are linked with the corresponding physical points at system generation time. For events, a physical point may be a single hardware interrupt, a group of such interrupts, or a "software interrupt" (executive operation); their specification is dependent on the hardware system. For external variables, the type and number of the peripheral equipment and the connection point is to be specified; in PEARL, the complete data path [must also be specified]. Further, system description in PEARL also comprises specification of the computer including type, features of the CPU, core size, and channels.

Tasking will be discussed . . . along the lines of PEARL. Note that tasking facilities in PROCOL may be considered a subset of those in PEARL. The particular areas to be treated are task generation, task activation, other task operations, and scheduling.

Tasks are generated statically or dynamically. Static task generation means that task names are introduced and always associated with only a given task code. Under dynamic generation, only the name of the task is initially declared, and the code is associated with the task upon activation. Activation of a statically generated task is done according to a programmable schedule and priority. Further tasking instructions are: SUSPEND, CONTINUE, DELAY, TERMINATE, PREVENT. The schedule facility of tasking makes it possible to attach a tasking operation to an event, to have a tasking operation performed at a certain instant of time or after a specific delay, to have a tasking operation performed repeatedly with a specific frequency, and to prescribe any meaningful combination of the above.

To synchronize tasks and to control usage of common resources by several tasks, *semaphores,* special integer variables, are used in both PEARL and PROCOL. Semaphores are accessible only for the special instructions REQUEST and RELEASE. A REQUEST operation decreases the value of the semaphore variable by one should the result be nonnegative; otherwise the task containing the REQUEST operation is suspended. A RELEASE operation increases the value of the semaphore by one, clearing the way for the highest priority request among the eventual pending ones to be serviced. Semaphores may be used, for example, to synchronize two tasks, that is, to ensure that a task does not proceed beyond a given point, an instruction, before another task performs a certain operation; to block access by the other tasks to a common data area while one task is exclusively using it; and to indicate whether or not there is free space in a limited-length buffer attached to some equipment jointly used by several tasks.

The way process *input–output* is handled is slightly different in the two languages discussed.

In PEARL, there is a special statement for process I/O, having the form MOVE source TO sink. In case of an input, "source" is the symbolic name of the communication register of a device and "sink" is the name of a memory location; in case of an output, vice versa. The MOVE statement does not imply any transformation of data. If such a transformation (conversion, coding, decoding, or calibration) is necessary, a GAUGE option is attached to the

MOVE statement. This contains the call of a previously declared procedure which, with the appropriate actual parameters, performs the required transformation.

In PROCOL, there are separate INPUT and OUTPUT statements. They include, in addition to the symbolic designation of the data source and sink, reference to a formatting scheme. Formatting for an input consists of feasibility checking, filtering, conversion, and logical checking. For an output, formatting includes filtering, that is, eliminating drastic changes, conversion, and logical checking.

For each formatting item, the user may either choose the standard treatment, with specific parameters, or introduce new procedures.

1-2-2-3 Application Packages–Problem–Oriented Languages

All major manufacturers provide with their process control systems several application packages. These packages are prewritten computer programs that operate in close connection with, and utilize several internal facilities of, the real-time executive system, and take care of a particular functional area common in a class of process control applications.

When dealing with application packages from a user's point of view, one has to concentrate on two basic aspects:

  a. What is the particular functional area it is intended for and, within this [area] what are the services it provides.

  b. What is the programmer's interface to the package, that is, how to program the software–hardware system for a specific task. Note that in most cases this interface is a special problem-oriented language.

Functional Areas.   The major functional areas encountered in many process control systems are as follows: data acquisition and conditioning, direct digital control, supervisory control, and sequence control.

Note that the borderlines between the separate packages of a particular vendor are not quite definite; data acquisition and processing is included in most control packages; also, some higher level control packages contain elements of the lower ones and there are possibilities for interpackage referencing.

The systems to be dealt with here are general-purpose process control packages. Apart from these, several special packages have also been developed to meet the needs of particular industries, for example, steam power generation [C 11].

Data acquisition and conditioning packages [C 1, C 2, C 5–C 7, C 9] include, as basic steps, scanning, filtering, conversion, and limit checking.

a. Scanning is the acquisition of rough process data through the respective input devices. The user selects the appropriate scanning rate for each variable. A first-limit checking is performed on these data to detect faults in the measuring system.

b. Rough measurements are digitally filtered to reduce noise effects. The user may choose between first- and second-order digital filters and specify his filter parameters.

c. Conversion of the measured data is generally performed in two steps. First the nonlinearities of the sensor are taken care of. Typical nonlinear sensors are thermocouples and flowmeters. In the latter case, temperature and pressure are also taken into account as correcting quantities. In the second step, the linearized or linear measurements are converted into the appropriate engineering units.

d. For limit checking, most systems allow two upper and two lower limits. The user may prescribe different response actions to the violation of the inner and outer limits. Further, user-defined deadbands may be attached to each limit value to filter "return to normal" actions, or messages. Also limit checking for the rate of change of variables is available.

Direct digital control packages [C 1, C 2, C 5–C 7] are primarily based on the digital implementation of the conventional three-term (PID) control algorithm. The user may choose sub-algorithms (P, I, PI) and specify his control coefficients.

The input to the algorithms is either the control error or its signed square $(e \mid e \mid)$. In some systems, the user may indicate if he wishes to have setpoint changes neglected in the differential term. Also available is adaptive tuning with changing coefficients, or neglected terms, upon high error or significant setpoint changes [C 1].

The output is either position or incremental type. Upper and lower limits are specified for the absolute position value of the output and maximum-per-step for its increments. If a calculated output leads to violation of any of these limits, it will be reduced accordingly [C 7]. Also, a deadband for the output increments may be defined to make control operation more quiet [C 3]. In some systems, incremental control is combined with position feedback to base the calculation of increments and checking for position limits on the real position instead of recursive computations [C 5].

A simple ratio-control algorithm is also available in most DDC packages. In addition, some systems offer special compensator algorithms like pure time-lag, sum of multiple inputs, and lead-lag [C 1].

Supervisory control packages [C 3, C 9] are meant for computing setpoint values or changes for analog or DDC controllers in continuous processes. Supervisory control is generally done in a steady-state or quasi-steady-state manner. There are two ways to describe the basic computation:

a. Using a standard adjustment equation [C 9]. This equation provides the necessary change of manipulated variable, based upon the actual deviation of the controlled (feedback) or some measured (feed-forward) variable. There is a possibility to consider deviations of three further variables. Up to four adjustment equations with common variables may be handled simultaneously.

b. Using special simplified procedural languages involved in the package [C 3, C 9].

Additional facilities [C 3, C 9] include limit checking on the inputs of the algorithm; minimum output deviation (deadband) below which no control action will be performed; absolute or incremental limits for the output; and special actions or programs to obtain initial values for the control calculations.

As far as timing of the control action is concerned, the user may specify [C 9] a minimum time between two adjustments; a setpoint movement rate; a stair function of up to four steps, expressed as fractions of the calculated change of setpoint versus fractions of a specified delay time.

Sequence control packages [C 7, C 12] serve for programming batch processes or start-up/shut-down operations in continuous processes. Their basic feature is the evaluation of logic conditions, involving functions like AND, OR, EXOR, INVERT. Inputs to the logic equations are ON/OFF type status information from the process or console; logic results of process variable comparisons, with respect to limits or to each other; and timing conditions, in logic form. In addition to the special sequencing facilities, these packages include some reduced data acquisition and control features as well.

PROBLEM-ORIENTED LANGUAGES. To make an application package operable, it has to be programmed for the given job. The objective of this programming is to fill up the data files of the package, that is, to inform the software of the actual numerical parameters; to specify the [method] of execution of the package, that is, to include/omit and link different program blocks; and to describe nonstandard operations.

Fitting packages to the particular job is implemented by means of problem-oriented languages which are provided as part of the package. Those languages meant for file building and program linking are of specification type: their statements describe specifications for a previously programmed sequence of operations instead of the operations themselves. On the other hand, languages for describing nonstandard operations are of procedural type, similar in this sense to the general-purpose process control languages.

Looking at the formal aspects of these languages, they may be strictly formatted languages, "fill in the blanks" systems, assemblylike languages, high-level, English-like languages, or conversational systems.

Note that some packages include two languages, one for specification and another for describing nonstandard operations.

The *strictly formatted languages* are meant for skilled programmers. They use low-level, numeric and alphanumeric symbols. There are strict rules to govern the length and order of the symbols, the use of delimiters, and the card layout. Such a language was developed as a means of specification for the OPO optimization package [C 4].

The *"fill in the blanks" technique* has been devised for unskilled programmers. Basically this is also a strictly formatted system, but the programmer need not care about formatting. He just has to fill in preprinted forms where the sequence and format of the answers are fixed. Cards are then punched mechanically on the basis of the forms. "Fill in the blanks" technique is used in the supervisory control packages BICEPS [C 3] and PROSPRO [C 9] for file building and program linking. The forms contain blanks (1) for the different numerical parameters of data acquisition and conditioning, such as filter and conversion coefficients, and so on; and control, such as a deadband or time delay; (2) for the numerical codes of execution specifications, such as the type of filter and conversion equation, absolute or incremental output and so on; and (3) for references to programs describing nonstandard operations.

In PROSPRO, the "fill in the blanks" technique is extended to some nonstandard arithmetic operations. This is achieved by introducing a "general equation" and an "adjustment equation". The user may select his particular equation within the given scheme by specifying his own coefficients which may also be zero. This too is performed by filling in blanks on some special forms.

Instructions in an *assemblylike problem-oriented language* consist of a mnemonic operation code and up to two operands. An assemblylike procedural language is provided in the PROSPRO package [C 9] for programming nonstandard operations (general action). The available instructions are arithmetic operations, comparisons, conditional and unconditional branch, time operations, adjustment, and program control operations.

High-level problem-oriented languages have free-format English-like statements, similar to those of FORTRAN and other well-known languages.

A characteristic example of the use of high-level languages in programming process control packages is the DACS-AUTRAN system [C 1]. This comprises two free-format English-like languages, one for building files and linking program parts of DACS (Data Acquisition System) and another for programming nonstandard supervisory control.

The AUTRAN specification language has the following sorts of statements: group specifications, input and output specifications, control operation specifications, input and output processing, control processing, alarm response specification, and timing (cycling) specification.

The supervisory control (procedural) language involves a version of FORTRAN as a subset. Additional statements are I/O variable list; output, semi-output, and semi-input statements, equipment control statements; tasking statements; and logging statements.

Another high-level problem-oriented language is the procedural BPL

(Biceps Programming Language) [C 3], added to the BICEPS supervisory control package to program nonstandard operations. BPL is a very simple language having only a few fundamental features. These are constant and variable declarations, FETCH and STORE statements, basic arithmetic operations, conditional jump, simple standard functions, such as ABS, and printing.

Conversational systems assume the least skill of the programmer. Programming is performed through an alphanumeric I/O device, such as a typewriter or display. After the programmer has indicated his intention to communicate, the system asks a set of questions. The programmer has to type in his answers either [by] (1) using an assemblylike language [C 6, C 7]; or (2) by making the right selection from the choice of answers offered, together with the questions, by the system [C 2].

The conversational technique can only be applied for specification purposes. This approach has been taken in the OMNIBUS-DDC [C 2] and PM/C [C 5] packages as well as in the CONRAD [C 7] and CONSUL [C 6] systems.

Though very convenient, the conversational technique is too slow to handle large amounts of information. Therefore, most systems provide an optional punched tape or card input with an assemblylike specification language for system initialization, while conversational programming is mainly reserved for additions and modifications [C 5, C 7].

1-2-2-4 Man-Machine Communication Software

The existence of appropriate communications, between man–machine and machine–plant, is one of the characteristic properties of industrial control systems. To accomplish these communications, we need an appropriate hardware, devices of the controlled plant, instruments, a control computer, terminals, and a good software.

Man–machine interfaces, serving the process operator, control engineer, or programmer, should obey the following rules:

a. The communication system should be able to display numerical values of the variables and technical parameters, messages, to register trends, also multiparameter, and to enter new plant parameters or values.

b. Each parameter to be entered into a control system must possess a functional specification, that is, scan, alarm, control, log, and so on.

c. It should be possible to make visible all input data before entering them into the system.

d. All input data, changing parameters or conditioning operations, must be registered automatically. This registration should reflect contents of the respective memory address.

e. The possibility of the registration optionally of all the alphanumeric requests which are displayed within the communication system, should also exist.

Note that items c and d simultaneously perform checks for frequently occurring human errors.

Man–machine communication software is implemented on three levels:

a. *Basic software:* that is, real-time executives, assemblers, compilers, program development utilities, for example editors, re-entrant routines, and database manipulation software.

b. *Communication software:* that is, peripheral device control packages and drivers, terminal communication packages, software for multiplexors, buffering, and core mapping for multiprogramming.

c. *Special programming systems for nonprogrammers:* that is, form or dialog based.

MAN–MACHINE COMMUNICATION IN BASIC SOFTWARE.   Communication between man and basic software is [made possible] by the use of special syntactical units of programming languages. For instance, a flexible macroinstruction language may serve to accomplish this [A 1]. In addition to a language like this, the programmer's console is generally available with an access to a keyboard and a printer. These facilities mainly permit one to

a. Introduce new programs and names of entities for data file handling.

b. Change the specification of programs, necessary core/bulk store, identification of source text, and control of peripheral units.

c. Cause program activations.

d. Provide the system with operational data.

e. Initialize calendar and real-time clocks.

COMMUNICATION SOFTWARE.   In process control . . . the [following] equipment . . . is used for communication: conversational typewriter (for programmers); conversational typewriter (for operators and technologists); output typewriter (or printer) for passive communication (alarm, log, various messages, trend records); pen recorders for operators; pen recorders (trend recording); displays; light panels; and punched tape and card I/O units.

Here the obvious [stipulation] is that all these units are connected with the central processor unit through a unified interface. Then also software can be built in a unified way in order that the following three basic facilities can be provided:

a. Routines to handle and react to real-time events, such as button pressings and light-pen interrupts, initiated by man through peripherals or terminals/modems.

b. Routines to build and manipulate data buffers and files, that is, display file, printer file, card file, and so on.

c. Routines to organize and present information for process–man communication, that is, input–output routines for teletypewriters–printers;

routines to create standard layout plotting patterns necessary for graphical aids, for example, points, lines, circles, characters, and so on.

Communication data structures realized by means of various I/O units can, of course, be diversified. With display interface for instance the following three properties of data structure are required [F 1]:

(1) It must represent the display sequence correctly, that is, it must imply the order in which the patterns are to be displayed.

(2) It must imply the number of words in the display file corresponding to each pattern so that editing may be performed.

(3) It must have a way of associating a "name" with a pattern. Names may be assigned either by the user or by the system. These names are used for all communications about the pattern between the user and the system.

From another aspect, most displayable files are [F 2]: maps movable within a page; one-page displays which can be updated but not moved, magnified, or rotated; scrolls—these are tabular lists which may be too large for a screen and can therefore be scrolled backward or forward.

Software for Nonprogrammers. Such software has been developed . . . for continuous process control and is built of separate preprogrammed algorithms for industrial data manipulation, general control actions, operator logs and console displays, and process output control. To accomplish man–machine communication, special control panels are used equipped with keyboards, functional and numerical, and simple displays to picture, as a rule, loop identifications, current values, new values, and various visible signals. Let us present the facilities as provided by one of these software systems [F 2], cf. Section 1–2–2–3.

a. Basic modular facilities:
     on-line assembly, modification and removal of control loops in the control system;
     opening and closing cascade switches;
     monitoring of process and control variables and checking parameters;
     interface with auto/manual stations.

b. Optional facilities:
     measured value logging for all the loops in the system;
     trend logging for selected loops;
     alarm logging for all loops in alarm state;
     loop logging of all loop variables for adjusting the loop;
     chart recording of selected measured values, set points, and valve positions;
     background-mode running of standard compiler and editing programs and of user-written background programs.

1-2-3 SERVICING OF PROCESS CONTROL SOFTWARE

Once we have finished the analysis of the algorithm of an industrial control system from the programming point of view, we can write the program in a chosen language. Then there are two main activities awaiting us around the computer, namely removal of syntactical and semantical errors from the program (debugging); and verification that the program actually realizes the algorithm (testing).

Of course, these two activities are very often interleaving. Formally, testing starts when debugging is "finished." However, the errors found during testing lead to program modifications which, having been performed, must go through "a new" debugging. Such a successively approximating activity is especially exacting in program development with real-time objectives. Unfortunately, there is no exact rule as to when to stop this and pass on to the phase of verifying the algorithm on a real plant. Here it is necessary to combine computer science results . . . with general experience. . . . The around-the-computer preparation of the "right" program should be associated with an automatic creation of documentation on the program (including all the program modifications). For this reason, it is not surprising that the right, high-quality outfit of service programs brings a fair economic benefit during realization of control algorithms. However, relatively [little] attention has been paid to these questions in the literature.

Let us now mention the services performed by the individual utility programs as they are successively met by the user: program preparation (PP), debugging (DB), testing (TS), and tuning (TN).

A simplified diagram of links between these activities is presented in Fig. 1-2-3, together with a list of the subjects which these activities work with. The

Figure 1-2-3 Servicing software for process control.

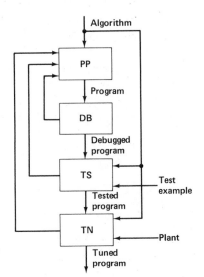

PP, DB, TS and TN activities are of course partially realized by means of the computer. For this reason, servicing software has its specific structure as indicated in Fig. 1-2-4. If S(PP) stands for software for PP and S(DB), S(TS), S(TN) alike, the following relation is valid: S(PP)⊂S(DB)⊂S(TS)⊂S(TN). Let us now try to characterize, briefly and gradually, the traits of these parts of servicing software.

Program Preparation Software.   During compilation and assembly, syntactical and semantical analysis of the source program text is important. Here it is convenient that both the usual messages about the errors found and the so-called *directives* [F 2], that is, control commands about the service activity of translators, be contained in our programming languages. The individual service routines then provide . . . the following services:

a. *Editing* [F 2] and modification [A 5] of programs at any language level used. Editing programs, developed in any programming language and for on-line or off-line use, can update the source text with the corrections required.

b. *Loading* data or absolute or relative programs in binary format from any input device/file into core/bulk memory. During loading, error checking and global label linkage is performed.

c. [*Comparing*], for checking purposes, of information read from any input device or a file with the contents of core/bulk memory. The differences found are indicated on the programmer's console–teletypewriter.

d. [*Dumping*] of selected core area or bulk memory on any output device. The information thus dumped is suitable for reloading.

e. *Reporting* about the different stages of program preparation. Message level, that is, depth of reporting, is selectable.

f. *Changing* the time–date, task parameters, and peripheral designation.

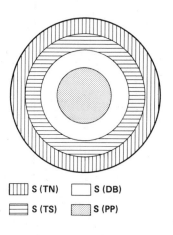

Figure 1-2-4 Structure of service software for process control.

[||||] S (TN)   [ ] S (DB)

[≡] S (TS)   [▒] S (PP)

g. *Listing* for documentation purposes, especially for activities DB, TS and TN. Useful documentation items include: source program listing, programs in intermediate languages, intermediate language listing, external references, routine entry names, data names referred from external programs, external routine/data names, common data names, symbol tables, physical memory maps, program unit name listing, program structure listing.

Debugging Software.   We can distinguish the following debugging aids:

a. *Tracing* . . . is provided for each programming language, [as is] editing. The interpretative software package usually enables the programmer to obtain various printout formats [F 2]. Tracing at the machine-level language includes:
   (1) instruction-only printout,
   (2) fully-executed-instruction printout including the resultant contents of all the registers affected by the instruction,
   (3) printout in either mode on program branching only,
   (4) printout on tagged (preidentified) instructions only, and
   (5) omitting n executions of some tagged instructions.
   Similarly, formats are provided for higher level programming languages. The formats are obviously based on their syntactical elements (macro, statement).
b. *Examining* . . . program and data storage contents. A selected sequence of core-memory locations is printed out in a selectable format, that is, program, octal number, integer, character, and so on.
c. *Changing* the contents or types of numbers
   (FIXED→FLOAT, FLOAT→FIXED).
d. *Searching* uses a breakpoint technique to check a program at selected points. The programmer can stop the program at preidentified points and then use some of the previous aids.
e. *Hardware debugging* for an integrated check of computer systems by test programs running in foreground.

Observations: (1) The debugging software may be used in foreground or background. (2) "Long-Term Procedural Language" [B 1] is intended to have syntactical units especially designed for setting the conditions for debugging operations; executable statements for debugging operations; auxiliary listings useful for debugging; and reporting, error messages, and so on, for debugging.

Testing Software.   In accordance with the diagram shown in Fig. 1-2-3, during testing of the algorithm of an industrial control system, a debugged program and a testing example form the subject of testing. The testing example contains some known data, generated by a small routine, and expected answers as well as selected program checking points. The testing example must also contain bases for evaluating time parameters of tasks. Therefore, there are two stages of testing, namely static and dynamic (cf. Section 1-2-1-3). Both states of course require their specific software; they involve and utilize also the activities discussed earlier as shown in Fig. 1-2-4.

  a. *Static testing software* consists particularly of the following elements
      Routines for generating example data.
      Testing procedures for testing task modules, these procedures being able first of all to compare preidentified results of the tested module with expected answers and then to halt the execution of the module under test if a specified condition is met.
      Core image software [A 1, G 2] provides additional information about the state of the program system at the time when the dump was taken. Thus we can receive a report which is not included in the dump. Among different types of messages are: system status, program (task) status, core map, trace history, peripheral status, bulk status, background (free-time) status.
      Query option facility, built into some macroinstruction systems [F 2], permits the programmer to insert in the tested program extra program instructions for monitoring intermediate data values at strategic program points. Subsequent translations can then progressively eliminate option items as knowledge of the correct performance is increased. This query option also permits several alternative sequences of code to be held on the same program file which implies a system having great program modularization.
  b. *Dynamic testing software* is closely connected with the real-time executive used. This testing software performs primarily the following activities
      Testing the intertask cooperation (user programs), this cooperation being controlled under time conditions and priorities in a multiprogramming environment.
      Testing the behavior of the program with respect to time, with the registration of the actual path of execution, for example, reporting on task's/routine's/subroutine's labels as they are passed.

  Tuning Software. This software operates mostly through real-time executive calls, cf. Section 1-2-2-1. Some of the software pieces discussed previously in the present Section are also incorporated. Tuning itself can start when the installation testing is finished. By means of this software are realized the flexible modifications of the control algorithm as inferred from the application of this algorithm on a real plant. A choice of the necessary programming facilities to accomplish such depends on the extent and depth of the required modifications as needed for the industrial control system.

1-2-4 STANDARDIZATION

Standardization of industrial programming languages has long been a desire of many people active in the field. As in many other areas, standardization would result in considerable savings of human effort. The primary benefit of standardized programming techniques consists in transferability of software products from one system to another, but the advantage of having to learn only one language is also significant.

This desire and recognition led to the formation of the Purdue Workshop on Standardization of Industrial Programming Languages in 1969. The Workshop, by far the most significant effort in this direction, has been established with the very ambitious program of producing standard proposals for the different levels of industrial languages within a couple of years. Five committees were formed to start work in the fields of glossary, functional requirements, problem-oriented languages, industrial Fortran, and long-term procedural language.

It should be noted that a Technical Committee of Industrial Computer Languages was also formed in Japan. Its three subcommittees, on Problem-Oriented Languages, Fortran, Long-Term Procedural Languages, maintain close cooperation with the respective Purdue bodies. Also, a very active subcommittee of the Long-Term Procedural Language Committee exists in Europe.

To unify the usage of special terms of the field, the Glossary Committee of the Workshop developed a *Dictionary for Industrial Computer Programming* which was published by ISA (Instrument Society of America) in 1972 [D 1]. Now a second edition is being prepared.

The role of the Functional Requirements Committee was to prepare the way for the language committees, that is, to produce functional requirements for industrial computer systems to serve as a basis for the development of standard industrial computer programming languages. This work was completed and the results published in 1971 [D 6, D 7].

The main objective of the Workshop has been developing the proposed language standards. In this respect, however, the outcome is well behind the original expectations. One of the reasons is certainly the voluntary nature of the work: many people, active for one period or another, drop their affiliation because of their changing working conditions and interest. The most serious reason, however, is probably the difference between company, and, in some cases, national interests.

The Problem-Oriented Language Committee has, for a long time, been attempting to find its way of operation. After studying functional requirements for and general features of problem-oriented languages, they arrived at the intermediate result that these languages, or at least their procedural parts, should be considered as macroforms of some general-purpose procedural language. Thus a wide class of problem-oriented languages could be handled by translating them into the standardized long-term procedural language. [Some] suitable translators are already available, but the lack of the definition of the object language prevents real progress in this direction.

Perhaps the overwhelming popularity of Fortran is the reason why an industrial extension of this language proved to be the most ripe, among the three levels, for standardization. Indeed, the Fortran Committee of the Workshop succeeded in developing a proposal containing special calls for process I/O, bit string manipulations, and elementary executive functions, that was standardized by ISA in 1972 [D 2]. A second proposal, dealing with Fortran procedures for handling random unformatted files, bit manipulation, and date and time information is just being considered by ISA [D 3]. A third one on task management, advanced functions is under final development [D 4]. Note that the first of the above extensions has been standardized also in Japan [D 5], while the two others are being considered.

The Long-Term Procedural Language (LTPL) Committee was formed with the aim of developing a high-level general-purpose process control language that might replace industrial Fortran in the long run. The Committee first decided to base this language on PL/1, a choice later attracting much criticism. This aspect of the work has since then been shifted to the X3J1.4 committee of ANSI (American National Standards Institute), explicitly dealing with the definition of a process control version of PL/1. Meanwhile, the European subcommittee of LTPL has been formed and has gained strength gradually; now most of the LTPL work is being done in this group. They compare and evaluate existing process control languages to find the best mixture recommendable as an international standard. They have also established contacts with the respective committees of ISO (International Standards Organization). Unfortunately, conflicting national interests sometimes also hinder the productivity of this group.

Just recently, the Purdue Workshop has been drastically reorganized. It was combined with the Purdue–ISA Computer Control Workshop (covering hardware and system aspects of computer control). Also, it was given an international structure with three regional workshops in North America, Europe, and Asia (Japan) and an international workshop, named the International Purdue Workshop on Industrial Computer Systems, integrating the regional ones.

The Purdue Workshop is affiliated with ISA and IFIP. Similar affiliation with IEEE and IFAC is under negotiation.

1-2-5 CONCLUSION

The increasing importance of process control software has drawn the attention to the special techniques and problems of this field. On the one hand, the changing balances between hardware and software costs have led to the increased use of high-level techniques. These result in a saving of programming manpower at the expense of computing time and memory. On the other hand, attempts to introduce unified or, if posible, standardized techniques have been initiated. It has been realized that much would be saved, if transferability of the programs or, at least, that of the trained programmers could be achieved through the use of such techniques. This recognition led to setting up organizations and starting serious efforts, first in the US and later in Japan and Europe. By now, there have been promising developments and some initial results, especially in the field of high-level general-purpose process control languages. However, it has also been seen that the difficulties of the task are far greater than expected originally. Thus, in spite of the highly esteemed efforts and devotion of those who have undertaken and promoted this work, success is still a long way off.

1-2-6 ACKNOWLEDGMENTS

The authors would like to thank the Brown, Boveri and Cie Aktiengesellschaft; Control Data Corporation; Digital Equipment Corporation; Ferranti Ltd.; Foxboro Company; GEC–Elliott Process Automation Ltd.; General Electric Company (now Honeywell Inc.); Gesellschaft für Kernforschung MbH; Hewlett-Packard Company; International Business Machines Corporation; Societe de Realisations en Informatique et Automatisme for providing source material for this survey. Further, they wish to thank Professor T. J. Williams, Chairman of the International Purdue Workshop on Industrial Computer Systems, for making the Minutes of the Workshop meetings available.

They also express their gratitude to their master institutions, the Institute for Computing and Automation, Hungarian Academy of Sciences (Budapest, Hungary), and the Institute for Industrial Management Automation, INORGA (Prague, Czechoslovakia) for supporting this work.

1-2-7 REFERENCES

[E 1] J. Sedlak: Development of programming means in the regions of production scheduling, production control in real-time. Ref. 6.8, IFORS 70, Karlovy Vary, Czechoslovakia, September (1970).

[E 2] O. W. Holt: General purpose programming systems. *Comm. ACM* **1,** 7–12 (1958).

[E 3] J. Y. De Latourne et H. Garelly: Tour d'horizon sur la programmation des calculateurs industriels. *Automatisme* **XVI,** 559–570 (1971).

[X 1] H. E. Pike, Jr.: Process control software. *Proc. IEEE* **58,** 87–97 (1970).

[A 1] Ferranti Argus 500 Director 6, General Description. Ferranti Ltd., Wythenshawe, D56 190 (1973).

[A 2] RTMOS Real-Time Multiprogramming Operating System for Honeywell 4400 Systems. Summary Manual. Phoenix, Arizona, PTS-001 (1974).

[A 3] RTMOS-30 for GE–PAC 3010/2 Computer Systems. General Electric Co., GET 6314 (1972).

[A 4] RTOS User Manual. GEC–Elliott Automation Ltd., SP–UM S 25 238 (1973).

[A 5] Real-Time Executive Software System. Programming and Operating Manual. Hewlett-Packard Co., Palo Alto, Cal., No. 02005–90001 (1971).

[A 6] Real-Time Executive File Manager. Programming and Operating Manual. Hewlett-Packard Co., Sunnyvale, Cal., No. 29033–98000 (1973).

[A 7] RSX-11D Concepts and Capabilities. Digital Equipment Corp., Maynard, Mass., DEC-11-OXDCA-B-D (1974).

[A 8] RSX-11D Executive Reference Manual. Digital Equipment Corp., Maynard, Mass., DEC-11-OXERA-A-D (1974).

[A 9] IBM 1800 Functional Characteristics. IBM System Reference Library, GA 26–5918–8.

[A 10] IBM System/7 Functional Characteristics. IBM Systems, GA 34–0003–5.

[B 1] H. E. Pike, Jr: Procedural language development at the Purdue Workshop on the Standardization of Industrial Computer Languages. *V World Congress of IFAC,* Paper 10.3, 12–17 June. Paris (1972).

[B 2] *Minutes, Eighth Workshop on Standardization of Industrial Computer Languages,* Purdue University, October (1972).

[B 3] FORTRAN reference manual. GE Process Computer Department. Manual YPG14M, May (1965).

[B 4] W. Diehl and M. Mensh: Programming Industrial Control Systems in FOR-TRAN. IFAC-IFIP Symposium on Digital Control of Large Industrial Systems, Toronto, Canada (1968).

[B 5] FORTRAN IV in a process control environment. *IEEE Trans. Industrial Electronics and Control Instrumentation* **15,** 61–63 (1968).

[B 6] R. E. Hohmeyer: CDC 1700 FORTRAN for process control. *IEEE Trans. Industrial Electronics and Control Instrumentation* **15,** 67–70 (1968).

[B 7] J. C. Mecklenburgh and P. A. May: PROTRAN, a FORTRAN based computer language for process control. *Automatica* **6,** 565–579 (1970).

[B 8] An introduction to CONTRAN. Honeywell Inc. Special System Division, Pottstown, Penn. SSD-20-ICMP 4/65–750 (1965).

[B 9] J. D. Schoeffler, T. Wilmott and J. Dedourek: Programming languages for industrial process control. IFAC-IFIP Second International Conference on Digital Computer Application to Process Control, Menton (1967). *ISA,* Pittsburgh, Penn., U.S.A., W. E. Miller (ed.), pp. 371–388.

[B 10] BCS Specialist Group: A language for real-time systems. *Computer Bull.* 202–212 (1967).

[B 11] Processalgol (PROGOL) I. SINTEF, AVD. Reguleringsteknikk, Trondheim, 68 17E 480 165 (1968).

[B 12] P. I. P. Boulton and P. A. Reid: A process control language. *IEEE Trans. Computers* **C-18,** 1049–1053 (1969).

[B 13] J. D. Schoeffler and R. H. Temple: A real-time language for industrial process control. *Proc. IEEE* **58,** 98–111 (1970).

[B 14] J. Gertler: High-level programming for process control. *Computer J.* **13,** 70–75 (1970).

[B 15] Official definition of CORAL 66. Prepared by the Inter-Establishment Computer Applications as a language standard for military programming. H.M.S.O., London (1970).

[B 16] J. Brandes: PEARL—the concept of a process- and experiment-oriented programming language. *Elektronische Datenverarbeitung* **12**, 429–442 (1970).

[B 17] K. H. Timmesfeld: A proposal for a process- and experiment-automation real-time language. Gesellschaft für Kernforschungs MbH, Karlsruhe (1973).

[B 18] Industrial Programming Language: LAI. CERCISESA. In: *Minutes, Fourth Workshop on Standardization of Industrial Computer Languages,* pp. 145–153, Purdue University, October (1970).

[B 19] PAS 1, Process Automation Language Description. BBC Aktiengesellschaft, Mannheim (1971). ZEKED and ZPF/L.ED1004 E (872.01).

[B 20] An Introduction to RTL/2. ICI Corp. Laboratory, Reading, England. In: *Minutes, Eighth Workshop on Standardization of Industrial Computer Languages,* pp. 217–257, Purdue University, October (1972).

[B 21] RTL/2 Language Specification. In: *Minutes, Eighth Workshop on Standardization of Industrial Computer Languages,* pp. 259–320. Purdue University, October (1972).

[B 22] M. Ritout, P. Bonnard, and P. Hugot: PROCOL: a programming system adapted for process control. *V World Congress of IFAC,* Paper 10.1, 12–17 June, Paris (1972).

[B 23] Systeme PROCOL T 2000. Notice Technique. STERIA Le Chesnay, France, Ref. 1 162 220/00 39 00.

[C 1] Control Data 1700 Computer System AUTRAN DACS, Software Manual Version 2.0., Control Data Corporation, La Jolla, Cal., No. 88762000.

[C 2] GE-DDC Direct Digital Control. Summary Manual. Honeywell Inc., Phoenix, Arizona (1974).

[C 3] BICEPS Supervisory Control. Summary Manual. Honeywell Inc., Phoenix, Arizona (1974).

[C 4] OPO On-Line Process Optimization Summary Manual. Honeywell Inc., Phoenix, Arizona, PTS–016 (1974).

[C 5] Process Monitor and Control (PM/C). User's Manual. General Electric Co., Phoenix, Arizona, GET–6256 (1972).

[C 6] Ferranti Argus 500. Consul General Description. Ferranti Ltd., Wythenshawe, D 54 180 (1973).

[C 7] MARCH Industrial Software for GEC 2050 Computer. GEC–Elliott Automation Ltd., New Parks, Leicester, A 1001-80, A 1002-200-205 (1972).

[C 8] Process Supervisory Program (PROSPRO/1800) User's Manual. IBM, GH20–0474-1.

[C 9] IBM 1800 Process Supervisory Program (PROSPRO/1800) Language Specification Manual. IBM, GH20–0472-2.

[C 10] Process Monitor and Control (PM/C) for GE-3010/2 Process Computers. General Electric Co., GEA–9643 (1972).

[C 11] SEER (Steam Electric Evaluating and Recording) Functional Description. Honeywell Inc., Phoenix, Arizona (1974).

[C 12] FOX 2/30 Batch Control System. Foxboro Co., Foxboro, Mass., 73002AY (1973).

[F 1] D. E. Thornhill, J. W. Brackett and J. E. Rodriguez: A sample interactive graphics program. Course Notes for Two-Day Seminar on Programming Techniques for Interactive Computer Graphics, NEL, Glasgow, Great Britain (1968).

[F 2] M. E. McLaughlin: Argus software for process control, message switching and general real-time applications. Ref. 4.9., IFORS 70, Karlovy Vary, Czechoslovakia, September (1970).

[G 1] F. Gruenberger: Program testing and validating. *Datamation,* **14,** 39–47 (1968).

[G 2] DEACON/CIA User's Manual, General Electric Co., GET–6257 (1972).

[D 1] Glossary Committee, Purdue Workshop on Standardization of Industrial Computer Languages: Dictionary of Industrial Digital Computer Terminology, Instrument Society of America, Pittsburgh, Penn. (1972).

[D 2] Anon.: Industrial Computer System FORTRAN Procedures for Executive Functions and Process Input–Output, Standard ISA–S61.1. *ISA,* Pittsburgh, Penn. (1972).

[D 3] Anon.: Industrial Computer System FORTRAN Procedures for Handling Random Unformatted Files, Bit Manipulation, and Date and Time Information, Proposed Standard ISA–S61.2. In: *Minutes, Eighth Workshop on Standardization of Industrial Computer Languages.* Purdue University, West Lafayette, Indiana (1972).

[D 4] Anon.: Industrial Computer FORTRAN Procedures for Task Management. Working Paper. In: *Minutes, Ninth Workshop on Standardization of Industrial Computer Languages,* Purdue University, West Lafayette, Indiana (1973).

[D 5] FORTRAN Subprograms for Industrial Computer Systems. JEIDA–20–1073. In: *Minutes, Ninth Workshop on Standardization of Industrial Computer Languages,* Purdue University, West Lafayette, Indiana (1973).

[D 6] Functional Requirements for Industrial Computer Systems. In: *Minutes, Fifth Workshop on Standardization of Industrial Computer Languages,* Purdue University, West Lafayette, Indiana (1971).

[D 7] R. L. Curtis: Functional requirements for industrial computer systems. *Instrumentation Technology* **18,** 47–50 (1971).

1-3 DIFFICULTIES OF REAL-TIME PROGRAMMING*

JAMES MARTIN

There are many problems associated with the programming of real-time systems. This [section] attempts to describe these.

Fortunately not all of the problems catalogued below apply to all types of real-time systems. However, many of the more complex systems do have to face . . . all of these difficulties. This [section] attempts to associate the type of system with the problems that are likely to arise.

1-3-1 DYNAMIC SCHEDULING

A computer used for a conventional data-processing application normally follows a repetitive cycle which may be planned and timed in detail by the programmer. Input and output operations are normally of a known length and time and may be balanced with each other and against the processing that is to be done. *The pattern of events is constant.*

In an on-line system this is unlikely to be true. Messages arrive at *random times* and are probably *varied in their length and nature.* For example, enquiries enter a credit checking system or an inventory system at unplanned times. When a clerk requires information he sends a message to the computer. Transactions enter a real-time banking system at times when customers pay in or withdraw cash at a bank counter. This occurs at random.

In addition to being random with respect to time, it is probable that different messages reaching the computer of a real-time system will require different programs. *Different functions will be executed in an unplanned sequence.* Because of this, dynamic scheduling . . . may be needed, that is, scheduling which changes with the changing requirements instead of being fixed as it would be on a conventional computer application. Unlike a conventional application, the timing pattern can constantly change from second to second. Therefore, it is necessary to schedule this unpredictable sequence of operations so that the data are still handled in the minimum time and the computer facilities are used to their best [advantage]. This will be a function of a *Control* or *Supervisory Program.* The Supervisory Program is often complex

*From James Martin, *Programming Real-Time Computer Systems,* © 1965, pp. 35–49. Reprinted by permission of Prentice-Hall, Inc., Englewood Cliffs, N.J.

and much more difficult to plan and write than normal data processing programs. . . .

1-3-2 DYNAMIC CORE ALLOCATION

In the system that varies continuously in the manner described, it is possible that the requirements for computer core storage will change from transaction to transaction. An area of storage needed at one time for one type of program may be needed shortly afterwards for a different type of program. For this reason a *dynamic allocation of computer memory* is required. The [uses for] an area of core . . . may change from second to second. Core is allocated to different functions as required.

If the system uses dynamic core allocation in this way, the continuously changing assignment of core to its various functions will be the work of the Supervisory Program. It may be necessary to write the Application Programs so that they can operate in different areas of core at different moments of time. In other words, programs would be *relocatable*.

New segments of programs may have to be called into the memory of a complex computer from a backing file, second-by-second. The organization needed to call in programs when required, to branch to them, and branch from one segment of a program to another can become very complex. Again, this organization is carried out continuously by a Supervisory Program.

1-3-3 ALLOCATION OF PRIORITIES

Different clerks operating the terminals of a real-time system are quite likely to send in messages to the computer at the same instant in time. For example, in an airline reservation system, attempts to book seats or to carry out other functions may be made in various agents' offices at the same instant in time. In fact, the system may have many messages contending for the use of the central processing unit at one time, and these messages may be of different types.

Some means of *allocating priority between the various messages* may be necessary. In some systems all messages have the same priority, but in others high priority messages must jump the queue and be processed quickly. The latter is likely to be the case in some commercial data processing systems or in technical systems such as those which control a chemical plant or monitor a defense network. Some systems utilize many different priority levels.

. . . The processing in a moderately complex real-time system does not follow a constant predictable routine. Rather, the pattern changes moment to moment. . . . This means that the planning of the processing and the selection of the computer with appropriate memory size and speed may become more complex than in a system in which the events are repetitive and predictable.

1-3-4 MULTIPROGRAMMING

Another factor that adds to the difficulties of real-time is multiprogramming, that is, the concurrent operation of more than one program. In a simple system only one transaction or message at a time will be processed. Work will not start on the next message until the preceding message is completed. In this type of system it may be necessary to jump from one program to another when different types of messages are received, but transactions will not be processed *in parallel.* However, in more complex systems it becomes necessary to process transactions in parallel, because the time taken to handle one transaction is greater than the interval of time between the arrivals of transactions. When two or more transactions have to be processed simultaneously in this manner, this is referred to as multiprogramming. *The degree of multiprogramming* varies considerably from one type of system to another, but it always adds complications to the program writing and particularly to the program testing.

A system with a computer handling several messages at the same time is like a juggler trying to keep several balls in the air at once. The more balls he keeps in the air, the more difficult it becomes. Similarly, the higher the degree of multiprogramming, the more complex is the Supervisory Program, and the more difficult the program testing.

A system designer may be forced to use multiprogramming because the time taken to read data from the files or to update them is long. Imagine, for example, a system with clerks sending messages from several hundred terminals at various locations. Messages may arrive at the average rate of one every half-second. Each message requires six references to random-access files and these references take an average time of a quarter of a second each. This means that [on an average] the computer will . . . process three or more transactions at the same time. In the large airline reservation systems as many as twenty transactions may be handled in parallel by the computer.

The random-access file references themselves are not of a predictable time. They may vary from thirty milliseconds up to 600 milliseconds and because of this the timing pattern of the processing changes constantly.

The computer may have allocated priorities between different messages. It may now also be necessary to *allocate priorities between different functions of the system.* The functions, such as file references, that are taking place at any one instant are unpredictable and constantly variable. Just as the programs in the computer may differ from one instant to another, so is the timing pattern in the system continually changing, and there are an almost infinite number of variations. . . .

1-3-5 INTERRUPTS

. . . On computers used in real-time work [it is necessary] to have some form of *interrupt* mechanism. When messages reach the computer, their arrival may trigger an interrupt in the processing so that the computer can read them into the appropriate part of its storage and hold them until it is ready for work on them. Similarly, if a real-time clock is used, it may be necessary for the clock to interrupt the computer periodically so that the time stored in the computer memory is updated. Events which have to occur at a specific time may be triggered in this way. In a multiprogrammed system it is desirable that there should be an interrupt associated with all input–output operations. For example, when reference to random-access files is made, this reference will take an unpredictable amount of time. When the file reference is complete, the computer should be interrupted so that it can read this item from the file into the appropriate place in its memory. [Then it can] take action on it as soon as is convenient. The structure of the interrupts and interrupt routines may be simple or complex depending upon the application. Large multiprogrammed applications may have many interrupts per second. When a program is interrupted, control must later be returned to that program at the point at which it broke off. To do this, sufficient information must be [stored] about the program status at the moment of interrupt. This can become complicated, especially if the [interrupted] program [was] using input or output devices at the moment the interrupt occurred. This is rather like comparing an office worker who is able to complete one job at a time, with one for whom the telephones are constantly ringing with urgent work and who has to be switching . . . from one vital job to another.

1-3-6 QUEUES

In most real-time systems the rate at which messages arrive varies from one moment to another. If one hundred clerks all decide to use their separate terminal sets at the same instant, it may be possible that one hundred messages [will] arrive at the computer all at the same instant. These cannot all be processed at once and therefore *queues* will develop. There are various methods for handling queues that must be available to the real-time programmer. It may also be necessary to queue the output messages. On a multiprogrammed system where there are several partially completed messages, these will also be queued. . . . Thus several queues may be waiting for the attention of the processing unit. A complex system may make several references in parallel to its random-access files. Under such conditions, items from the files which are waiting to be used may also have to be put into queues.

    The queues build up and are depleted in a probabilistic manner; at one time they will contain many items, but at another time they may be small. This further complicates the work of designing the system and planning the layout of those parts of the memory in which queues are handled. The queues are commonly in the core storage of the computer. In other words, they are programmed queues. Some means must be programmed of *scanning the queues* and taking appropriate items from them for processing. It is the work of a Supervisory Program to decide which item in which queue to process next.

1-3-7 OVERLOADS

Because the transactions or messages arrive at random *the system will occasionally become overloaded.* If all the clerks happen to use their terminals at [the same] moment, the queues of new transactions may grow too large. The computer will be in danger of running out of core storage, or possibly running out of processing time. An input or output channel or an access arm on a disk file may be given too much work, and . . . excessive queues of items waiting for this facility may build up. It is possible that the computer may begin the processing of several transactions in parallel and be unable to complete them because, in attempting to do so, it causes an overload. Such overloads are a normal, but exceptional, state of affairs in many real-time data-processing systems. The sudden flood of messages that produces such overloads will, in a well-designed system, be only a short-lived state of affairs. However, programs must be available to handle it. In the multiprogrammed system it may be necessary for the computer to detect a potential overload before it actually occurs, in other words before the computer starts processing all the messages that would cause the overload. . . .

1-3-8 MULTIPROCESSING

Sometimes more than one computer is used. These are normally interconnected by a data channel which enables one computer to read from or write in the memory of the other. This use of coupled computers is referred to as *multiprocessing.* It may, for example, be used as an alternative to multiprogramming. Instead of having one computer do two jobs at once, two computers are used, each doing one job at a time. It may be used to increase the reliability of the system. If one computer breaks down the other one takes over. In some systems the computers execute different functions. For example, one computer may do all the reading and writing on files, and the other computer may process the transaction. Sometimes one computer handles all the input and output on the communication lines, and the other computer does the remainder of the work. In this way it may be possible to use a small or specialized computer for line control, and a large or conventional computer for the rest of the work. The machine handling all the input and output on the communication lines may also be able to handle the queuing of the messages. Where multiprocessing is used, additional control problems are added. One computer may be the "master" and the other the "slave." It will be the job of the Supervisory Program to coordinate the operations of processing units connected . . . in this way. It may be necessary to have a different Supervisory Program in each of the computers used.

1-3-9 COMMUNICATION LINES

Many of the problems outlined above are connected with the difficulties of handling data that arrive at random and which vary in their nature. Other problems in real-time programming are caused by the new types of hardware that are used on this kind of computer system. The use of large random-access files, . . . telecommunication lines and terminals, . . . special equipment, and the real-time clock, all introduce new complications into the programming.

Where a computer has attached to it a network of communication lines and each of these communication lines may have one terminal or more, and possibly a very large number of terminals, a program must scan the lines and accept data from them in parallel. One bit is read from one line and one bit is read from the next line and so on. All of these bits must be assembled into messages. The words and messages must be carefully checked for errors because on communication lines many more errors are likely to occur than in normal computing hardware. Similarly, output messages have to be transmitted bit by bit in parallel. When a terminal has a message to transmit, this may cause an interrupt of the computer. Alternatively, a terminal may have to wait until the computer requests it to transmit.

The computer may compose instructions which tell the terminal to send data. These instructions may be passed down the line from one terminal to another until a terminal has a message to transmit, or the computer may address individual terminals. The computer would scan all the lines in this manner. Some lines or some terminals may be "polled" more often than others because they have higher priority. . . .

1-3-10 RANDOM-ACCESS FILES

Large random-access files also present a whole family of new problems in programming and *data organization*. Where should data be placed on the files in order that they may be located in minimum time? How can additions and deletions be made to random files in such a way that the information may still be readily found, and the packing of the file is not too low? And perhaps the most difficult problem of all, how can the file addressing be organized?

The basic problem of file addressing is the following: records in the files are identified by a number or key which is characteristic of the application. This may, for example, be an account number in a bank, a part number in a factory, a flight number and date in an airline reservation scheme, or perhaps a passenger name. A clerk or a factory hand will key this number or name into his terminal; it is this number which will reach the central processing unit in the input transaction. From this the machine address of the record, that is, its precise location in the files, must be determined so that the record can be read. To convert the original number into the required machine address can be a difficult problem. There are various possible techniques for generating the required file address. . . .

1-3-11 SUPERVISORY PROGRAMS

In considering all these problems, it becomes apparent that the Supervisory Programs in a large real-time system have much work to do. They are indeed complex programs, and in some systems . . . they have taken as many as twenty [person-years] to write. It is very important that the Supervisory Programs . . . be planned well and written correctly. Much of the performance of the system depends upon the skill with which these programs are written.

The Supervisory Program may be compared to the production manager in a small engineering company. Imagine a factory machining metal parts. There is no mass production or batch production. Each part is a one-off item to be made individually, just as messages in a real-time computer are processed individually. Orders for parts to be made arrive at the factory continuously but at random, and the nature of the parts varies considerably. Some parts will have a high priority attached to them, but others need not be made immediately. The shop floor of the factory has various groups of machine tools: lathes, milling machines, drills, and so on. These may be compared with the input–output units and files on a real-time system or possibly with the programs for carrying out specific tasks. The work of the production manager is to route the parts being made through the factory in such a way that the necessary operations are performed in the correct sequence and with as little delay as possible. He must optimize the utilization of the machine tools.

Each group of machine tools may have its own foreman who supervises the work on this section. The production manager coordinates the work of these foremen, and they organize the movements of the parts from one section to another. In a similar way an *Input/Output Control Program* may be used for certain input/output units of the computer system. Each input/output channel may have a *Channel Scheduler*. A Supervisory routine coordinates the work of these programs. They may perhaps be regarded as subroutines of this Supervisory routine. When exceptional conditions arise or when emergencies occur, the Supervisory routine should be able to take the necessary action, just as the production manager in the factory [would do].

1-3-12 APPLICATION PROGRAMS

Important though the production manager is, the actual manufacturing is done by the workers. Similarly, in the computer the processing of transactions and the calculations and the assembly of output messages are done by Application Programs—the programs which correspond, broadly, to the data-processing programs of conventional computer systems.

The Application Programs will normally be written separately from the Supervisory Program. The question, therefore, arises: How do the Application Programs interface with the Supervisory Program? What are the connecting links?

Application Programs will normally be written in a language of the level of *Autocoder* or FAP, in which one line of code may result in one machine instruction, or sometimes a macroinstruction, in which case it generates a complete subroutine. To connect the Application Programs to the Supervisory Program, macroinstructions would be written which provide these links. These macroinstructions would normally form part of the Supervisory Program Package.

The Application Programmer would write his programs for a machine which is provided with a clearly defined Supervisory Program and its associated macroinstructions. If the Supervisory Package is written well, he would be able to think about the processing of one message and ignore the relationship of this with any other messages that may be in the system at the same time. He would not have to consider the input/output timing of this program as this will have been taken care of by the Supervisory Program. . . .

1-3-13 COMMUNICATION WITH THE COMPUTER OPERATOR

The person operating the computer on the real-time system has a comparatively easy job, although his status as an operator may be high because he is in charge of a roomful of complex and sophisticated computers and mature judgment is required in times of trouble. For a conventional application the operator is constantly loading up the computer with punched cards or changing magnetic types. A real-time system is designed to be as automatic and as independent of its operator as possible. However, situations will arise when the computer needs the assistance of its operator, and this must be obtained as promptly and efficiently as possible. It will be another job for the Supervisory Program to detect when operator intervention is necessary. The Supervisory Program must ask for help, telling the operator exactly what is wrong or what is required. Similarly, if the operator wishes to communicate with the system, to change its action in some way, or to monitor its performance, this action will also be via the Supervisory Program.

1-3-14 HIGH RELIABILITY

In general real-time systems need to be much more reliable than conventional computers. There are two reasons for this:

First, the system is more automatic. Because of the nature of their job, most real-time systems are planned not to stop if it is possible to avoid stopping. Messages entering the system are processed and are returned to the appropriate terminals without any human intervention. If an error occurs during this cycle it may not be detected unless it is obvious to the person operating the terminal. If an error occurs which damages the files, this could be particularly disastrous because it might go undetected. The system would continue in operation with damaged or incorrect file records.

It has often been said that the computer is a moron. Its advantage lies in the fact that it is a high-speed moron. If it should deviate from its planned program, it is likely to take action that is wildly irrational or produce results that are stupid. If it is doing scientific calculations or batch-processing, this does not matter too much because its wild errors can be detected. If a check total on a batch does not agree, the matter is investigated, and the batch is processed again. If a set of equations are solved incorrectly, this too can be detected and put right. However, if a computer goes wrong on a real-time run this may not be detected. A clerk at the terminals may ignore the "rubbish" that he gets in reply and merely repeat his last message. Unless steps are taken to prevent it, it is possible for a real-time computer to overwrite the file records. It is as though the Dickensian clerk went berserk and scribbled all over his ledgers and ripped out pages. A high degree of system reliability is necessary to rule out the possibility of this happening.

Mistakes of the type described are more likely to happen because of faults in the programming than because of faults in the electronic circuitry. Good quality computing equipment today is [so reliable] that undetected errors caused by the hardware are very rare indeed. It is interesting to note that when errors occur on the large and complex real-time systems . . . these are usually programming errors and not hardware errors. Reliability is thus another programming problem of real-time systems. *Reasonableness checks* must be built into the programs. *Means of protecting the files* must be devised and *memory protection aids* must be used. In a system with a high degree of multiprogramming it is especially difficult to achieve high reliability in the programs. The program testing needed to ensure this reliability is particularly complex because there are an almost infinite number of combinations of circumstances that must be tested.

Second, . . . high reliability is needed in a real-time system . . . because of the nature of the system. It is usually very inconvenient when it ceases to function. For example, the system used by a firm of stockbrokers to maintain immediate contact with brokers on the floor of the stock exchange would impede business if it failed to function. When a computer controlling a chemical plant fails, the plant must be operated manually until the computer is back in operation, and for this period the process cannot be optimized. When an information retrieval system goes down, its users cannot obtain the information they require. An extreme example for the need for reliability is the use of computers in the manned space flight. In the critical seconds after launching, a computer makes a decision whether or not [to put] the missile . . . into orbit. If it is not, it must be brought down immediately into a safe landing area. Similarly, a Ballistic Missile Early Warning System and other defense networks need very trustworthy computers.

1-3-15 DUPLEXING AND SWITCHOVER

One way to improve reliability in a real-time system is to duplicate all of the critical components, so that when one computer fails a standby computer takes over automatically. Whenever information is written on the files, it is written twice on separate files. Duplexing is, of course, expensive, and whether or not it is used depends upon the need for very high reliability. When duplexing is used, the Supervisory Program must detect the need for a switchover of any of the components, including the computer itself, and must initiate the switchover, whether it is to be done manually by the operator or whether it is to be automatic. There are many programming problems associated with switchover because the need for it may occur when an Application Program is half-completed, when a file has been read but not completely updated, or when a message has been half-received, or when several messages in the system are half-processed. All this half-completed work must be sorted out and, in particular, caution is needed in updating the files; otherwise it may be possible that a file is updated twice and so becomes incorrect. . . .

1-3-16 FALLBACK

If it can be achieved, it is desirable that a failure of part of the system should not knock out the entire system. If one communication line fails, the computer continues to operate with the other lines. If one file fails, then, as far as possible, work goes on without this file. If one computer fails in a system with more than one computer, those remaining may do a portion of the job. This technique of making the most of a bad situation and continuing to do a portion of the job, is referred to as "graceful degradation." If possible, the system must "fail softly," rather than failing suddenly and perhaps catastrophically. The Supervisory Program initiates a *fallback*. The system may continue to limp along in the "fallback" mode until the component that caused the trouble has been put right. The Supervisory Program must then initiate a *recovery*. "Fallback" and "recovery" may become complex. For example, it may be necessary to change the file on which the data are written. If this is done, all the file addresses referred to by an Application Program must be modified by a Supervisory Program before the file in question is written on. . . .

Not all real-time systems need duplexing or elaborate fallback procedures. This depends upon the application. However, the designers of any application must always have in their minds the thought: What will happen if the computer or any other part of the hardware fails? In many types of applications it will be possible to devise some form of manual bypass procedure by means of which a very limited but tolerable service can be given until the computer system is fully working again.

1-3-17 PROGRAM TESTING

Because of the high degree of reliability that is needed on real-time programs, thorough program testing is very important. However, program testing on real-time systems presents far more problems than program testing on conventional computer applications. On some of the large systems that have been installed . . . it has proved extremely difficult. The crises and delays associated with testing have been considerable. It is apparent that this is one of the fundamental problems of real-time and that techniques more advanced than those for conventional systems are required.

The difficulties of real-time program testing are caused by several factors not found in conventional systems. First, there is the use of terminals and lines for input and output.

It will normally be impractical to use actual terminals and lines for the testing as this would be too slow. Therefore the input and output devices must be simulated. Other special equipment may be needed. If a Supervisory Program is not completed at the time when it is necessary to test the Application Programs, and similarly, if some of the Application Programs are not available at the time they are required to interface with other Application Programs, this gap must somehow be bridged.

Multiprogramming introduces additional difficulties, because a wide variety of different combinations of circumstances must be investigated in the testing. When errors occur it may be difficult to say which of the programs in a multiprogrammed system caused the error. If more than one computer is used the problems of testing are multiplied, especially if overload and switchover conditions have to be investigated. The complexity of large real-time systems also adds to the difficulties. Where so many programs tie together to make a tightly integrated whole it is necessary to test them working in cooperation with one another. This needs much organization.

Solutions to these problems have been worked out. . . . In general, they involve writing programs which are designed to assist only in the testing of the system. These programs must be available at the time when they are needed for the testing; they may take several [person-years] to write. To neglect the planning of these testing aids early in the implementation schedule could prove disastrous.

1-3-18 PROBLEM OF PROGRAMMER COORDINATION

This chapter has described some of the details of a real-time system that make its programming difficult. However, none of the problems so far mentioned are beyond the ingenuity of a reasonably inventive and skilled programmer. There is one problem, however, that needs more than just good programming to solve it. Some of the more ambitious systems have become immensely complex. Some of them have taken as many as a hundred programmers writing routines which must eventually tie together to form one tightly integrated system. If the hundred programmers had been writing separate routines to run on the computer at separate times, this would have presented no problem for a conventional installation. But here the routines must all be capable of working together in the same real-time system. If any programmer makes a change in his programs this may affect the work of many of the other programmers.

Here is the main source of many problems. Programmers constantly find a need to change what they are writing. In fact, the writing of a program is a process of evolution. The first idea crystallizes into the first block diagram. This is elaborated upon and grows. As it grows, it changes constantly. Intricacies are added, and procedures are modified. Almost like the growth of a city over the years, so a program is built up stage by stage. But now a hundred programmers are all building a part of a complex machine. Eventually all these parts have to be put together and mesh smoothly with one another. When this constant evolution is taking place, how can the programming management be sure that all the parts are developing in such a way that they will all fit together to form the integrated system? This is a problem of a new order in programming management. More rigorous techniques are needed than those in common use in the computer world today.

1-3-19 DESIGN PROBLEMS

The *design* of a real-time system can also be very complex. When planning a magnetic tape installation for batch processing, the program sizes and core requirements can be estimated and the time taken to do the job calculated with sufficient accuracy to enable the selection of the right computer. On the larger real-time installation it has proved much more difficult to make accurate estimates of the program size, and because the contents of the core storage are continually varying, it is difficult to predict how much core storage is needed. The size to which the queues may grow in the memory of the computer is uncertain. The time that will be taken to deplete these queues cannot be stated exactly. Indeed, even the input to the computer is not certain, and on many installations it will vary from moment to moment. Ascertaining the time and core requirements of the computer now involves *probability and queuing theory*. To assist in this design work the technique of *simulation* is frequently used. A model is built of the system and its programs. Into this model input can be fed which corresponds to the input of the actual system when it will be in operation. This input can be varied easily. The delays and the size of the queues can be measured. The model may be adjusted to make these conform with the requirements. If a multiprogrammed system is simulated in this way the model itself can become quite complicated, but it is the only sure way to estimate the computer requirements.

1-3-20 MONITORING THE PROGRAMMING PROGRESS

Unfortunately, when a real-time system is being planned, there are many unknowns, especially connected with the programming. When eventually a program is being done, many justifiable decisions may have been made by the programmers which cause the system to drift away from the original design concepts. It has commonly been the experience on complex real-time systems that a large drift away from the original design has been experienced when a system is being implemented. This drift can have catastrophic results. It may be found that the equipment ordered is no longer able to do the job. An expenditure which cannot be justified is needed to put matters right, or else the programming must be thought out afresh, which may delay the implementation of the system by a year or more. This again is a problem in programming management. How can management be sure that, as these complex programs are being written, they are not drifting away from the original specifications? Again, simulation techniques may be needed. The development of the programs is monitored by adjusting or elaborating the simulation model of the system whenever programming decisions are made or whenever the sizes or timings of programs become more clearly known.

In general, the management problems on a large real-time system are much more complex than on previous types of computer installations. New techniques are needed for monitoring and control. Good documentation techniques are needed, and there must be intricate coordination between the work of different programmers. . . .

1-3-21 SUMMARY

To summarize, the following reasons can make real-time programming more difficult than conventional programming:

(a) Control of communication lines and terminals.

(b) Control of multiple input/output devices.

(c) Organization and addressing of random-access files.

(d) Variable message types and variable processing requirements.

(e) Dynamic program read in and memory allocation.

(f) Fluctuating message input rate.

(g) Handling of occasional overloads.

(h) Input messages of different priorities.

(i) Handling of queues.

(j) Multiprogramming: Processing two or more transactions at once.

(k) Handling of multiple processor interrupts.

(l) Multiprocessing: Control of multiple processing units.

(m) Switchover of faulty units, including the central processing unit while work is in progress.

(n) Fallback to a limited mode of operation, and recovery from fallback.

(o) Error control.

(p) An intricate Supervisory or Control Program.

(q) The relationship between the Supervisory and the Application Programs.

(r) The relationship between associated Application Programs.

(s) The fitting together of a complex integrated system written by many different programmers.

(t) Many new difficulties in program testing.

(u) Increased reliability requirements.

(v) Design problems and the use of simulation.

(w) New difficulties in programming management.

REAL–TIME
APPLICATIONS

Real-time computing systems, as we have seen, have a number of things in common. What we will see in this chapter is something they do not have in common: similarity of application. The real-time computing solution may be applied to an amazing diversity of problems, ranging from a guidance system on a space probe to a hand-held language translator.

To set the stage for this diversity, we rely on James Martin again. In section 2–1, Martin briefly describes each of seven real-time *reference* applications. He discusses the kind of information processed and the frequency with which it is received at the computer; the database which may (or may not) be accessed; and the response time and reliability required of the system. These reference systems might be found in a bank, an industrial plant, a warehouse, or at an airport ticket counter. It is the requirements of the system, in terms of information, access, response, and reliability, which the software person must understand most clearly in order to satisfy the banker, industrialist, or airline executive who has a problem to be solved.

Faced with this diversity of application problems, the real-time novice may wonder whether there is any commonality to real-time problems at all. We rely on Martin again to bring order out of potential chaos. In section 2–2, Martin points out that any real-time software will consist of three kinds of program—the application software itself, the supervisory system which provides execute-time services to the application program, and the support programs which assist in the preparation of application programs. The simplicity of this concept and of Martin's explanation is deceptive—many a real-time software system has had problems because its developers blurred this distinction too badly, for example, by putting too many application functions into the systems' supervisor.

Many of today's most complex real-time systems are procured by the government. In section 2–3 we are introduced to what may be the largest software system ever attempted, an antiballistic missile system built by TRW. It required 400 programmers at peak workload and utilized the fastest mainframe computers available. The distinctions made by Martin regarding types of systems and software are borne out by the specifics of the TRW software. In section 2–4 we see a more commonplace system, a fire department dispatching system for the city of New York. In this case, the focus is on both the real-time system itself and the support system—an environment simulator—used for rigorous testing of the system.

From TRW's huge, exotic system to the more commonplace, we then move to a tiny but complex real-time system. One of my favorite software articles is found in section 2–5. There Paul Heckel describes the complexity of a system caused by the *smallness* of the constraining problem and its computer hardware solution. Struggling with the need to "fit ten pounds of spinach in a five-pound sack," where the "sack" is a hand-held electronic language translator, Heckel shows us the other side of the real-time coin in contrast to larger systems discussed in sections 2–3 and 2–4. Heckel's problem is just as difficult to grasp in its own small way as was the TRW antiballistic missile system. So a prototype, throwaway system is built to explore the requirements and solution options. Heckel's article regarding this prototype approach is a rich learning experience in the alternatives open to real-time software builders.

2-1 SEVEN REFERENCE SYSTEMS *

JAMES MARTIN

[The previous chapter] illustrated real-time systems ranging from small and relatively simple computers to large and very complex multicomputer systems. Some of the characteristics of real-time apply to all of these systems, but in general the descriptions, suggestions, and principles in the remainder of the book apply to specific sections of this wide spectrum. Different techniques are used for different parts of the range.

In order to impose a sense of perspective on the remainder of this book, seven reference systems are used. These are landmarks from which the reader may take his bearings. . . .

2-1-1 REFERENCE SYSTEM NO. 1

2-1-1-1 Small Commercial System, for Example, a Savings Bank

Commercial records are referred to and updated, and decisions made.

Input from terminals by human operators at random times.

Input rate: 500 to 5000 transactions or enquiries per hour.

Number of file references: 2000 to 20,000 per hour.

Figure 2-1-1 Reference System No. 1.

Random–Access Files

Printer,
Card Reader,
etc.

Small
computer,
e.g., 16,000
characters
of core

Small line
control unit
without its own
stored program

Communication
lines to terminals

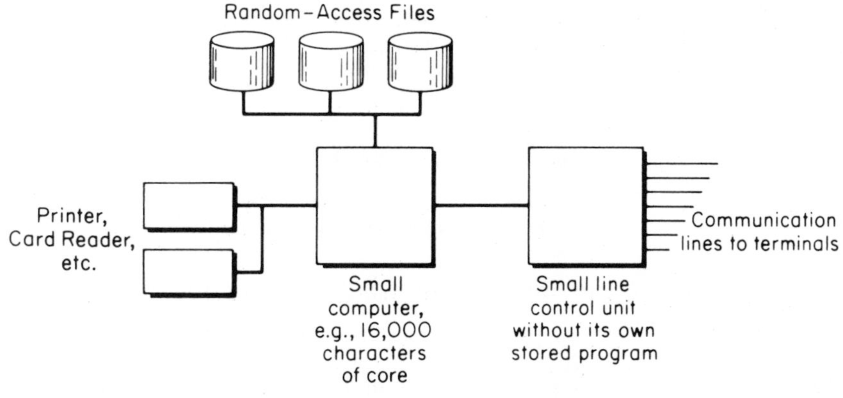

*From James Martin, *Programming Real-Time Computer Systems,* © 1965, pp. 53–60. Reprinted by permission of Prentice-Hall, Inc., Englewood Cliffs, N.J.

Required response time: Ten seconds or less.

Processing is strictly serial, that is, processing a transaction does not begin until the previous transaction is completed.

All frequently used programs are in core. Exceptionally used ones are on the files.

2-1-2 REFERENCE SYSTEM NO. 2

2-1-2-1 Small Process Control System, for Example, Petroleum or Chemical Plant Control

Inputs are pressure and temperature readings and other plant data read under program control. Calculations are made using this, and the output is used to set valves, heaters, and other plant controls, or to instruct the plant operator how to set these.

Input rate: Quick scan of 100 or so instruments approximately every minute.

Number of file references: Very few, if any.

Required response time: One to five minutes or more.

All or most of the Application Programs are in core.

One Application Program may be much more complex than one segment of a commercial program.

No multiprogramming except for interrupts by high-priority data.

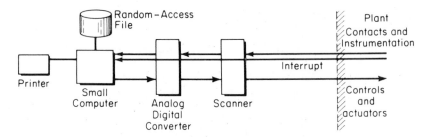

Figure 2-1-2 Reference System No. 2.

2-1-3 REFERENCE SYSTEM NO. 3

2-1-3-1 Hybrid System, for Example, Warehouse Control, Insurance Company

The main computer does any form of nonreal-time work. The small satellite computer collects and stores on its file messages arriving on the communication network. It interrupts the main computer at preset intervals or when it has a certain number of messages. The interruptions may take place . . . once every half minute [or] once every half hour. When they occur, the main computer removes its nonreal-time work from core and processes the messages. The replies are sent by the small machine while the large computer continues its other work.

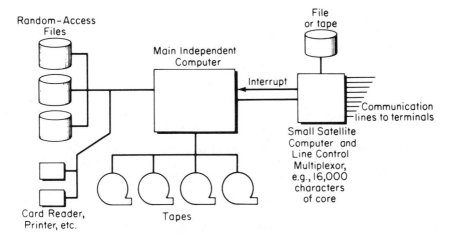

Figure 2-1-3   Reference System No. 3.

2-1-4 REFERENCE SYSTEM NO. 4

2-1-4-1 Medium-Size Commercial System, for Example, Warehouse Control

Commercial records are updated and referred to and decisions made.

Input from terminals by human operators at random times.

Figure 2-1-4   Reference System No. 4.

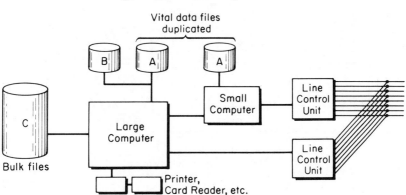

A portion of the file data must be available at all times, so this is duplicated. A hierarchy of fallback procedures is used rather than the expense of a fully duplexed system. The vital files are still accessible if any one unit fails.

The large computer may at times do off-line work while the small one does on-line real-time work.

2-1-5 REFERENCE SYSTEM NO. 5

2-1-5-1 Medium-Size Commercial System, for Example, a Large Stockbroker

Commercial records are referred to and updated, and decisions made.

Input from terminals by human operators at random times.

Input rate: 2000 to 20,000 transactions or enquiries per hour.

Number of file references: 12,000 to 120,000 per hour.

Required response time: Ten seconds or less.

Small degree of multiprogramming: Two or three messages may be processed in parallel.

Not all the frequently used programs can be held in core.

Extreme reliability is required; therefore, the system is duplexed.

Figure 2-1-5 Reference System No. 5.

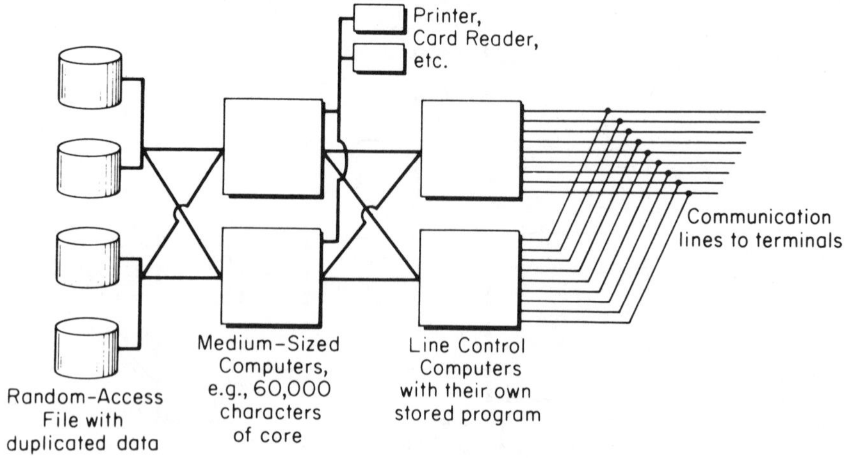

2-1-6 REFERENCE SYSTEM NO. 6

2-1-6-1 Large Commercial System, for Example, Airline Reservation System

Commercial records are referred to and updated, and decisions made.

Input from terminals by human operators at random times.

Input rate: 6,000 to 60,000 transactions or enquiries per hour.

Number of file references: 40,000 to 400,000 per hour.

Required response time: Three seconds or less.

High degree of multiprogramming: Three or more transactions are processed in parallel.

The majority of the programs are held on the files as there is not room for them in core.

Extreme reliability is required; therefore, the system is duplexed.

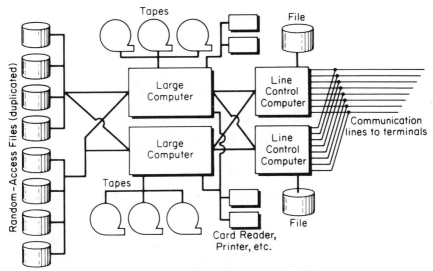

Figure 2-1-6   Reference System No. 6.

2-1-7 REFERENCE SYSTEM NO. 7

2-1-7-1 A Multicomputer System, for Example, for Information Retrieval

Several small computers are used in one system where no complex processing is required. This avoids the complications of multiprogramming and gives added reliability. However, it is expensive and can give logic difficulties if the files are updated by real-time transactions.

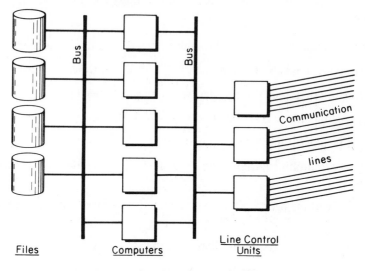

Figure 2-1-7   Reference System No. 7.

2-2 THE THREE KINDS OF PROGRAM*

JAMES MARTIN

In programming a real-time system three kinds of program are needed. A clear-cut distinction among the three types should be made from the outset. In systems which have not established this division from the start confusion has often resulted. The three kinds of program are:

1. Application Programs. These are the programs that carry out the processing of transactions or messages. They correspond to the data-processing programs of conventional applications and are unique to each system. They contain no input-output coding except in the form of macroinstruc-

---

tions which transfer control to an input/output control routine or monitor, which, in a real-time system, is part of the Supervisory Programs.

2. Supervisory Programs. These programs coordinate and schedule the work of the Application Programs and carry out service functions for them. It is possible to consider the many Application Programs as subroutines of the main Supervisory Program. The Supervisory Programs handle input and output operations and the queuing of messages and data. They are designed to coordinate and optimize the machine functions under varying loads. They process interrupts and deal with error or emergency conditions.

3. Support Programs. The ultimate working system consists of Application Programs and Supervisory Programs. However, a third set of programs is needed to install the system and to keep it running smoothly. These are referred to as Support Programs and include testing aids, data generator programs, terminal simulators, diagnostics, and so on.

The Application Programs are like the workers and plant in a factory, while the Supervisory Programs are like the office staff, management and foremen. The Support Programs are similar to the maintenance crew, helping to install new plant and to keep the machinery working.

Different terms are used by different organizations to describe these programs. The Application Programs are called *Operational Programs, Processors, Ordinary Processors,* and so on. The Supervisory Programs are called *Control Programs, Executive, and Monitors.* A variety of terms are used for the Support Programs. . . .

2-2-1 SUPERVISORY SYSTEM

The Supervisory Programs may be written by one team and classed together as the *Supervisory System.* A manual should be written for this package which the writers of the Application Programs must study. These programmers are then faced with the task, not of programming a computer in the normal way, but of programming a computer plus Supervisory System. In some ways this simplifies their work, but in other ways it restricts it. It gives them tools to use but imposes rules upon them. For example, the programmers are limited in their use of index registers and core storage, but input–output operations are done for them, and they do not have to time these as on a conventional system.

The Supervisory Programs may be provided by a computer manufacturer or may be written by the user. These are intricate programs. For a large system they take a long time to write and need skilled programmers. They are inevitably hardware-dependent and cannot be written in higher languages. Furthermore, they must be well defined before detailed work can start on the Application Programs. It is, therefore, a big advantage to the user if these are provided for him. Often, however, it may be necessary to tailor them to a particular application. Little success has been achieved so far in the standardization of Supervisory Programs for complex real-time systems, although portions of them have been provided successfully as standard packages. The customer may also find a need to modify the Supervisory Programs. If his system is a success he is likely to expand the work on it. If it is not, he will want to change its way of operating. Either could mean a change in the Supervisory Programs. It is, therefore, advisable for some of the user's programming team to understand fully the way these programs were designed and coded.

2-2-2 INTERRUPTS

Real-time systems make extensive use of some sort of *interrupt* feature. For example, a new message arriving from a distant terminal operator may interrupt what the computer is doing so that it may be read into the core. The end of a "seek" on a random-access device causes an interrupt, so that the computer can initiate the reading of the record found; and when reading is complete there may be another interrupt, so that the computer knows that the record is available for use and, also, so that the random-access device may be given another instruction if work is waiting for it. Either a Supervisory Program or an Application Program may be interrupted. When an interrupt occurs it is serviced by a short "priority" routine which is normally part of the Supervisory System.

When the cause of the interrupt has been dealt with, control will usually be returned to the point at which the interrupt occurred. . . . In order that the computer may resume what it was doing before the interruption occurred, the priority routine must retain the exact conditions that existed at that time. If it changes any of these it must restore them and make sure that the interrupted program continues as though no interrupt had occurred.

2-2-3 MAIN SCHEDULER

Figure 2-2-1 illustrates this and shows the relationship between the programs on a typical real-time system. The heart of the system is the small routine labelled *Main Scheduler*. When a chunk of Application Program or of Supervisory Program has finished its work it returns control to the Main Scheduler, and this decides what is to be done next. All portions of the system, with the exception of the interrupt processors, are entered from the Main Scheduler, and they all return control to the Main Scheduler as shown. This routine is the master of the system. It determines the sequence in which jobs are done, and allocates work to the other programs as required.

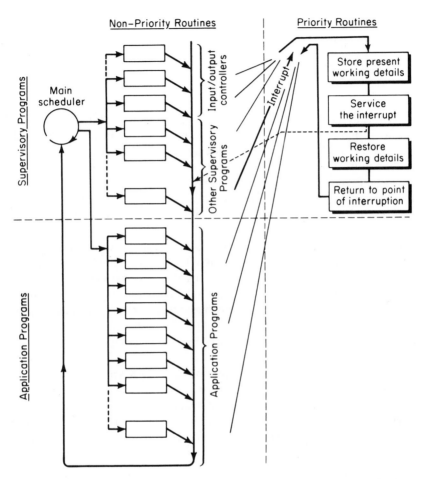

Figure 2-2-1   The relationship between the Application Programs and Supervisory Programs.

The Application Programs, which actually perform the processing on the real-time data, have no direct contact with the outside world. They receive data from the Supervisory Programs, process them, and then return them to the Supervisory Programs. They may, however, be the largest part of all the programming. Some systems . . . have 200,000 or so instructions in the Application Programs but not more than 20,000 in the Supervisory Programs.

The Main Scheduler transfers control to some of the Supervisory routines. These may, in fact, be written in the same way as Application Programs, that is, obeying the same rules. They may be routines for handling errors, for generating file addresses, or for preparing a message to the computer. These three functions might, indeed, be regarded as the work of Application

Programs. There is an area in which the distinction between the two becomes rather vague, and they would be differently defined for different systems.

2-2-4 COMMUNICATION LINES

The control of a *communication network* may be an important function of the real-time programs. The impulses on a communication line are translated by the hardware into bits. The bits are assembled either by hardware or program into characters or words. The characters or words are assembled by program into messages or transactions ready for processing. This may be happening on many lines at the same time. The lines must be constantly scanned. If the program is assembling bits, it must be sure that it never stops scanning long enough to lose a bit.

Conversely, outgoing messages must be broken down into words or characters, and these split into bits. The bits are transmitted down the line by the hardware in the form of pulses. Among the messages being sent down the line will be signals controlling the terminals. If a line has many terminals attached to it they cannot all send their messages at once. Normally they must wait until they are instructed by the computer to send. The instruction is one form of control message. Such messages have to be composed and sent at appropriate intervals.

The work of controlling the communication lines is normally a duty of the Supervisory Programs. The programs for doing this may or may not be in the main computer. Often a separate line control unit or multiplexor has its own core storage and stored program. Alternatively, a small subsidiary computer may be attached to the main computer, and has the duty of controlling the communications network and feeding complete checked-out messages to the main machine.

In Reference System No. 1 in Figure 2-1-1 the line control unit does not have a stored program. It may interrupt the computer when it has assembled a character or word, and the computer reads this. The computer has a routine to assemble the characters or words into messages and to break down the output messages ready for transmission. The line control unit interrupts the computer when it needs another character or word to transmit.

In Reference System No. 5, however, the multiplexor has its own stored program. It assembles complete messages, performs an error check on them, queues them if necessary, and sends them ready for processing to the computer.

When more than one machine has a stored program the Supervisory System must coordinate their operation. The programs in a Line Control Computer may be regarded as a part of the Supervisory Programs of the System. In Reference System No. 6, there are four machines with a stored program. The Supervisory Programs for the system must coordinate all of these, arrange that when they interrupt each other the interrupts are processed correctly, and control the transfer of data from one system to another.

2-2-5 FILES

Real-time systems often have large random-access files attached to the computer for retrieving and updating information. Various programs are needed for organizing and locating data in these. . . . Locating an item in a large file is rather like looking up a number in a telephone directory, or finding an item in a room full of filing cabinets. In a commercial system this may take a much longer time than processing the item in question, and therefore a number of file operations are carried out at the same time. Where several such operations of varying length overlap, control becomes difficult. Interrupts signal the end of file operations, and the Supervisory Programs are made more complicated by this.

Items may be constantly added to the files or deleted from them. When items are deleted this leaves empty space which is wasteful, and when items are added they cannot be placed in the most convenient location immdiately. A telephone list makes a good analogy. If names are struck off the list they leave unused lines. This does not matter on a sheet of paper, but on computer files it becomes expensive to have too much empty space. Similarly, when an item is added, it cannot be placed in alphabetical sequence but is added at the bottom of the list. For this reason . . . a computer file with additions and deletions has to be reorganized periodically. It is rewritten with the items in the most convenient place.

2-2-6 SUPPORT PROGRAMS

The file reorganization programs are one example of the many Support Programs that may be needed. Like that part of an iceberg below the surface, the Support Programs have sometimes not been viewed in their true significance by teams planning and installing real-time systems. The [person-years] of effort they require may be considerable. It may be surprising to a new team to note that on most systems the Support Programs have taken considerably more programming manpower than the Supervisory Programs. In some systems the ratio has been as high as four to one.

A list of Support Programs for a typical real-time system will include such items as the following:

System loading and initializing programs
Restart programs

Diagnostics

File reorganization programs

Fallback programs

Library tape and file maintenance programs

Data generation programs for program testing

File loading routines

Supervisory Program Simulators for use in testing

Application Program Simulators for use in testing

Operator set and line control unit simulators

Testing Supervisory Routine

"Introspective" testing aids

Core print programs

Debugging aids

Testing output analysis programs and sorts

2-3   SYSTEM TECHNOLOGY PROGRAM *

Site Defense (SD) was intended to be an antiballistic missile terminal defense system. It was designed to possess a performance credibility sufficient to deter an aggressor from a first-strike attack against the Minuteman Missile force and to ensure that an acceptable number of Minutemen would survive in the event of a first strike. Furthermore, the SD System would be capable of countering attacks of various levels and tactics, and of degrading gracefully in the event of subsystem overloads or failures, or in the event of attacks of greater severity than the design threat parameters. The SD System development has been redefined to be a Ballistic Missiles Division (BMD) Systems Technology Program (STP), to provide objective evidence of the performance of the key functions of a tactical SD System. The primary objectives of STP are:

1. Validating the data processing subsystem by demonstrating the performance of the engagement software (the tactical applications program and the tactical operating system) executed by the computer, a CDC 7700, against both real targets and simulated threats.

* From "Impact of Modern Programming Practices on System Development," RADC–TR–77–121, 1977.

2. Providing the framework for incorporating currently deferred data processing subsystem elements.

3. Supporting data gathering during system tests at Kwajalein missile range.

The STP software being developed by TRW has been organized into engagement software, test support software, and development support software categories. The software in these categories consists of ten major computer programs.

The engagement software is the software necessary to identify and track ballistic reentry vehicles through the use of STP system resources. Its logic and algorithms consist of those needed to satisfy functional and performance requirements that support the system engagement functions: detect and designate objects, track objects, and discriminate objects.

The software that actually runs on the CDC 7700 (the STP processor) is referred to as a *process*. A process is composed of a data base, an operating system, and one or more application programs. The Tactical Application Program is composed of tasks, which are composed of several levels of routines. The operating system is a table-driven, real-time system designed specifically for the CDC 7700. The Application Program and the Test Support Programs operate under its control. It provides the following basic functions: task supervision, scheduling, dispatching, real-time input and output, system timing, data management, history logging, error detection, error processing, initialization, and termination.

The primary component of the Test Support Software is the Kwajalein Test Support Program. It is required to test key functions of the engagement process and to support system test operations. Additional test support functions have been provided in the Data Processing Subsystem Simulator and a variety of test tools used in the generation of test data and evaluation of test results. Development of two other test support components (that is, the System Environment and Threat Simulator and the System Test Driver) was initiated, but continued development was deferred.

The Development Support Software consists of the Basic Operating System, the Process Construction Program, specialized development support tools, and the Data Reduction and Report Generator. The basic operating system, the primary operating system used in software development, consists of a specially tailored version of the SCOPE 2 operating system for the CDC 7600/7700 plus the associated loaders, compilers, assemblers, and utilities. The functions of Process Construction are data base definition, data base generation, task–routine compilation, process consolidation, and process adaptation using a higher level, Fortran-like language which facilitates construction of the real-time software. Using the process designer's input directives and definitions and a library file of coded routines and tasks, Process Construction assembles the application program, constructs the tables defining the program operation to the tactical operating system, and links the entire process together.

Specialized tools consist of a number of utility programs that aid developers in the design, execution, and evaluation of SD software. They provide information useful in static and dynamic analysis of the software and relieve developers and testers of many repetitive and tedious tasks.

Data Reduction is an off-line program used to postprocess in a nonreal-time environment the data generated by the test processes. It supports analysis and reduction of real-time execution history logs and generates reports based on user requests.

The major elements of the computer hardware system consist of CDC 6400, 7600, and 7700 computers. The CDC 6400 computer is used primarily as an input and output station for the 7600 and 7700. The 7600 was used in the early phase of software development and was replaced by the 7700, which is essentially two 7600s with a shared large core memory. The 7600 and 7700 mainframes have been supported by an extensive complement of peripherals driven by the CDC 6400. At the peak of the configuration, the system contained two card readers, one card punch, six tape drives, eleven disk packs, six printers, one large disk file, and three operators' consoles. Off-line peripherals consisted of one IBM 360–20 and three Calcomp plotters. . . .

At its peak the project staff exceeded 400 personnel. A history of the project population through mid-1976 is shown in Figure 2–3–1. The figure also

Figure 2–3–1 STP staffing.

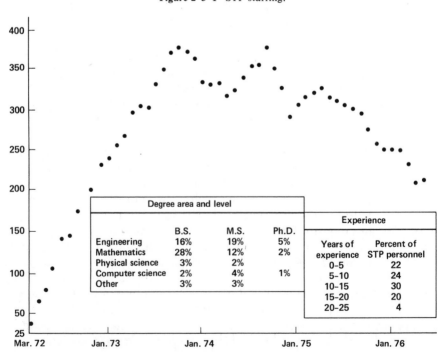

Degree area and level			
	B.S.	M.S.	Ph.D.
Engineering	16%	19%	5%
Mathematics	28%	12%	2%
Physical science	3%	2%	
Computer science	2%	4%	1%
Other	3%	3%	

Experience	
Years of experience	Percent of STP personnel
0–5	22
5–10	24
10–15	30
15–20	20
20–25	4

illustrates the personnel mix (educational background, degree level, and experience) which has remained relatively constant despite the large variation in project size.

The programmers on the STP project fell into three major categories: (1) CDC operating systems support programmers, (2) real-time systems programmers, and (3) application programmers. . . .

〰〰〰〰〰〰〰〰〰〰〰〰〰〰〰〰〰〰〰〰〰〰〰〰〰〰〰〰〰〰〰〰〰〰〰〰〰〰〰

2-4 AN ENVIRONMENTAL SIMULATOR FOR THE FDNY COMPUTER-AIDED DISPATCH SYSTEM*

John Mohan, FDNY

AND

Michael Geller, Bradford National Corporation

〰〰〰〰〰〰〰〰〰〰〰〰〰〰〰〰〰〰〰〰〰〰〰〰〰〰〰〰〰〰〰〰〰〰〰〰〰〰〰

2-4-1 ABSTRACT

FDNY's MICS computer-aided dispatch system is designed about dual PDP 11/45s and supported in fallback by dual INTEL 8080 microprocessors. The computer processes alarms, assigns available units, notifies these units by voice and hard copy terminals located in the fire stations, monitors status changes of firefighting units and incidents, and dynamically adjusts firefighting coverage for maximum effect.

This paper describes the MICS environmental simulator that was used to test and validate the MICS development effort. Some results of system performance are presented to depict how the environmental simulator was used for system acceptance testing. Finally, encouragement is given to developers of other large real-time systems to adopt a design approach which considers simulated load generation and performance monitoring to be an integral part of the overall applications and systems software. . . .

2-4-2 INTRODUCTION

The New York City Fire Department (FDNY) presents a complex problem in the deployment of men and equipment. Over 500 pieces of apparatus, manned

*From the Proceedings of the Second IEEE International Conference on Software Engineering, 1976; and with the permission of the authors: John Mohan, consultant, Douglaston, N.Y., and Michael Geller, Bell Laboratories, Whippany, N.J. Reprinted with permission.

by more than 13,000 men, are distributed throughout the five boroughs of New York City. In 1975, there were 400,000 fire alarms of which half were false. The variety of demands for service and the spiralling alarm rates required more sophisticated methods of deploying firefighting resources.

To meet these demands, FDNY embarked on the development of a new computer-based Management Information and Control System (MICS) to replace the manual dispatch procedures and to improve the effectiveness of the department's operations.

The MICS computer-aided dispatch system is designed about dual PDP–11/45s and supported in fallback by dual INTEL 8080 microprocessors. (The dual designation is used to connote that the backup computer runs in hot standby mode.) The computer processes alarms received by telephone, new electronic street boxes and older mechanical street boxes; assigns available units; notifies these units by voice and hard copy terminals located in the fire stations; monitors status changes of firefighting units and incidents, dynamically adjusts firefighting coverage for maximum effect, and provides management with timely and concise activity reporting for up to three alarms per minute. As with MICS, the performance requirements for a real-time system are chosen to satisfy throughput rates projected years hence. But even with the abundance of literature on the subject, performance requirements are stated prior to system development without a precisely defined procedure for achieving and measuring the requirements. FDNY felt there was significant advantage to be gained by a planned integration of load generation, performance monitoring, and training in an environmental simulator. Although MICS did include test support for unit and modular testing, the term *environmental simulator*[1] is not used here to include this capability. The MICS environmental simulator placed the emphasis on volume testing in a multiprogrammed context for final system acceptance.

FDNY required an environmental simulator to be developed as an integral part of the MICS. This concept has proven to be propitious for the system development. The environmental simulator has provided a threefold advantage: an invaluable debugging aid and design tool, the means for demonstrating the performance criteria for systems acceptance, and a training vehicle for operators.

The environmental simulator consists of an off-line scenario generator, an on-line load generator module, and a performance monitor module. The scenario module creates alarms and subsequent activity associated with the alarm from an alarm history model using Monte Carlo techniques. Field responses, request for additional equipment, status and incident updates, and CRT operator interactions associated with each alarm history are generated from this model. The alarm history model is built into a FORTRAN program which creates the desired scenario storing the alarms and their corresponding histories including arrival times, operator actions, and updates on magnetic tape. Each message generated is defined as originating from the hardware device associated with that message. Operator availability for incoming alarms is also included in the simulation. The messages are generated according to alarm rates and mixes specified in the input stream to the scenario generator.

The load generator module, residing in the standby PDP 11/45 (the driver system), reads the scenario tape. The actions and times associated with the alarms are sorted into a separate data file corresponding to the hardware device from which the action originated. When this initialization is completed, the real-time load generation is triggered. Each input device file is scanned for an action; at the appropriate time the driver system transmits the input message to MICS residing in the prime computer via the proper communications interface. The approach of using the standby computer to drive the on-line computer was taken to eliminate the effect of interference on performance monitoring. The prime computer receives the input message exactly as if it were coming from the real input device. If the device is also an output device (that is, CRT), MICS responds by generating its normal output message. The output message is transferred to the driver system. If the output message is a data entry format screen, the driver system simulates the CRT operator interaction and transmits the completed data entry screen back to MICS. The structure of the load generator module permits any combination of simulated and real devices or operators.

The performance monitor module gathers statistics on MICS as related to input message rates, CPU utilization, core utilization, system queue lengths, response time to operator requests, task execution times, and I/O analysis. Other system parameters representative of functional performance time from alarm receipt through dispatch, notification and so on, are also generated. The performance monitor module can be used either stand-alone in the on-line MICS or in conjunction with the load generator module. When used with the load generator module, system measurements can be analyzed in light of a known and controlled environment [2].

This paper describes the MICS environmental simulator architecture and how it was used to facilitate MICS development effort. Some results on system performance are presented to depict how the environmental simulator was used for system acceptance testing. Finally, encouragement is given to developers of other large real-time systems to adopt a design approach which considers simulated load generation and performance monitoring to be an integral part of the overall applications and systems software.

2-4-3 MICS SYSTEM DESCRIPTION

Briefly, MICS hardware is composed of dual PDP-11/45 systems with a channel-to-channel link for interprocessor communications, 96K words of core, three 88M byte disks, two tape drives on each system, line printers, card reader, CRT terminals and other special purpose terminals for Central Office operations, and a microprocessor Alarm Teleprinter terminal in each fire station. An automated fallback subsystem (dual INTEL 8080s) is included to take over alarm processing at the central office in the event both systems fail at the same time (Figure 2-4-1). All device communications are switched through a line switch for maximum configurability.

The fallback subsystem is designed about dual INTEL 8080 microprocessors with 8K bytes of ROM and 2K bytes of RAM that operate as an intelligent controller for an automated map, an automated chipboard, and four Status Entry Panels. The fallback subsystem is designed to operate as a peripheral to the PDP 11/45s in prime mode and as a stand-alone subsystem when both PDP 11/45s fail. The Status Entry Panels are specially designed terminals that are used to enter firefighting unit and incident status changes. These entries are transmitted to the PDP 11/45s when operating in prime mode and processed locally in fallback mode. The fallback system was designed to facilitate the transition from an automated environment to a total manual operation if all electronics fail.

MICS maintains the current status of incidents and units throughout the city. Using programmed rules, it computes the quickest and most suitable

Figure 2-4-1 MICS hardware.

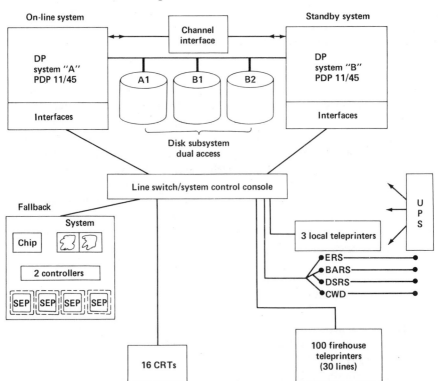

response to each alarm and displays it for a dispatcher to approve or modify according to his knowledge of the situation. MICS also indicates the need for changing the deployment of units and recommends specific moves which are subject to higher level review and modification before execution. MICS functions in six modes of operation: alarm receipt, decision dispatch, display/fallback, notification, status monitoring, and management.

ALARM RECEIPT.   The alarm receipt mode of operation supports three methods of receiving alarms: telephone, street boxes, and the Emergency Reporting System (ERS).

ERS uses a newer electronic street box which provides a voice transmission capability to supplement the electronic coded box number. The more traditional mechanical street boxes are decoded by the Box Alarm Readout System (BARS) that interfaces directly with the alarm circuits. Alarms originating from street boxes enter MICS through BARS and are automatically processed by the system. Telephone and ERS alarms are switched to Alarm Receipt Operators who obtain the pertinent information from the concerned citizen and enter this into MICS via a computer terminal. The telephone alarm information is processed by a phonetic address translation program to determine the closest company for response. The phonetization capability provides the operator with phonetically equivalent alternatives for incorrectly spelled names [3]. Each alarm is then checked by the computer with the alarms in progress to determine whether it has already been received and is being processed. After the alarm is identified as unique, the decision dispatch mode is entered.

DECISION DISPATCH.   When an alarm is received by MICS, an automatic determination is made regarding the appropriate response. This determination is made in terms of how many units should be sent and which units they should be. The system-determined response is automatically directed to the operator for his or her review and action. The operator can inform the system of any one of several actions which he desires to take, such as deleting or adding units to the recommended response.

The supervisor also interacts with the computer to perform the all important relocation function. Assisted by the computer, the supervisor must decide when firefighting resources in an area have been reduced below an acceptable level that requires other available units to be moved or relocated into the uncovered area. Relocation recommendations, concerning which units are to be relocated and to where, are generated based on the dynamic state of the system at the time.

DISPLAY-FALLBACK.   The display mode functions both as a visual aid to the dispatching process and an automated fallback system. The display system contains a geographic map that pictorially represents the coverage area by displaying the availability of each company. The purpose of this map is to provide a visual aid for the determination of the relocations of companies to depleted areas. This map and an automated chipboard are driven electronically by the dual INTEL 8080 microprocessor system. The chipboard has a slot that holds a plastic chip for each company and next to the slot, a light that describes the company's availability. During normal operation, the computer will electronically drive the indicator lights on both the chipboard and map. If the computer system fails, the system supervisor will be able to determine the availability of a company by the state of the associated light. With this information, the supervisor immediately reverts to the manual backup operational procedures. This involves removing the plastic chip from the slot and placing it on the side in an array containing the units dispatched to the associated incident.

Notification.　　After the decision has been made concerning which units to send, the system enters the notification mode. Notification of the responding units depends on whether the units are in quarters or not. The order to respond is printed in the fire station on the alarm printer with the time of alarm. The alarm order is forwarded to the Voice Operator for notification on the voice alarm system if the unit is in quarters. So the fire station receives both written and verbal notification. When a responding company is out of quarters and available on the air, MICS notifies the Radio Operator to dispatch the company by radio. Notification is not complete until an acknowledgment from the selected unit is received. A specially designed microprocessor response terminal that also functions as controller for the 30 cps alarm teleprinter is located at each fire station. This response panel enables acknowledgments, return to service, and out of service messages to be transmitted to the Central Office.

Status Monitoring.　　Status monitoring mode involves monitoring of both the status of units and incidents. MICS maintains an accurate up-to-second status of all firefighting units in terms of their availability and their location. Units report when they have completed their work and are leaving the scene, and when they arrive back at the fire station. Units being relocated from one fire station to another report when they leave the old location and when they arrive at the new one.

MICS receives and acknowledges all unit reports and updates the file records in which the current location and availability status of all units are maintained via a Status Entry Panel. This information is thus available for display and for use by the various application programs. MICS also provides an automatic monitoring function which causes the radio dispatcher to be alerted if a unit has not taken action to respond after a preset length of time. In this way, he is alerted to take whatever actions are necessary to insure adequate and timely response. Status is also maintained on incidents so that the supervisor can tell at a glance how many incidents are in progress and what units are assigned to each incident.

Management.   Management mode is a term used to describe a variety of functions that are performed as support to the actual dispatching process. These functions include: data recording, activity reporting, information retrieval, message switching, training vehicle, and also includes load generation and performance monitoring.

The stated performance requirement for MICS is that all terminal inputs associated with the first five modes of operation (alarm receipt, decision dispatch, display–fallback, notification and status monitoring) have an average response time of one second and a 99 percent probability that the response time not exceed three seconds for message rates up to one message per second. An input message is a buffer generated by an event external to MICS (for example, an operator pressing one of the function keys at a CRT or Status Entry Panel). Alarms from the Box Alarm Readout System (BARS) and the Emergency Reporting System (ERS) are also input messages. Each input message is processed by the communications control program which transfers control to the appropriate application program for the particular message. The result is an output message to a CRT or other output device.

The response time is measured from the time the input is received by the computer until the first character is output to the terminal I/O bus. These response time requirements must hold true for input message rates up to and including one message per second. (A rate of one message per second is functionally equivalent to three alarms per minute, if twenty input messages per alarm is assumed.) The MICS performance monitoring module is the vehicle used to determine what computer response times actually are.

Using the load generator to drive the system, the performance monitoring measures response times. The performance criteria must be demonstrated using the 1974 incoming alarm rate mix.

2-4-4 ALARM HISTORY SIMULATION MODEL

In order to properly measure the effectiveness of the MICS data processing system, and to test the various functions that it performs, a mechanism for creating test data representation of well defined and controllable scenarios was developed. A simulation program, ALMSIM, was written in FORTRAN which simulates the arrival of alarms and their subsequent histories according to input parameters specified. The input data which determines the nature of the scenario consists of: alarm rate, duration of the simulation, percent of alarms by source (BARS, ERS, PHONE), percent false alarms, percent duplicate alarms, and number of Alarm Receipt operators.

The history of each alarm consists of its arrival time, the source of the alarm, the box number associated with the alarm, which Alarm Receipt

Operator handled the alarm, the operator service times for completing each screen, the time until all units acknowledge their dispatch orders, and finally, all signals from units at the incident that would occur for the alarm and their respective times. These histories are generated by the ALMSIM program according to the alarm history model (Figure 2–4–2) and stored on magnetic tape. The tape is later compared to performance monitoring history printouts which depict the processing of alarms by MICS. The comparison checks whether all incidents were properly handled by MICS. For example, if a signal is sent requiring additional units to be dispatched, it is easy to verify whether or not the additional dispatch was made.

The stored scenarios are then converted into device dependent files containing appropriate messages for each device (that is, alarm messages for the BARS and ERS simulators, function key messages and screen modifications for each CRT and Status Entry Panel). The result is one file for each hardware device to be simulated during the load generation experiment. These files are used by the corresponding device simulators which are part of the load generation system described in the next section. For example, a file is created for each Alarm Receipt Operator consisting of the times and canned messages that he will send to initiate telephone alarms, the service time for completion and the actual completed alarm screen to be sent for that telephone alarm.

The alarms are created with exponential interarrival times at the mean rate specified. The interarrival time t_n is obtained from the inverse cumulative exponential distribution.

Operator service times are similarly chosen, using their respective mean service rates. Similar techniques were used to simulate the time until various signals arrive and until the different types of alarms are complete. The type of signals that are associated with a particular alarm depend on the nature of the fire; for example, whether it is structural or not. The type of fires simulated and the corresponding signals were selected randomly using distributions based on 1974 statistics gathered by the FDNY.

The availability of Alarm Receipt Operators is simulated since these operators respond to messages which originate external to MICS, namely ERS and telephone alarms. For example, if an ERS alarm arrives and there is no Alarm Receipt Operator available, the simulation program must create two types of messages. The first will be treated as a BARS alarm (dispatch is automatic), the second will cause an ERS screen to be sent immediately when an operator next becomes available (determined by the simulation) for additional information to be entered. This portion of the simulation was instrumental in determining the quantity of alarm receipt equipment required at different communication centers. Note the other types of operators respond to messages which are queued to them by MICS. These queues are measured directly by the performance monitor and have been analyzed with respect to known input rates created by the load generator.

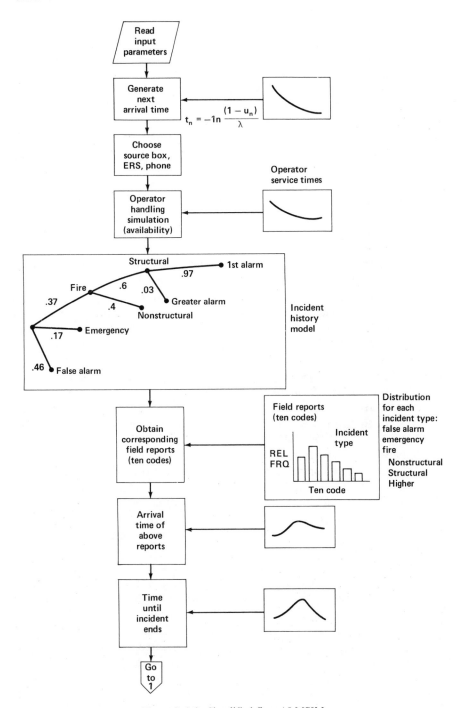

Figure 2-4-2 Simplified flow-ALMSIM.

2-4-5 LOAD GENERATION MODULE

The load generation module outline in Figure 2-4-3 exercises MICS with simulated alarms and subsequent operation interaction. It is a set of assembly language programs, one for each device simulated, and resides in the driver PDP-11/45 computer. The driver-computer is loaded with a version of MICS that was modified to transmit BARS and ERS alarms, to accept polls by MICS, and to emulate the CRTs and the Status Entry Panels. The lines normally terminating at the CRTs and Status Entry Panels are connected to the driver-computer for a load generation experiment through the line switching equipment. By integrating the load generator into the MICS framework, the MICS line control table and communication control program was utilized, thus minimizing the amount of communication effort required. Also, MICS provided us with the ability to schedule programs at specified times, passing along the input data through the parameter block.

The line handling tables and communication control program (SIMQUE) are written so that a MICS message bound for a particular hardware device is scanned by SIMQUE which passes control to the proper entry point of the appropriate device simulator. For example, if a prompting light (message waiting) is sent by MICS to the Decision Dispatcher's CRT, it will instead be sent to the standby computer where SIMQUE determines the appropriate entry point of the simulator to call. In this case, the entry point begins a program which decides if the Decision Dispatcher is available and, if so, returns the proper NEXT message to MICS via the SIMQUE program. If the Decision Dispatcher is not available, a flag is set so that when it becomes available (releases current screen) a NEXT is transmitted. If a screen is being transmitted to the Decision Dispatcher's CRT, SIMQUE must pass control to the entry point of the simulator where the appropriate completed times are read from the response file. After the time to complete the screen elapses, the response is returned. So, in effect the output message which under normal circumstances is processed by an operator at his CRT is instead transferred to the driver system where the operator's interactions are simulated by programmed rules. Thus, the driver system is not only an input load generator but is also simulating the real world environment including operator interactions.

The use of separate files for each hardware device makes it possible to mix simulated and real activity. This is especially useful in training because one or more types of operators can be on-line, entering information and responding to computer generated screens, while simulated hardware devices [4] are inputting alarms and actions of other operators. It is also possible to perform individual experiments while background activity is being created by the simulator. All communication between computers is logged for automated post analysis. All messages from the backup system are transmitted over the lines which correspond to the hardware where they are actually generated, line disciplines and protocols being emulated exactly.

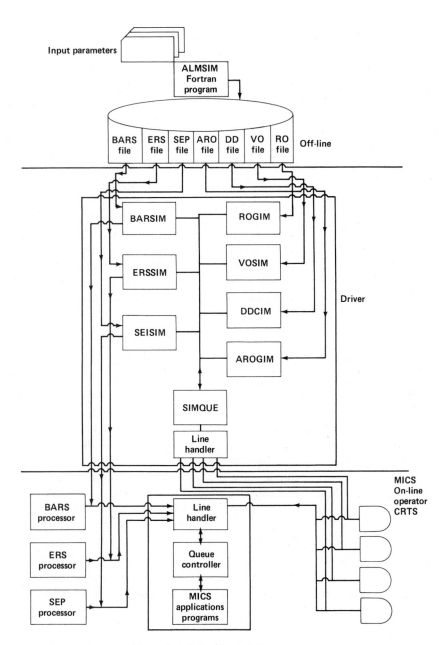

Figure 2-4-3 Load generation system.

The following are brief descriptions of the various simulators:

BARSIM: Reads the file of BARS alarm messages and their inter-arrival times. It schedules the transmission of each message which is transmitted in the exact manner of a BARS alarm at the specified time.

ERSIM: Similar to the above but with communication hand-shaking emulating the ERS processor.

SEPSIM: This program transmits all status reports from the field entered via the Status Entry Panel. The SEP file which it reads contains the box number, time of arrival and all reports from the field created by the ALMSIM program and stored according to arrival time in the SEP file.

AROSIM: There is one module for each Alarm Receipt Operator being simulated. The program reads a record from the ARO file. The first record indicates that a telephone or ERS alarm is to be transmitted and will contain the corresponding transmission time and canned message. AROSIM then schedules the transmission of the canned message. If it is a telephone alarm, AROSIM will cause a telephone alarm entry message to be sent to the operator. When the alarm screen is returned, AROSIM reads the next record from the ARO file which will contain the operator service time and the canned alarm screen to return. The service time is simulated by the program waking itself at the appropriate time to return the canned screen. The next record is read from the file and will contain the time and next alarm to be sent and hence the process starts again.

If it is an ERS, the canned ERS message is transmitted. The program responds to a message waiting light by transmitting a NEXT. When the ERS screen is received, AROSIM reads the next record which contains the service time and canned screen to return. It schedules the transmission and, after it is done, reads the next record for the next alarm and time.

DDSIM: This module simulates the Decision Dispatcher's actions. It responds, when available, to a message-waiting prompt with a NEXT command. After receiving the screen, it simulates the Decision Dispatcher's service time stored in the DD file and sends a RELEASE command when the time elapses. After the screen is released, a check is made to determine if another message is waiting.

VOSIM: Performs same function as DDSIM for the Voice Operator.

ROSIM: Performs same function as DDSIM for the Radio Operator; in addition, a message is sent that all units have acknowledged before the screen is released.

2-4-6 PERFORMANCE MONITORING

An on-line software performance monitoring module is incorporated into MICS. It lies dormant until activated from the system console. When activated, it gathers information pertinent to system performance. Data associated with input message rates, operator queue lengths, CPU, memory and peripheral hardware utilization are continuously accumulated and logged periodically at a specified rate. Data associated with tasks such as their execution times, files accesses, amount of I/O and so on, is logged on the system log tape at the termination of each task. A task is a unique set of programs responding to an operator entry or other appropriate input message (alarm) or conditional event. Since each task corresponds to a set of actual programs, it is possible to pinpoint inefficient code, program bugs, I/O problems, bottlenecks and their reasons (for example, waiting for core, I/O). The performance monitoring reports are developed by off-line programs that read the appropriate sorted and filtered versions of the system log tape created during a performance monitoring session.

A system profile is obtained from the aggregate of the performance monitoring reports. When used in conjunction with input from the load generator, the statistics gathered are analyzed in the light of known and controlled environment with minimal artifact being introduced by the performance monitoring. These reports are the Task Monitor, File Monitor, Response Monitor, Incident Monitor, Session Monitor, Queue Monitor, Message Monitor, and CPU Monitor.

A task parameter block is carried through all programs associated with a particular task and is used for gathering statistics corresponding to that task (I/O, files accessed). A task initiator-terminator module measures the execution time and logs the task record. The task parameter block is used to develop the Task Monitor report. Since this data contains I/O accesses, a File Monitor report is generated by inverting these blocks on the files accessed.

Tasks associated with operator function keys are analyzed with respect to response time. The tasks corresponding to operator entries are flagged and a complete response time analysis is produced as part of the Response Monitor report.

In addition to measuring the internal performance of MICS, the functional system performance is also considered. This is summarized in the Incident Monitor report which includes an analysis of elapsed times between alarm receipt, dispatch, voice and radio notification for all alarms. The task parameter block is also used to provide data on the CRT operator's performance. The Session Monitor report is used as an integral part of the operator training program to evaluate the efficiency of operators completing the various system screens.

A queue record is periodically logged, containing for each queue the number of entries, maximum queue size, a cumulative waiting time, and the time since the cumulative time integral was last updated. The queue statistics for the Queue Monitor report are obtained from this data.

CPU and core utilization records are obtained by modifying the wait function and block allocation portions of the MICS operating system.

These records are also logged periodically and reported in the CPU Monitor report.

In addition, the delay-time distributions for each communication line to the fire station teleprinters are measured. The time the message is queued for transmission and the time transmission is actually completed is included in the log of the message. The time from alarm receipt through teleprinter notification is also computed by the off-line programs.

2-4-7 SUMMARY AND CONCLUSIONS

The environmental simulator was used throughout the development of MICS. It was used during the system-design phase, the implementation phase, the testing phase, and operator training during parallel operation. Although the environmental simulator was itself being developed along with MICS, the fact that this concept was built into the system from inception insured a high degree of attention to performance considerations. For example, in the preliminary implementation stage, the ALMSIM program was run simulating various data mixes and operator service times in order to estimate basic system requirements, such as memory requirements, operating system requirements, line baud rates, quantity of operators and associated hardware, and checkpoint procedures. A three-minute snapshot of input messages and tasks resulting from an alarm rate of three alarms per minute (peak design load) was used in conjunction with independent timing estimates to produce a gross system profile. This effort revealed that the proposed operating system software (DEC RSX–11D, version 6) had two important deficiencies. The memory management capability of the PDP–11/45 was not fully supported at all hardware levels and the software overhead associated with I/O support was significant. These factors working together produced a CPU utilization in excess of 70 percent for the three-minute snapshot. These results created serious doubt as to whether MICS would achieve its stated performance goal. A decision was made not to use the DEC RSX–11D Operating System, all of whose features were not required by MICS, but instead develop a more limited and efficient one for this application. It was also concluded that an additional 32K words of memory would provide an important contribution to system performance and reduce waits for memory. Further into the implementation phase, key application programs were written and integrated into a skeleton system exercised by the load generator. Because the data provided by the load generator is known a priori, it was possible to determine whether programs were working properly. Performance monitoring reports revealed system bottlenecks early in the integration process and action was taken before problems were compounded. The Task Monitor demonstrated the effects of new programs as they were integrated. For example, the most complex task is a mathematical algorithm for relocating units in order to assure evenly distributed coverage with adequate response capability. This task was run while load generation simultaneously provided background activity. The effect of the algorithm on overall performance was measured by analyzing performance monitoring reports with and without the relocation algorithm executing. The impact on system performance is similarly measured whenever any new major function is added. The environmental simulator was used as the vehicle to ascertain whether MICS met the system acceptance criteria. It was used to drive the system under peak alarm conditions of three alarms per minute and greater for one hour of simulated time. The performance monitor reports were obtained for each series of runs. The key test of the system was to maintain adequate response times to the CRT operators (average of one second and three seconds response within 99 percent). The Response Monitor report was used to develop a graph (Figure 2–4–4) of response time versus throughput that describes the results. As depicted by the graph, MICS system performance was more than adequately met. These same runs were used to train the CRT operators by suppressing the CRT simulation modules. The reproducibility of the training runs provided for uniformity of training and a means for detecting operator errors. Since these alarm rates were beyond what is currently experienced, the only means of obtaining this input rate as well as sustaining the subsequent activity associated with it was with artificial methods. As is the case with most real-time systems, a source of test data that is representative of the real world environment is needed for effective testing but is not readily available. However, many system implementors question load generator models such as the alarm history model in

Figure 2–4–4   Response time vs. task rate.

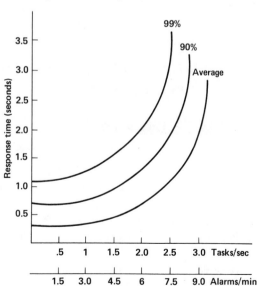

ALMSIM as unrepresentative of the real world and then proceed to use very rudimentary test data for the system testing phase.

This paper has attempted to demonstrate how load generation and performance monitoring can be readily integrated into the development of a real-time system as complicated as MICS. This scaffolding [5] is usually done in a token form anyway. However, if formally structured into the total development effort, many benefits result. It is especially beneficial in a contracting environment where a performance criteria is almost always stated but the means to determine that the performance objective is achieved is almost always lacking. It is the hope of the authors that environmental simulator scaffolding becomes as much a part of any real-time system as the application software itself.

2-4-8 REFERENCES

[1] Ginzberg, M. G., "Notes on Testing Real-Time System Programs," *IBM Systems Journal,* Vol. 4, No. 1, 1965, pp. 58–72.
[2] Pinkerton, T. B., "Performance Monitoring in a Time-Sharing System," *Communications of the ACM,* Vol. 12, No. 11, November 1969, pp. 608–617.
[3] Russell Soundex system developed by Remington Rand Corporation's American Filing Bureau.
[4] Morgan, David E., "A Computer Network Monitoring System," *IEEE Trans. Software Eng.,* Vol. SE–1, No. 3, September 1975, pp. 299–311.
[5] Brooks, Frederick P., *The Mythical Man–Month, Essays on Software Engineering.* Addison-Wesley Publishing Co., 1975.

2-5 DESIGNING TRANSLATOR SOFTWARE*

PAUL HECKEL

The Craig Translator, designed to translate words from one language to another, is also a general purpose computer that can run a variety of programmed cartridges. Along with similar products such as Texas Instruments' Speak and Spell, it is a forerunner of many inexpensive, small, handheld, intelligent products with alphanumeric i/o. Because hardware is now composed of a few common components such as microprocessors and memories, the role of software and the challenge in its design is becoming singularly crucial. So, as we expected, the task of designing the software for the Craig Translator was formidable indeed.

The prototyping approach used by those of us responsible for developing the product should be useful to developers of other microprocessor-based products where human factors are important. Attention to human factors in the beginning of the software design accounted for the later success of the product in performing the difficult task of translation.

The software engineers responsible for the translator faced four major problem areas.

First, what the translator would do and how it would do it, as perceived by the user, would mean the difference between success and failure in the marketplace.

Second, in order for the translator to have a large enough vocabulary to be useful, a good data-storage compression structure had to be designed.

Third, the microcode was going to be sizable, yet the space available to run it was limited. Cost considerations required the selection of a single-chip microprocessor. Thus the software engineers were confronted with the blivit problem: how to fit ten pounds of spinach in a five-pound sack.

Finally, the designers faced a tight time schedule; even worse, the pressure to complete the design became more severe when it was discovered that a competitor was making a similar product. (The total software effort took about seven months. The beginning of product design to product in the marketplace was one year.)

While all these problems proved solvable, attempting to deal with them simultaneously provided a real challenge.

The first major decision was to build a black box prototype configured on an 8085 microprocessor. The prototype used a sixteen character display, a forty-four key keyboard and was about 3 × 5 × 7 inches in size, operating on an internal battery (Figure 2-5-1). It ran programs either from internal 2716 eproms or from an Intel program development system operating in debug mode. Some of the 2716 eproms were used to store test languages.

Once the program had been debugged, the emulator could be disconnected and the 8085 replaced in its socket. proms for the program could be blown and plugged into the other 2716 sockets. The result was a portable self-powered prototype that could be readily demonstrated anywhere.

The prototype software was written in plm rather than machine language, thereby speeding the programming and making it easier to change. During this initial programming stage, some critical decisions were bypassed. For example, we had yet to select the microprocessor for the production version. We had not designed the final data structure.

During the initial two months of the project we implemented the original

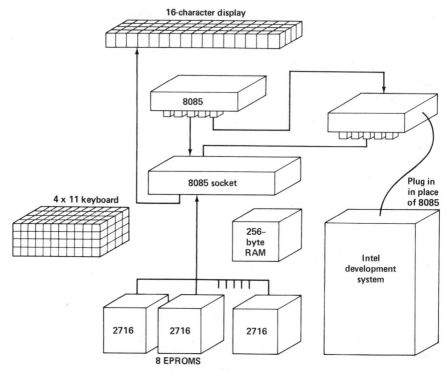

Figure 2-5-1 Prototype black box.

specification. Also during that time, and to a lesser extent during the following months, we provided new versions. Each version was tested by various engineers and assessed as a marketable product; as a result, several problems were discovered. More than thirty versions of the prototype were tested. At the same time, progress seemed slow and painful, but the result was a product that was easy to use, had a number of useful features, and was capable of being implemented on a single-chip microprocessor.

2-5-1 FOCUS ON USER PROBLEMS

The prototype forced us to focus on some problems of human engineering. We were convinced we had to address the problems users would actually experience, rather than those problems the designers imagined might be important, and we used the prototype to help us do this.

First, because the designers could play with the black box, they focused upon what the black box actually did, rather than on the abstraction of a specification. By so doing, the frequent trap of writing and rewriting a software specification was avoided. Although software, marketing, and engineering were occasionally unhappy, they all shared some common perceptions of the final product. The repeated updating of the prototyping reduced the number of last minute, unpleasant surprises.

We caught some potential problems early. Certain features had undesirable side effects. Other features were just plain misunderstood. For example, in the beginning "rotate" was implemented to handle the problem of fitting more than 16 characters on the display. We changed it to establishing operation like the moving sign in Times Square to give the translator more pizzazz. We had misinterpreted the original specification, but we were able to catch the specification ambiguity and fix it.

We also developed the idea of flashing question marks. It was our policy to try out as many suggestions as possible as quickly as possible. This kept ego involvement in specific ideas to a minimum. Several ideas worked their way into the final product, while others were discarded.

Ideas that were discarded were singular and plural case endings, past tenses, and masculine and feminine genders. It was of utmost importance that new ideas could be evaluated more objectively when people could implement them rather than merely discuss them.

Throughout the prototyping phase we were quite aware of the limits imposed by a single-chip microprocessor. The 3870 we chose contained only 64 bytes of RAM, whereas the prototype 8085 had used a 256 byte RAM chip. Thus, in prototyping we could ignore the restrictions on ROM and RAM as long as we were careful not to commit ourselves to design decisions which would prove impractical in the 3870 production version. By avoiding such restrictions during the prototype stage we focused on developing the ideal product. We postponed dealing with the constraints of the final 3870 version until we had to.

In several cases we were able to come up with elegant solutions to quite complex problems. For example, we were able to solve the homograph problem. Many words in a language are homographs—words that are spelled the same but have two distinct meanings. "Watch," for example, can mean "to look at" or "wristwatch." In French, the first is: *regardez,* the second *montre.* Our initial response to such words was to ignore them. That is, we chose to leave "watch" out of the dictionary altogether, or to assign, arbitrarily, one of the two meanings. While only a small percentage of dictionary words are homographs, they occur frequently enough to become problems in almost every language.

We solved the "watch" problem by adding a parenthetical qualifier at the end. Thus "watch" has two dictionary entries: WATCH (SEE) and WATCH (CLOCK). When the user types WATCH, the translator alternately flashes question marks, because WATCH, as such, is not in the dictionary. The user can then hit the Search key, and the device alternately displays WATCH (SEE) and WATCH (CLOCK). He then hits a space key when the one he wants is displayed. It turned out that the additional code required to program this procedure was quite small.

2-5-2 DATA STRUCTURE CHOSEN

The black box was critical to the human engineering, but it proved invaluable in other areas as well. In the first prototype we employed a very simple data structure: we just stored words, one after another, in the language cartridge. Thus, in the English cartridge we stored the ASCII characters THE*A*IS*, and in the French cartridge LE*UN*EST* (Figure 2-5-2). The asterisks served as "end of word" characters. If the user keys in the word IS, the program counts the words until it finds the word IS, which is word number three. If translating to French the translator counts to the third word in the French cartridge, EST, and displays it. This approach would be unacceptable in the production translator. First, 8 bit characters would limit us to about 650 words in a 32,000 bit ROM. However, we eventually achieved 1,150. Second, accessing any word could require searching the entire dictionary cartridge. (We evaded the problem of building a language compiler at this point by using the 8085 assembler to generate the language cartridges.)

Early in the project Richard Schroeppel, a specialist in data compaction, joined the project. Working with him we designed the final data structure. This data structure was first implemented in the prototype. Schroeppel built a language compiler to generate the language ROMs. During the initial prototyping we had defined the interface to the symbol table routines in a general way. Thus, we were able to redefine the data structure by replacing the data structure subroutines.

This is another place where prototyping really paid off. By keeping the data structure decision and language compiler out of the critical path, we gained two additional months that enabled us to explore alternatives before

Figure 2-5-2 Prototype data structure.

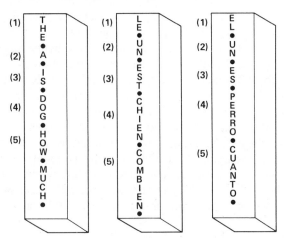

reaching a decision. Then we tore out the old data structure routines and replaced them with the new ones without affecting the user interface.

In the production data structure, words are stored in alphabetic order; a table provides bidirectional mapping between a word's alphabetic position and its language invariant word number (Figure 2-5-3).

If we had been forced to make the data structure decision much earlier, we would probably have picked an inferior structure. In fact, one major data structure decision was postponed to within a few weeks of releasing the final code. We were faced with two alternatives for one of the data substructures, and our concern was centered about the amount of code the preferred one would require in the single-chip processor. One method was a list of alphabetic positions indexed by the language word number. A second method was a bidirectional mapping algorithm. We chose to implement both in the prototype and thus had the compiler generate both. Not until almost all of the production code was debugged and running did we make our final decision to choose the bidirectional mapping algorithm.

The index list of alphabetic positions was simple to implement. It was fast when mapping from the alphabetic position to the language invariant word number—it required only one indexed load. However, mapping from the language invariant word number to its alphabetic position required searching the list, which required referencing on average half of its entries—500 items for a 1,000-word dictionary.

We also implemented a bidirectional mapping algorithm, a sophisticated mathematical technique that allowed mapping in each direction by referencing only about $2 \log_2 (N)$ words. For a 1,000-word list this meant referencing only 20 words in each direction (rather than 500 in one direction, one in the other). This algorithm took substantially more code, however, and thus we could not be sure we would be able to use it in the production version.

After the production prototype was working and we realized the bidirectional algorithm would fit, we decided to use it. If we had been forced to make the decisions earlier we undoubtedly would not have been willing to take the

Figure 2-5-3   Bidirectional mapping table.

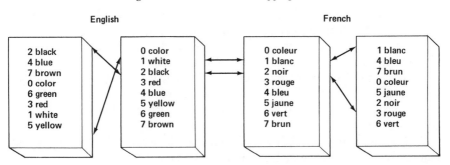

risk that the bidirectional algorithm would fit, and would not have committed to it.

During the time we considered which mapping algorithm to use we generated both from the language compiler and ran both on the 8085 prototype and eventually the production version.

Once the prototype was working, we concluded the code would not fit in the single-chip microprocessor without taking out several features. This was a critical point in the project. We had selected the 3870 because it could store 2,048 bytes of program memory, was sourced by three vendors, and was inexpensive compared to the alternatives. However, the instruction set made it difficult to program. Furthermore, the development tools were abysmal. Our initial estimates indicated that the code would just barely fit in the 3870. These estimates proved wrong because the code ended up requiring 5,000 bytes instead of 2,000. However, the original estimate did not include a calculator or several other features that we added later.

2-5-3 TWO COURSES PURSUED

We decided to pursue two independent courses of action: we would do straight 3870 machine coding of the prototype code, and simultaneously, we would bring up an interpreter version. As it turned out, the interpreter version had several advantages over the machine-coded version.

* It enabled the translator cartridges to store code as well as data.
* It provided calculator functions.
* If our code size estimates were wrong, it permitted us to use an external ROM for part of the application code.

A company that had developed a FORTH interpreter was brought into the project. It brought up an 8-bit version of its interpreter for the translator. It quickly became obvious that, for the reasons specified above, the interpreter version should be employed in the production machine: the code would not fit without it.

Eventually we not only added an external ROM but also 32 bytes of RAM (to the 3870's 64 bytes) to make the program fit (Figure 2-5-4). While we had hoped to avoid both courses of action, we were able to integrate these changes within a few weeks once they proved to be necessary.

While the 3870 software effort was in progress, the prototyping effort continued, but at a slower rate. New data structures were implemented. Several new ideas were tried. Some, such as recognizing phrases (how much = *combien*) were retained.

Continuation cartridges were also discarded because they made the code run too slow. During the concluding phases of the project, the 3870 software

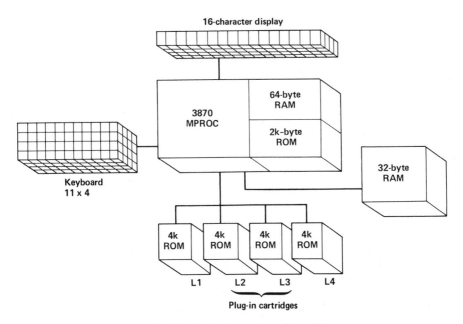

Figure 2-5-4   Production version of translator.

group was deliberately not advised of all the changes in the user interface. Its problem was hard enough without having to track a moving target. For this reason it was told only about major changes.

Some features, such as case endings, were implemented in the prototype, then taken out. Others evolved over time. An example of a feature that evolved was the Search mode. The original version of the Search mode did not subtract letters from the end of the words. Until we added the subtraction feature, Search was limited in its ability to identify words that were similar in spelling to the word the user had keyed in.

When the 3870 effort began, we gave it a final target but continued to modify the prototype. During this period, the prototype effectively buffered the 3870 effort from ideas that didn't work out, such as case endings. Only when the 3870 version began working did we redirect the people's aim toward the somewhat changed prototype.

The prototype approach had still another advantage. The 3870 dictionary cartridges were identical to those of the prototype, so language cartridges could be debugged on the prototype. Thus the 3870 programmers could eliminate bad test ROMs from their list of potential problems.

We did not write the traditional software specification for the project until we were more than half through the 3870 development effort. In fact, our initial plan was to do without a specification entirely. Instead, we intended to use the prototype as the specification. There were several reasons for this decision.

First, two distinct versions of the specification evolved, the black box and the high-level PLM program listing. Any questions about what the translator should do could be answered by either running the prototype or looking at the PLM listing. Second, the inevitable misunderstandings and contradictions in a written specification were avoided. Finally, the absence of the specification directed everyone's attention to what the prototype did, rather than to a piece of paper that represented an abstract version of the final product. In general, this proved to be a good approach. However, lack of a software specification did create some problems. We had no list of the features in the prototype to ensure that

> we had implemented everything.
> we had tested everything.
> we could determine all of the capabilities quickly.

We were obliged to write an English language specification. As it turned out, the prototype and the English language specification complemented each other.

When the first version of the specification was written, we considered it complete. However, it went through several changes during the remaining two and one-half months. (We maintained the specification on the development system and used the text editor to update it.)

Features alone do not make a product better, although unused features can sometimes be important for marketing reasons. What makes the better product is how the features help the typical user in normal circumstances. A translator is a dynamic product. Thus, the best way to evaluate it is to play with it to see whether it seems useful, friendly, easy to use, and interesting—or, alternately—gimmicky, frustrating, difficult, and dull.

In looking back over the project, there were some disappointments. It took longer than we originally expected. Seven months were required for the software effort. It took more memory than expected, requiring the addition of ROM and RAM.

However, the software prototype proved beneficial in four ways:

> We could keep trying new things.
> The prototype was a good model of the final product, and thus everyone involved had similar expectations about what the product would do.
> Several decisions could be postponed for a few months without affecting the critical path.
> We could focus our efforts on opportunities rather than problems.

There may be development projects where such advantages are not so crucial, but these advantages are clearly beneficial in the development of innovative products.

The prototyping approach is not a cure-all; there are many ways to misuse it. An important part is the person in charge of the prototyping. He must be able to single out and eliminate pitfalls that will prove impractical in the production version. It is also important to be receptive to trying several different features, even if the manager doesn't believe in them.

REAL–TIME
METHODOLOGIES

Many of the methodologies useful to real-time programmers are the same as those needed by other programmers. But just as real-time software has unique applications, there are unique methodologies which the real-time programmer may use. This chapter explores those methodologies. The papers which follow may talk about methodologies common to all software development, but they were chosen because they also discuss unique *real-time* problems and solutions.

This chapter is organized so that early software life cycle activities are dealt with first (for example, requirements definition), and later life cycle activities follow in order.

Requirements definition methodologies used in the field tend to be pragmatic and varied (some people would use the term *ad hoc;* however, that has come to be a derogatory term which seems unfair in the highly people-oriented world of requirements definition). The first paper, by Kathryn Heninger Britton, is an especially interesting one because it tells the story of a requirements definition exercise for a large real-time project—the A–7 Navy aircraft avionics—to which some of the recent computer science research concepts were applied. David Parnas, a noted computer scientist, also participated in the project although he is not mentioned. The author's analysis of the problems will be familiar to anyone who has worked on requirements for a large real-time system—''None of the available documents were entirely accurate; no single person knew the answers to all of our questions; some questions were answered differently by different people; and some questions could not be answered without experimentation with the existing system.'' The paper describes, in a useful, step-by-step way, how these problems were overcome.

There are few ''classic'' papers in the literature of real-time software. Section 3-2, a paper by Niklaus Wirth, is one of those. Wirth takes the position that (1) real-time software is the most complex software there is; (2) what characterizes real-time software is its ''processor-time dependency'' in that program validity depends on the execution speed of the processor (computer hardware); and (3) tasking with its attendant synchronization and shared data problems is a key real-time problem area.

Wirth evolves the programming language Modula to address these problems, and defines a "recipe" for making real-time programs manageable: (1) formulate the program without concern for execution time, relying on synchronization signals where needed; (2) analyze each signal's time dependencies; and (3) evaluate the need for each signal based on computer timing. Although Wirth emphasizes tasking more than contemporary real-time practice might require, his insights are "required" reading in the real-time software world.

As this book is written, the impact of microcomputers on real-time systems is similar to that of the pebble at the top of an avalanche-prone slope . . . nothing much has happened yet, but it won't take much to start something big. In section 3–3, Patricia Molko describes the use of a Z–80-based microcomputer to attack the management maxiproblem. The setting is the Galileo space probe, a Space Shuttle-based exploration; the problem is how to manage the software development for this huge and cost-critical project. It is a fascinating juxtaposition of the tiny Z–80 and the simplistic CP/M operating system with the control of the exotic complexities of a space mission. The microcomputer is used to produce automated work breakdown structures, schedule charts, action item status reports, computer resource consumption analysis, and more, in support of the real-time software project managers. It is more power than most real-time managers have ever had at their disposal in a surprisingly small package.

Nelson Prentiss looks closely at one of those problems, computer resource consumption analysis, in section 3–4. On-board computer timing and sizing is a critical problem in the resource-constrained world of real-time software, and Prentiss does an in-depth analysis of the treatment of that problem on the Viking Mars space probe project. A 50 percent growth margin up front was insufficient to avoid the necessity of "optimizing algorithms and designs already coded." But planned-for management visibility allowed in-process recovery from what could have otherwise been project-killing problems.

Moving farther back in the software life cycle, we come to two papers written by your editor. In section 3–5, a "lost world" of archaic practices is discovered in the checkout of real-time software. Via a ten-company survey, it is found that the "primitive" techniques still in use in one of these companies are common to all. Primitive, in this case, means such things as debugging software with no operating system support and no debugger support, with the programmer twirling dials at the console, and with in-process patching of memory practices which were abandoned in the 1950s in the world of nonreal-time software. The suggestions for evolving a solution to this problem begin in section 3–5 and are expanded in 3–6, which advocates a "source error first" approach. This means concentrating first on removing programming errors in the code, using a friendly "host" computer environment with lots of powerful debugging tools; and later looking for the target computer specific errors: timing and sizing, device interface specifics, accuracy problems, support software errors, and target-computer hardware errors. Surprisingly, this is the opposite of the engineering-oriented thrust of most real-time projects, where programmers are usually urged to move swiftly into the austere checkout environment of the target computer.

An important touch of reality is presented in section 3-7 by John Connet and others. Ideally, checkout practices should remove all software errors, but in actual fact they do not. Acknowledging that, fault-tolerant software—that which expects unidentified errors to reside in the software and defends itself against them—is discussed. The application in this case is a telephone company system with a requirement for no more than two hours downtime in *forty years*! Dynamic "audits" (similar to what others call *assertions*) are used to determine whether the software is operating correctly, using redundant information for self-checking. Recovery techniques include restoring a faulty database from a low volatility backup memory. The fault-tolerance techniques in this paper are very application-specific, but the concepts could be useful to any application with high reliability requirements. Since fault-tolerant software is still generally thought of as a research concept (whereas fault-tolerance *hardware* techniques have been in use for over ten years), this is an especially interesting pragmatic paper.

Telephone switching systems are the subject of section 3-8 by R. D. Stinaff. Several important real-time checkout concepts are discussed in this paper. An environment simulator is used to provide simulated inputs to the software under test to enable testing in an environment which does not yet include the devices which will generate that input. This technique, totally foreign to nonreal-time systems, is quite common in real-time checkout work. In this case, the simulator is built to include some important software debugging facilities. Source language debug—which allows the programmer and the debugger to communicate in programmer language rather than machine language—is provided by the simulator, as is the ability for multiple users to concurrently test separate systems on the network. This paper describes a simulator-debug facility as fine as any available in the real-time world—and one eons ahead of the "lost world" depicted in earlier sections.

Contrasting with the modern world of source debug described in section 3-8, your editor provides a short paper on that archaic software technique, patching. The practice is "thriving" in the real-time world. What is bad about this practice, why it continues to be used, and what can be done about it make up the content of section 3-9.

We reach the final phase of real-time software development in section 3-10 with a discussion of the maintenance of real-time software by W. K. Sharpley, Jr. His viewpoint is that old software should be updated to new technology without major cost impact (Sharpley says that approximately 32 percent of software's cost is spent on maintenance while other authors, reinforcing Sharpley's point, put the figure as high as 80 percent). Special emphasis is placed on tools and facilities for maintenance. The latter is especially appropriate as real-time systems frequently use a special laboratory of computers and environment devices to check out and maintain their software.

Part of the task of maintenance is the removal of residual software errors. Your editor explores real-time software error reports in the two papers found in sections 3-11 and 3-12. In the first paper, we look at the errors which cost the most in both system impact and repairs. These are called "persistent" errors, which remain in the software even after checkout and acceptance testing are completed. There is a pattern to such errors; a surprisingly large percentage of them are the result of "the software is too simple for the complex problem being solved." The implication is that neither the designer's nor the programmer's minds stretched far enough to encompass all aspects of the problem. Unfortunately, although the pattern is identified, no comprehensive solution is proposed. In section 3-12, we step back a few paces to view real-time software in the context of a total real-time system. From this perspective, we explore the relative reliability of real-time computer software and real-time computer hardware. The motivation for the study is the frequently expressed belief that software is unreliable. The methodology for the study is the tallying of actual software and hardware error reports from four real-time systems. The conclusion that software is several times as reliable as hardware may be questioned from several points of view identified in the paper, but according to the paper, that finding is fairly consistent across the examined systems.

All of the preceding sections on real-time software methodologies have tacitly assumed that the software developers were doing the whole job. The final sction of this chapter, 3-13, explores a different alternative. Suppose the software is so important that an independent, unbiased team should analyze the emerging software product to ensure that it meets its requirements. This alternative is called Independent Verification and Validation (IV and V) and is surprisingly common in the world of supercritical software such as that used in space missions. Donald Reifer takes an in-depth look at IV and V and identifies tasks to be performed, organizational alternatives, costs of various levels of IV and V (development plus from 10 to 60 percent), and methods of contracting for IV and V. Although Reifer's report is written for the U.S. Air Force Program Managers, the ideas he presents may easily be applied to more common applications.

3-1 SPECIFYING SOFTWARE REQUIREMENTS FOR COMPLEX SYSTEMS: NEW TECHNIQUES AND THEIR APPLICATION *

KATHRYN HENINGER BRITTON
Computer Science and Systems Branch
Naval Research Laboratory

3-1-1 ABSTRACT

This paper concerns new techniques for making requirements specifications precise, concise, and easy to check for completeness and consistency. The techniques are well-suited for complex real-time software systems; they were developed to document the requirements of existing flight software for the Navy's A-7 aircraft. The paper outlines the information that belongs in a requirements document and discusses the objectives behind the techniques. Each technique is described and illustrated with examples from the A-7 document. The purpose of the paper is to introduce the A-7 document as a model of a disciplined approach to requirements specification; the document is available to anyone who wishes to see a fully worked-out example of the approach.

3-1-2 INTRODUCTION

Much software is difficult to understand, change, and maintain. Several software engineering techniques have been suggested to ameliorate this situation, among them modularity and information hiding[11,12], formal specifications[4,9,10,13,16,20], abstract interfaces[15], cooperating sequential processes[2,18,21], process synchronization routines[2,8], and resource monitors[1,6,7]. System developers are reluctant to use these techniques both because their usefulness has not been proven for programs with stringent resource limitations and because there are no fully worked-out examples of some of them. In order to demonstrate feasibility and to provide a useful model, the Naval Research Laboratory and the Naval Weapons Center are using the techniques listed above to redesign and rebuild the operational flight program for the A-7 aircraft. The new program will undergo the acceptance tests established for the current program, and the two programs will be compared both for resource utilization and for ease of change.

*From the Proceedings of the IEEE 1979 Specifications of Reliable Software Conference. U.S. Government work not protected by U.S. copyright.

The new program must be functionally identical to the existing program. Stated differently, the new program must meet the same requirements as the old program. Unfortunately, when the project started no requirements documentation existed for the old program; procurement specifications, which were originally sketchy, are now out-of-date. Our first step was to produce a complete description of the A–7 program requirements in a form that would facilitate the development of the new program and could be updated easily as the requirements continue to change.

Writing down the requirements turned out to be surprisingly difficult in spite of the availability of a working program and experienced maintenance personnel. None of the available documents were entirely accurate; no single person knew the answers to all our questions; some questions were answered differently by different people; and some questions could not be answered without experimentation with the existing system. We found it necessary to develop new techniques based on the same principles as the software design techniques listed above to organize and document software requirements. The techniques suggested questions, uncovered ambiguities, and supported cross-checking for completeness and consistency. The techniques allowed us to present the information relatively concisely, condensing several shelves of documentation into a single 500-page document.

This paper shares some of the insights we gained from developing and applying these techniques. Our approach can be useful for other projects, both to document unrecorded requirements for existing systems and to guide software procurers as they define requirements for new systems. This paper introduces the techniques and illustrates them with simple examples. We invite anyone interested in more detail to look at the requirements document itself as a complete example of the way the techniques work for a substantial system.[5]

First this paper addresses the objectives a requirements document ought to meet. Second it outlines the general design principles that guided us as we developed techniques; the principles helped us achieve the objectives. Finally it presents the specific techniques, showing how they allowed us to achieve completeness, precision, and clarity.

3-1-3 A-7 PROGRAM CHARACTERISTICS

The A–7 flight program is an operational Navy program with tight memory and time constraints. The code is about 12,000 assembler language instructions and runs on an IBM System 4 PI model TC–2 computer with 16K bytes of memory. We chose this program because we wanted to demonstrate that the run-time overhead incurred by using software engineering principles is not prohibitive for real-time programs and because the maintenance personnel feel that the current program is difficult to change.

The A–7 flight program is part of the Navigation-Weapon Delivery

System on the A-7 aircraft. It receives input data from sensors, cockpit switches, and a panel with which the pilot keys in data. It controls several display devices in the cockpit and positions several sensors. Twenty-two devices are connected to the computer; examples include an inertial measurement set providing velocity data and a head-up display device. The head-up display projects symbols into the pilot's field of view, so that he sees them overlaying the world ahead of the aircraft. The program calculates navigation information, such as present position, speed, and heading; it also controls weapon delivery, giving the pilot steering cues and calculating when to release weapons.

3-1-4 REQUIREMENTS DOCUMENT OBJECTIVES

In order for documentation to be useful and coherent, explicit decisions must be made about the purposes it should serve. Decisions about the following questions affect its scope, organization, and style: a) What kinds of questions should it answer? b) Who are the readers? c) How will it be used? d) What background knowledge does a reader need? Considering these questions, we derived the following six objectives for our requirements document.

1. *Specify external behavior only.* A requirements document should specify only the external behavior of a system, without implying a particular implementation. The user or his representative defines requirements using his knowledge of the application area, in this case aircraft navigation and weapons delivery. The software designer creates the implementation, using his knowledge of software engineering. When requirements are expressed in terms of a possible implementation, they restrict the software designer too much, sometimes preventing him from using the most effective algorithms and data structures. In our project the requirements document must be equally valid for two quite different implementations—the program we build and the current program. For our purposes it serves as a problem statement, outlining what the new program must do to pass acceptance tests. For those maintaining the current program, it fills a serious gap in their documentation—they have no other source that states exactly what the program must do. They have pilot manuals, which supply user-level documentation for the entire avionics system, of which the program is only a small part. Unfortunately, the pilot manuals make it difficult to separate the activities performed by the computer program from those performed by other devices and to distinguish between advice to the pilot and restrictions enforced by the program. The maintainers also have implementation documentation for the current program: mathematical algorithm analyses, flowcharts, and 12,000 lines of sparsely commented assembler code. But the implementation documents do not

distinguish between the aspects that are dictated by the requirements and those that the software designer is free to change.

2. *Specify constraints on the implementation.* In addition to defining correct program behavior, the document should describe the constraints placed on the implementation, especially the details of the hardware interfaces. As is usually the case with embedded systems*, we are not free to define the interfaces to the systems, but must accept them as given for the problem. A complete requirements description should therefore include the facts about the hardware devices that can affect the correctness of the program.

3. *Be easy to change.* Because requirements change, requirements documentation should be easy to change. If the documentation is not maintained during the system life cycle, control is lost over the software evolution; it becomes difficult to coordinate program changes introduced by maintenance personnel.

4. *Serve as a reference tool.* The primary function of the document is to answer specific questions quickly, rather than to explain in general what the program does. We expect the document to serve experienced programmers who already have a general idea about the purpose of the program. Precision and conciseness are valued. Indispensable reference aids include a glossary, detailed table of contents, and various indices. Since tutorial material has different characteristics, such as a narrative style, it should be developed separately if it is needed.

5. *Record forethought about the life cycle of the system.* During the requirements definition stage, we believe it is sensible to exercise forethought about the life cycle of the program. What *types* of changes are likely to occur?[22] What functions would maintainers like to be able to remove easily?[17] For any software product some changes are easier to make than others; some guidance in the requirements will help the software designer assure that the easy changes correspond to the most likely changes.

6. *Characterize acceptable responses to undesired events.* Undesired events [14], such as hardware failures and user errors, should be anticipated during requirements definition. Since the user knows the application area, he knows more than the software designer about acceptable responses. For example, a pilot knows better than a programmer whether a particular response to a sensor failure will decrease or increase his difficulties. Responses to undesired events should be stated in the requirements document; they should not be left for the programmer to invent.

---

*An embedded system functions as a component of a significantly larger system. Parnas [15] has a discussion of embedded system characteristics.

3-1-5 REQUIREMENTS DOCUMENT DESIGN PRINCIPLES

Our approach to requirements documentation can be summarized by the three principles discussed below. These principles form the basis of all the techniques we developed.

1. *State questions before trying to answer them.* At every stage of writing the requirements we concentrated first on formulating the questions that should be answered. If this is not done, the available material prejudices the requirements investigation so that only the easily answered questions are asked. First we formulated the Table of Contents in Figure 3-1-1 in order to characterize the general classes of questions that should be answered. We wrote it before we looked at the A-7 at all, basing it on our experience with other software. Then we generated questions for the in-

Figure 3-1-1   A-7 requirements table of contents.

Table of Contents	
Chapter	Contents
0 Introduction	Organization principles; abstracts for other sections; notation guide
1 Computer characteristics	If the computer is predetermined, a general description with particular attention to its idiosyncrasies; otherwise a summary of its required characteristics
2 Hardware interfaces	Concise description of information received or transmitted by the computer
3 Software functions	What the software must do to meet its requirements, in various situations and in response to various events
4 Timing constraints	How often and how fast each function must be performed: This section is separate from section 3 since "what" and "when" can change independently.
5 Accuracy constraints	How close output values must be to ideal values to be acceptable
6 Response to undesired events	What the software must do if sensors go down, the pilot keys in invalid data, etc.
7 Subsets	What the program should do if it cannot do everything
8 Fundamental assumptions	The characteristics of the program that will stay the same, no matter what changes are made
9 Changes	The types of changes that have been made or are expected
10 Glossary	Most documentation is fraught with acronyms and technical terms. At first we prepared this guide for ourselves; as we learned the language, we retained it for newcomers.
11 Sources	Annotated list of documentation and personnel, indicating the types of questions each can answer

dividual sections. Like any design effort, formulating questions requires iteration. We generated questions from common sense, organized them into forms, generated more questions by trying to fill in the blanks, and revised the forms.

2. *Separate concerns.* We need the principle of *separation of concerns*[3] to organize the document so that each project member could concentrate on a well-defined set of questions. This principle also serves the objective of making the document easy to change, since it causes changes to be well-confined. For example, hardware interfaces are described without making any assumptions about the purpose of the program; the hardware section would remain unchanged if the behavior of the program changed. The software behavior is described without any references to the details of the hardware devices; the software section would remain unchanged if data were received in different formats or over different channels.

3. *Be as formal as possible.* We avoided prose and developed formal ways to present information in order to be precise, concise, consistent, and complete.

The next two sections of the paper show how these principles are applied to describe the hardware interfaces and the software behavior.

3-1-6 TECHNIQUES FOR DESCRIBING HARDWARE INTERFACES

3-1-6-1 Organization by Data Item

To organize the hardware interfaces description, we have a separate unit called a *data item,* for each input or output that changes value independently of other inputs or outputs. Examples of input data items include barometric altitude, radar-measured distance to a point on the ground, the setting of the inertial platform mode switch, and the inertial platform ready signal. Examples of output data items include coordinates for the flight-path marker on the head-up display, radar antenna steering commands, and the signal that turns on and off the computer-failed light. The A–7 computer receives seventy input data items and transmits ninety-five output data items.

In order to have a consistent approach, we designed a form to be completed for each data item. We started with an initial set of questions that occurred to us as we read about the interfaces. How does the program read or write this data? What is the bit representation of the value? Can the computer tell whether a sensor value is valid? As we worked on specific data items, new questions occurred to us. We added these questions to the form, so that they would be addressed for all data items. The form is illustrated in Figures 3-1-2 and 3-1-3 at the end of this section.

3-1-6-2 Symbolic Names for Data Items and Values

The hardware section captures two kinds of information about data items: *arbitrary details* that might change if a device were replaced with a similar device, and *essential characteristics* that would be shared by similar devices. The bit representation of a value is an arbitrary detail; the semantics of the value is an essential characteristic. For example, any barometric altitude sensor provides a reading from which barometric altitude can be calculated—this information is essential. But the resolution, representation, accuracy, and timing might differ between two types of barometric altitude sensors—this information is arbitrary.

Essential information must be expressed in such a way that the rest of the document can use it without referencing the arbitrary details. For example, each data item is given a mnemonic name so that it can be identified unambiguously in the rest of the document without references to instruction sequences or channel numbers. If a data item is not numerical and takes on a fixed set of possible values, the values are given mnemonic names so that they can be used without reference to bit encodings. For example, a switch might be able to take the values "on" and "off". The physical representation of the two values is arbitrary information that is not mentioned in the rest of the document in case it changes. The names allow the readers and writers of the rest of the document to ignore the physical details of input and output, and are more visually meaningful than the details they represent.

We bracket every mnemonic name in symbols indicating the item type, for example, /input-data-items/, //output-data-items//, and $nonnumeric-values$. These brackets reduce confusion by identifying the item type unambiguously, so that the reader knows where to find the precise definition. Moreover, the brackets facilitate systematic cross referencing, either by people or computers.

3-1-6-3 Templates for Value Descriptions

The values of the numerical data items belong to a small set of value types, such as angles and distances. At first we described each data item in an ad hoc fashion, usually imitating the descriptions in the documents we referenced. But these documents were not consistent with each other and the descriptions were not always complete. We made great progress when we developed informal templates for the value descriptions, with blanks to be completed for specific data items. . . . The template for angles might read

angle (?) is measured from line (?) to line (?) in the (?) direction, looking (?)

[For] example, *magnetic heading* is measured from *the line from the aircraft to magnetic north* to *the horizontal component of the aircraft X axis,* in the *clockwise* direction looking *down.*

Although templates were not used as hard and fast rules, their existence made values easier to describe, made the descriptions consistent with each other, and helped us apply the same standards of completeness to all items of the same type.

3-1-6-4 Input Data Items Described as Resources, Independent of Software Use

When describing input data items, we refrain from mentioning how or when the data is used by the software, to avoid making any assumptions about the software function. Instead, we describe the input data items as if taking inventory of the resources available to solve a problem. We define numerical values in terms of what they measure. For example, the value of the input data item called /RADALT/ is defined as the distance above local terrain as determined by the radar altimeter. Many nonnumerical inputs indicate switch positions; these are described without reference to the response the pilot expects when he changes the switch, since the response is accomplished by the software. For example, when the pilot changes the scale switch on the projected map display, he expects the map scale to change. Since the response is achieved by the software, it is not mentioned in the input data item description, which reads, "/PMSCAL/ indicates the position of a two-position toggle switch on the projected map panel. This switch has no hardware effect on the projected map display."

3-1-6-5 Example of an Input Data Item Description

Figure 3-1-2 shows the completed form for a nonnumerical input data item. The underlined words are the form headings. *Value encoding* shows how the mnemonic value names used in the rest of the document are mapped into specific bit representations. Switch nomenclature indicates the names of the switch positions as seen by the pilot in the cockpit. *Instruction sequence* gives the TC-2 assembler language instructions that cause the data to be transmitted to or from the computer. We are not usurping the programmer's job by including the instruction sequence because there is no other way to read in this data item—the instruction sequence is not an implementation decision for the programmer. The channel number is a cross-reference to the computer chapter where the general characteristics of the eight channels are described. *Data Representation* shows the location of the value in the 16-bit input word. Notice how the *Comments* section defines the value assumed by the switch while the pilot is changing it. This is an example of a question we asked about all switches, once it had occurred to us about this one.

Input data item: IMS mode switch

Acronym: /IMSMODE/

Hardware: Inertial measurement set

Description: /IMSMODE/ indicates the position of a six-position rotary switch on the IMS control panel.

      Switch nomenclature: OFF; GND ALIGN; NORM; INERTIAL; MAG SL; GRID

Characteristics of values	$Offnone$	(00000)
Value encoding:	$Gndal$	(10000)
	$Norm$	(01000)
	$Iner$	(00100)
	$Grid$	(00010)
	$Magsl$	(00001)

Instruction sequence: READ 24   (channel 0)

Data representation: Bits 3-7

Comments: /IMSMODE/ = $Offnone$ when the switch is between two positions

Figure 3-1-2 Completed input data item form.

3-1-6-6 Output Data Items Described in Terms of Effects on External Hardware

Most output data items are described in terms of their effects on the associated devices. For example, the description of the output data items called //STEERAZ// and //STEEREL// shows how they are used to communicate the direction to point the antenna to the radar. This section does not explain how the software chooses the direction. For other output data items we define the value the peripheral device must receive in order to function correctly. For example, the description of the output data item called //FPANGL// shows that the radar assumes the value will be a certain angle which it uses to determine the climb or dive angle the aircraft should use during terrain following. We avoid giving any meaning to an output value that is not a characteristic of the hardware.

3-1-6-7 Example of an Output Data Item Description

Figure 3-1-3 shows the completed form for a numerical output data item. Notice how the value is described in terms of its effect on a needle in a display, rather than in terms of what the needle is supposed to communicate to the pilot. The value is characterized by a standard set of parameters, such as range and resolution, which are used for all numerical data items. For *Data Representation,* we show how the sixteen-bit output word is constructed, including which bits must be zero, which bits are ignored by the device, and which bits encode

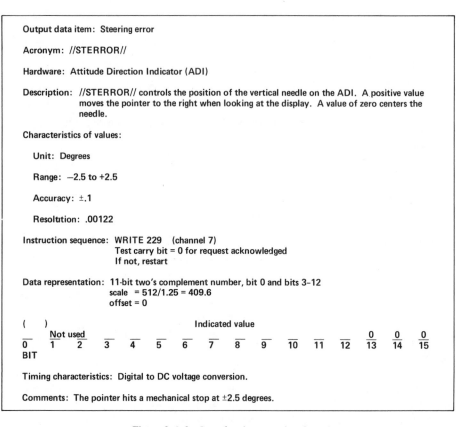

Output data item: Steering error

Acronym: //STERROR//

Hardware: Attitude Direction Indicator (ADI)

Description: //STERROR// controls the position of the vertical needle on the ADI. A positive value moves the pointer to the right when looking at the display. A value of zero centers the needle.

Characteristics of values:

  Unit: Degrees

  Range: −2.5 to +2.5

  Accuracy: ±.1

  Resolution: .00122

Instruction sequence: WRITE 229 (channel 7)
                     Test carry bit = 0 for request acknowledged
                     If not, restart

Data representation: 11-bit two's complement number, bit 0 and bits 3–12
                    scale = 512/1.25 = 409.6
                    offset = 0

( )	Not used						Indicated value						0	0	0
0	1	2	3	4	5	6	7	8	9	10	11	12	13	14	15

BIT

Timing characteristics: Digital to DC voltage conversion.

Comments: The pointer hits a mechanical stop at ±2.5 degrees.

Figure 3–1–3 Completed output data item form.

the output value. Since the actual output value is not in any standard units of measurement, we also show how it can be derived from a value in standard units, in this case degrees. The relation between output values and values in standard units is given by the equation:

$$\text{output value} = \text{scale} \times (\text{standard value} + \text{offset})$$

Since the same equation is used for all numerical data items, we need only provide the scale and offset values for a particular data item. Thus the output value for the data item //STERROR// in Figure 3–1–3 is derived from a value in degrees by the following expression:

$$\text{output value} = 409.6 \times (\text{standard value} + 0)$$

The timing considerations section contains a pointer to another section; since many output data items have the same timing characteristics, we describe them once, and include cross references. The comment shows a physical limit of the device.

3-1-7 TECHNIQUES FOR DESCRIBING SOFTWARE FUNCTIONS

3-1-7-1 Organization by Functions

We describe the software as a set of functions associated with output data items—each function determines the values for one or more output data items and each output data item is given values by exactly one function. Thus every function can be described in terms of externally visible effects. For example, the function calculating values for the output data item //STERROR// is described in terms of its effects on a needle in a display. The meaning conveyed to the pilot by the needle is expressed here.

This approach, identifying functions by working backward from output data items, works well because most A-7 outputs are specialized; most output data items are used for only a small set of purposes. The approach breaks down somewhat for a general-purpose device, such as a terminal, where the same data items are used to express many different types of information. We have one general-purpose device, the computer panel, where the same set of thirteen 7-segment displays can display many types of information, including present position, wind speed, and sensor status. We handled this situation by acting as if each type of information had its own panel, each controlled by a separate function. Thus, we have forty-eight panel functions, each described as if it always controlled a panel, and a set of rules to determine which function controls the real panel at any given moment. This approach, creating *virtual panels,* allows us to separate "what" the values are from "when" they are displayed. It also causes the description to be less dependent on the characteristics of the particular panel device than it otherwise would be.

Software functions are classified as either demand or periodic. A *demand function* must be requested by the occurrence of some event every time it is performed. For example, the computer-fail light is turned on by a demand function when a computer malfunction is detected. A *periodic function* is performed repeatedly without being requested each time. For example, the coordinates of symbols on the head-up display are updated by periodic functions. If a periodic function need not be performed all the time, it is started and stopped by specific events. For example, a symbol may be removed from the head-up display when a certain event occurs.

This distinction is useful because different performance and timing information is required for demand and periodic functions. To describe a demand function one must give the events that cause it to occur; an appropriate timing question is "What is the maximum delay that can be tolerated between request and action?" To describe a periodic function, one must give the events that cause it to start and stop and the conditions that affect how it is performed after it is started; an appropriate timing question is "What are the minimum and maximum repetition rates for this function?"

3-1-7-2 Output Values as Functions of Conditions and Events

Originally we thought we would describe each output as a mathematical function of input values. This turned out to be a naive approach. We found we could seldom describe output values directly in terms of input values; instead we had to define intermediate values that the current program calculated, but that did not correspond to any output value. These in turn had to be described in terms of other intermediate values. By the time we reached input values, we would have described an implementation.

Instead, we expressed requirements by giving output values as functions of aircraft operating conditions. For example, the output data item named //LATGT70// should change value when the aircraft crosses 70° latitude; how the program detects this event is left to the implementation. In order to describe outputs in terms of aircraft operating conditions, we defined a simple language of conditions and events. *Conditions* are predicates that characterize some aspect of the system for a measurable period of time. For example, /IMSMODE/ = $Gndal$ is a condition that is true when the IMS mode switch in the cockpit is set to the GND ALIGN position (see Figure 3-1-2). If a pilot expects a certain display whenever the switch is in this position, the function controlling the display is affected by the value of /IMSMODE/. An *event* occurs when the value of a condition changes from true to false or vice versa. Events therefore specify instants of time, whereas conditions specify intervals of time. Events start and stop periodic functions and they trigger demand functions. Events provide a convenient way to describe functions where something is done when a button is first pushed, but not if the pilot continues to hold it down. Before we distinguished clearly between events and conditions, situations of this sort were very difficult to describe simply.

3-1-7-3 Consistent Notation for Aircraft Operating Conditions

TEXT MACROS.   To keep the function descriptions concise, we introduced over two hundred terms that serve as text macros. The terms are bracketed in exclamation points and defined in an alphabetical dictionary. A text macro can define a quantity that affects an output value, but that cannot be directly obtained from an input. An example is "!ground track angle!", defined as "the angle measured from the line from the aircraft to true north to !ground track!, measured clockwise looking down." Although the derivation of such values is left to the implementation, text macros provide a consistent, encapsulated means to refer to them while specifying function values.

Text macros also serve as abbreviations for compound conditions that are frequently used or very detailed. For example, !Desig! is a condition that is true when the pilot has performed a sequence of actions that designates a target to the computer. The list of events defining !Desig! appears only in the dictionary; while writing or reading the rest of the document, these events need not be considered. If designation procedures change, only the definition in the dictionary changes. Another example of a text macro for a compound condition is !IMS Reasonable!*, which represents the following bulky, specific condition:

> !IMS total velocity! 1seq 1440 fps AND
> change of !IMS total velocity! from .2 seconds
> ago 1seq 50 fps

Even though this term is used many times in the function descriptions, only one place in the document need be changed if the reasonableness criteria change for the sensor.

The use of text macros is an application of stepwise refinement—while describing functions, we give names to complicated operating conditions or values, postponing the precise definitions. As the examples above show, we continue introducing new terms in the definitions themselves. This allows us to limit the amount of detail we deal with at one time. Furthermore, like the use of /, //, and $ brackets in the hardware descriptions, the use of ! brackets for text macros indicates to the reader that reference is being made to something that is precisely defined elsewhere. This reduces the risk of ambiguity that usually accompanies prose descriptions (for example, !Desig! vs. designated).

Conditions.   We represent these predicates as expressions on input data items, for example, /IMSMODE/ = $Gndal$, or expressions on quantities represented by text macros, for example, !ground track angle! = 30°. A condition can also be represented by a text macro, such as !IMS Reasonable!. Compound conditions can be composed by connecting simple conditions with the logical operators AND, OR, and NOT. For example, (!IMS Reasonable! AND /IMSMODE/ = $Gndal$) is true only when both the component conditions are true.

Events.   We use the notation @T(condition 1) to denote the occurrence of condition 1 becoming *true* and @F(condition 2) to denote the occurrence of condition 2 becoming *false*.

For example, the event @T(!ground track angle! ls 30°) occurs when the !ground track angle! value crosses the 30° threshold from a larger value. The event @T(!ground track angle! = 30°) occurs when the value reaches the 30° threshold from either direction. The event @T(/IMSMODE/ = $Gndal$) occurs when the pilot moves the switch to the GND ALN position. In some cases,

---

*This text macro represents the condition that the values read from the inertial measurement set are reasonable: the magnitude of the aircraft velocity vector, calculated from inertial measurement set inputs, is less than or equal to 1440 feet per second and has changed less than 50 feet per second from the magnitude .2 seconds ago.

an event only occurs if one condition changes when another condition is true, denoted by

@T(condition 3) WHEN (condition 4).

Thus, @T(/ACAIRB/ = Yes) WHEN (/IMSMODE/ = $Gndal$) refers to the event of the aircraft becoming airborne while the IMS mode switch is in the GND ALN position, while @T(/IMSMODE/ = $Gndal$) WHEN (/ACAIRB/ = Yes) refers to event of the IMS mode being switched to GND ALN while the airplane is airborne.

USING MODES TO ORGANIZE AND SIMPLIFY.   Although each function is affected by only a small subset of the total set of conditions, we still need to organize conditions into groups in order to keep the function descriptions simple. To do this, we define *modes* or classes of system states. Because the functions differ more between modes than they do within a single mode, a mode-by-mode description is simpler than a general description. For example, by setting three switches, deselecting guns, and keying a single digit on the panel, the pilot can enter what is called the visual navigation update mode. In this mode several displays and the radar are dedicated to helping him get a new position estimate by sighting off a local landmark. Thus the mode affects the correct behavior of the functions associated with these displays. The use of modes has an additional advantage—if something goes wrong during a flight, the pilot is much more likely, when he makes the trouble report, to remember the mode than the values of various conditions.

Each mode is given a short mnemonic name enclosed in asterisks, for example, *DIG* for *D*oppler-*i*nertial-*g*yrocompassing navigation mode. The mode name is used in the rest of the document as an abbreviation for the conditions that are true whenever the system is in that mode.

The current mode is defined by the history of events that have occurred in the program. The document shows this by giving the initial mode and the set of events that cause transitions between any pair of modes. For example, the transition list includes the entry

```
*DIG* TO *DI*
   @T(!latitude! gt 70°)
   @(/IMSMODE/ = $Iner$) WHEN (!Doppler coupled!)
```

Thus the system will move from *DIG* mode to Doppler-inertial (*DI*) mode either if the aircraft goes above 70° latitude or if the inertial platform mode switch is changed to Iner while the Doppler Radar is in use.

The table in Figure 3–1–4 summarizes conditions that are true whenever the system is in a particular navigation mode. Thus, in *DIG* mode, the inertial platform mode switch is set to NORM, the aircraft is airborne, the latitude is less than 70°, and both the Doppler Radar and the inertial platform are func-

MODE	/IMSMODE/	/ACAIRB/	!latitude!	Other
DIG	$Norm$	Yes	1s 70°	!IMS Up! AND !Doppler Up!
DI	$Norm$ OR $Iner$	Yes	1s 80°	!IMS Up! AND !Doppler Up! AND !Doppler Coupled!
I	$Iner$	X	1s 80°	!IMS Up!
IMS fail	X	X	X	!IMS Down!

Figure 3-1-4 Section from the navigation mode condition table.

tioning correctly. "X" table entries mean the value of that condition does not matter in that mode.

The mode condition tables are redundant because the information can be derived from the mode transition lists. However, the mode condition tables present the information in a more convenient form. Since the mode condition tables do not contain all the mode transition information, they do not uniquely define the current mode.

3-1-7-4 Special Tables for Precision and Completeness

In an early version of the document, function characteristics were described in prose; this was unsatisfactory because it was difficult to find answers to specific questions and because gaps and inconsistencies did not show up. We invented two types of tables that helped us express information precisely and completely.

CONDITION TABLES are used to define some aspect of an output value that is determined by an active mode and a condition that occurs within that mode. Figure 3-1-5 gives an example of a condition table. Each row corresponds to a group of one or more modes in which this function acts alike. The rows are mutually exclusive; only one mode affects the function at a time. In each row are a set of mutually exclusive conditions; exactly one should be true whenever the program is in the modes denoted by the row. At the bottom of the column is the information appropriate for the interval identified by the mode-condition intersection. Thus to find the information appropriate for a given mode and given condition, first find the row corresponding to the mode, find the condition within the row, and follow that column to the bottom of the table. An "X" instead of a condition indicates that information at the bottom of the column is never appropriate for that mode.

In Figure 3-1-5, the magnetic heading value is 0 when the system is in mode *IMS fail* and the condition (/IMSMODE/ = $Offnone$) is true.

Condition table: Magnetic heading (//MAGHDGH//) output values		
MODES	CONDITIONS	
DIG, *DI*, *I* *Mag sl*, *Grid*	Always	X
IMS fail	(NOT/IMSMODE/=$Offnone$)	/IMSMODE/=$Offnone$
//MAGHDGH// value	angle defined by /MAGHCOS/ and /MAGHSIN/	0 (north)

Figure 3-1-5 Example of a condition table.

Whenever the system is in *IMS fail* mode, (/IMSMODE/ = $Offnone$ OR NOT /IMSMODE/ = $Offnone$) is true, showing that the row is complete, while (/IMSMODE/ = $Offnone$ AND NOT(/IMSMODE/ = $Offnone$)) is false, showing the row entries are mutually exclusive.

Condition tables are used in the descriptions of periodic functions. Periodic functions are performed differently in different time intervals; the appropriate time interval is determined by the prevailing mode and conditions. Each row in the table completely characterizes the intervals within a mode that are meaningful for that function. The conditions must be mutually exclusive, and together they must describe the entire time the program is within the mode. These characteristics ensure that condition tables be complete, that is, all relevant intervals are indicated. They also ensure that condition tables be unambiguous, that is, given the aircraft operating conditions, the correct interval can be determined.

EVENT TABLES show when demand functions should be performed or when periodic functions should be started or stopped. Each row in an event table corresponds to a mode or group of modes. Table entries are events that cause an action to be taken when the system is in a mode associated with the row. The action to be taken is given at the bottom of the column.

The event table in Figure 3-1-6 specifies that the autocalibration light controlled by output data item //AUTOCAL// be turned on when the two listed modes are entered and off when they are exited. We use the symbol ": = "

Figure 3-1-6 Example of an event table.

Event table: when AUTOCAL light switched on/off		
Modes	Events	
Lautocal *Sautocal*	@T(In mode)	@F(In mode)
Action	//AUTOCAL//:=On	//AUTOCAL//:=Off

to denote assignment. The event @T(In mode) occurs when all the conditions represented by the mode become true, that is, when the mode is entered. @F(In mode) occurs when any one of the conditions represented by the mode becomes false, that is, when the system changes to a different mode.

3-1-7-5 Function Description Examples

Figures 3-1-7 and 3-1-8 illustrate the forms we created for demand and periodic functions respectively. All function descriptions indicate the associated output data items, thereby providing a cross reference to the hardware description. The list of modes gives the reader an overview of when the function is performed; the overview is refined in the rest of the description.

The event table in Figure 3-1-7 shows both the events that request the function and the values output by the function at different times. For example, if the //IMSSCAL// value is $Coarse$ when the *LandaIn* mode is entered, the function assigns it the value $Fine$. Notice how the table uses the symbolic names introduced in the hardware section for data items and data item values.

Demand function name: Change scale factor

Modes in which function required:
   Lautocal, *Sautocal*, *LandaIn*, *SINSaIn*, *HUDaIn*, *AiraIn*

Output data item: //IMSSCAL//

Function request and output description:

Event table: When the scale factor is changed

Modes	Events	
Lautocal *LandaIn*	@T(In mode) WHEN (//IMSSCAL//=$Coarse$)	X
HUDaIn	@T(In mode) WHEN (/IMSMODE/ = $Gndal$ AND //IMSSCAL//=$Coarse$)	@T(In mode) WHEN (NOT (/IMSMODE/=$Gndal$) AND //IMSSCAL//=$Fine$)
Sautocal *SINSaIn* *AiraIn*	X	@T(In mode) WHEN (//IMSSCAL//=$Fine$)
ACTION	//IMSSCAL//:=$Fine$	//IMSSCAL//:=$Coarse$

Figure 3-1-7 Completed demand function form.

In Figure 3-1-8, the initiation and termination section gives the events that cause this periodic function to start and stop. This function starts when another output data item, //HUDVEL//, is assigned the value On, and stops when //HUDVEL// is assigned the value Off. The function positions a symbol on a display device. The position of the symbol usually represents the direc-

Periodic function name: Update flight path market coordinates

Modes in which function required:
DIG, *DI*, *I*, *Mag SI*, *Grid*, *IMS fail*

Output data items: //FPMAZ//, //FPMEL//

Initiation and termination events:
Start: @T(//HUDVEL// = On)
Stop: @T(//HUDVEL// = Off)

Output description:
The Flight Path Marker (FPM) symbol on the head-up display shows the direction of the aircraft velocity vector. If the aircraft is moving straight ahead from the nose of the aircraft, the FPM is centered on the display. The horizontal displacement from display center shows the lateral velocity component and elevation displacement shows the vertical velocity component.
Although the means for deriving Flight Path Marker position varies as shown in the table below, the position is usually derived from the current !System velocities!. The velocities are first resolved into forward, lateral and vertical components. Then FPM coordinates are derived in the following manner:

$$//FPMAZ// \text{ shows } \frac{\text{lateral velocity}}{\text{forward velocity}} \quad //FPMEL// \text{ shows } \frac{\text{vertical velocity}}{\text{forward velocity}}$$

Condition Table: Coordinates of the flight path marker

Modes	Conditions		
DIG, *DI*	X	Always	X
I	/ACAIRB/=No	/ACAIRB/=Yes	X
Mag sl, *Grid*	/ACAIRB/=No	!ADC Up! AND /ACAIRB/=Yes	!ADC Down! AND /ACAIRB/=Yes
IMS fail	/ACAIRB/=No	X	/ACAIRB/=Yes
FPM coordinates	//FPMAZ//:=0 //FPMEL//:=0	based on !System velocities!	//FPMAZ//:=0 //FPMEL//:/AOA/

Figure 3-1-8 Completed periodic function form.

tion of the aircraft velocity vector, but under some conditions the output data items are given other values. The output description consists of two parts: a brief prose description of the usual meaning of the symbol, and a condition table that shows what will happen under different conditions. Notice that every mode in the mode list is accounted for in the table. The relevant conditions for this function are !ADC Up! or !ADC Down!, that is, the operating status of the Air Data Computer Sensor (ADC) which provides a measurement of true airspeed, and /ACAIRB/ = Yes and /ACAIRB/ = No, that is, whether the aircraft is airborne. Thus, if the system is in the inertial mode (*I*) and the aircraft is not airborne (/ACAIRB/ = No is true), both coordinates of the symbol are set to zero.

3-1-8 TECHNIQUES FOR SPECIFYING UNDESIRED EVENTS

3-1-8-1 Lists of Undesired Events

In order to characterize the desired response of the system when undesired events occur, we started with a list of undesired events and interviewed pilots and maintenance programmers to find out both what they would like to have happen and what they considered feasible. The key was the list of possible undesired events. To derive this list, we used the classification scheme shown in Figure 3-1-9 as a guide.

```
Undesired event classification

derived from Parnas[19]

1.  Resource failure
        1.1  Temporary
        1.2  Permanent
2   Incorrect input data
        2.1  Detected by examining input only
        2.2  Detected by comparison with internal data
        2.3  Detected by user realizing he made a mistake
        2.4  Detected by user from incorrect output
3   Incorrect internal data
        3.1  Detected by internal inconsistency
        3.2  Detected by comparison with input data
        3.3  Detected by user from incorrect output
```

Figure 3-1-9

For example, in the class "Resource failure—temporary," we include the malfunctioning of each sensor since the sensors tend to resume correct functioning; in the class "Resource failure—permanent," we include the loss of areas of memory.

3-1-9 TECHNIQUES FOR CHARACTERIZING TYPES OF CHANGES

In order to characterize types of changes, we looked through a file of change requests and interviewed the maintainers. To define requirements for a new system, we would have looked at change requests for similar systems. We also made a long list of fundamental assumptions that we thought would always be true about the system, no matter what. In a meeting with several maintenance system engineers and programmers, all but four of the fundamental assumptions were rejected: each rejected assumption was moved to the list of possible changes. For example, the following assumption is true about the current program, but may change in the future: "The computer will perform weapon release calculations for only one target at a time. When a target is designated, the previously designated target is forgotten." By writing two complementary lists—possible changes and fundamental assumptions—we thought about the problem from two directions, and we detected many misunderstandings. Producing a list of fundamental assumptions forced us to voice some implicit assumptions, so that we discovered possible changes we would have omitted otherwise. One reason for the success of this procedure is that it is much easier for a reviewer to recognize an error than an omission.

Listed below are examples of feasible changes.

1. Assignment of devices to channels may be changed.
2. The rate of symbol movement on the display in response to joystick displacement might be changed.
3. New sensors may be added. (This has occurred already in the history of the program.)
4. Future weapons may require computer control after release.
5. Computer self-test might be required in the air (presently it is only required on the ground.)
6. It may be necessary to cease certain lower priority functions to free resources for higher priority functions during stress moments. (Presently the program halts if it does not have sufficient time to perform all functions, assuming a program error.)

3-1-10 DISCUSSION

We expect the document to be kept up-to-date as the program evolves because it is useful in many ways that are independent of our project. The maintainers of the current program plan to use it to train new maintenance personnel, since it presents the program's purpose in a consistent, systematic way. It is the only complete, up-to-date description of their hardware interfaces. One of the problems they now face when making changes is that they cannot tell easily if there are other places in the code that should be changed to preserve consistency. For example, they changed the code in one place to turn on a display when the target is twenty-two nautical miles away; in another place, the display is still turned on when the target is twenty nautical miles away. The unintended two-nautical-mile difference causes no major problems, but it adds unnecessary complexity for the pilot and the programmer. Inconsistencies such as this show up conspicuously in the function tables in our document. Besides using the document to check the implications of small changes, the maintenance staff want to modify it to document the next version of the program. They expect major benefits as they prepare system tests, since the document provides a description of accceptable program behavior that is independent of the program. In the past, testers have had to infer what the program is supposed to do by looking at the code. Finally they also intend to derive test cases systematically from the tables and mode transition charts.

The usefulness of these ideas is not limited to existing programs. They could be used during the requirements definition phase for a new product in order to record decisions for easy retrieval, to check new decisions for consistency with previously made decisions, and to suggest questions that ought to be considered. However, a requirements document for a new system would not be as specific as our document. We can describe acceptable behavior exactly because all the decisions about the external interfaces have been made. For a new program a requirements document describes a set of possible behaviors, giving the characteristics that distinguish acceptable from unacceptable behavior. The system designer chooses the exact behavior for the new product. The questions are the same for a new system; the answers are less restrictive. For example, where we give a specific number for the accuracy of an input, there might be a range of acceptable accuracies for a new program.

3-1-11 CONCLUSIONS

The requirements document for the A-7 program demonstrates that a substantial system can be described in terms of its external stimuli and its externally visible behavior. The techniques discussed in this paper guided us in obtaining information, helped us to control its complexity, and allowed us to avoid dealing with implementation details. The document gives [us] a headstart on the design phase of our project. Many questions are answered precisely that usually would be left to programmers to decide or to discover as they build the code. Since the information is expressed systematically, we can plan for it systematically, instead of working each detail into the program in an ad hoc fashion.

All of the techniques described in this paper are based on three principles: formulate questions before trying to answer them, separate concerns, and use precise notation. From these principles, we developed a disciplined approach including the following techniques:

1. symbolic names for data items and values
2. special brackets to indicate type of name
3. templates for value descriptions
4. standard forms
5. inputs described as resources
6. outputs described in terms of effects
7. demand vs. periodic functions

8. output values given as functions of conditions and events
9. consistent notation for conditions and events
10. modes for describing equivalence classes of system states
11. special tables for consistency and completeness checking
12. undesired event classification
13. complementary lists of changes and fundamental assumptions

This paper is only an introduction to the ideas that are illustrated in the requirements document.[5] The document is a fully worked out example; no details have been left out to simplify the problem. Developing and applying the techniques required approximately seventeen months of effort. The document is available to anyone interested in pursuing the ideas. Most engineering is accomplished by emulating models. We believe that our document is a good model of requirements documentation.

3-1-12 ACKNOWLEDGMENTS

The techniques described in this paper were developed by the author together with David Parnas, John Shore, and John Kallander. The author thanks Edward Britton, Honey Sue Elovitz, David Parnas, John Shore, and David Weiss for their careful and constructive reviews of the manuscript.

3-1-13 REFERENCES

[1] P. Brinch Hansen, *Operating Systems Principles;* Englewood Cliffs, NJ: Prentice-Hall; 1973.

[2] E. W. Dijkstra, "Co-operating Sequential Processes"; in F. Genuys (ed.), *Programming Languages;* New York: Academic Press, pp. 43–112, 1968.

[3] E. W. Dijkstra, *A Discipline of Programming;* Englewood Cliffs, NJ: Prentice-Hall, 1977.

[4] J. V. Guttag, "Abstract Data Types and the Development of Data Structures"; *Comm. ACM,* vol. 20, no. 6, pp. 396–404, June 1977.

[5] K. Heninger, J. Kallander, D. L. Parnas, and J. Shore, *Software Requirements for the A-7E Aircraft;* Naval Research Laboratory, Washington, D.C. 20375; Memorandum Report 3876, 27 Nov. 1978.

[6] C. A. R. Hoare, "Monitors: an Operating System Structuring Concept"; *Comm. ACM,* vol. 17, no. 10, pp. 549–557, Oct. 1974.

[7] J. Howard, "Proving Monitors"; *Comm. ACM,* vol. 19, no. 5, pp. 273–279, May 1976.

[8] R. Lipton, *On Synchronization Primitive Systems;* Ph.D Dissertation, Carnegie-Mellon University, 1973.

[9] B. Liskov and S. Zilles, "Specification Techniques for Data Abstractions"; *IEEE Transactions on Software Engineering,* vol. SE-1, no. 1, Mar. 1975.

10   B. Liskov and V. Berzins, "An Appraisal of Program Specifications"; *Proceedings of the Conference on Research Directions in Software Technology,* pp. 13-1—13-24, October 10-12, 1977.

11   D. L. Parnas, "Information Distribution Aspects of Design Methodology"; *Proceedings of IFIP Congress 71;* North Holland Publishing Company, TA-3, pp. 26-30, 1971.

12   D. L. Parnas, "On the Criteria To Be Used in Decomposing Systems into Modules"; *Comm. ACM,* vol. 15, no. 12, pp. 1053-1058, Dec. 1972.

13   D. L. Parnas and G. Handzel, *More on Specification Techniques for Software Modules,* Fachbereich Informatik, Technische Hochschule Darmstadt, 1975.

14   D. L. Parnas and H. Wurges, "Response to Undesired Events in Software Systems"; *Proceedings of Second International Conference on Software Engineering,* pp. 437-446, 1976.

15   D. L. Parnas, *Use of Abstract Interfaces in the Development of Software for Embedded Computer Systems;* Naval Research Laboratory, Washington, D.C. 20375; Report 8047, 1977.

16   D. L. Parnas, "The Use of Precise Specifications in the Development of Software"; *Proceedings of the IFIP Congress 1977;* North Holland Publishing Company, pp. 861-867, 1977.

17   D. L. Parnas, "Designing Software for Ease of Extension and Contraction"; *Proceedings of the Third International Conference on Software Engineering,* pp. 264-277, 10-12 May 1978.

18   D. L. Parnas and K. Heninger, "Implementing Processes in HAS"; in *Software Engineering Principles;* Naval Research Laboratory, Washington, D.C. 20375; Document HAS.9, 1978.

19   D. L. Parnas, "Desired System Behavior in Undesired Situations"; in *Software Engineering Principles;* Naval Research Laboratory, Washington, D.C. 20375; Document UE.1, 1978.

20   O. Roubine and L. Robinson, *SPECIAL Reference Manual,* SRI, Menlo Park, CA; Tech. Report CSL-45, SRI project 4828, 3rd ed., 1977.

21   Alan C. Shaw, *The Logical Design of Operating Systems;* Englewood Cliffs, NJ: Prentice-Hall, 1974.

22   David M. Weiss, *The MUDD Report: A Case Study of Navy Software Development Practices;* Naval Research Laboratory, Washington, D.C. 20375; Report 7909, 1975.

3-2   TOWARD A DISCIPLINE
OF REAL-TIME
PROGRAMMING*

Niklaus Wirth
Federal Institute of Technology (ETH),
Zürich, Switzerland, and
Xerox Palo Alto Research Center

Programming is divided into three major categories with increasing complexity of reasoning in program validation: sequential programming, multiprogramming, and real-time programming. By adhering to a strict programming discipline and by using a suitable high-level language molded after this discipline, the complexity of reasoning about concurrency and execution time constraints may be drastically reduced. This may be the only practical way to make real-time systems analytically verifiable and ultimately reliable. A possible discipline is outlined and expressed in terms of the language Modula.

3-2-1 CONCEPTS AND TERMINOLOGY

Conventional programs describe actions that change the values of variables in discrete steps. Execution of these actions by any processor takes a finite amount of time. This time is not a characteristic property of the program, but rather of the employed processor. In the interest of generality, programs are usually designed such that the computed results are independent of the execution speed of their processor(s). The obvious way to obtain time independence is to restrict programs to describing purely sequential chains of actions. Each action is initiated when its unique predecessor has been completed. Such a program is called a *sequential program.*

  Apart from the commercial necessity of cost accounting, the reasons for introducing the notion of time into the programmers' considerations are purely technical. The principal reason is that computation can be speeded up by the use of several concurrently operating processors. Often processors are needed with special capabilities not shared by others (such as input–output devices). The viable aim is to utilize them as effectively as possible. Programs using several processors consist of several routines, called *processes,* which are themselves purely sequential, are executed concurrently, and communicate via shared variables and synchronization signals. A program that specifies (possible) concurrency is called a *multiprogram*.

It is prudent to extend the conceptual framework of sequential programming as little as possible and, in particular, to avoid the notion of execution time, in spite of the fact that time was the ultimate reason for multiprogramming. Multiprograms should, whenever possible, be designed with sufficient generality that they specify the computed results independently of the absolute and relative speeds of employed processors. The only indispensable assumption is that these speeds are greater than zero. Adherence to execution time independence affords the tremendous advantage that a program's validity can be deduced solely from the static program text containing logical assertions on the state of the computation after each statement and signal exchange. If we depart from this rule and let our programs' validity depend on the execution speed of the utilized processors, we enter the field commonly called *"real-time"* programming. (From the foregoing it appears that "processing-time-dependent" programming would be a more descriptive term.)

Which are the reasons for designing execution-time-dependent programs? A serious reason is that certain processes—which are not programmable at discretion, as they may be part of the environment—may fail to wait for synchronization signals indicating completion of the cooperating partner's task. As a result, cooperation with such processes will necessarily have to depend on processor speed. For example, a sensor in a traffic control system emits a signal each time a car passes, but will not await acknowledgment of signal registration before emitting another signal. Hence validation of the computerized part of the system will depend on, for instance, a lower bound on the interval between two consecutive sensor signals. In other examples, the non-programmable partner may well be a human unwilling to wait for the results of his request longer than a certain duration.

The essential point here is that the sets of concepts (for reasoning) and facilities (for description) of real-time programming should be small extensions of those governing multiprogramming, which in turn should be small extensions of those used in sequential programming. Only very few fundamental concepts are added in each of the two steps, namely synchronization signals and mutual exclusion for multiprogramming, and execution speed for real-time programming. Yet in each step, the complexity of reasoning about programs has been increased by a new dimension. Only by adhering to a restrictive discipline can validation problems be kept intellectually manageable. Such a discipline is decisively shaped by the programming language used. We have developed the high-level language *Modula* with the aim of making the advantages of reasoning in terms of high-level languages amenable to the realms of multiprogramming and real-time programming[6]. Here we shall illustrate the relevant parts of that experimental language by means of a few examples and attempt to outline a set of rules to cope with real-time phenomena. These rules are still tentative and incomplete. Further research is needed to achieve a full understanding of the subject. But perhaps such rules will ultimately lead to a discipline.

3-2-2 AN EXAMPLE

Consider first the purely sequential process in which repeatedly a data portion is produced and deposited in a buffer, and thereupon fetched and consumed.

```
PROCESS PRODUCERCONSUMER;
    VAR BUFFER: BUFFER TYPE;

BEGIN
    LOOP PRODUCE; DEPOSIT;
        FETCH; CONSUME
    END

END PRODUCERCONSUMER
```

Now assume that the operations *produce* and *consume* can be executed by two—perhaps different—processors and that we wish to express this possibility explicitly by a multiprogram, taking advantage of concurrency by multiple buffering. Hence we need to express coordination: the producer must wait when the buffer is full, and the consumer when it is empty. Using the synchronization primitives offered by the language Modula, namely shared variables and so-called signals, we can express the program as follows:

```
MODULE PRODUCERCONSUMER;
    VAR N: INTEGER; (*NO. OF OCCUPIED BUFFER SLOTS*)
        NONFULL, NONEMPTY: SIGNAL;
        BUFFER: BUFFERTYPE (*N SLOTS*)

    PROCESS PRODUCER;
    BEGIN
        LOOP PRODUCE;
            IF N = N THEN WAIT(NONFULL) END;
            (*BUFFER NOT FULL*) DEPOSIT;
            N := N + 1; SEND(NONEMPTY)
        END
    END PRODUCER;

    PROCESS CONSUMER;
    BEGIN
        LOOP IF N = 0 THEN WAIT(NONEMPTY) END;
            (*BUFFER NOT EMPTY*) FETCH;
            N := N - 1; SEND(NONFULL);
            CONSUME
        END
    END CONSUMER;

BEGIN (*INITIALIZE N AND START PROCESSES*)
    N := 0; PRODUCER; CONSUMER
END PRODUCERCONSUMER
```

This scheme guarantees that the processes synchronize at the appropriate moments and hence execute exactly the same number of *produce* and *consume* operations. But in general the scheme depends on the two statement sequences starting with "if" and ending with "send( )" being *mutually exclusive*.

To ensure this mutual exclusion in a Modula program, the critical statement sequences must be formulated as procedures which are declared in a so-called *interface module*. This module also contains declarations of all shared variables and shields them from external access. Brinch Hansen[1] and Hoare[3], who call the interface module a *monitor*, proposed this scheme. As it ensures that shared variables are accessed under mutual exclusion only, it makes sequential programming verification rules applicable to multiprograms adhering to the scheme's discipline[3,4].

The define- and use-lists in the heading of a module explicitly define its precise transparency. The define-list indicates the local objects to be visible outside, and the use-list enumerates the nonlocal objects to be visible inside the module. Hence there is no dogmatic rule ensuring safety against every possible blunder (for example, the buffer could also be declared visible to the outside), but instead there are facilities that cater to the recommended discipline and encourage the programmer to adhere to it wherever applicable.

```
MODULE PRODUCERCONSUMER;
    TYPE ELEMENTTYPE = . . . ;

    INTERFACE MODULE BUFFERING;
    DEFINE FETCH, DEPOSIT;
    USE N, ELEMENTTYPE;

        VAR n: INTEGER: (*NO. OF FILLED BUFFER ELEMENTS*)
            NONFULL, NONEMPTY: SIGNAL;
            BUFFER: BUFFERTYPE; (*N SLOTS*)
    PROCEDURE FETCH(VAR x: ELEMENTTYPE);
    BEGIN IF n = 0 THEN WAIT(NONEMPTY) END;
        (*n > 0*) FETCH(x); n := n − 1; SEND(NONFULL)
    END FETCH;
    PROCEDURE DEPOSIT(x: ELEMENTTYPE);
    BEGIN IF n = N THEN WAIT(NONFULL) END;
        (*n < N*) DEPOSIT(x); n := n + 1; SEND(NONEMPTY)
    END DEPOSIT;
    BEGIN (*INITIALIZE BUFFER MANAGEMENT*) n := 0;
    END BUFFERING;

    PROCESS PRODUCER;
        VAR y: ELEMENTTYPE;
        BEGIN
            LOOP PRODUCE(y); DEPOSIT(y)
            END
        END PRODUCER;

    PROCESS CONSUMER;
        VAR z: ELEMENTTYPE;
```

```
BEGIN
    LOOP FETCH(z); CONSUME(z)
    END
END CONSUMER;

BEGIN PRODUCER; CONSUMER
END PRODUCERCONSUMER.
```

Now assume that the producer is designed such that it fails to await the *nonfull* signal. It may, for example, be a card reader initiated to read a card, or a tape unit reading a block of characters. The card (tape), once in motion, cannot be stopped; the eighty characters are "produced" whether or not the consumer is ready to accept them. Under these unsafe circumstances, the scheme works properly if and only if the consumer is always faster than the producer. In [that] case, the consumer would never have to send its *nonfull* signal, as the producer would be bypassing its *wait* statement if there were one. This, however, implies that we rely on some knowledge of execution speed; we have entered the domain of real-time programming. The assertion *buffer not full* in the producer must now be derived from the premise that it is a consequence of the statement *fetch,* and that

$$T(\text{"fetch; full} := \text{false; send( ); consume"}) <$$
$$T(\text{"produce"})$$

where T(S) denotes the (maximum) time to execute statement S.

3-2-3 A FIRST CONCLUSION

Program verification is best manageable in the case of purely sequential programs, where assertions on the state of the computation provide an effective handle for keeping track of the effects of each statement. The problem is considerably more complicated in multiprogramming. However, the disciplined use of common variables and synchronizing signals in explicitly designated interface sections with mutual exclusion reduces the added complexity of validation drastically. Such a disciplined use is aided (and can even be enforced) by high-level language features such as monitors and conditions[3] or modules and signals[6]. In effect they make multiprograms which adhere to this discipline amenable to the verification techniques of sequential programs.

Similarly, dependence on execution-time constraints makes the verification task almost intractable unless a discipline is observed that confines time dependence to certain isolated parts in some standard pattern. From the foregoing, my conclusion for making real-time programs manageable can be condensed into the recipe:

1. First formulate the entire program *without* any reliance on execution times. Explicitly provide all synchronization signals needed for this generality.
2. For each signal that is not made available by the machinery to be used, analytically derive the time constraints that allow the absence of the signal.
3. Check whether these constraints are met by your computer system.

The first step constitutes a task in "ordinary" multiprogramming with—more or less—established validation techniques. The second step is relatively straightforward, provided the time-dependent parts of the program are few, simply structured, and without loops with an unknown number of repetitions.

3-2-4 AN INTERLUDE: SIGNALS AND SEMAPHORES

The above rule may even be useful in situations where a priori the notion of time does not seem to play a role at all. In certain situations programmers make assumptions—perhaps unconsciously—about relative execution speeds of processors. If they consciously refrained from doing so, the programs might become slightly more complicated. Specifically they use *signals* where they should use *semaphores*. Because this mistake does not seem to be uncommon in spite of its disastrous effects, we shall briefly characterize it.

Semaphores have been postulated as synchronization primitives by Dijkstra[2]. Hoare and Brinch Hansen have instead proposed *conditions*[3] and *queues*[1]. We have renamed them *signals* in Modula,[6] in analogy to pulse or trigger signals in electronic circuits. Semaphores can be expressed in terms of signals and ordinary variables. Signals must therefore be considered as more primitive entities. We subsequently present a formulation of binary semaphores (bs) and general semaphores (gs) and their P and V operations in terms of Modula (declared as an interface module).

```
TYPE BS =                          TYPE GS =
   RECORD s: SIGNAL;                  RECORD s; SIGNAL;
      b: BOOLEAN                         n: INTEGER
   END                                END

PROCEDURE P(x: BS);                PROCEDURE P(x: GS);
BEGIN                              BEGIN
   IF x.b THEN WAIT(x.s) END;         IF x.n = 0 THEN WAIT(x.s) END;
   x.b := FALSE                       x.n := x.n − 1
END                                END

PROCEDURE V(x:BS);                 PROCEDURE V(x: GS);
BEGIN x.b := TRUE; SEND(x.s)       BEGIN x.n := x.n + 1; SEND(x.s)
END                                END
```

Evidently the semaphore is equivalent to a signal with associated memory. It remembers whether or not the corresponding signal had been sent (bs), or even counts the number of past unresponded signal emissions (gs).

Now assume that two processes P1 and P2 start executing respective statements S1 and S2 simultaneously and that it is requested that before continuing after S2, P2 wait for the completion of S1 by P1. If we happen to know that S2 is executed (considerably) faster than S1, we are (much) tempted to use the following schema involving a completion signal s:

$$P1: \ldots \ S1; \ \text{send}(s); \ \ldots$$
$$P2: \ldots \ S2; \ \text{wait}(s); \ \ldots$$

However, if for some—of course not unforeseeable but nevertheless unforeseen—reasons sometimes S2 is not completed before S1, then the signal may be emitted without P2 noticing it, and, when S2 is finally completed, P2 will wait forever. This very mistake is often the cause of deadlocks in systems said to be "basically correct, but susceptible to heavy load." In fact, the "heavy load" is precisely what causes the execution time T(S2) to exceed the unrecognized, implicit limit T(S1).

Perhaps it might be wiser to define the emission of a signal that is not awaited as an error instead of an empty operation, that is, to declare *awaited*(*s*) as a necessary precondition of *send*(*s*). The culprit of system crashes might then be more easily located.

3-2-5. LANGUAGE AND SYSTEM REQUIREMENTS FOR REAL-TIME PROGRAMMING

It is futile to make an attempt to provide an exhaustive list of necessary features and detailed language facilities for real-time programming. Instead, it seems sensible to concentrate on basic issues. It is unquestionably the form and *structure* of a language that plays the dominant role in the development of well-structured and reliable programs, be they sequential or "real-time." In this respect, a "real-time language" appears to require no more structural concepts than a good multiprogramming language. The most important single item is a notational unit for describing *processes* that are themselves purely sequential, but can be executed concurrently. In particular, this implies the absence of the notion of an interrupt. We must be able to think of each logical process as being sequential and coherent. The second item that appears to be necessary is a collection of shared variables together with their operators for which mutual interference is excluded (monitors, *interface modules*). The third item is an object to trigger continuation after waiting (*signals*).

Whereas real-time programming calls for no additional language structures, and for hardly any added facilities, a new requirement must be imposed on implementations: they must be able to provide accurate execution time bounds for any compiled statement or statement sequence. Such a facility, although unusual at present, is readily provided by additions to existing compilers. In the case of straightforward code generation without optimization, a simple table indicating the times for each kind of statement may even be satisfactory. Particularly important figures in this table are the times for the *send* and *wait* operations. They may be taken as reliable indicators for the effectiveness (or overhead) of a real-time language implementation.

The postulate that the programmer must be able to think of each logical process as being coherent, that is, behaving as if executed by its private processor, does not of course imply that actual implementations cannot deviate from this schema as long as they satisfy the defining axioms. In reality, most implementations *share* processors among processes, and several processors may take turns in the execution of the same process. The reason for insisting that a program should not rely on assumptions about any particular processor-sharing strategy is twofold: to *simplify the logical foundations* of the program and to provide implementations with a maximum degree of *freedom for choosing such a strategy*. This reason is the sole motivation behind the distinction between logical coherent processes and physical interruptible processors. The "ban" on the notion of interrupt is merely a corollary because interrupts pertain to shared processors but not to coherent processes.

The acceptance of processor-sharing implementations has, however, one grave consequence: the determination of execution-time bounds can no longer be based on static timing figures only. We must take into account that during execution of any statement the processor may be diverted to work on another process for an unknown "time slice." This difficulty is perhaps the most convincing reason why hitherto real-time programming remained the unchallenged domain of assembly coding, where programmers feel most confident to have all details under their control. However, if the influence of processor sharing (that is, of interrupts) can be ignored in considerations about a system's computational state (that is, in logical assertions) and can be confined to timing considerations only, then the goal of a discipline of real-time programming appears noticeably more realistic.

3-2-6 REAL-TIME PROGRAMMING IN HIGH-LEVEL LANGUAGES USING PROCESSOR SHARING

It does not appear feasible at this time to postulate any generally valid and at the same time practically useful rules for the determination of execution-time bounds for systems using processor sharing. Rather we shall investigate techniques used to cope with real-time problems when using assembly code. We may then be able to identify a frequently used program schema that seems manageable and to suggest a formulation in terms of high-level languages.

First and most important, we find that time-critical operations most frequently occur in close connection with peripheral devices such as readers, sensors, and equipment to be controlled. It is customary to associate a process with each device (or array of identical devices). If a separate processor is available for this purpose, the process is called a *driver,* if a general processor has to be shared, it is called an *interrupt handler.* In either case, both the device itself and the associated routine effectively constitute a pair of cooperating sequential processes. This typical situation is abstracted by the following schema, expressed for the case of an input device. The completion signal is customarily called *the interrupt.*

```
VAR INTERFACEBUFFER: REGISTER;
    INITIATION, COMPLETION: SIGNAL;
PROCESS INPUTDEVICE;
BEGIN
  LOOP WAIT(INITIATION); READDATA; PUTDATA; SEND(COMPLETION)
  END
END INPUTDEVICE;

PROCESS DRIVER;
BEGIN
  LOOP SEND(INITIATION); WAIT(COMPLETION); GETDATA; PROCESSDATA
  END
END DRIVER
```

The characteristic of this schema is that the two processes effectively *alternate* in being active. Moreover, the first process represents an essentially nonprogrammable device. In Modula, this typical example of cooperating sequential processes is therefore condensed into a single so-called *device process.* The *send(initiation)* statement is replaced by commands determined by the specific hardware device, and the *wait(completion)* statement is replaced by a generic statement called *doio,* representing the device's entire activity.

```
PROCESS DRIVER;
⟨DECLARATIONS OF DEVICE STATUS AND BUFFER REGISTERS⟩
BEGIN ⟨INITIALIZATIONS⟩;
  LOOP STARTDEVICE; DOIO; GETDATA; PROCESSDATA
  END
END DRIVER
```

The driver communicates with other processes; in the example this is hidden in the statement *ProcessData.* Communicating procedures would have to be declared in an interface module. Since, however, the statements in the cycle (apart from *doio*) are few and take a very short time anyway, it appears appropriate to move the entire driver process text into that interface module and to explicitly declare the *doio* statement to be exempted from the mutual exclusion condition. This kind of special interface module is called *device module* in Modula. The *doio* statement and declarations of hardware specific facilities, such as device control and buffer registers, are allowed in such device modules only.

```
DEVICE MODULE READER;
  DEFINE READ;
  VAR BUFFER; BUFFERTYPE;
    NONFULL, NONEMPTY: SIGNAL;

  PROCEDURE READ(VAR x: CHARACTER);
  BEGIN IF ... THEN WAIT(NONEMPTY) END;
    FETCH(x); SEND(NONFULL)
  END READ;
  PROCESS DRIVER;
    VAR CARDREADERBUFFER: REGISTER;
        CARDREADERSTATUS: REGISTER;
  BEGIN INITIALIZE;
    LOOP STARTREADER; DOIO;
      IF ... THEN WAIT(NONFULL) END;
      GET CHARACTER FROM CARDREADERBUFFER AND DEPOSIT;
      SEND(NONEMPTY)
    END
  END DRIVER;
  BEGIN INITIALIZE LOCAL DATA AND BUFFER;
    DRIVER
  END READER
```

We now return to the important question of how to take real-time constraints into consideration. Remember that we cannot rely on timing information obtained from the static program text since we assume that the processor may be shared among the various processes. Evidently we need to know something about the strategy by which it serves individual processes and, in particular, whether or not certain processes are served with priority.

The common technique is that so-called interrupt routines are given priority, that is, upon receipt of an interrupt signal the processor is unconditionally diverted to that routine. The analogy now becomes apparent: because the device process corresponds to the interrupt routine, it must be executed with priority in noninterruptible mode. In systems with several devices, interrupts are queued when arriving while another is being served. In Modula, this effect therefore manifests itself as a hidden delay statement behind each *doio*. Its minimal duration is 0, and the maximum duration d is equal to the sum of the execution times of all other interrupt responses: $0 \leq d \leq \text{sum } T(S_i)$, where $T(S_i)$ is the time to execute the longest statement sequence S_i between any two instances of *doio* in the *i*th device process, measured in noninterrupted mode, and where *i* ranges over all other processes.

The recommended discipline of real-time programming in Modula can now be summarized as follows:

1. Confine time-dependent program parts to device processes which are executed in noninterruptible mode.
2. Execution time of statements in device processes is determined statically, that is, as if there were no processor sharing.
3. Each *doio* statement is assumed to be followed by a hidden delay statement whose bounds are given above.

Note: The lower bound of the delay is not exactly 0, but is equal to the "overhead" of processor switching upon interrupt. This is another characteristic performance figure of a multiprogramming language implementation.

In practice, the typical system operates a large number of devices, a few of which require fast response. As no appreciable delays in the associated drivers are tolerable, the value d—being the sum of a large number of terms—might easily become unacceptably high. The solution lies in the use of a priority interrupt system. Its essence is that the shared processor, when operating at priority level p, is interruptible only by devices assigned an interrupt strength $k > p$ ($0 \leq p \leq pmax$, $0 < k_i \leq pmax$). Processors without this feature appear as a special case with $pmax = 1$.

Unfortunately the situation becomes hopelessly more complicated and eludes exact analysis because now device processes can be interrupted by other device processes of higher priority. Yet, the situation becomes manageable again if we adhere to the following constraints:

1. Every device process P_i is cyclic, the cycle consisting of a statement sequence S_i executed by the shared processor and the statement *doio*, representing the waiting for the device completion.
2. The cycle time
   $$t_i = T(S_i) + T(doio_i)$$
   of process i at any priority level k is considerably larger than that of all processes at level $k - 1$. Note that $T(doio_i)$ is determined by the ith device.
3. Over every cycle, the ratio
   $$r_i = T(S_i)/(T(S_i) + T(doio_i)) \ll 1.$$
   This is the fraction of time that the processor is needed to serve the ith device process.

Under these conditions we may approximately compute the effective execution time T of any statement S in a device process at priority level k as

$$T(S) = T'(S)/(1 - \text{sum } r_j),$$

where $T'(S)$ is the execution time of S without processor sharing, and where i ranges over all processes at priority levels greater than k.

Let us now formulate, as a brief example, a time-dependent card reader driver in terms of Modula:

```
DEVICE MODULE CARDREADER [PRIORITY];
    DEFINE READ;
    VAR BUFFER: BUFFERTYPE;
    PROCEDURE READ( ); . . .
    PROCESS DRIVER [INTERRUPT ADDRESS];
        ⟨DECLARATIONS OF DEVICE REGISTERS⟩
    BEGIN
        LOOP . . . STARTMOTION;
            LOOP DOIO (*DELAY MAY OCCUR HERE*);
            WHEN ENDOFCARD EXIT
                FETCH NEXT CHARACTER FROM DEVICE REGISTER;
                DEPOSIT IN BUFFER
            END;
            DEPOSIT ENDOFCARD MARK IN BUFFER
        END
    END DRIVER;
    BEGIN INITIALIZE LOCAL DATA AND BUFFER;
        DRIVER
    END CARDREADER
```

Assuming that reading a character takes $t = T(doio)$ milliseconds, we must conclude that the necessary constraint is

$$T(\text{``}\{(*delay*)\}; \textbf{when} \ldots \text{deposit''}) < t.$$

If no other device drivers operate at priority level greater than or equal to p, the hidden delay is zero. If no other driver operates at a level greater than p, the execution times can be determined statically without considering a slowdown factor.

3-2-7 PROBLEMATIC PRIORITY

We have seen that the notion of process priority is necessary if real-time programs are to be executed by systems using processor sharing. Even so, explanations of a program's validity are often intricate and complex. Unfortunately the notion of priorities also imports a dilemma in connection with the presented concept of synchronization through signals.

We started out with the recommendation to design programs in a timing-constraint-free manner whenever possible and instead to rely on logical assertions on the state of the computation. The signal facility must therefore also be defined in an axiomatic way. The following is commonly accepted:

$\{P_s \& Q\}$ SEND(s) $\{Q\}$,
$\{Q\}$ WAITS(s) $\{P_s \& Q\}$.

Here Q is a condition over the variables of the interface module in which the signal s is declared. Q must hold before and after each *send* and *wait* (and *doio*) statement, and also at the entrance and exit of each interface procedure. Q is called the *interface invariant*. P_s is the condition associated with the signal s. It must be established before each signal emission and is therefore guaranteed to hold whenever a process resumes after waiting for the signal. This definition of the semantics of signals—including the association of a transmitted condition (message)—is certainly sensible and intuitively correct. However, it also has the effect of enforcing an effective switching of the processor for each *send* statement (when sharing is employed), for, if a process would not immediately be resumed after signal receipt, no guarantee could be given for the condition P_s still to hold when at a later time the waiting process obtains the processor. After all, other processes might have invalidated P_s in the meantime[5].

But now the following awkward question arises: Should the processor still be switched if the sending process is declared to have a higher priority than the receiving one? If the answer is yes, unreasonably frequent processor switching may be the consequence, and—worse—timing considerations become exceedingly difficult if not impossible. If the answer is no, then the axioms governing signals must be revised, and they become inherently more complex. Considering that signals are a truly basic concept, that would look like a symptom of inadequacy.

The question remains open. In Modula, the negative answer was adopted. It seems counterintuitive to release a processor to a process of lower priority. The following additional constraints on signals emitted by device processes are sufficient, but perhaps too strong, and certainly cumbersome:

1. Each signal s which is emitted by a device must be awaited by a single (regular) process only.

2. A device process itself must never invalidate the condition associated with a signal which it emitted.

Acceptance of these rules yields the benefit of applicability of the presented framework of reasoning about timing constraints and the possibility of an extremely efficient implementation of signalling. The latter is truly important for real-time applications and low-level device handling.

3-2-8 SUMMARY AND CONCLUSIONS

We have divided programming into three categories with ascending complexity in required reasoning: sequential programming, multiprogramming, and real-time programming. The former two categories are characterized by the property that the validity of programs is independent of the execution speed of processors used. In order to keep real-time programs intellectually manageable, we recommend that they first be designed as time-independent multiprograms and that only after analytic validation they be modified in isolated places, where the consequences of reliance on execution time constraints are simple to comprehend and document.

The advantages of high-level languages are even greater in real-time programming than in sequential programming. This is because appropriate language structures help in isolating those parts of a program that rely on timing conditions (device processes) from those parts where time is irrelevant. The important idea is that all processes can be considered as purely sequential and coherent. In many cases, the consequences of using an actual system with a shared processor are relatively simple to take into account: they manifest themselves as virtual delay after each *doio* and, if the implementation is based on a priority interrupt system, by a virtual slowdown of actual processor speed by a computable factor.

The notion of priority is important when dealing with systems using the technique of processor sharing. The presented rules apply only if the processes of any given priority level require an order of magnitude less processor time than all processes at the next lower level. In all other cases, the problem of analytically verifying a system's validity appears formidable, if not impossible. Then, as often in engineering, it is wiser to avoid the problem than to solve it. With rapidly decreasing hardware cost, it is best to avoid the technique of sharing and to dedicate a processor to each process. This appears even more attractive if we consider problems of reliability in the sense of hardware fault tolerance. This subject was not covered here, as it is based on engineering experience rather than language design.

In summary, the use of a suitable high-level language, together with adherence to a strict programming discipline, is instrumental in making analytic validation of real-time programs possible. It may be the only viable way toward genuine reliability in real-time systems.

3-2-9 ACKNOWLEDGMENTS

The author gratefully acknowledges the valuable comments made by S. L. Graham, S. Knudsen, J. H. Morris, and I. C. Pyle, and the support received from the Xerox Corporation.

3-2-10 REFERENCES

[1] Brinch Hansen, P., *Operating System Principles*. Prentice-Hall. Englewood Cliffs, N.J., 1973.
[2] Dijkstra, E. W., Cooperating sequential processes. In *Programming Languages,* F. Genuys. Ed., Academic Press. New York, 1968.

[3] Hoare, C. A. R., Monitors: An operating system structuring concept. *Comm. ACM 17,* 10 (Oct. 1974), 549–557.

[4] Howard, J. H., Proving monitors. *Comm. ACM 19,* 5 (May 1976), 273–279.

[5] Howard, J. H., Signaling in monitors. Proc. 2nd Int. Conf. on Software Engineering, IEEE Cat. No. 76CH1125–4C. San Francisco, Oct. 1976, 47–52.

[6] Wirth, N., Modula: A language for modular multiprogramming. *Software—Practice and Experience, 7,* 1 (Jan. 1977), 3–35.

3-3 SAMS: ADDRESSING MANAGERS' NEEDS*

PATRICIA M. MOLKO
Jet Propulsion Laboratory
California Institute of Technology

ABSTRACT

Project Galileo's Orbiter Spacecraft, developed and managed by the Jet Propulsion Laboratory (JPL), is scheduled for launch from the Space Shuttle in early 1984. The size and complexity of the on-board and ground software systems demand a strong management control methodology to be integrated into the software development approach. The purpose of this paper is to describe the Software Automated Management System (SAMS), which provides an ensemble of software tools to aid the Galileo Project in controlling software development. On a project the size of Galileo, it is imperative that computer technology be used to facilitate the necessary communications among software developers and managers. Past JPL projects have automated portions of the management task, such as configuration management and some level of schedule monitoring; however, the additional automation afforded by the use of SAMS will simplify the management task associated with the development of this large software system.

* © 1980 IEEE. Reprinted, with permission, from the Proceedings of IEEE Compsac 80, pp. 691–697.

The work reported in this paper was carried out at the Jet Propulsion Laboratory, California Institute of Technology, under NASA Contract NAS7-100. Provided through the courtesy of the Jet Propulsion Laboratory, California Institute of Technology, Pasadena, California.

3-3-1   INTRODUCTION

In the past ten years, considerable research has been done to broaden our knowledge regarding the development and maintenance of software. Studies have been conducted to increase our understanding of the distribution of costs and incidence of errors in the software life cycle.[1,2] Tools, techniques, and management approaches have been proposed, implemented, and evaluated in an effort to make the final product both cost-effective and reliable. Software engineering techniques emphasize the use of systematic software development methodologies, supplemented by support tools, such as PSL/PSA[3] and PDL[4], which are applied to specific stages in the software development cycle. Software management techniques such as chief programmer teams, program support libraries, configuration management, software factories[5], cost estimation, and monitoring and reporting software development status have provided increased opportunity for improving the software product. The successful application of technical methods for producing and operating software systems is creating a basis for the software engineering discipline which continues to evolve.

Project Galileo is aggressively pursuing the use of modern management practices to meet the challenges summarized in D. J. Reifer's introductory paper.[6] This paper presents an overview of SAMS followed by a description of each of the processors comprising SAMS. In order to understand the use of the system, the reader is presented with a typical operational scenario occurring during software development. The current status of SAMS is described and the experiences to date are summarized.

3-3-2   SOFTWARE AUTOMATED MANAGEMENT SYSTEM

3-3-2-1   Overview

Advances in technology resulting in shared database techniques and the availability of moderately-priced intelligent terminals have made it possible for a computer system to be the main repository for information regarding a system under development. The advantages of having information retrievable by computer instead of documented only in memos and program listings is that the latest data is always available, and can be selected and organized according to the requestor's needs. Additionally, a database provides historical information for the evaluation and improvement of the techniques applied.

SAMS, which consists of several databases and a set of both independent and integrated processors, has four basic characteristics, as follows:

1. Its architecture was created using current software engineering principles.
2. It incorporates human engineering techniques, making it operable by people with a wide variety of computer skills.

3. It allows an incremental development of tools–processors, which provides for a systematic integration approach and phased operations training.
4. It provides both technical and management views of the evolving software system.

SAMS operates on an Automated Office Data Center (AODC), a micro-processor-based computer workstation. The AODC hardware configuration includes a Zilog Z–80 microprocessor as the basic computer mainframe, up to three CRT terminals, a dual or quad floppy disk system, a hard disk, and a character printer. Telecommunications and interfaces with an IBM 3032 or a UNIVAC 1100/81 are provided. The software components of the standard system include the following:

1. Control Program Monitor, CP/M©, is a single-user, disk file manage-ment system, marketed by the Digital Research Corporation, which pro-vides a general environment for program construction, storage, retrieval, and execution. A multi-tasking, multi-user operation system with the same applications interfaces as CP/M has been developed by JPL. It permits up to three users and various background tasks to operate within a single AODC system.
2. Many high-level languages (BASIC, FORTRAN, PASCAL, and so on) and numerous utilities, which operate under CP/M, are available.
3. WORDSTAR©, produced by MicroPro International Corporation, is a CP/M compatible, full-screen text edit/word processing system.
4. VULCAN is a database management tool, produced by Software Con-sultation, Design, and Production, that allows creation and easy manipulation of small- and medium-sized database files.

3-3-3 OPERATIONAL CONCEPT

A central SAMS Operations Staff, consisting primarily of data-entry opera-tors, is responsible for operating SAMS to provide management with data and reports. The databases are configuration-controlled, and data entry by this staff to the master files is made only with the approval of the Configuration Management Staff. Each member of the Project SSM Staff is provided with an AODC for easy access to the database. Additional AODC units are dedicated to the line organizations to support both the technical software development pro-cess, and via SAMS, a view of the evolution of that process.

3-3-4 MAJOR COMPONENTS

In addition to the AODC software components previously described, the set of processors which comprise SAMS includes the following:

1. Automated Work Breakdown Structure Processor
2. Schedule Generation Processor
3. Information Display Processor
4. Distribution List Processor
5. Action Item List Processor
6. Document–Memo Index Processor
7. Software Delivery Processor
8. Computer Margin Summary Processor
9. Configuration Management Processor

Although not part of SAMS, several other processors allow software documentation to be generated on the AODC and become part of a documentation database. The AODC text edit/word processor, WORDSTAR, is used to create Galileo software documents. Design documents and "as-built" program description documents are entered using the Software Design and Documentation Language Processor[7], which is similar to PDL.

3-3-4-1 Automated Work Breakdown Structure Processor

A survey conducted by R. Thayer and J. Lehman on software engineering project management listed planning, control, and resource estimation as being among the biggest software management problems.[8] Project Galileo has adopted detailed scheduling and monitoring practices for software development based on the Work Breakdown Structure (WBS) supported by an automated processor. A prototype of the processor is currently in use and therefore the description that follows is more detailed than some of the other processor descriptions.

A WBS is an enumeration of all work activities in hierarchic refinements of detail, which organizes work to be done into short, manageable tasks with quantifiable inputs, outputs, schedules, and assigned responsibilities.

The Automated Work Breakdown Structure Processor (AWBSP) provides management with rapid access to a database containing manpower allocation and schedule information. It also provides the capability to request reports designed to provide visibility into the development process, so that problems may be discovered and resolved before becoming crises. The processor is based on the major program management function of organizing and planning the job in advance, accounting for and measuring the work completed to date, and analyzing variances from the plan and taking corrective action as necessary.

The statistical accuracy with which predictions can be made concerning costs and the completion date of future milestones is directly related to the number of tasks contained in the WBS, the accuracy of the estimate of resources and duration assigned to each, and the reporting frequency. Project Galileo has set goals and policies for each of these parameters. Both the WBS philosophy and methodology are described in a Galileo Software Technical and Administrative Procedure (STAP)[9] and in a paper by R. Tausworthe.[10]

Although the AWBSP supports the definition of any group of tasks to make up a schedule, software development as defined by the Project Galileo Software Management Plan[9] is accomplished by completing the thirteen milestones listed in Table 3-3-1. These thirteen events are established as project milestones to provide consistent reporting for each program that is included in the software system.

The programmer and engineer responsible for a given program begin by creating a schedule with the thirteen milestones specified in Table 3-3-1. Although distant activities cannot be scheduled in precise detail, it is important to preserve a valid plan for future work, because the interrelationships of the entire plan determine the time requirements of the work which can be scheduled.

Prior to each software development phase (requirements definition, design, code, etc.), the milestones for that approaching phase are expanded to a unit-task-level breakdown of activities. A "unit task" is characterized by the following attributes:

Sized for a single individual.

No further breakdown into subtasks.

Input needs, precedent tasks, and interfaces with other tasks are identifiable.

Outputs are identifiable.

Completed status is sharp (yes, no).

TABLE 3-3-1 Galileo Software Milestones

1. System–Subsystem Functional Requirements Document approved.
2. Integrated Software Functional Diagram approved.
3. Software Requirements Document, Software Interface Specification–Phase 1, User's Guide–Phase 1; preliminary versions approved.
4. Software Requirements Document, Software Interface Specification–Phase 1, User's Guide–Phase 1; final versions approved.
5. General Design Document approved.
6. Software Interface Specification–Phase 2 approved.
7. Operational Scenario Simulation Verification complete.
8. Acceptance Test Plan approved.
9. Software Integration and System Test Plan approved.
10. Program Implementation complete; Program Description Document and User's Guide–Phase 2 approved.
11. Acceptance testing complete; acceptance approval.
12. Delivery to Central Software Library.
13. Software integration and system testing complete; delivery to operations.

A detailed WBS checklist is provided to aid engineers and programmers in generating subtasks dependent on program architecture . . . and those independent of program architecture, such as project administration and management.

The goal of scheduling is to continually validate plans. Engineers and programmers can plan the work they must perform. Supervisors can observe progress, foresee problems, and institute solutions. Managers can monitor status, understand resource needs, and plan utilization of resources. The AWBSP has been designed to facilitate the operational decision-making process, but does not make decisions itself. The managerial decision is required to close the loop.

A database of schedule and cost data is built which absorbs a maximum of information and provides reports based upon the user's needs. Reporting requirements differ for each level of management, and the AWBSP, in addition to detailed reporting, provides exception information tailored to each level of management. In this way, project management is able to concentrate on major problem areas, while minor problem areas are left to the individuals responsible, with upper management being involved on request or when overall project schedule or budget is affected. Reports generated include summary reports of progress by milestone or by person. Task-dependency trees and summaries of overdue or upcoming milestones can also be produced.

Current Galileo policy is for each WBS to be kept current, updated biweekly, and reviewed by the cognizant line manager. Schedule–resource and appropriate recovery plans are required to be provided to the project if project-specified constraints are violated. The AWBSP supports a minimal level of security such that approved schedules cannot be altered without proper authorization.

3-3-4-2 Schedule Generation Processor

The Schedule Generation Processor (SGP) utilizes the WBS data base to generate project-level software schedules based on user input of the items to be selected. For example, in order to generate a project-level schedule for a given program, the SGP would select the thirteen milestones in Table 3–3–1 from among the unit tasks in the WBS for that program. In this way, managers have access to the schedule data of interest to them, while the full set of detailed information is available to the developers. The SGP maintains the previously generated schedules and indicates all changes since the last generated schedule.

3-3-4-3 Information Display Processor

The Information Display Processor (IDP) aids one in simulating program operation scenarios. It includes a full-screen data entry capability which aids an engineer–programmer in designing the input–output capability and format of an application program in consultation with the users of the program. It allows experimentation, testing, and modification of the capability before the application program is coded.

The IDP is used to aid in generating the requirements and design of the various SAMS processors. Because SAMS is to be operated by persons with a wide variety of computer skills, this processor allows operators to take part in designing the input format; users can experiment with various interactive display formats; designers can simulate the general logic flow through the processor and its interfaces.

3-3-4-4 Distribution List Processor

Designed primarily to aid in the timely dissemination of project information, the Distribution List Processor (DLP) depends on a centralized personnel database. For each project individual there is a corresponding database entry which contains an address, telephone number, job title, program responsibility, supervisor, organization, and assigned distribution list identifiers. The DLP provides the capability to selectively extract any portion of the data associated with an individual, facilitating the construction of concise and complete "qualified" distribution lists and mailing envelope labels. Consequently, duplicate distributions can be avoided.

3-3-4-5 Action Item Processor

With hundreds of documents to review and numerous reviews to attend, the Project SSM Staff must have immediate access to data which summarizes action item status, to aid in making the decision to affix signature approval to a document.

Using the Action Item Processor, action items from software reviews can be recorded, their progress tracked, and closure identified in a central database. The Action Item Processor is a processor which uses the database tool VULCAN and generates reports based on selection of any of the following data:

Action item identifier-title-description-priority-status,
system-subsystem-program-identifier; responsible individual,
documents affected; other areas affected,
schedule information,
memo-document closure number.

The Configuration Management Processor (CMP) interfaces with this processor to verify completion of documentation for the software delivery process. Refer to the operational scenario section for a further explanation.

3-3-4-6 Document/Memo Index Processor

All Galileo software documents will be part of a documentation database, with the master configuration-controlled disks under control of the Configuration Management Staff. Documents will be entered using either WORDSTAR or the Software Design and Documentation Language Processor.[6] Use of these tools will allow easy updating of software documents and to some extent aid in solving the problem of documents being out of date. It is recognized that management enforcement of configuration control procedures is required to keep documents current.

The Document–Memo Index Processor (DIP) uses the database tool VULCAN to maintain a database and to generate reports based on the following data:

Document number–title–date–location–status–author–signature list,

configuration management related data, such as change requests applicable to the document, and so on; schedule date for modification per each change request.

In addition, if the document is a software interface specification document, the program producing the data for the interface, as well as those programs receiving the data, are recorded and may also be reported.

The DIP database is accessible by the CMP to provide it with information regarding the status and location of Galileo software documents. Refer to the operational scenario section for a further explanation.

3-3-4-7 Software Delivery Processor

When a program has completed the first eleven milestones of Table 3-3-1, it is ready for delivery to the project's Central Software Library.

The Software Delivery Processor (SDP) aids the software developer in gathering the items necessary to make such delivery. The AODC full-screen data entry capability allows a form to be displayed and filled in with the appropriate data, rather than an item-by-item interactive prompting of required information. The current status of deliverable documents is displayed [along with] a checklist to aid the software developer in making sure all required items are in order.

The SDP produces summary reports regarding the status of the various program deliveries. These reports are useful to the Project SSM Staff, the Configuration Management Staff, and the Quality Assurance Staff.

3-3-4-8 Computer Margin Summary Processor

Project Galileo recognized early the need to control critical parameters, whose untimely consumption can lead to major design problems, especially in the case of on-board software. A computer margin management policy and procedure was implemented which provides for establishing, measuring, and reporting margins for resource usage including memory sizing, CPU execution, bus–channel traffic, and ground commutation channel processing.

The Computer Margin Summary Processor accesses a database compatible with VULCAN to provide reports containing computer memory, timing, and bus–channel, traffic-data utilization of programs comprising the software system.

3-3-4-9 Configuration Management Processor

A method of managing change is a must for project management. A change can be viewed as a correction to a problem or the addition of some capability. Managers require accurate information about the status of any change and also statistical data, such as the numbers and identity of changes in any given status, for example, all "open" change requests for a given program.

The Configuration Management Processor (CMP) supports multiple views of the current system at the configuration item level. A configuration item is defined to consist of a software program and all of its documentation. Information contained in the CMP database is described in the operational scenario section. The CMP also provides system-level control for updating databases under the control of other SAMS processors. It is not capable of accepting module source changes and generating an equivalent object change. That task is outside the scope of this processor and is left to the programmers.

3-3-5 TYPICAL OPERATIONAL SCENARIO

The use and operation of SAMS is best understood by considering a typical operational scenario. To aid in understanding the process, the example that follows is represented pictorially in Figure 3-3-1.

The configuration baselines established for Galileo software are the requirements or "build-to" baseline, the design or "code-to" baseline, the "as-built" baseline, and the "as-tested" baseline.

3-3-5-1 Submitting a Change Request

For this scenario, assume a user requests a change in requirements to operational program ALPHA against the as-tested baseline. Using a standard Galileo Software Change Request (SCR) form,[9] which could be accessed as a full-screen entry page on the AODC, the user would fill out information regarding the change. Information includes other areas or programs affected by the change. The SAMS Operations Staff would enter this data into the CMP data base, assigning a unique SCR number, for example, SCR 100.

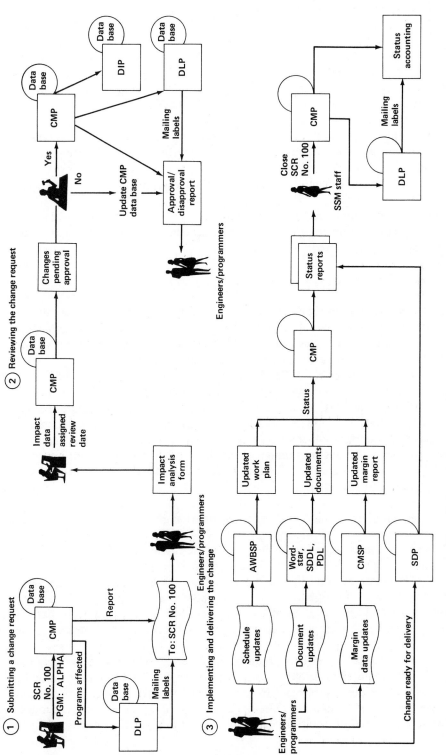

Figure 3-3-1 Pictorial representation of SAMS operational scenario.

151

A copy of the report would be sent to the appropriate engineers and programmers by the CMP initiating the DLP to list persons responsible for program ALPHA or other programs affected by the change. The DLP would produce the appropriate set of mailing envelope labels.

The Computer Margin Summary Processor and WBS Processor would provide the current data required by the programmers and engineers to make a margin–cost–schedule impact analysis of the change. This data is recorded on a standard Galileo Software Impact Analysis form,[9] and the engineer is responsible for attaching the change pages of the Software Requirements Documents of the affected programs. The requirements analysis must be completed at this stage to ensure valid impact analysis data. To minimize the preapproval workload, all other document modifications are scheduled, but the inputs are made after approval of the requested change.

3-3-5-2 Reviewing the Change Request

The SAMS Operations Staff enters the impact analysis and status data into the CMP database for SCR 100. The database contains all of the change request information, all of the impact analysis information, and the date when it will be reviewed by the Software Change Control Board (SCCB).

The SCCB receives a CMP report specifying the changes pending approval at that particular meeting. If it does *not* approve SCR 100, the SAMS staff updates the CMP database to reflect this. If it does approve the change, the CMP database is updated and the document index database is updated to reflect the dates when documents will be updated as a result of the change. A report is sent to the engineers and programmers to reflect approval–disapproval of the change request. The date and the project build for which the change is targeted is also indicated.

3-3-5-3 Implementing and Delivering the Change

Current schedules are red-lined and sent by the engineers and programmers to the SAMS Operations Staff; WBSs are updated.

The change is implemented, tested, and made ready for project delivery. During this time, the operations staff has updated all affected documents and reflected this in the DIP database and the CMP database. Margin data is updated using the Computer Margin Summary Processor and reflected in the CMP database.

The SDP is then utilized to aid the software developer in generating the paperwork required to deliver software to the project. A CMP report would be used by the Project SSM Staff to verify all delivery items were in order and therefore SCR 100 should be closed. The CMP would produce status accounting and summary information regarding all programs in the new project build.

3-3-6 CURRENT STATUS

The standard AODC software components, WORDSTAR, VULCAN, and so on, are already in use. Prototypes have been developed for the AWBSP, the IDP, the DLP, the Action Item Processor, and the CMP. A WBS schedule, which specifies the milestones given in Table 3-3-1, exists for each of the Galileo software programs, including SAMS.

Requirements are currently being written for the overall system and database architecture, as well as for each of the SAMS processors. SAMS was expected to be complete and operational by January 1982.

3-3-7 EXPERIENCES TO DATE

Galileo is the first large project at JPL to put all of its software documentation on a computer. Experience with the word processing capabilities of the system have been very favorable. Fast turnaround service is essential to the success of its use. A person is much more likely to update a document if he does not have to wait days or weeks to receive the updated version.

One of the major efforts by the Galileo SSM Staff in the past year has been the implementation of the WBS methodology; therefore, the knowledge and experience gained to date is primarily in that area. Considerable time was spent in determining how the methodology would be applied to Galileo, in obtaining line management approval of the policies and procedures, and then in documenting the methodology, policies, and procedures for the technical staff. A prototype WBS processor was built and the SAMS Operations Staff trained in its use.

A three-hour training session for the technical staff was held. How to create a WBS for a given program and how to partition the job into unit-level tasks, filling out the user-input forms, was explained. The updating of an existing WBS was also described.

Experience to date with the WBS processor has indicated several things:

1. Additional time with the technical staff on a one-to-one basis was required to provide further training in partitioning a job.
2. The SAMS operations staffing level had to be increased to provide one day turnaround service. This was felt to be important to gain the support of the technical staff.
3. Summary reports listed in the WBS processor description section were requested to make the data more usable to management.
4. The operator interface with the processor was simplified by the addition of a full-screen data entry capability.

5. The benefits of having schedule data on a computer, where it can easily and quickly be summarized, far outweighs the effort expended to learn the methodology and procedures.

The staff will continue to closely monitor the overhead associated with the implemented WBS methodology to assess its cost effectiveness.

3-3-8 SUMMARY

The successful development of a large-scale software system depends on many elements among which are experienced management, an environment which affords proper management control, and good supporting tools to execute and control the development.

SAMS is being created by the Project Galileo SSM Staff to cope with the problems of managing a large-scale system. The underlying concepts and design can be applied to the management of any software development effort. SAMS provides a highly automated environment with tools which gives the manager visibility into and control of the evolving systems.

3-3-9 ACKNOWLEDGMENTS

The concepts presented here have drawn upon the ideas formulated by the Project Galileo Software System Management Staff, and, in particular, Robert E. Loesh and Dr. Robert C. Tausworthe.

3-3-10 REFERENCES

[1] Wolverton, R. W., "The Cost of Developing Large-Scale Software," *IEEE Transactions on Computers, 23,* 1974, pp. 615–636.

[2] Endres, A., "Analysis of Errors and Their Causes in Systems Programs," *IEEE Transactions on Software Engineering,* June 1975, pp. 140–149.

[3] Teichrow, D., and E. A. Hershey, III, "PSL/PSA: A computer-aided technique for structured documentation and analysis of information processing systems," *IEEE Transactions on Software Engineering,* January 1977, pp. 41–48.

[4] Caine, Farber, and Gordon, Inc., "Program Design Language Reference Guide (Processor Version 3)," February 1977.

[5] Bratman, H., and T. Court, "The Software Factory," *Computer,* May 1975, pp. 28–37.

[6] Reifer, D. J., et al., "Lessons Learned from the Galileo Project–Introduction," IEEE, COMPSAC 80.

[7] Kleine, H., "Software Design and Documentation Language," JPL Publication 77-24, July 1, 1977.

[8] Thayer, R., and J. Lehman, "Software Engineering Project Management: A Survey Concerning U.S. Aerospace Industry. Management of Software Development Projects," *AIAA, Computers in Aerospace Conference Proceedings,* 31 October–2 November 1977, Report No. TR-77-02.

[9] *Project Galileo Software Management Plan,* Volume I; "Technical Development and Management Policies and Approach;" Volume II, "Software Technical and Administrative Procedures;" JPL 625-510, Revision C, June 10, 1980.

[10] Tausworthe, R. C., "The Work Breakdown Structure in Software Project Management," *The Journal of Systems and Software* 1, 1980, pp. 181–186.

3-4 ON-BOARD COMPUTER TIMING AND MEMORY SIZE MONITORING*

Nelson H. Prentiss, Jr.

3-4-1 SUMMARY

Classically, memory size and worst path timing are critical in aerospace applications. A 50 percent margin for each was allocated at preliminary design time on the Viking Lander system. Accepting the fact of inevitable change, a margin allocation curve was also established at preliminary design time in order to control margins throughout the project development phase. The plan originally called for a few hundred words margin at launch time to accommodate last-minute changes during operations.

3-4-2 APPLICATION CONSIDERATIONS

The high relative cost per change with low margins has been well established. Changes made with limited spare room or time often lead to redesign of existing code with attendant ripple effects. Some published results indicate that relative costs begin to rise where margins are less than 50 percent. With many of the Viking Lander devices and subsystems at the state-of-the-art, 50 percent margins at preliminary design time was deemed essential. Perhaps more important, was the realization that margin monitoring was also essential. Where con-

---

*From "Viking Software Data," RADC-TR-77-168, May 1977. Martin Marietta Corp.

tinuing system change can be anticipated, software changes rapidly consume margins unless they . . . become a part of the change controls.

3-4-3 RECOMMENDATION

Management is well advised to pay close attention to timing and memory size when a relatively small computer is to be used to perform a significant real-time task. This requires a considerable effort to obtain accurate estimates of the impact of proposed changes. The 50 percent growth margin used by Viking was not great enough to avoid the necessity of optimizing algorithms and designs already coded.

3-4-4 HISTORY

During the development of the Viking Lander on-board program, constant control was exercised over the growth of the program within the time and space domains of the computer hardware. This was done because there were several precedents of program development problems due to unchecked growth. In order to achieve good control several tools were developed and used throughout the life of the project.

The first problem with respect to obtaining good control was to establish realistic values for the memory and time margins. The approach used was to define a hypothetical computer and then to program the descent guidance and control equations for it. The descent phase was picked for two reasons. First, a significant amount of analysis had yielded a set of descent control equations which could be coded. Second, the descent phase represented the major area of concern about timing. Based on this exercise, the number of instructions to be executed was obtained along with their frequency of execution.

The sources of good size values were: first, the code size defined by the descent software; and second, the code size estimated by coding the flow charts established for the remainder of the on-board program. Together, these produced the initial program memory size requirement. To this memory size was added a 50 percent growth margin. That value was defined to be the limit for program size growth. The two values defined a linear growth curve, starting with the program size at the date the analysis was made and terminating with a full computer at program delivery. This growth curve defined, at any given time when an audit was made, whether the program growth was being contained.

The hypothetical computer characteristics were included within the computer procurement drawing as a statement of desired instruction set and timing. This also allowed for the generation of memory and timing impact summaries for each of the prospective computer vendors. Then once the vendor's machine characteristics were known, the impact to timing was well defined. In addition, there are instruction set versus memory requirement relationships defined by information theory. Using them, a memory impact was defined for each of the possible computers. This exercise informed the project management that the selected computer would have little impact timewise but . . . the memory would have to be 2000 words larger if the initial 50 percent margin was to be maintained.

Following selection of the on-board computer, a software change control mechanism was installed. This provided a definition of what changes were outstanding and their associated time and size impact. Management could then weigh changes against any possible growth violations. In order to make this accurate, all changes were forced through this control system.

During the course of the on-board program development there were several major stresses on the control mechanism. Each of these involved the definition of a significant violation of the size or time margin curves. The first was the incorporation of a generalized on-board executive. The design change was necessitated by the total program requirements, but presented an unknown risk to the time margins. In order to gain an insight into the timing of the then current sequencing algorithm and the proposed processing, a discrete simulation model was constructed. The model was used to define the worst case time consumption by the executive. With this known, it became apparent that there was minimal risk [in incorporating] the generalized executive.

The second major stress occurred when the development of coded modules for nearly all of the on-board program was completed. The resultant code size violated substantially the size-growth curve. As a result a set of code reduction changes were proposed. Incorporation of the changes brought the program size back within the established growth curve. However, this necessitated substantial changes to the already coded and partially tested program.

The third major stress was due to the violation of time margins by the descent control code. This was isolated through the use of an emulator for the on-board computer. The descent code, run in an emulated mode, was shown to take too long during certain descent phases. As a result, the descent control equations were changed in order to reduce the number of calculations required. In addition, some algorithms used during descent were optimized with respect to time. This problem had been brought to management's attention quite early, due primarily to the enforcement of regular time and size audits. Because of this, there was ample time to analyze and correct the problem.

3-4-5 DESCRIPTION

The components of a good timing and memory size monitor system are: accurate software audit reports, timely report generation and total software change control. One cannot emphasize enough the importance of [each] of these components. Without any one of them, the process of monitoring is susceptible to failure. In describing each, one can take the Viking on-board program development and show why each is required.

The generation and reporting of the current program size and time requirements was basically an audit. For the audit to be effective, the process of generating realistic data had to be accurate. In the case of the on-board software, this was done directly by timing the known worst case loops via an emulator. The availability of an emulator greatly simplified and improved the accuracy obtained from this task. Because the landed phase development was significantly behind the descent development, the size values obtained were prone to error. However, by coding candidate modules from flow charts, relatively good size values were obtained. In fact, some module size values as originally defined were within 10 percent of the final size of the coded flight module.

Since the on-board program was constantly changing, the size and time requirements were audited monthly by management with approximate values maintained between audits. This provided, given an accurate audit process, an actual input. The input was then used to update the graph for memory growth. Using this graph, management readily established trends of rapid growth. When they were recognized, the change traffic was interrupted and a status meeting was held to define which changes to reject and which requirement or design changes to incorporate.

The audit process depends upon an accurate sampling process. This, in turn, depends upon accurate reporting of current size, impact of changes in progress, and impacts for proposed changes. Software changes were forced to proceed through a control system for the on-board program. This initially entailed the complete definition of the change requirements. The on-board software development group used these requirements statements to define the impact of the proposed change on memory usage and, for descent control changes, the impact on timing. The proposed change and associated impact were then presented to a management team for consideration. The team could then approve or reject the changes as too large an impact, or as an unnecessary requirement. In this manner the modifications to the memory and time requirement were made by one group. This caused the auditing of the memory and time margins to be quite accurate.

3-4-6 QUALITATIVE RESULTS

As a result of timing and sizing monitoring, the on-board program was developed and delivered successfully. The concept of regular and highly visible audits seemed to allow for ample time to recover from major stresses. In addition, management was provided with sufficient information to control a highly volatile software development task. . . . The system seemed to fail when the entire software group was devoted [only] to the development process to the detriment of the audit process. As a result, the audit would encompass a very long time period and nominally would define a significant change to the size and time margins. In addition, continual auditing seemed to force a more disciplined development.

The growth constraint curve was a linear line connecting a 13K memory size in July 1971, to an 18K memory size in October 1974. On two occasions large accumulations of new code caused the current memory size estimate to violate the constraint curve. The first occurred between March and May 1973, when as-built code rapidly grew from 15.5K to 18.5K. The second occurred between February and June 1974, when as-built code grew from 16.5K to 19K. On each occasion management was forewarned that an unacceptable growth was taking place, thus permitting them time to assess the need for and the ramifications of candidate redesign efforts. On both occasions management required the implementation of agreed upon design changes that brought the as-built code below the memory size constraint curve. These two instances demonstrate the practicality of using the technique.

3-4-7 QUANTITATIVE IMPACT

The process of monitoring the memory size and timing margins of the flight computer was a planned event that did not require additional staffing. As such, there was no manpower cost impact.

3-5 REAL-TIME: THE "LOST WORLD" OF SOFTWARE DEBUGGING AND TESTING*

ROBERT L. GLASS
Boeing Aerospace Co.

3-5-1 INTRODUCTION

Many years ago, Sir Arthur Conan Doyle, best known for his ventures into the intricacies of the investigative mind in the character of Sherlock Holmes, wrote

*From *Software Soliloquies,* Computing Trends, 1981. A similar paper was published in Communications of the ACM, May 1980, Vol. 23, No. 5.

a non-Holmesian book called "The Lost World." Later made into a movie, it was about a plateau in South America where the advance of civilization had been stopped, with the area remaining primeval.

We have a lost world in software as well. Over the years, the march of software civilization has given us first the operating system, removing the programmer from the console and hardware intimacy; then the high order language, removing the programmer further from hardware intimacy; then fast compilers and link-loaders, relieving the programmer of the need to create machine language "patches"; and now, the beginnings of symbolic or source language debugging, transferring the language advances made earlier into the testing phase of the software life cycle.

Very few, if any, of these civilizing advances, however, have penetrated the world of real-time software debug and test. This world, like Conan Doyle's, is primeval. The typical real-time program is still tested on a computer with no operating system; written in assembler language; patched to a fare-thee-well; and tested by programmers at the console, taking octal or hexadecimal readings of absolute machine address contents.

It is the purpose of this article to present a survey of real-time debug and test practices across several projects and companies, to be specific about the state of the art as defined by that survey, and to suggest ways of bringing the "lost world" up to date.

Conan Doyle may be leaned on for another analogy. Software debug and test specialists operate somewhat like super sleuths, sifting through software evidence such as traces and dumps, looking for clues left behind in a software mishap. However, the sophisticated Sherlock Holmes, employing all the power of a scientific and focused mind, is in stark contrast to the inhabitants of the lost world of real-time software debugging, where science is unknown and the focus is on survival.

3-5-2 THE DICHOTOMY

The literature on software reliability reports many tools and techniques available to support the harried tester (GLAS79). None, however, are panaceas; the route to reliable software requires hard work and a suite of methodologies, as well as good intentions (DEWO77), (SEIF76), (WIRT77). Fortunately, in the last few years, heavy governmental spending on research and renewed academic and industrial interest has helped to create techniques for making software more trustworthy. Now, new knowledge is available to testers keeping up with the literature (DEWO77), (GAY78), (KOPE75), (LAUE79), (STIN78).

The gap between the literature and practices is a chasm when viewed from the perspective of real-time software. The researcher who advocates symbolic execution or proof of correctness or even automated verification systems, is so far from real-world real-time reality as to be ludicrous. The real-time tester needs all of those things when they are feasible, of course; but the tester needs a lot more rudimentary support capability first. For programmers who spend most of their time reading hexadecimal lights on a minicomputer console, trying to replace nonworking machine language code with better machine language code, some sort of software debug package—perhaps even symbolic debug—must be available before more sophisticated concepts can be considered. Even Wirth's contributions in the Modula area (WIRT77) are irrelevant in view of this operational consideration. It is the purpose of this report to attempt to overcome this researcher–real-world dichotomy, by letting the researchers understand why they are not being heard, and by letting the real-time tester know that there is a problem—the tester is being left behind by technological advances in the field.

3-5-3 THE REAL-TIME OVERVIEW

So far, this article has suggested that the real-time practitioner might be at fault. That is not entirely fair. To understand why the lost world exists, it is necessary for the reader to understand what real-time software is really all about.

First of all, let us define some terms:

Real-time software   is software that drives a computer which interacts with functioning external devices or objects. It is called real-time because the software actions control activities that are occurring in an ongoing process. For example, real-time software may drive an acceleration–deceleration controller in a rapid transit system vehicle; or it may capture data from other physical devices in a nuclear physics experiment; or it may interpret radar data onboard an antisubmarine aircraft and translate it into displays for a military operator at a console.

Embedded computer system   defines a computer and its software embedded in some larger system. "Real-time" and "embedded" are largely interchangeable concepts, except that the embedded computer is physically included in the system it serves.

Debug   is the act of seeking and removing errors in computer software.

Test   is the act of executing software to see whether it is functioning correctly. Testing has come to be viewed as a more formal process than debugging, including executing the integrated components of a large software system and the final acceptance test process.

It is crucial to the understanding of real-time software testing practices to be aware that this software is part of a larger system. The requirements of the larger system are paramount in the design of the real-time software. If it takes extra work and extra complexity in the software to make the total system function better, then that work and complexity will be delegated by the system architects to the software. In fact, as systems people come to understand the role of software better, albeit gradually and sometimes grudgingly, they begin to see software as a weightless, spaceless sink in which all the system problems can be dissolved. This is, in fact, not a bad practice—the economic and technical reasons for this trend are compelling—but it does mean that the real-time software developer is constructing software which is a long way from classroom exercises in complexity.

Now another forcing function enters the world of the real-time practitioner. Not only are the system designers complicating the practitioner's life, but the hardware developers are constraining it. For a variety of reasons, real-time computer hardware needs to be cheap, small, and light. It needs to be all of those things in order not to perturb the physical design and economics of the total system. For example, if a real-time computer is driving a missile system, it is actually a throwaway piece of hardware. Clearly, the hardware designer's goal is to minimize the cost, and therefore the capability, of this hardware. Consequently, complexity must be transferred from hardware to software.

There is also the issue of multipliers: n copies of software cost no more than one copy; n copies of computer hardware multiply the cost of one unit by n; and if n is very great, it may dictate a further shift in complexity from hardware to software.

Still another forcing function is the schedule. Total system schedules are important to an extreme degree, with enormous amounts of money sometimes imperiled in schedule overruns. As an example, consider the impact if software for the avionics system in a new bomber is late, and several squadrons of bombers are sitting on the ground waiting for the last known software catastrophe to be repaired. As a result, the schedule pressures on the real-time software developer are sometimes nearly unbearable. Voluntary overtime is not at all unknown in this schedule-driven world.

Thus, at the same time the system designers are adding complexity to real-time software, the computer hardware developers are squeezing that complexity into smaller and less capable computers. The schedule managers are also adding to the pressure. The real-time software practitioners are caught in a squeeze not of their own making, and one of which the practitioners are often unaware. A rash of recent papers, for example, (FOST78), (RAMA75), have followed the pattern of software people wringing their hands over the unreliability and the elastic cost–schedule results of software construction, and promising to do better next time because magical tools and techniques will be used. This is naive. Software practitioners do not need to apologize for their emerging technology, given that they have supported, without complaint, the burden of added complexity and constrained hardware. What is needed instead is better knowledge of the outside factors impacting the computing practitioner, and decisions as to what to do about them.

3-5-4 REAL-TIME: CLOSEUP VIEW

Now that we have seen that real-time software is always part of a larger and more important world, complex, constrained, and pressurized, let us look at some of the details in this picture. There are some good details and some bad details.

The good details include an admirable attention to overall system considerations. The important goals of real-time software development and testing are well in focus. System needs are well defined in software requirements, and system considerations are prominent in software test practices. In the lost world of real-time software testing, for example, the modern concept of an environment simulator (STIN78), an automated replication of the external system world built for computer hardware–software test, is almost universally used.

It is around the software developer that the bad details are found. Many resources are poured into system level environment simulators, while almost nothing "extra" is spent on the software tester. The software developer is constrained to test on the barebones mission computer, and is often discouraged by management from building nondeliverable (to the customer) support software, such as debug tools. One is encouraged to code in high-level language (ELZE77), (RUBE78), (WIRT77) and increasingly often does, but the developer is left alone to check out code at the assembler or machine code level. No analogous drive by anyone encourages the software developer to advance this archaic technology (GLAS78), (STEE77). Tools that do exist, such as instruction-level simulators (GILL77), almost universally function exclusively at the machine language level and compel the user to think and do likewise. Not only is the real-time software tester lost in the lost world, but *there are currently no factors at work to correct that situation.* The bad details in the real-time software picture are, as far as can be seen, bad.

To descend another level of detail into the real-time test world, let us categorize the characteristic phases of that test process. Commonly, there is a host (larger) computer and a target (smaller) [computer]. The host is often a commercially available computer used for construction of programs for the target. For example, it will contain either a cross compiler or a cross assembler for the target, or both; a link-loader for the target; and in many cases an instruction-level simulator (described further below) for the target. The target is the mission or onboard or process control computer—the real-time computer—and it is sometimes a special-purpose, hardened, militarized, or weatherized computer procured just for this project. It is worth noting that this is one reason why an instruction-level simulator is used—to stand in for the target until it is available.

Given the roles of the host and the target, the phases of the real-time test process may be broken down as follows:

HOST-HOST. Some testing is done purely on the host computer. Its purpose is to eliminate errors from the programmer's code. Of course, there are more errors than are found here, as will be seen later. Usually, the testing at this point is so-called "unit testing" of small program components. If a high order language (HOL) is used and a code generator is available for the host, considerable valuable testing may be performed on the host. If assembler language is used, then it may only be tested on the host if there is an instruction-level simulator. Full system testing is done on the host only . . . occasionally. To do this, a software environment simulator is built which runs on the host computer. Considering the economics of host usage and the debug facilities available there, this still rare practice holds considerable hope for the future.

HOST-HOST (INSTRUCTION-LEVEL SIMULATOR). Some target testing may even be done on the host. The purpose of this testing is to remove errors from the support software, such as the compiler target code generator or the assembler, and to begin to detect target dependent errors in the programmer's code. Support software errors are no idle concern—just as real-time computers are sometimes nonstandard, so is their support software. New compilers frequently turn from 500 to 1,000 errors in their first several years of heavy production use.

One tool used for this target testing is the instruction-level simulator (ILS), a software program which allows the host to pretend it is the target. Typically, the ILS thinks and speaks machine language. That is, its output is a trace of all instructions executed, with the contents of significant registers or stacks after each. Obviously, this is a highly machine language-oriented function. Rarely is the compiler or assembler symbol table passed to the ILS to allow a more mnemonic readable level of ILS test. This too, is a little-used practice that holds hope for the future.

A similar tool, with similar historic limitations, is the hardware In-Circuit Emulator (ICE). Again, symbolic debug is possible in this environment, but rarely done. Intel microcomputers are an exception; in the Intel system, several compilers communicate with an execute-time debug package via symbol tables and an ICE system.

TARGET. The proof of the real-time software test process is execution on the target. In this environment, all facets of the software—the code the programmer wrote, the support software, and the real-time executive program —receive their real and final test. In addition, the computer itself is tested— nonstandard computers are often as error prone as nonstandard support software.

Execution on the target is the most primitive part of the lost world. Often the only tools the software practitioner has for debugging are those prepared for the system debugger—a recording function, which saves system relevant data for post-mortem review, and the environment simulator, which does system relevant I/O and permits the use of system relevant scenarios to drive test sessions. It is obvious that the software worker in this environment has been given short shrift in favor of the system worker. That is not necessary, of course. It is possible and necessary to provide both system level and software level test facilities.

The picture is not entirely black. Sometimes a rudimentary software or hardware debug package is available which permits stopping the computer at specified absolute locations, and inspecting–changing memory contents. The programmer must be at the console to use this (dark grey) technology in most installations. Ironically, the new kid on the block, the microcomputer, often has a somewhat more advanced facility. This is a firmware package which retains certain history, such as the execution results from the last sixty instructions, for programmer examination when necessary. Rarely, however, may the programmer preplan a debugging session by inserting dynamic probes. To the author's knowledge, source or symbolic language debug capability has almost never been made available on a target computer. Reference (STIN78) describes the only exception with which the author is familiar. The concept of passing the compiler or assembler symbol table to the target computer, as is occasionally done to the ILS, to allow mnemonic testing on the target, is simply unknown.

Interestingly, most other advanced tools, such as automated verification systems or test coverage analyzers, have also apparently never been used on target computer software. This problem area is casually passed over in most of the literature on tools. It appears that researchers and tool builders are not aware of or ignore the target environment.

There are several flavors of target computer testing. Initially, just the raw hardware box is available, and software unit testing is all that may be performed. Later, the environment simulator is hooked to the target and integration testing may begin. Finally, the environment simulator is replaced by the real world, and full system testing is begun. However, the variety of ways in which testing occurs does not change the basic underlying software fact— virtually no tools are available in any of these aspects to support the real-time software tester.

Source vs. Object Checkout.   The key issue here is, how does the programmer communicate with the software/computer during test? Ideally, this communication occurs in the language in which the software was coded. In today's state of the real-time art, this is only likely to occur on the host computer with host-mode checkout. It could occur in host-ILS mode, but rarely does; and it almost never occurs in the target environment. In fact, the norm in real-time software test is to communicate in the language of the computer. This means the programmer must learn several difficult skills: the assembly–machine language of the target, and its register–stack conventions; operation of the target from some sort of console; hex–octal to decimal conversion and back; and perhaps worst of all, how to construct and inject machine language patches.

Real-time software debug and test are about as far on the wrong side of the key issue as is possible.

3-5-5 ACCURACY OF THE PICTURE

This picture of paucity in real-time software debugging and testing methodologies has emerged from an in-the-field study of industry practices. It results from a survey of ten projects within the author's own company (Boeing), as well as ten projects from outside institutions.[1]

In summary, the in-house (Boeing) survey results are as follows (also see Table 3–5–1):

Size: Projects varied in size from four programmers and 3,000 instructions to 150 programmers and 500,000 instructions.

Source language: Five projects used HOL (usually JOVIAL, since most projects were Air Force related), five used assembler.

Host environment: Five projects used HOL host code generators, but only two had a software environment simulator for integrated testing on the host.

Host-ILS environment: Seven projects used an ILS, but only one had compiler symbol table input to permit mnemonic ILS debug. Three others used a host computer whose instruction set was the same as the target's, thus alleviating the need for an ILS.

Target environment: Nine projects used an environment simulator. All ten had some sort of system-related recording facility. Only three used any kind of software debug package.

Results from outside companies were nearly identical to those from Boeing. HOL was used by five companies. ILSs were used by five, one of which had a mnemonic (symbol table) interface to the compiler. One used a host which is a larger version of the target, and one, interestingly, compiled on the target but uplinked to the host to use the ILS. Target computers had rudimentary software debug in seven cases, but none used a source language interface.

The picture is consistent and clear; the lost world is truly lost.

---

[1]General Dynamics, General Research, Grumman, Honeywell, Hughes, Lockheed, Rockwell, Texas Instruments, TRW, Vought.

TABLE 3-5-1 Real-Time Software Checkout: An Overview

Project	Max No. Programmers	No. Instructions	Source Language	Host Environment	ILS	Target Environment Simulator	Target Recording Facility	Target Debug
A	—	100,000	Assembler	—	Yes	Yes	Yes	—
B	30	100,000	JOVIAL	Unit Test	Yes	Yes	Yes	—
C	6	15,000	Assembler	—	Yes	Yes	Yes	—
D	150	500,000	JOVIAL	Environment Simulator	Yes	Yes	Yes	Core dump, breakpoint
E	6	13,000	Assembler	Host = Target	Not needed	Yes	Yes	Trace
F	3	20,000	JOVIAL	Unit Test	Yes	No	Yes	—
G	—	—	JOVIAL	Statement Simulator	Yes, with symbol table	Yes	Yes	—
H	27	75,000	Fortran	Host = Target	Not needed	Yes	Yes	Vendor package
I	4	3,000	Assembler	Environment Simulator	Not used	Yes	Yes	—
J	15	35,000	Assembler	—	Yes	Yes	Yes	—
Summary:	Average = 30	Average = 100,000	Half HOL, Half assembler	Usually unit test only	Usually	Nearly always	Always	Rarely

3-5-6 UNDERLYING PROBLEMS

The first thing wrong with the real-time software test world is that it is stuck at the 1950s level. The literature may picture a Greased Lightning fantasy, but the real-time practitioners are still coaxing along their De Soto clunkers and using machine language, patching and bailing wire to hold them together. The result is a product that usually works, but not always; a product that may be very economical, if the developers are skilled, but may on the other hand cost a fortune; a product that is virtually unschedulable; and a product whose quality is intimately tied to the skill of the software mechanic. The result can be satisfying and satisfactory; but when it is bad, it is very bad.

The problem is not simply one of a technological lost world. We also have a management unaware of, and therefore unconcerned about, the problem. The forces which would normally correct this sort of problem do not appear to be at work.

Finally, we have a dichotomy between the research world and the real-time world. Real-time software practitioners are so far behind the state of the art that the onrushing research world isn't even aware that they fell off. Government agencies supporting the research are equally oblivious, in this author's opinion. Judging by performance and the arguments presented in this paper, we have a stuck technology with no positive forces at work to modernize it.

3-5-7 A LOOK AT THE FUTURE

What kinds of solutions might help the real-time practitioner? The key word in the solution domain is "evolution." Only a process that begins with an evaluation of the real-time practitioner's present condition holds any promise of freeing the retarded technology. It is not just that reality must be acknowledged in order to deal with human inertia, it is that there are many economic-political-technical reasons why the technology is backward, mainly focused on the factor of risk in change; . . . only a low risk technological upgrade has hope of moving the field forward.

The list of potential evolutionary solutions below is intended to be comprehensive. Fortunately, most of these solutions are achievable without incurring greatly increased risk and cost.

The first part of the list is most promising. The programmer needs to do testing as much as possible in the "friendly" host computer environment, where adequate debug and other resources are available. The goal should be to remove as many source code errors as possible before venturing into the target computer world. A host computer environment simulator is a vital part of this "source error first" approach to real-time checkout.

This is not to say that the target environment can be ignored—target specific problems, such as hardware errors, cross compiler code generator errors, timing problems and errors, sizing problems, and hardware interface and accuracy problems—will all have to be dealt with before the testing is finished. It is simply true that, given this multitude of target problems, the target checkout process should be contaminated as little as possible with source code errors which could more easily be removed elsewhere.

Also, there is a desperate need for all programmers—real-time or otherwise—to be able to debug their code in the same language in which it was developed. Symbolic or source debug is the name given this frequently missing capability. In the real-time world, it may be present on the host computer, but it is almost never present in either the instruction-level simulation or the target mode. Correction of this problem would go a long way toward modernizing the real-time practitioner's debug world.

The list of possible solutions, presented as a menu of worthwhile ideas for both real-time practitioners and researchers, follows:

(1) Heavier use of host computer facilities, with HOL code tested on host computers using vendor or user group supplied HOL debug packages, and software environment simulators to permit host integration testing. The result will be software which is largely error-free *before* it begins target computer checkout.

(2) Introduction and use of ILS packages with mnemonic capabilities tied to an HOL compiler symbol table. Source debug techniques may then be used in simulation mode.

(3) Establishment of hardware downlinks from host to target and back, permitting fast recompilation, relinking, and retesting when an error is found. The temptation to generate machine code patches will be nullified by a more convenient source update capability.

(4) Use of software (or firmware) debug packages on target computers, tied to an HOL compiler symbol table. Source debug can then be used on the target computer as well as on the host.

(5) Augmentation of debug hardware on laboratory (test) target computers, such as larger memory to support debuggers, and more and better peripherals (disks/tapes/printers) to support debug output. The programmer will then find the target environment becoming increasingly friendly.

(6) Standardization of host and target computer hardware, and support tool software, in order to provide the stability to promote the development of checkout tools; perhaps even the introduction of compatible host-target computer instruction sets. New projects can then count on the existence of well-checked-out hardware and software facilities.

(7) Development of operator-oriented target computer labs, with programmers preplanning debug runs and absent from the lab during test. This will result in (1) more efficiently run labs (programmers often make

clumsy operators), (2) even less temptation for programmers to write patches, and (3) better utilization of software's scarcest resource, programmer time.

(8) Deployment of a small nucleus of target specialists, who consult on target optimizations, target dump reading, and through whom all patching (if any) must be performed. Then not every programmer would need to learn all about the machine-intimate technologies.

(9) Increased management awareness of testing and checkout technology (as well as project requirements and productivity technology). The attention such awareness will bring should result in resources being devoted to the other solutions discussed in this section.

(10) Improved liaison with systems people who better appreciate and provide for the problems of software. A broadened outlook among such specialists is necessary if the new software portions of traditional engineering systems are to receive the attention they must have.

(11) Closer contact with researchers who deliberately keep in touch with real-world problems. Solution domains will then be achievable in a low-risk manner from existing problem domains.

These prescriptions represent this author's approach to the problems. They also represent an admittedly optimistic look at the future. The challenge lies with the reader to play a part in advancing the lost world.

3-5-8 ACKNOWLEDGMENTS

The author wishes to thank the many interviewees who contributed time, knowledge, and a critique of results with which they did not always concur; Nancy Bethel, who helped conduct many of the interviews; and especially Dave Feinberg, Lee MacLaren, and Ron Noiseux, for stimulating the creation of this paper.

3-5-9 REFERENCES

[DEWO77] DeWolf, J. B., and Wexler, J. Approaches to software verification with emphasis on real-time applications. Computers in Aerospace Conf., Los Angeles, Calif., Oct. 1977, pp. 41-51.

A good survey of software verification methodologies; less effective at making the methodologies relevant to the unique aspects of the real-time environment.

[ELZE77] Elzer, P., and Roessler, R. Real-time languages and operating systems. Proc. Fifth Int. Conf. on Digital Computer Applications to Process Control, The Hague, Netherlands, June 1977, pp. S-2, 1-12.

An excellent summary of (1) the international political mechanisms impacting real-time software; (2) real-time programming languages and their properties; (3) the unique aspects of real-time language/operating system interfaces.

[FOST78] Foster, R. A. It's time to get tough about computer software. *Quality Progress 11,* 8 (Aug. 1978), 10–12.

Expresses alarm about "rising costs and poor quality of software being produced," and recommends quality assurance approaches to solve this problem.

[GAY78] Gay, F. A. Evaluation of maintenance software in real-time systems. *IEEE Trans. Computers C–27,* 6 (June 1978), 576–582.

Describes a real-time "Trouble Locating Program" which relies on error seeding (the deliberate introduction of known errors) to evaluate the number of errors in software.

[GILL77] Gill, C. F., and Holden, M. T. On the evolution of an adaptive support software system. Computers in Aerospace Conf., Los Angeles, Calif., Oct. 1977, pp. 77–1420 1–7.

Describes the Boeing Support Software System and its use. The system contains an HOL compiler (JOVIAL J3B); a meta cross assembler; a meta linker/loader; and instruction level simulation capability.

[GLAS78] Glass, R. L. Patching is alive and, lamentably, thriving in the real-time world. *SIGPLAN Notices (ACM) 13,* 3 (March 1978), 25–28.

Defines patching, explains why it is bad and why its use is rising, and suggests a variety of techniques for minimizing or eliminating its use.

[GLAS79] Glass, R. L. *Software Reliability Guidebook.* Prentice-Hall, Englewood Cliffs, N.J., 1979.

Surveys the available technological and managerial software reliability techniques; makes value judgments about each technique; illustrates each by example.

[KOPE75] Kopetz, H. Error detection in real-time software. Proc. IFAC-IFIP Workshop on Real-Time Programming, Boston, Mass., Aug. 1975, pp. 81–87.

Advocates fault tolerance on real-time software as an accommodation to the inability to remove all software errors; suggests a programming language mechanism for error processing.

[LAUE79] Lauesen, S. Debugging Techniques. *Software-Practice and Experience 9,* 1 (Jan. 1979), 51–63.

Contrasts top-down and bottom-up debugging; recommends and describes ten debugging techniques; presents case studies of their usage.

[RAMA75] Ramamoorthy, C. V., and Ho, S. F. Testing large software with automated software evaluation systems. *IEEE Trans. Software Engineering SE–1,* 1 (March 1975), 46–58.

Calls most software development projects "unsuccessful in terms of specification, time and cost," and recommends automated software tools to solve this problem.

[RUBE78] Rubey, R. J. Higher order languages for avionics software—a survey, summary and critique. NAECON, Dayton, Ohio, May 1978, pp. 945–951.

Traces the history of avionics (real-time) HOL usage; cites problems and resolutions in HOL vs. assembler tradeoffs; sees trends leading toward more HOL usage.

[SEIF76] Seifrick, J. M. Structured programming experiences in a minicomputer real-time process control environment. Proc. Int. Symp. Mini and Micro Computers, Toronto, Canada, Nov. 1976, pp. 56–67.

An honest report on experiences using structured programming (chief programmer team, HIPO, development support library, structured coding, design walkthroughs) on a real-time project.

[STEE77] Steele, S. A. Characteristics of managing real-time software development for military systems. Computers in Aerospace Conf., Los Angeles, Calif., Oct. 1977, pp. 174–181.

Defines a management environment for real-time software development.

[STIN78] Stinaff, R. D. An integrated simulation and debugging facility for a distributed processing real-time system. Int. Conf. on Communications, Toronto, Canada, June 1978, pp. 44.5.1–44.5.5.

An excellent example of an environment simulator and debug package used to test a telephone switching system. Multiple user debug is provided; compiler symbol table output is used by the debugger.

[WIRT77] Wirth, N. Toward a discipline of real-time programming. *Comm. ACM 20,* 8 (Aug. 1977) 577–583.

Advocates the use of high level languages for real-time work, especially to allow the isolation of time dependent portions of code; recommends dedicating separate processors to separable processes; describes a discipline for using HOL in this environment.

3-6 REAL-TIME CHECKOUT:
THE "SOURCE ERROR FIRST" APPROACH*

ROBERT L. GLASS
Boeing Computer Services

3-6-1 SUMMARY

This paper proposes some improvements to the archaic methodologies currently used for checkout of real-time software. The emphasis is placed on removing errors from the computer program source code in the host computer environment, and deferring target computer checkout until those errors have been largely removed. Specific tools and techniques to make this possible are described. This improvement is seen to be risk-free and to reduce cost. It is, however, controversial.

3-6-2 INTRODUCTION

The checkout of real-time software is said to be a "lost world" of obsolete practices.[1] Whereas other phases of the software life cycle are receiving considerable attention, checkout continues to be a programmer-at-the-console practice, with the technologies employed essentially the same as those used in the late 1950s.

On one hand, we have progress in the early life-cycle phases:

1. Increasing use of high-order languages.
2. Improvements in those languages (for example, Ada, Pascal).
3. Program Design Languages.
4. Automated checkers for those languages.
5. Requirements languages.
6. Requirements traceability tools.
7. Documentation standards (especially strong for U.S. Department of Defense software).

On the other hand, we have stagnation in the checkout phase:

1. Programmer at the console.
2. Octal or hexadecimal readouts.
3. Machine code patching.

*From Software-Practice and Experience, Jan. 1982.

4. Inadequate resources (for example, no printers, no memory for debug systems, no preplanning of debug functions).

In essence, what has happened is that technology advances for the real-time programmer have stopped part way through the software life cycle. Checkout, [which] consumes . . . more developer time than any other life-cycle phase, is also the most neglected of those phases.

3-6-3 THE CHECKOUT PHASE

It is worth looking a little more closely at this checkout phase. For a large real-time system, checkout actually breaks down into several subphases—module testing (the checkout of small units of the total system); integration testing (where the modules are linked together to test the complete software system); and system testing (where the software and its real-time operational environment are tested together). In terms of time spent, according to Boeing Aerospace real-time programmer experience, module testing dominates these phases (perhaps 50 percent module test, 25 percent integration test, and 25 percent system test).

There is a blurring of the borderline between module test and integration test. As modules in a large system are developed, it is increasingly difficult to test them in isolation. For example, a large system database may be necessary to test individual modules, and data may at times be created only by the interaction between modules. In addition, the top-down development technique demands the use of increasingly complex layers of integration testing, and the programmer using this technique swiftly moves past pure module testing.

Considering this, the area of greatest need in real-time software checkout is the combined module-integration test subphase. It consumes approximately 75 percent of the checkout resources, and is often inseparable in practice.

3-6-4 WHAT CAN BE DONE?

Given that real-time software checkout is archaic [and] that module and integration testing is the area of greatest need, what can be done to improve this situation?

There is a distinction which, once made, helps to clarify this problem. Any programmer knows that a program is written in source code which in some way is translated into executable object code. In the real-time world, the traditional emphasis—an engineering emphasis—has been on checking out the object code. Somewhere along the way, the real-time programmer has lost track of the importance of checking out the *source* code.

This distinction is important. In the real-time world, source code is usually processed on a *host* computer—a mainframe which offers such amenities as compilers, linkers, printers, debuggers (sometimes even symbolic), data traces, snapshot dumps, test coverage analyzers—all the capabilities which make up a modern programmer's toolkit. By contrast the *target* computer where the object code executes usually has none of this friendliness.

Clearly it is desirable to perform as much checkout as possible on the host computer, processing the source code. (There are some problems with this approach—they will be discussed later). It will be possible to perform source code checkout on the host computer—even in the integration subphase—if the following criteria are met:

1. The initial version of the system is coded entirely in a high order language.
2. A compiler exists on the host computer which produces both host object code and target object code at user option.
3. A host computer environment simulator is constructed to allow host checkout to interact with a simulated version of the true real-time environment.
4. Host computer memory is large enough to support the integrated software system and the environment simulator.

Now the source code may be compiled, linked together to form an integrated system, executed on the host computer, and provide environment-sensitive results. The goal here is to detect as many *source* code errors as possible on the friendly host computer.

3-6-5 WHY CONCENTRATE ON SOURCE ERRORS?

What is the significance of removing errors from the source code? For one thing, most software errors are source errors, and there are usually plenty of them. Getting rid of those errors in a friendly environment is clearly faster and cheaper than getting rid of them in the target environment.

But, for another thing, in the complex real-time world there are plenty of non-source-detectable errors. There can be:

1. Target-sensitive timing errors.
2. Timing problems (the code is too slow to meet specifications).
3. Sizing problems (the code is too large to meet specifications).
4. Interface problems (the hardware behaves differently from the environment simulator).
5. Accuracy problems (the target's usually-shorter word length causes too much loss of algorithmic accuracy).

6. Support software errors (the compiler's target code generator is all too often bug ridden).
7. Target hardware errors (these are sometimes astoundingly prevalent).

Consider the complexity of trying to locate source code errors in an environment where there are seven or more other kinds of possible errors! Two things rapidly become apparent here—source code errors *must* be removed in a friendly environment, and target computer checkout *cannot* be eliminated.

There are two motivations, then, for emphasizing source checkout on the host—to remove those errors where it is simple to do so, and to postpone as long as possible putting the programmer into the inefficient, computer-intimate target environment. *Programmer time is probably the most scarce resource in the computing world today.* The goal here is to optimize the use of that time.

The question naturally arises, is this different from how real-time software is currently developed? The answer is a resounding "yes"—Reference 1 shows that projects typically move as swiftly as possible to target code checkout, often preclude the use of debug code (on the grounds that there is no explicit requirement for it), and in general seem to use a hardware engineer's approach to software checkout. In fact, the average real-time software engineer seems unaware of this situation, or else accepts it as correct. No one, for instance, has commented publicly on the irony of writing software in the latest high-order language, and then checking it out in hex or octal!

3-6-6 WHAT ELSE CAN HELP?

Source code checkout is the most exciting prospect for upgrading the real-time software checkout art. There are, however, others. Many of them are not limited to real-time applications.

1. The peer code review is a tedious but important way of removing software errors. Reference 2 shows that it was capable of detecting 90 of 124 real-time software errors examined.

   The peer design review also holds promise for warding off software errors. Most contemporary design reviews are customer- and management-oriented. The peer review should supplement these.
2. Self-checking and debug code inserted in a program can help the software detect its own errors.
   (a) Data traces, according to Reference 2, could assist in detecting 41 of 124 errors.
   (b) Assertion checking[3] could help detect 37 of 124 errors.[2]
   (c) Snapshot dumps, a very old technique, could help detect 35 of 124 errors.[2]

(d) Logic traces could help detect 14 of 124 errors.[2]

(e) Conditional compilation is an important methodology that allows self-check and debug source code to be left in a program but not compiled when a "clean" version of the program is desired.

3. The cross-reference list has traditionally been understood to be a vital software development and maintenance tool. A cross-reference list which spans a whole system, not just a compilation unit, is obviously just as vital for large software systems. Unfortunately, tools to produce them are rarely provided.

4. Target computer hardware must be more friendly, given that some software checkout will always happen there. It should include:

(a) A link to the host computer, for fast down and up loading (for example, recompile, relink, and reexecute a program).

(b) Printers (often the target has none, only a console for readouts).

(c) More memory to support debug software.

5. Communication among real-time programmers on different projects about common concerns and solutions is vital.

6. It is usually assumed that timing errors are only detectable by testing. This is not necessarily true. The most obnoxious kind of timing error—where data shared across tasks is clobbered by one task when another needs it—is statically detectable. It requires identifying all shared data, flagging it (for example, bracketing references to it with a LOCK–UNLOCK mechanism call), using a system cross-reference-like tool to detect unflagged data, and statically analyzing all such data for conflicts.

7. Another promising tool is the Test Coverage Analyzer.[4] According to Reference 2, it could detect 40 of 124 errors.

8. Fault-tolerant software[5] may be an especially important concept for life-critical software. As a research concept, it warrants cautious project use but continuing study.

3-6-7 WHAT ABOUT COST AND RISK?

The pragmatic software person naturally wants to know about the cost and risk of a new concept. This is especially true in real-time software, where solutions are frequently constrained by nearly cruel cost and schedule considerations. Those issues are dealt with in what follows.

The risk of source code checkout is nil. There is no new technology in the concept at all; it is simply a reordering of functions currently performed. There is, however, some cost impact. The environment simulator, traditionally developed to support programmer-at-the-console use in the target environment, must now be written for the host. (Note, however, that if it is written in the same high-order language as the application software, it can be reused on the target). In addition, an all high-order-language version of the application code must be written, even if some of it must later be rewritten in assembly language for optimization reasons. (This is not necessarily bad practice, however; it may well be the most cost-effective optimization technique for high-order-language programming). And there may be a requirement for an extra-large host computer memory. (Fortunately, memory is cheap today, and virtual memory is becoming increasingly common). But balanced against all this added cost is the cost reduction of more efficient use of programmer time. The net cost impact is likely to be very favorable.

Peer code review is also largely risk-free. We all know how to review code; we just don't like to do it! Because of that dislike, and the tedium which begets it, there is a measurable cost impact to the peer code review—100 lines of code per hour for a peer review group is the generally accepted progress rate.[6] For a large system, that can be a significant cost. It is, of course, an up-front cost, which should result in reduced testing costs. . . . In addition, the peer review should result in better quality code, technology sharing among programmers, and the creation of backup programmers. These are potent fringe benefits.

Self-check and debug code is risk-free (we know how to do it, we just don't take the time) and has only minor cost impact. A system cross-reference tool is also a risk-free concept (it does not impact deliverable software functions), but there is cost in constructing the necessary tool. Enhanced target computer hardware is risk-free, and the cost (with today's declining hardware costs) is minor except for the smallest of projects. Cross-project communication is obviously largely risk- and cost-free.

Static timing analysis is [also risk- and cost-free,] and in addition, if it is successful, it will cause significant testing savings. The Test Coverage Analyzer, like the system cross-reference tool, is risk-free but entails implementation cost. Fault-tolerant software, on the other hand, has both risk and cost impact. In summary, the approaches to improved real-time checkout suggested here are almost entirely risk-free and in general have minor negative, with potentially large positive, cost impact.

3-6-8 RELEVANT TRENDS

There are some relevant trends which make this way of doing real-time software checkout even more promising. They revolve around a series of standardization efforts:

1. The U.S. Department of Defense is driving toward a standard programming language, Ada,[7] and a standard environment for it, including compilers.[8] When this effort stabilizes, the use of high-order language should increase, and the incidence of compiler errors should begin to fall. As we have

seen, source code checkout only makes sense in a high-order language environment. Stabilizing of that environment can be expected within the next five years.

2. The DoD is also moving toward standard target computer hardware. Two such efforts, MIL-STD-1750 (a 16-bit architecture) and MIL-STD-1862 (a 32-bit architecture) define common software interfaces for two computer families. Nearly a dozen manufacturers are said to be building such computers. The existence of such a standard will not only stabilize the computer hardware world, but the compiler code generator world as well. Thus a reduction of computer hardware and code generator errors can be expected.

3. Many institutions are standardizing on software development host computers. Boeing Aerospace has chosen a Digital Equipment Co., VAX, for this role. Again, the impact on support software systems should be stability. In addition, it begins to make sense to invest in project-independent tools, such as system cross-reference listers and test coverage analyzers. Whole integrated families of support tools, in fact, become feasible. The Boeing Military Airplane Co. Support Software System,[9] currently being upgraded to a new design, is an example of the kind of generalized support system which an institution can afford to implement in a more stable environment.

4. Even real-time executive programs have undergone standardization efforts. The Air Force Digital Avionics Information System (DAIS), and its follow-on activities, include one such attempt.[10] Stability in the executive area could result in a more predictable application software development environment.

In summary, it is beginning to be possible to predict large portions of the environment for the next generation real-time software project. This predictability should tend to lessen many of the classes of real-time software errors (for example, target hardware, support software). Thus, the source code error will stand out even more as the prime problem to be worked.

3-6-9 CONCLUSION

Real-time checkout activities currently focus on debugging object code in an unfriendly target computer environment. This is a mistake. It intermingles a complicated multiplicity of error types, making it difficult for the programmer to know what kind of error is being sought. Worse yet, it wastes programmer time, which is probably the most valuable resource today in the computing field.

This paper suggests that source code checkout on the host computer should be nearly complete prior to proceeding to the target environment. Techniques are suggested which allow even integration testing on the host computer.

This new methodology is shown to be nearly risk-free, with moderate up-front cost impact balanced by probably heavy downstream cost savings. The savings of programmer time, and the creation of more reliable software sooner, may well produce dramatic quality and schedule results.

It is worth mentioning that this new methodology is controversial. There are those who believe in the contemporary methodology and are suspicious of any solutions which separate the software engineer from the final system environment. Those beliefs are fundamental, are supported by some elements of truth, and are generally held by the most key people in the real-time software profession. Thus the process of change, even with a relatively risk-free approach such as this, is expected to be slow. Less risk-free and more revolutionary proposals would have considerably less chance of success.

3-6-10 REFERENCES

[1] R. L. Glass, "Real-time: The 'Lost World' of software debugging and testing," *Communications of the ACM,* May (1980).

[2] R. L. Glass, "A benefit analysis of some software reliability methodologies," *ACM Software Engineering Notes,* April (1980).

[3] L. G. Stucki and G. L. Foshee, "New assertion concepts for self metric validation," Proceedings of the 1975 IEEE International Conference on Reliable Software.

[4] J. C. Huang, "An approach to program testing," *ACM Computing Surveys,* Sept. (1975).

[5] "Special issue on fault-tolerant software," *ACM Computing Surveys,* Dec. (1976).

[6] *Structured Programming Series, Vol. 15 (Verification and Validation),* RADC-TR-74-300, 1975.

[7] *Reference Manual for the Ada Programming Language,* U.S. Department of Defense, July 1980.

[8] *Requirements for the Ada Programming Support Environment-'Stoneman',* U.S. Department of Defense, Feb. 1980.

[9] C. F. Gill and M. T. Holden, "On the evolution of an adaptive support software system," Computers in Aerospace Conference, 1977.

[10] W. H. Vandever, "The DAIS executive: An introduction," Proceedings of NAECON, 1978.

3-7 SOFTWARE DEFENSES IN REAL-TIME CONTROL SYSTEMS*

JOHN R. CONNET, EDWARD J. PASTERNAK, and BRUCE D. WAGNER
Bell Telephone Laboratories, Incorporated
Holmdel, New Jersey

3-7-1 ABSTRACT

The ability to tolerate faults is essential in a high reliability, real-time control system. The design of systems which can tolerate hardware faults has been discussed extensively. However, in systems employing stored program control, software problems can contribute significantly to the deterioration of processing capability. The means for dealing with such problems have received little attention.

Software errors can originate because of residual design errors, hardware troubles, and human mistakes in maintaining and administering the system. Each can result in the mutilation of memory.

To permit continuous operation in the presence of such errors, three types of defenses can be provided: circuits which monitor program operation, in-line program checks, and independent software error detection and correction programs known as audits. Audit techniques are the subject of this paper.

Audits can be used to check for errors in any volatile memory. In a real-time system, they are of primary value in maintaining transient data associated with processing clients and with system facilities (software and hardware). Specifically, audits can use the redundancy in the software structure to locate errors and inconsistencies, thereby preventing performance degradation due to loss of facilities and incorrect processing actions. Audits can return the memory to a viable state, permitting processing to continue virtually uninterrupted.

Audits are integrated into the system software so that they normally consume only a small portion of the system processing capacity. However, when software troubles arise, audits play a wider role; in an emergency, they may take over full program control for an extended duration until stable processing can resume.

Audits have been found essential to achieve the high reliability required for several of the Bell System's stored program telephone switching systems. They have reduced the frequency of system outages and provided tools for analyzing elusive design weaknesses. It is believed that similar approaches may be applicable to other types of real-time, stored program control systems.

*Republished through the courtesy of Bell Laboratories and IEEE.

3-7-2 INTRODUCTION

The dependence on large, real-time program-controlled systems for providing vital services could not be popularly accepted if they could not operate continuously. Stringent reliability criteria apply to such systems as: telephone switching systems, network control systems (power, vehicular traffic), and communications systems. For example, the objective for the Bell System's Traffic Service Position System (TSPS No. 1)[1] specifies that system downtime may not exceed two hours in forty years; requirements are also specified on the duration and frequency of periods of less severe service degradation.

In order to achieve sufficiently high reliability, these systems must tolerate a statistically predictable rate of hardware problems, and a low but unpredictable rate of software problems, with only infrequent service interruptions of short duration. Considerable study has been done on the design of systems which can tolerate hardware faults; techniques such as redundancy and automatic fault diagnosis, for example, are widely used. As a result, systems can continue to operate despite hardware troubles. Bell System experience with stored program telephone switching systems indicates that software errors, if not corrected, will contribute significantly to system downtime. Consequently, methods must be provided to correct such troubles; frequently only manual techniques are available. But even with powerful, automatic recovery capabilities which permit a system restart, the effects of software mutilation may seriously degrade system performance for several minutes at a time. Therefore, to ensure high reliability, defensive techniques must be applied to minimize the effects of software errors and reduce the incidence of severe recovery actions.

The term "software" applies to all information stored within the system; this includes programs, transient data (which is rapidly changing, such as data associated with a particular telephone call), and semipermanent data (which changes infrequently, such as that associated with the type of equipment installed at a telephone subscriber's station.) Each class of software can be stored in various types of devices. Much of the following discussion applies to information stored in random access memory, such as core, but similar considerations apply to sequential access devices as well.

Errors in software can occur for several reasons. First, despite extensive testing prior to its introduction, the system program may contain residual design errors. While the operational environment can generally be simulated fairly well with development testing, it is difficult (if not impossible) to completely test programs. Especially error-prone are the complex interfaces among programs produced by several individuals.

A second source of software errors is hardware troubles. Faults or transient errors occurring in hardware devices can result in improper processing actions. In particular, problems in the central processor or the memory access circuits can cause severe mutilation.

Software errors can also result from human mistakes which, for example, would include problems in semipermanent data. Such data typically distinguishes one application of the system program from another, and can change in time. As a result, when the data is changed, errors and inconsistencies can be introduced in the data because of human mistakes. Also, new combinations of data can exercise a program in an unanticipated manner, revealing incipient program design weaknesses.

All the above can cause the mutilation of memory. If the mutilation is not well-contained, a catastrophic failure can result, requiring the setting of transient data and hardware to an initial state in order to recover the system. However, if the frequency of such errors is low and adequate defenses are provided, the effects of software errors can be limited and processing need not be interrupted.*

Three types of defenses are used to permit system operation in the presence of software errors. First, circuits can monitor proper program operation and trigger recovery action before the effects of errors are too severe. One such technique uses an external "watchdog" timer which must be reset periodically by program action. Second, defenses in processing programs can check data on which the program is operating. Such checks can identify out-of-range data, "impossible" conditions, and so on. However, these checks are necessarily limited in scope, since performing exhaustive checks during each processing action would cost too much additional time and would reduce the system's processing capacity.

To incorporate more extensive software defenses than could be economically provided by hardware or in-line processing checks alone, all Bell System stored program switching systems have employed independent check programs known as audits which detect and correct errors in memory content. The Bell System has used audit techniques since 1960, with the introduction of their first stored-program controlled switching system.[3]

The remaining sections of this paper consider more fully the third type of defense, audits. The paper discusses various software structures which must be audited, the types of errors amenable to detection by audits, and techniques used by audit programs to find and correct software errors. Finally, based on Bell System experience with audits, broader questions of system design are covered. This discussion is intended to aid designers in incorporating similar techniques in other types of real-time, stored-program control systems.

3-7-3 SOFTWARE TO BE AUDITED

Audit techniques may be applied to each of the classes of memory mentioned previously, that is, program, transient data, and semipermanent data. Tran-

---

*Reference 2 characterizes memory mutilation problems and broadly discusses techniques used to combat them.

sient data must be capable of being changed quickly and is, therefore, normally vulnerable to mutilation. An example is the data associated with the states of system hardware or software facilities. These facilities generally are provided in just sufficient quantity so that the probability of a facility not being available is small. Loss of some or all facilities of a given type can degrade (or ultimately stop) processing. For example, in a telephone switching system, the number of circuits that supply dial tone is calculated using traffic engineering formulae so that excessive delay is rarely encountered by a caller. Loss of several circuits during high traffic periods would cause noticeable delay in obtaining dial tone.

Also subject to mutilation is transient data associated with the activity of a particular processing client, such as a telephone call in a switching system. Should memory mutilation occur, individual calls could be mishandled and facilities lost to the system; if errors propagate through the transient data, the effects can be more serious.

In some systems, programs and/or permanent data are protected from unintentional mutilation by placing them in permanent (read-only) or semipermanent (restricted write) memories. In the absence of such protection, defenses are needed for this information as well. When feasible, backup records are available on-line. Clearly, even small errors in program or permanent data can have disastrous effects on system operation, so that audit techniques should be applied here as well.

3-7-4 TYPES OF ERRORS FOUND BY AUDITS

The effects of software errors on system performance can range from limited to rather severe. Errors which are well-contained and do not propagate through the memory (*quiescent* errors) often result only in minor performance degradation. For example, loss of one dial tone circuit in a telephone switching system might only slightly increase the average delay in obtaining a circuit. However, certain combinations of quiescent errors, occurring simultaneously, can result in serious error conditions. For example, if enough single facilities are lost, eventually all processing will suffer from lack of facilities.

More serious are errors which are propagated through memory when the program operates on incorrect data. If such errors (*volatile* errors) propagate widely and rapidly, they can result in loss of many facilities and, potentially, in an interruption of processing.

When considering the design of software defenses, it is more meaningful to classify errors by their nature. Three categories will be covered: state data errors, linkage errors, and loss facilities. These errors are typical of those encountered in a real-time system.

State data describes the current processing or service state of the facility with which it is associated. Errors in state data might cause a facility to erroneously appear idle, busy, and so on. Usually such errors are localized and thus quiescent.

When a processing client requires use of several facilities simultaneously, software registers used to administer these facilities can be linked together. For example, on a telephone call, registers associated with each of the two network terminals to be connected and with the switching path between them are linked by having each register contain the memory address of another. An error in this linkage structure could result in improper processing of the affected call. If the error is not corrected quickly it could easily propagate, resulting in the mishandling of other clients as well.

Linkage structures also susceptible to error are those in which program addresses are stored in temporary memory to specify a future processing action. Errors in such data can result in the loss of program continuity.

When facilities are administered, it is convenient to group together, possibly on a work list, software registers associated with facilities of a given type in a specific processing state. Errors in the list structure could result in the "loss" of facilities, interrupting the servicing of that facility and resulting in a volatile error.

Indefinite lockout of a program is another type of lost facility. When a program performs certain kinds of activities, it may lock out other programs from running to prevent potentially interfering actions. Should the program lose processing control, the lockout state might never be released.

3-7-5   AUDIT TECHNIQUES

3-7-5-1 Error Detection

Several techniques are used by audit programs to detect and correct software errors such as those just described. These techniques include consistency checks, linkage checks, integrity checks, unconditional corrections, and timeouts.

Consistency checks are made by comparing data or program stored in a writeable memory with a less volatile on-line backup record. This permits a more flexible system design without a loss of reliability. For example (Figure 3-7-1), if the program and permanent data are stored in an unprotected memory, a backup record can be placed on a cheaper, slower-access memory. When changes are made, records are kept of both the previous and changed versions. Comparison of the changed backup record with the primary memory provides a means for detecting errors in the primary memory. Since data in the backup memory is generally much less volatile than that in the primary memory, errors can be corrected by simply overwriting the record in the primary memory.

Example
Verify unprotected program and permanent data memory

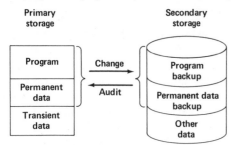

Detect: By comparing with backup
Correct: By overwriting primary storage

Figure 3-7-1 Example of consistency check.

Linkage checks verify that registers associated with facilities are validly linked together, using the redundancy inherent in the linkage structure. For example, when a linked list is audited, redundancy permits the last entry on the list to be identified in two ways. Similarly, a "loop-around" check can also be made of the registers linked in a circular fashion for a single processing client.

Figure 3-7-2 illustrates a one-way linked list structure in which a head cell points to the first and last member on the list. The first word of each facility register on the list contains the address of the next register. The list integrity can be checked in two ways: (1) by identifying the last member on the list using both methods of identifying it, and (2) by determining whether the "next" address in each register is that of a potential member of the list. In the example, the

Figure 3-7-2 Example of linkage and integrity checks.

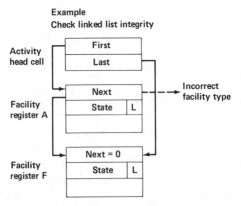

Detect: By determining consistency of linkages and validity of states
Correct: By placing register in "safe" state, then restoring to list on
          deferred basis

"next" address in facility register A violates the second check. When an error is detected, the list can be truncated after the last "good" register; the remaining registers can be restored by a subsequent audit. Registers which pass all checks will have their "lost" (L) bits set for use by the follow-up audits to be described with Figure 3-7-3.

Integrity checks are made on state data associated with facilities. These checks determine whether the state data is consistent with the work list on which the software register is located. This technique is a way of identifying lost facilities. For example, in Figure 3-7-2, state data associated with a facility is encoded within its register. An integrity check is made by comparing the state data with those states which are valid for this linked list.

When integrity or consistency checks would be extremely complex or error-prone, *unconditional correction* techniques may be used. For example, having identified all nonidle facilities of a given type using previously-discussed techniques, the audit can construct a list of idle facilities simply by including those facilities not already identified. This technique does not provide error detection. Figure 3-7-3 shows seven facility registers (A through G) of a given type. Registers A, B, and F were found by earlier audits on the "active" list (Figure 3-7-2) and "maintenance" list, as indicated by having their lost bits set to one. If the only other valid state for these registers is "idle," the "idle" linked list can be formed by identifying those registers with lost bits still zero. No checks are made on the current "idle" linked list, but this technique ensures that the "idle" linked list is correct.

Finally, *timeout* auditing locates facilities that do not violate logical checks, but are unavailable for processing. If an absolute limit can be placed on the holding time of a facility (without being idled), the facility can be examined

Figure 3-7-3   Example of unconditional correction.

Example
Locate idle facilities

Facility register			State
A		1	Active
B		1	Maintenance
C		0	Idle
D		0	Idle
E		0	Idle
F		1	Active
G		0	Idle

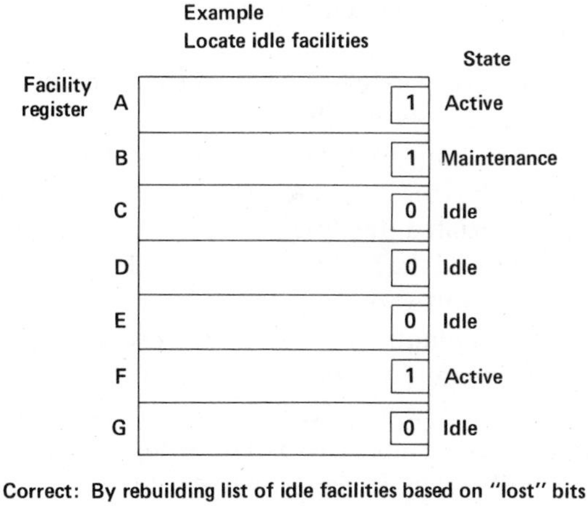

Correct: By rebuilding list of idle facilities based on "lost" bits

at a period equal to the maximum holding time. A timeout bit is associated with the facility, and the bit is zeroed when the facility is idled. If an audit sets the timeout bit when the facility is in use, on its next entry the audit should find the timeout bit zeroed. If the bit is found set, the facility is assumed lost and can be idled. This limits the time a facility can be lost to two holding times. In a similar way, where no absolute holding time limit is appropriate for a facility or program, a probabilistic timeout can be applied. Specifically, if all facilities of a given type are continuously nonidle for a long period of time, loss of facilities is suspected and detailed integrity checks should be made. Figure 3–7–4 shows the facility register used previously with a timeout bit (T) added.

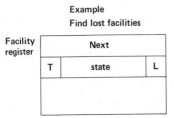

Example
Find lost facilities

Facility register

	Next	
T	state	L

Detect: By determining whether facility has been in continuous use for period exceeding maximum holding time

Correct: By delinking register; complete correction on deferred basis

Figure 3–7–4 Example of timeout check.

3–7–5–2 Error Correction

Having found an error using one of the methods just discussed, audits can correct the error in one of several ways. If the proper data is known, the error can be corrected absolutely. Thus, for consistency or unconditional correction error detection techniques, the erroneous data is simply replaced by the correct information.

More likely, however, are cases where the correction can only return the software to a "safe" state. Rather than determining the precise extent of error propagation and attempting to reconstruct the memory, the single affected facility can be returned to an idle state, or processing of a single client can be discontinued and associated facilities idled. If the software mutilation is suspected to extend beyond the immediate error, other audits can be called in to examine closely-related software.

Such correction techniques may affect the processing of several calls in a telephone switching system. For example, correction of a software error could result in the disconnecting of a limited number of calls. But the sacrifice of a few calls is preferable to the alternative of allowing the trouble to grow to proportions where overall system integrity is jeopardized.

3-7-6 SYSTEM DESIGN ASPECTS

Integration of audit programs into a program system can be done in a number of ways. In this section, some of the major system considerations will be explored, and the approaches used in systems such as TSPS No. 1 and No. 1 ESS[4] discussed.

Audits use the redundancy in the software structure to locate errors and inconsistencies. Often the redundancy is inherent in the data structure, such as in a linked list. In some cases, it is necessary to expand the data structure to add memory needed only for audit purposes. The timeout bit in the timeout audit is an example of such memory.

The portion of the processing capability devoted to audits at a given instant in time depends strongly on the immediate health of the software. Their role can vary from a state of minimal usage under normal conditions to a position in a severe emergency wherein they take over full program control for an extended duration.

3-7-6-1 Normal Operations

Most real-time program controlled systems are limited in their processing capacity by unacceptably long delays which occur if the processor is overloaded. Whatever their throughput may be, there is almost always economic pressure to handle more. This is certainly true in telephone switching systems, such as TSPS No. 1, where added capacity would permit each system to handle a larger volume of telephone traffic, and hence fewer systems would be needed to process the total traffic. Since audit programs do consume processing time, they must be designed to have minimal effect on system capacity, yet be effective in maintaining system integrity. They must also be designed to operate in a time-shared mode, characteristic of the system they are protecting.

This is achieved by executing audits only a small fraction of the time. In the TSPS No. 1 system, a minimum of 3 percent of system time is spent on this work. The scheduling is elastic; as processing needs increase, audits are executed less frequently. In addition, to minimize the delay experienced by other programs, audit programs are divided into small segments. These segments, typically less than 10 milliseconds run-time, are interlaced with the processing programs. Various techniques can be used to interlace these programs, with the exact method chosen depending on the specific structure of the data being audited and whether an error state is considered quiescent or volatile.

Quiescent errors, as we have defined them, will generally not degrade normal processing activities. These errors can thus remain in the system for an extended period of time. Audit programs which can detect and correct this type of error state are usually placed on a fixed time schedule, running perhaps every few seconds or once per hour or once per day, depending on the consequences of the trouble if not corrected.

Volatile errors present a more difficult problem since these error states can rapidly escalate to serious proportions. For these error conditions, rapid detection and isolation of the error is essential, with final correction of the problem often handled on a deferred basis.

As discussed previously, defensive program checks coded directly in the mainstream of the processing programs are usually applied sparingly because of their excessive use of processing capacity. When real-time considerations permit such checks, the trouble state can be detected either at the instant of occurrence or before the mutilated data is used. Once the trouble state is isolated, the final clean-up of all the data can be performed at low priority. Defensive programming can thus limit the consequences of a volatile error to the level of perhaps one or maybe a few incorrect processing actions.

When processing time penalties make such defensive checks impractical, the volatile error states have to be detected on a more probabilistic basis. The audit program segments which guard against these potential error states are run at a high frequency, ranging from as often as once every few seconds to once per minute. The relative frequency of the different segments is set by the rate at which an error could propagate and by the consequences that could ensue from such an error. Structuring the audits in this manner to detect volatile error states represents a compromise between maximizing system processing capacity and minimizing system downtime.

One of the important secondary benefits derived from the audits is the detailed information obtained of the error conditions that were encountered. Whenever an error state is found, a printout is made of the error condition. Later analysis of these error messages aids in locating the cause of the trouble. Analysis may be difficult, but once a system is placed into continuous service, this is one of the few techniques available to gain insight into program malfunctions.

3-7-6-2 Emergency Conditions

On occasion, an error state occurs that causes normal system processing to deteriorate drastically and perhaps even stop. There are a number of techniques by which a processing system detects such severe malfunction. For the purposes of this paper, we assume that detection mechanisms exist, and we will be concerned only with the way the system reacts to the triggers.

Because of the complete inability of the processing system to carry out its assigned tasks under these emergency conditions, all attempts to operate in a time-shared mode are suspended and instead, the entire attention of the processing system is devoted to the task of effecting a recovery. When such an event occurs, the assumption is initially made that audits can correct the trouble, provided they have full system control. If the actual trouble state is not too severe, audits can correct it without too serious a loss of processing continuity and little or no disruption to unaffected areas of the data. But if the trouble is more serious, it may be necessary to clear the transient data completely and enact a full program restart.

This latter action, of course, causes extensive service disruption, both through the mishandling of existing work as well as through the inability to process new service requests until recovery is completed. For TSPS No. 1 a full restart can cause an outage of close to two minutes duration. The purpose of audits stated simply, is to clear the error states so that the occurrence of such program restarts is held to the minimum possible.

3-7-7 EXPERIENCE WITH AUDITS

The experience of most Bell System program controlled switching systems has been that errors in the transient data occur relatively frequently. TSPS No. 1 installations are experiencing a rate of 10 to 100 errors detected and corrected per day with rates of several hundred occasionally recorded. Yet program restarts are relatively rare, occurring presently at the rate of about once every two months. As good as this rate may seem, it is still a factor of four greater than our system objective. But without audit programs, the difference of some three orders of magnitude between errors and restarts could not be possible.

The audit error rate cited above for TSPS No. 1 is prevailing three years after cutover of the first installation on January 19, 1969. If numerous program corrections had not been made in the interim, the level would be much higher. Indeed, at the time of cutover, the error rate was in the range of 100 to 300 per day. The fact that data errors still occur, in spite of the intensive effort made over the last three years to correct the program troubles, indicates strongly that large complex program systems can never be fully debugged.

Audit error levels vary widely among offices, even though those offices have identical programs. In general, they increase with increasing traffic load, and with the amount of maintenance activity. Offices with high hardware trouble rates usually also experience a high software (that is, audit) trouble rate. This latter phenomenon is probably due to the strain placed on the software to maintain continuity of service with troublesome hardware. The program branches which are designed to handle these conditions are usually not as well debugged as the main program legs, and hence they are subject to subtle problems that initially go uncorrected.

3-7-8 SUMMARY

Audit programs provide the defenses needed to reduce significantly the frequency of outages due to software problems. They are especially valuable in an atmosphere which places a premium on rapid introduction of new systems or new service features on existing systems, and on the maintenance of reliable and continuous service. Audits permit a less than perfect software system to be placed in service. In a sense, they are a necessary evil since they consume system resources such as storage space and processing time. Naturally, systems should be designed to be as free from errors as possible. They should not be designed to depend directly on audits. But without audits, the timely introduction of some of the more complex Bell System program-controlled switching systems may not have been possible.

3-7-9 REFERENCES

[1] "TSPS No. 1" (Series of seven articles), *Bell System Technical Journal,* Volume 49, Number 10, December 1970, pp. 2417–2731.

[2] Nowak, J. S. and Tuomenoksa, L. S., "Memory Mutilation in Stored Program Controlled Telephone Systems", 1970 International Conference on Communications—Conference Record, pp. 43–32 to 43–45.

[3] Haugk, G. and Yokelson, B. J., "Experience with the Morris Electronic Switching System", IEEE Transactions, Part I, Communication and Electronics, No. 64, pp. 605–610, January 1963.

[4] Almquist, R. P., Hagerman, J. R., Hass, R. J., Peterson, R. W. and Stevens, S. L., "Software Protection in No. 1 ESS", 1972 International Switching Symposium Record.

3-8   AN INTEGRATED SIMULATION AND DEBUGGING FACILITY FOR A DISTRIBUTED PROCESSING REAL-TIME SYSTEM*

R. D. STINAFF
ITT Telecommunications

3-8-1 SUMMARY

This paper describes a simulation and debugging facility which is designed for use in the development of a highly complex distributed processing control system. Although the specific application of the control system is telephonic

*Originally published in the Proceedings of ICC '78. Reprinted with permission.

switching, the paper focuses on application-independent concepts of the simulation-debugging facility which are potentially applicable to a wide range of distributed processing system developments.

The facility described in this paper was designed as a software development aid for a system of the type shown in Figure 3-8-1a. In terms of control, the physical process is homogeneously partitioned into segments of comparable size, each of which is controlled by a microprocessor via a memory-mapped control interface. Interprocessor communication capability is provided via memory-mapped communication interfaces connected to a common Time-Division Multiplex bus.

The specific application to which this system is directed is telephone switching (1-3), but the discussion will focus on application-independent concepts present in the simulation–debugging facility which are potentially applicable to a wide range of similar distributed processing system developments. The only application-dependent feature which is perhaps relevant is the modularity of the control system. Each control partition corresponds to a group of terminal circuits, with each microprocessor-driven complex capable of controlling a certain maximum number of such circuits. The total system capacity, then, is modularly adaptable over a very wide range by varying the number of microprocessor complexes.

The need for an integrated simulation–debugging facility in the development of the system stemmed primarily from three factors. First, in order to adequately test and debug the software, it is necessary to exercise it in the context of the full hardware configuration under a wide range of driving conditions (for example, call initiation, dialing, and fault occurrence). Second, it is impractical

Figure 3-8-1a System configuration.

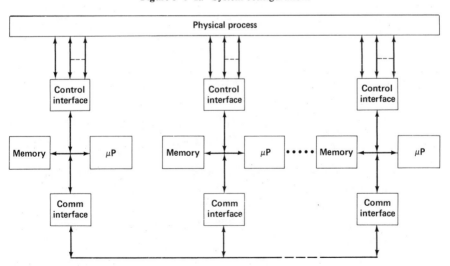

to physically configure the necessary hardware complexity. Finally, it would not be feasible, even with the actual hardware configured, to adequately test the software under certain low-probability driving conditions.

The general approach taken in providing the required simulation–debugging capabilities is illustrated in Figure 3-8-1b. In the context of the system description at this level, all that has been done is to replace the control interfaces and the physical process itself by a simulation–debugging system which, additionally, can exercise direct control over the execution of each microprocessor.

The simulator–debugger was configured as an external processor with special hardware interfaces to the system microprocessor complexes. The software was designed in the form of two independent packages, one for simulation and one for debugging functions, which can be used independently or in conjunction with one another. Details of each of these aspects of the simulator–debugger (configuration, hardware, and software) are provided in succeeding sections.

A significant amount of work in the area of simulation facilities for telephony systems has been reported previously (4–9), but to the author's knowledge, this is the first paper concerning a simulation facility designed for use with a distributed processing telephony system.

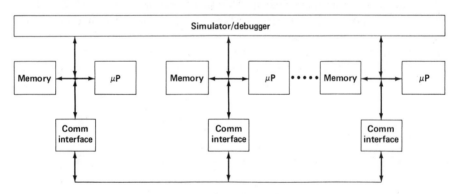

Figure 3-8-1b   Simulation configuration.

3-8-2 SIMULATION-DEBUGGING
FACILITY CONFIGURATION

The general configuration for the simulation-debugging facility is shown in Figure 3-8-2 in terms of the functional relationships among its major components. The heart of the facility is a minicomputer, with a real-time operating system, moving-head disk, mag tape, line printer, and multiple interactive CRT terminals, which serves as the external simulation-debugging processor. This

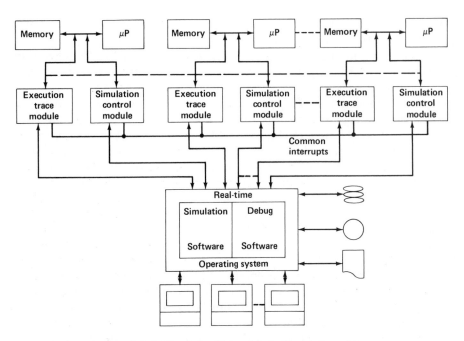

Figure 3-8-2   Simulation/debugging facility configuration.

processor is interfaced individually to each microprocessor complex in the system via two special-purpose hardware modules, which are connected to the microprocessor busses and also to identical modules in other complexes for control purposes. Figure 3-8-2 shows only a single test system configured with the simulation–debugging facility, but multiple systems may be simultaneously configured simply by providing separate common interrupt lines for each system. Systems are attached on a one-to-one basis to users associated with separate CRT terminals. The facility thus provides the capability for multiple users to concurrently test separate systems.

The software is designed such that multiple users may concurrently access the debug package, the simulation package, or both. In addition, both software packages are designed so that these facilities may be used either interactively, or in an offline mode, whereby a user may construct preset sequences of simulation and/or debug operations which can then be executed in batch mode by an operator at another time. This permits efficient use of the simulation–debugging facility in a heavily loaded software development environment, especially since the simulation and debug software packages can also be run for the purpose of batch run specification on software-only development systems similar to the minicomputer system used in the simulation–debugging facility itself.

The execution trace modules, which are used in conjunction with the debug package, provide the capability for monitoring microprocessor bus activity in real-time and maintaining traces of this activity under control of a number of user-specifiable conditions.

The simulation control modules provide the necessary I/O and control capabilities to permit synchronous input of simulated driving conditions from the simulation package to the appropriate microprocessor complexes, and to permit the simulation package to emulate responses of the physical process to I/O requests from the microprocessor complexes. Every execution trace module and every simulator control module has the capacity to halt or restart the applications software in all microprocessor complexes within a test system simultaneously via a common high-level interrupt line. Functional details of the execution trace module and the simulation control module will be subsequently discussed.

3–8–3 EXECUTION TRACE MODULE

In general, each microprocessor complex in a system under test will be interfaced to an execution trace module, whose functional organization is illustrated in Figure 3–8–3. The trace module contains its own microprocessor for setup of trace conditions as specified by ASCII command strings received over an RS–232C serial link from the simulation–debugging processor or directly from

Figure 3–8–3 Execution trace module.

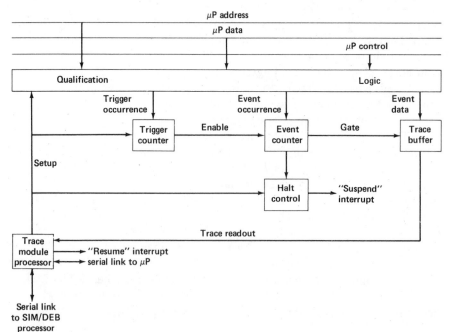

an ASCII keyboard. The serial link provides remote capability and the ASCII command format permits limited use of the trace module in field systems without the need for the full debugging processor configuration used.

The trace module contains qualification logic which samples the states of the microprocessor address, data, and control busses during every processor cycle. If the composite state matches any one of a number of such states which have been preset via the link language in terms of address range, data range, and memory access mode (for example, Read, Write, DMA, Execute), then the state is stored in a circulating trace buffer, a trigger occurrence signal is generated, or both, depending on whether the matched conditions have been specified as trace qualifiers, triggers, or both. When a trigger occurrence signal is generated, it decrements a trigger counter which has been preset (perhaps to '1') via the link language. When the trigger count reaches zero, a trace event counter is enabled which is then decremented each time another qualified trace event is stored. When the event counter reaches zero, event storage is halted and, if the halt control circuit has been so initialized via the link language, execution of applications software in all system microprocessors is suspended.

Control system execution and execution tracing are thus controllable by a compound condition which specifies that any given trigger condition must occur a certain number of times, followed by the occurrence of a certain number of qualified trace events, before execution is halted and/or the event trace is suspended. The trace event counter permits a trace which represents prehistory, posthistory, or a combination, relative to the occurrence of a trigger condition. Since events are stored in circulating FIFO fashion, if the event counter is initialized to zero, the contents of the buffer at the time tracing is suspended represents the series of events immediately preceding the occurrence of the trigger condition (the number of events stored is equal to the actual number of qualified events which have occurred, up to a maximum number equal to the buffer capacity). If the event counter is initialized to the buffer capacity, the trace buffer will contain the series of events immediately following the occurrence of the trigger condition. Initialization of the event counter to a number between zero and the buffer capacity results in a trace which represents a mixture of prehistory and posthistory. The event counter can even be initialized to a number greater than the buffer capacity, in which case a delayed posthistory results.

In addition to simple concurrent comparisons of trigger conditions against trace events, triggers may be set up to be sequenced in hardware, that is, a given trigger can be initialized to become "armed" (that is, active) only if another trigger occurs first. Thus, a measure of conditional execution tracing capability is afforded by the hardware.

The capability is provided to simultaneously resume application processing in all system microprocessors via link language command to any trace module processor in the system. This capability is provided via a high-level interrupt to a special utility routine in each of the system processors in the same manner as the simultaneous halt capability is provided. This suspend-resume capability allows for fully synchronized observation and control of applications software execution in the general multiprocessor control system. The simulation control module makes use of the same mechanism to attain a time-true representation of the simulated execution conditions.

The special utility routine in each system processor, in addition to providing the suspend-resume mechanism, also provides a number of additional functions, such as processor single-stepping, readout and modification of memory and register contents, and simple break-pointing. These functions are accessed via the same link language used to access the trace module facilities. When a trace module is configured with the system processor in question, such commands are forwarded to the utility routine by the trace processor, as shown in Figure 3-8-3. If no trace module is present, the trace processor is automatically bypassed, and the utility functions can be invoked directly by the simulation–debugging processor or via ASCII keyboard.

3-8-4 SIMULATION CONTROL MODULE

In the actual system configuration (Figure 3-8-1a), control is exercised by each microprocessor via an intelligent interface which can perform a number of functions related to the physical process based on commands received from the microprocessor. In addition, the control interface transmits driving signals to the microprocessor in the form of data and status words. The simulation method used replaces the functions of this interface for each microprocessor, as well as the behavior of the physical process itself, by software in the simulation–debugging facility processor. To accomplish this, each control interface is replaced by a simulation control module whose functions are illustrated in Figure 3-8-4. When a command is output by the microprocessor intended for the normal control interface, the address decoder of the simulation control module responds by gating the command into the input buffer and generating a "suspend" interrupt. The command is then sent to the simulation–debugging processor via serial link for interpretation, the simulation software generates an emulation of the actual response which would be generated by the physical process, and the response is sent via serial link to the control processor, which puts the response in an output buffer and generates a "resume" interrupt. Driving signal representations are input to the system microprocessors via the same mechanism except that the microprocessors will generally be in execution at the time. Commands received via the serial link for response emulation, driving signal emulation, and status inquiry, follow the same ASCII string philosophy used for the execution trace module and for the special utility routine in the same microprocessors. Thus, the simulation control module, too, can be exercised directly via ASCII keyboard for field use.

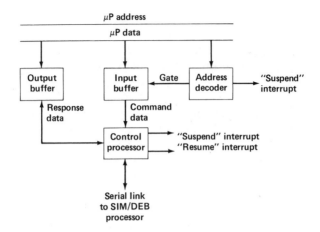

Figure 3-8-4   Simulation control module.

3-8-5 SIMULATION-DEBUGGING FACILITY SOFTWARE

The user can access the facilities of the simulation package and/or the debugging package either interactively via function menus and parameter prompts at a CRT terminal or in batch mode by executing commands directly from a disk file. Specification of a batch file is done interactively by the user exactly as though he were executing commands directly, except that the command stream is written to a disk file, rather than being executed.

The debugging package has several unique features in addition to batch mode execution. One such feature provides the user with symbolic reference capability at run time for debugging purposes. The applications software is written in a high-level language and is compiled and linked on a separate software-only system. The symbol table output of the linker is transported to the simulation-debugging processor and is used to generate tables which permit a user to make memory references in terms of symbolic memory locations plus offsets. The same symbol table is used in inverse fashion to provide the user with information as to which symbolic software module was executing when execution was suspended. The real-time operating system of the simulation-debugging processor provides a key-index file capability with hashed primary key which makes the symbolic reference feature very efficient.

Other features of the debugging package allow the user to define and maintain a library of triggers and event qualifiers, to list and/or modify register and memory contents directly or automatically under trigger control, to activate and deactivate triggers and qualifiers directly or under trigger control, to maintain counts of trigger occurrences, to locate data values in memory, and to run, single-step, or halt system processors.

Triggers and qualifiers are composed of four logically ANDed conditions with respect to the microprocessor busses: memory access mode (Read, Write, Execute, DMA), logical memory address range (memory mapping is used in system processors), physical memory address range, and data conditions (comparison of masked data value to a range which is specified either explicitly or indirectly). In addition, triggers can be specified to cause suspension of system processor execution or not to cause suspension.

The simulation package operates on the basis of a sequence of driving and conditional events specified by a user by means of a special event description language. An off-line preprocesser operates on the user-specified sequence and translates it into run-time files for control of simulator execution. Driving signals are generated by an event generator module according to these run-time files, and an emulation module intercepts control commands which have been generated by the system processors as a result of the driving signals and outputs emulated responses back to the system processors. As the event generator and emulator modules execute, they output simulator execution data to disk files. Information is gleaned selectively from these files following the simulation run by an interactive post processor to produce output reports containing the desired information. The organization of modules within the simulation package is illustrated in Figure 3-8-5.

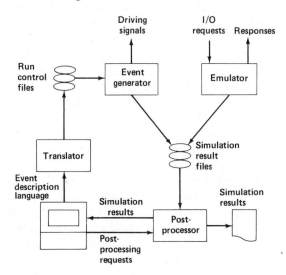

Figure 3-8-5 Simulator software structure.

3-8-6 CONCLUSIONS

The integrated simulation–debugging facility provides an extremely effective tool for the development of real-time software in a multiprocessing system. Although the facility was designed for use with a particular type of system in terms of application, the features provided, particularly in the way of debugging capabilities, make such a facility applicable to a fairly wide range of real-time multiprocessing system development tasks. The facility provides user convenience and flexibility by means of multiuser interactive control and also permits efficient use in a heavily loaded software development environment by providing batch execution capability. The simulation package provides the usual advantages associated with simulation, notably extremely flexible testing capability without the need for configuring a large, complex physical system.

3-8-7 ACKNOWLEDGMENTS

The author wishes to thank Mr. R. Sanders and Mr. W. Morgan for their invaluable aid in the development of the special interface hardware, and Mr. S. Morganstein, Mr. G. Couturier, and Mr. A. Thompson for their helpful suggestions regarding the manuscript.

3-8-8 REFERENCES

1. Bourbina, R. J. and Patel, P., "Structured Analysis, Design and Telephony," *Proc. 1978 Intl. Conf. on Communications,* June, 1978.
2. Yamasaki, D. T. and Morganstein, S. J., "Functional Partitioning of Telephonic Activities in a Distributed Load Sharing Environment," *Proc. 1978 Intl. Conf. on Communications,* June, 1978.
3. Libman, R. E., "Telephonic Maintenance Considerations in a Distributed System," *Proc. 1978 Intl. Conf. on Communications,* June, 1978.
4. Gruszecki, M. and Cornelis, F., "Environment Simulator for Traffic and Processor Capacity Studies in SPC Switching Systems," *Electrical Communication,* Vol. 51, No. 2, pp. 107-111, April, 1976.
5. Fontaine, B., "Real-Time Environment Simulation," *Electrical Communication,* Vol. 46, No. 3, pp. 188-190, July, 1971.
6. Cornelis, F., Gruszecki, M. and Salade, R., *Belgian Patent No. 809213.*
7. Kosten, L., "Simulation in Traffic Theory," *Sixth Intl. Teletraffic Congress,* Sept., 1970.
8. Dietrich, G., "Traffic Model for Common Control Switching Systems," *Electrical Communication,* Vol. 50, No. 1, pp. 28-34, January, 1975.
9. Grantges, R. F. and Sinowitz, N. R., "NEASIM: A General-Purpose Computer Simulation Program for Load-Loss Analysis of Multistage Central Office Switching Networks," *Bell System Technical Journal,* Vol. 43, No. 3, pp. 965-1004, May, 1964.

3-9 PATCHING IS ALIVE
AND, LAMENTABLY, THRIVING
IN THE REAL-TIME WORLD*

ROBERT L. GLASS
Boeing Aerospace Company

"Patching" is generally acknowledged to be a bad programming practice. It flies in the face of all positive directions in the language-compiler field. Yet its usage is definitely on the rise in at least the real-time sector of computing.

This material defines patching, explains why it is considered bad, why its usage is increasing, and suggests some strategies (both technical and managerial) for fighting it.

3-9-1 WHAT IS PATCHING?

Patching is the practice of correcting a program in object code, regardless of what language it was originally programmed in.

3-9-2 WHY IS PATCHING BAD?

Patching is highly error-prone as illustrated in the following:

a. Patches are coded in a numeric and specialized language with which the programmer may be unfamiliar.
b. Patches must be assigned vacant storage in memory, a task which is easier said than done. For example, assignment of a patch to an already assigned patch area is a common problem.
c. Patches are only a temporary expedient. The "real" correction probably must be made in program source code, meaning the correction is done twice, often not using the same algorithm.
d. Patch insertion into the computer requires unusual techniques. For example, patches may be entered into the computer from its console, an error-prone process in itself which also retains no written record. Or patches may be punched into "binary" card decks, a process for which no proper equipment has ever been defined, and one often requiring the circumventing of a card-reader error-check process called "checksumming."

*From SIGPLAN Notices, March 1978, Vol. 13, No. 3.

3-9-3 WHY IS PATCH USAGE ON THE RISE?

Patches are a solution of expedience. Several common problems, especially in the real-time environment, have led to increased usage:

a. Testing methodology and schedules, especially in the integration of large real-time systems, preclude taking the time to do the job right. For example, large system integration tests sometimes run for a day or more. Aborting and rescheduling such a test usually seems, at the time, more painful than patching and pressing on.

b. Configuration management practices often inhibit the making of source code changes. The patch is an expedient alternative to waiting for formal approval.

c. Compilation, assembly, and link-loading often occur on a "host" computer other than the one on which the program is to be run. This is done to take advantage of support facilities which large computers possess and small, typical real-time computers do not. However, large computers often have prohibitive turnaround time. Patches may be an attempt to overcome that time.

d. Support software, such as that mentioned in (c) above, may not be coded with proper concern for efficiency since it is often considered to be less important than the real-time software. The result may be extremely time-consuming code (one link-loader required several hours to link a large real-time system). Programmers may patch real-time code rather than go back through an expensive rebuild from source.

e. Transition from the support software host computer facility to the real-time computer facility is at best annoying. Synchronization of host and real-time runs is difficult, and if done conservatively, adds human wait time to a wait problem already aggravated by (c) and (d) above. Geographic locations of the host and the real-time computer may also be different.

f. Real-time computers are sometimes of a new design and are error-prone. Software workarounds are required for such hardware problems. It is undesirable to place such changes in program source, since they are temporal only; patches are used instead.

g. Many times support software, especially the compiler, is of a new design. Workarounds are sometimes required for these problems as well. The reasoning of (f) above, applies here also.

h. Maximization of programmer checkout time while on the real-time computer is always a goal. If a run aborts, typically the programmer wants to correct the abort and move further into the test. This may mean a patch just for the duration of this test.

    i. There is a psychological or ego factor involved. Programmers feel more intimate with the computer and further removed from management when operating at the machine code (patch) level.

Note for the above that patches may be characterized in three time-dependent ways:

    a. A "now" patch—just for this time on the computer.

    b. A "circumstances" patch—just until the hardware–compiler–other external cause is corrected.

    c. An "error" patch—to correct an error in the program itself.

3-9-4 WHAT CAN BE DONE TO STEM THE TIDE OF PATCHING?

The problems which cause patching to be utilized must be addressed if the practice is to be reduced. The suggestions which follow can aid in the correction of the noted problems. However, more in-the-field research into causes and effects will be needed before the problems surrounding patching are fully resolved.

    a. Place management emphasis on long-term rather than short-term goals. Make sure that schedule pressures do not force patching to occur. At the same time, ensure that configuration management practices are responsive to project needs and do not inhibit change needlessly.

    b. Improve compilation–assembly–link-load turnaround. This can be done by any of the following:
Use a timesharing host computer
Reduce host computer loading (buy another, if necessary)
Rehost support software on the real-time computer itself
Give high priority to real-time users (priority systems often seem to collapse of their own weight, however)

    c. Improve the quality of support software. Write tighter sizing-timing requirements and provide for correction of product limitations. Improve already-in-use support software.

    d. Improve host–real-time computer transition time. This can be done by building a computer-computer link between the two, or at least situating them in proximity to one another.

    e. Improve acceptance testing of computers and support software. More vigorously tested products will cause fewer in-the-field "circumstance" patches.

f. Provide operator and perhaps operating system support for real-time computer checkout. Make it easy for the programmers not to be at the console coding "now" and "ego" patches.

3-10   SOFTWARE MAINTENANCE PLANNING FOR EMBEDDED COMPUTER SYSTEMS*

W. K. Sharpley, Jr.
The Analytic Sciences Corporation

3-10-1   ABSTRACT

The transition of embedded computer system software from developmental to operational status requires careful planning and preparation. Providing a well-designed software maintenance capability is an essential part of an overall system maintenance plan. In this paper, key software maintenance issues are summarized and their resolution in terms of software maintenance goals and facilities requirements is described. Alternative configurations for software maintenance facilities and criteria for selecting a configuration are discussed, with illustrative examples based on ongoing maintenance planning activities for two Department of Defense (DoD) tactical systems.

3-10-2   INTRODUCTION

Software engineering technology has progressed rapidly in the last several years. Software developers are now provided with a comprehensive assortment of tools for developing high-quality software at an affordable price. This is especially important to the Department of Defense (DoD), for which the cost of software development for embedded computer systems[1] has become a major item of concern (1, 2, 3). The high degree of acceptance of modern software

---

[1] An "embedded computer system" is an automated system (for example, weapon system) in which dedicated digital computers provide all primary mission functional control.

engineering technology in system development will probably lead to dramatic improvement in embedded software cost–performance ratios in the near future. However, two important special classes of embedded computer systems exist, for which applicability of the new technology is not obvious:

Systems with a long (> 5 years) development cycle which are currently entering the inventory

Systems constructed by aggregating "off-the-shelf" equipment, including software.

The key software management problem for such systems is to find an optimal way to benefit from recent insights and "lessons learned," *without expending limited resources on cosmetic conformance to current ideals and standards.* One area in which significant cost savings potential exists is life cycle software maintenance. DoD experience indicates that approximately 32 percent of software-related life cycle cost is incurred during the Operations and Maintenance (O&M) phase (2). Current DoD emphasis on standardization and application of software engineering technology is partially motivated by the desire to reduce software O&M costs, and planning for effective software maintenance is a key element of the DoD approach.

This paper discusses planning for software O&M based on the following premises:

. The subject system belongs to one of the above special classes, and is to be dealt with as *delivered and documented*

Modern software engineering practices *applicable to the O&M phase* are to be utilized as appropriate

Software maintenance is to be performed by organizations and personnel *who were not involved in the software development.*

3-10-3 EMBEDDED COMPUTER SOFTWARE MAINTENANCE ISSUES

3-10-3-1 Software Life Cycle Management Considerations

Software development practices and the use of supporting documentation and configuration management disciplines have undergone serious study and refinement in recent years. Several design methodologies and software engineering approaches have been applied to the problems of software development and life cycle cost control (4). The currently accepted approach for real-time mission-related system software projects (Figure 3–10–1) is based on two principles:

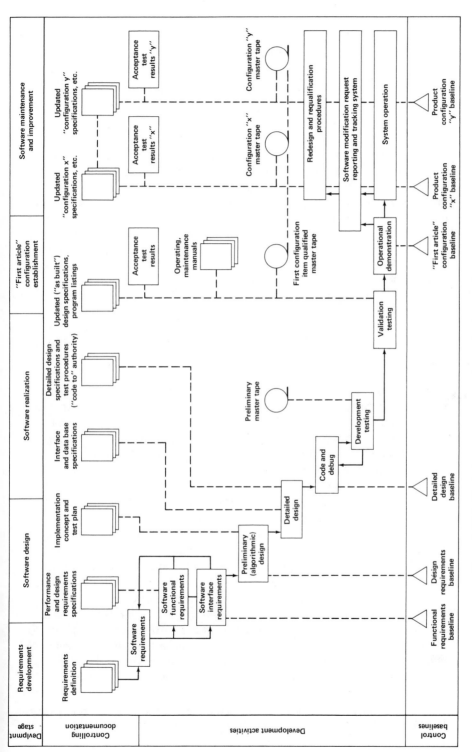

Figure 3-10-1 Typical weapons system software development/support approach.

207

Approved specifications must precede and guide specific development and modification activities

The establishment of a controlled baseline configuration is required to ensure (1) preservation of operational capability, and (2) repeatability of validation test results.

Development of embedded system software has often proceeded differently from the ideal process illustrated in Figure 3-10-1. Extended development cycles, with resources concentrated on "proof of principle" testing, sometimes preclude the development of a sophisticated software production capability. Establishment of *retroactive, formal* configuration management may not be in keeping with cost minimization goals. However, establishment of a reasonable level of O&M configuration tracking and control and a minimal software development and test capability are necessary to support the deployed systems.

3-10-4 KEY SOFTWARE MAINTENANCE COST FACTORS

Software maintenance is an expensive undertaking because it is *inherently both labor intensive and an inefficient use of labor.* It is *labor intensive* because the detection, confirmation, and correction of software design errors, and the development of software modifications, can only be performed by highly skilled individuals. The process is typically *inefficient* because a well-tested operational software system[2] exhibits symptoms of software errors only infrequently and under special conditions. *The personnel assigned to maintain such software do not get sufficient trouble exposure to maintain their knowledge of the details of and interactions within the software.*

Planning for a software maintenance capability should therefore include specific attention to developing tools and techniques which *complement the capabilities of the software maintenance personnel,* and *compensate for their lack of intimate familiarity with the detailed software design.* The overall software maintenance planning process *should include specific provision for prompt and complete error detection and reporting by the system users,* so that the operational situation which reveals a specific software problem can be understood by the programmer assigned to correct the problem. *The principal planning objective should be to minimize software maintenance costs by maximizing the productivity of the maintenance personnel.*

----

[2] "Operational software" as used hereafter will refer to both primary mission software and associated system maintenance software packages (system operability tests, and so on).

3-10-5 SOFTWARE MANAGEMENT TOOLS

Software maintenance includes the operations shown in the lower right portion of Figure 3-10-1. This activity should be performed under formal documentation and configuration control. The tools required to *manage* the software maintenance activity consist of the following:

A comprehensive system–software trouble reporting system

A complementary set of software-oriented test procedures for operating command use

A mechanism for controlling and tracking operational program revisions

A Software Configuration Control Board (SCCB) to review and authorize changes.

3-10-6 SPECIAL TOOLS FOR SOFTWARE MAINTENANCE

Figure 3-10-2 shows a software maintenance concept designed to bring possible software errors to the attention of a permanently assigned team of software experts. The resources required to support major activities in this concept are indicated in the lower part of the diagram. System–software test tools and software development tools are required to support this concept. Their use in operational software maintenance vs. software modification differs only in approach.

Table 3-10-1 summarizes the key requirements for a system software

---

TABLE 3-10-1   Software Maintenance/Modification Required Capabilities

- Problem Verification
    - —Reproduce trouble situations
    - —Verify reported symptoms
    - —Identify cause: software, hardware, interface
- Diagnosis
    - —System state specification-sequence control
    - —Software–hardware test points access
    - —Test data collection
    - —Test data analysis
- Reprogramming (new requirements or specific correction)
    - —Source code modification
    - —Object code generation
    - —System reload
- Baseline Verification-Reverification
    - —Scenario control
    - —Data collection
    - —Data analysis

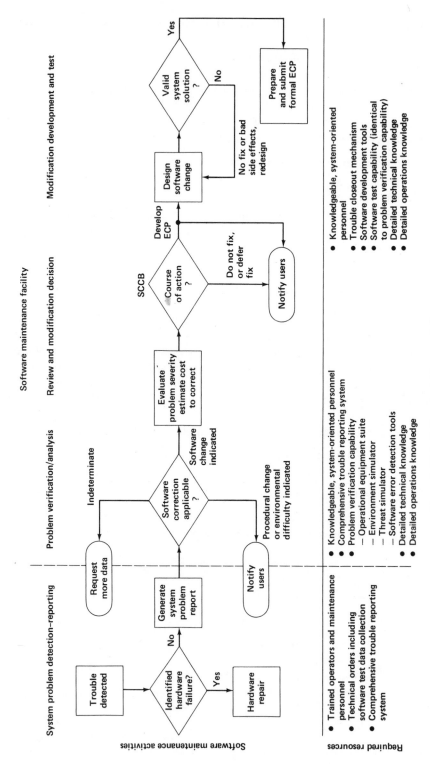

Figure 3-10-2 Software problem resolution sequence.

210

maintenance and/or modification capability, or software laboratory, which for practical systems typically involves interconnection of actual system hardware in a "hot mockup" arrangement. The major elements required, in addition to the embedded computer and other elements of the subject system, are:

Scenario generators, which interpret high-level user commands and generate test control command sequences

Real-time test drivers, which translate scenario command sequences and control the system environment

Environment simulators

Test data collection–reduction capability

All stages of system software maintenance involve detailed tests of software operation. Because of the extreme combined complexity of the hardware, program logic, and large memory of a computer system, practical testing never aims at complete execution. It depends instead on *verifying key states and major transitions on a selective basis.* This is analogous to the diagnostic problem of "identification" of a sequential machine, which in this case is composed of the program–computer system combination. In software development the same process is applied to debug and validate the operational programs. *This implies that an adequate set of software test access tools* (debugging tools) *will also provide adequate access for post-delivery software problem analysis and repair activities.*

A generally useful set of software test tools is outlined in Table 3–10–2. This is not a minimal set, in that it includes excess capabilities which would simplify and expedite software testing and thus minimize test manpower. *Provision of a standardized set of test tools which operate within the embedded computer is highly desirable, because it encourages concentration on the problem rather than the mode of attacking the problem.*

3-10-7 SOFTWARE MAINTENANCE GOALS

3-10-7-1 Support of Initial Deployment

Initial deployment of a complex hardware–software system is an important transitional phase in the development, as indicated in Figure 3–10–1. *This applies even in the case of a well-proven design because some modifications and adaptations are inevitable.* Furthermore, since qualification testing is necessarily limited by the law of diminishing returns, *transition to an operational environment will expose the system to environmental conditions and operational sequences which have not been specifically tested. The principal problems will be startup difficulties,* compounded by a heavy transient problem report load.

TABLE 3–10–2 Useful Software Test Access Mechanisms

Probe Type	Principal Stimulus (Monitor Point)	Options	Typical Outputs & Actions
Address Trap	Specific Program	Trap on Block of Addresses	Standard Utility Dumps Time of this Trap Enable New Trap(s) Load Data for Next Test
Transfer Trap	Transfer Instruction Reached	Trap All, Last "N", Next "N" Transfers Trap Ends of Loops	Standard Utility Dumps Time of this Trap
Tracer	Address Trap	N.A.	Accumulates Copy of Last "N" Instructions Executed Read Out by Utility Dump in Response to Traps
Timeout Trap	System Real-Time Clock	Count Only Trap when Preset Count Exceeded	Counts Time Between Trapped Points in Processing Standard Dumps, when Preset Count Exceeded
External System Event Trap	Special Conditions in Controlled System	Record Only Trap & Initialize	Standard Dumps, Time Enable Other Traps Adjust System State

3-10-7-2 Support of New Requirements

In most cases, it will be found that *no additional hardware or software is required to support major software modification versus routine software maintenance.* The principal impact of new requirements is to be expected in the form of increased manpower demands and support of different modes of activity, such as review, clarification, and modification of new requirements. This will divert key manpower from software maintenance, because the software maintenance personnel will be the most knowledgeable and capable people available for the purpose. Cost and workload factors can be individually predicted for each new requirement, based on procedures available in the literature (for example, 5). *The principal problems will lie in establishing priorities and adapting schedules.*

3-10-7-3 Normal Operational Support

The primary goal of embedded computer system software maintenance planning is to provide timely solutions to system problems in support of normal mission operations. Most of the required support workload and cost will arise from software errors and may be predictable on the basis of inherent software reliability (4, 6, 7). *The principal problems will arise from the difficulty of obtain-*

ing adequate and timely information about system problems when the individual tactical equipments are widely deployed.

3-10-8 SOFTWARE MAINTENANCE FACILITY DESIGN CONSIDERATIONS

A software maintenance facility must incorporate both a comprehensive software *test* capability and sufficient software *generation* capability to enable complete program reissues as required. Test Scenario Generators and Test Drivers are required to initialize, control and monitor missionlike real-time tests. For the PHALANX system,[3] an integrated hardware–software maintenance facility is being considered (Figure 3-10-3). This implies a capability to direct the Target–Projectile Return Simulation to present signals appropriate to the target trajectory being modeled, including multiple target conditions and noise–clutter effects. Similarly, either actual mount and gun hardware or digital simulations thereof must be driven in accordance with simulated ship's motion and Weapon Control Group output data. The corresponding elements of the planned E-3A NCS[4] software maintenance facility (Figure 3-10-4) can be and are significantly less elaborate, because (1) only software maintenance is to be supported, (2) the navigation equipment and process are well understood, and (3) external factors (for example, Omega radio navigation signal properties) are not imposed by offensive tactics.

Production versions of embedded computer systems generally do not provide for comprehensive test control or real-time test data collection capability. However, hardware and software interfaces for such "debugging" access are usually available in development versions. These can be utilized to provide a range of test tools and data access capable of supporting:

Software problem analysis
Temporary patching for solution modifications
Validation of operational software releases.

3-10-9 SYSTEM TEST DRIVER OPERATING MODE OPTIONS

The test driver function indicated in Figures 3-10-3 and 3-10-4 can be implemented in several ways. In Figure 3-10-3 the most complex implementation

---

[3] The U.S. Navy PHALANX Close-In Weapon System (CIWS) is an automatic, self-contained, radar-controlled gun system designed for "last-ditch" ship defense.

[4] The U.S. Air Force E-3A Navigational Computer System (NCS) is an integrated radio-inertial navigation system designed for accurate, long-duration navigation and station keeping.

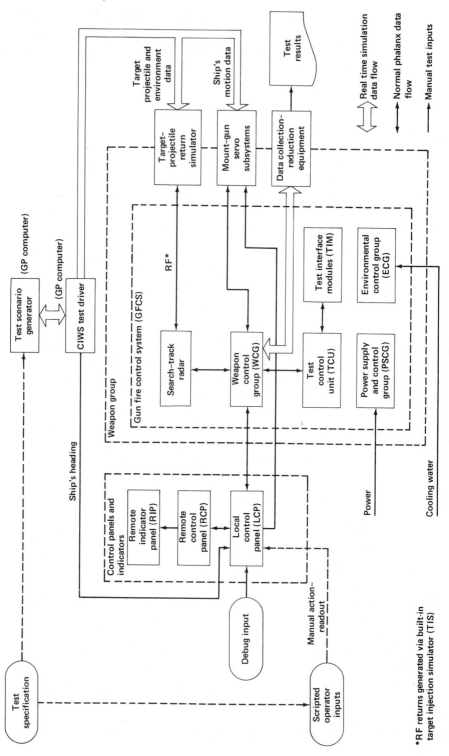

Figure 3-10-3 Possible configuration of Phalanx CIWS operational maintenance facility.

*RF returns generated via built-in target injection simulator (TIS)

214

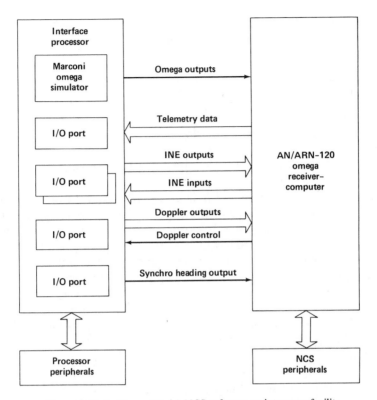

Figure 3-10-4   Planned E-3A NCS software maintenance facility.

is assumed, involving closed-loop responsiveness on the part of the driver. Other options are possible, based on the degree of realism provided by the driver.

A *static system driver* establishes and maintains a specific set of external conditions for the duration of a specific software test. Data channel timing and other mechanical reactions are provided for, but the environment does not change as a function of time. An *open-loop test driver* provides a much greater degree of test flexibility while avoiding much of the complex real-time mathematical modeling required to respond correctly to system responses. Essentially, an open-loop driver operates with a fixed script: it presents the tested system with a completely pre-determined sequence of environmental conditions.

A *closed-loop* driver simulation provides all of the advantages of the open-loop arrangement, since it can be operated in an open-loop mode if desired. At the same time, it provides the ability to continue to drive a malfunctioning system through its normal error response and back-up modes, and allows for operator intervention. The major difficulties arise from sensitivity to minor equipment variations, which may reduce the exactness and repeatability of results. Data analysis is also made difficult, since exact time-based matching is impossible in general. Both of these problems are solvable by judicious use of the open-loop mode.

3-10-9-1 Implementation Considerations

It is possible to execute and test operational software in an *emulator* or *simulator* environment, instead of the actual embedded system computer. However, there is usually a requirement for accurate reproduction of operational conditions which makes it advisable to use the actual system computer for the bulk of the testing.

There are several alternatives in the design of a test driver capability which should be examined. Many large software systems have been well-exercised by a driver program co-resident in the same computer as the tested software; the two processes operate asynchronously, "stealing" time from each other as required. However, this approach is often impractical for embedded systems because (1) the system computer is not capable of hosting an additional large program, and (2) the complications of stopping and restarting the system are too great, due to time-critical processes (such as radar return processing in the PHALANX system). The best òption appears to be the development of a real-time closed-loop driver, operating in a separate general purpose computer of appropriate power.

3-10-9-2 Special Software Maintenance Tools

Test setup for major system tests, such as simulated missions, will require *instrumentation of the embedded software* through mechanisms like those of Table 3-10-2, with provisions for generating large numbers of traps and specifying routine data collection. *The generation of test instructions by automatic preprocessors* should be investigated. If the available computer center facilities can support it, interactive data processing is a recommended way to prepare and verify test scenarios and test data collection instructions.

3-10-10 CONCLUSIONS

The preliminary planning and evaluation of strategies applicable to embedded computer systems operation and maintenance should begin with consideration of the general requirements of system software maintenance. This analysis should address at least the following:

> Applicability of actual system hardware in a "hot mockup" arrangement
> Applicability of a closed-loop, real-time driver simulation, with capability for open-loop operation

Consideration of a comprehensive scenario generation capability

Provision of capabilities for specifying and implementing test data collection and reduction

Implementation of system-hosted debugging tools

Implementation of software configuration control and system problem reporting procedures.

The outcome of this analysis effort will be reduced life cycle software cost and increased system utility, due to:

Improved software problem detection–isolation capability

Reduced software error correction time

Improved validation of the corrected software.

3-10-11 ACKNOWLEDGMENT

The work discussed herein was performed under two DoD contracts: U.S. Air Force Contract F19628-77-C-0033, "E-3A Navigational Computer System Analysis," AFSC/ESD, and U.S. Navy Contract N00024-75-C-7229, "PHALANX CIWS Engineering Support," NAVSEA PMS 404-30.

3-10-12 REFERENCES

1. *Proceedings of the Aeronautical Systems Software Workshop* (Dayton), April 1974 (see especially pp. 71–116 and 287–323).
2. Gansler, J. S., "Software Management in the Department of Defense," *Abridged Proceedings from the Software Management Conference* (Washington, D.C.), March 1976, AIAA.
3. Gansler, J. S., "The DoD Defense System Management Program—Overview," *Abridged Proceedings from the Software Management Conference* (Washington, D.C.), January 1977, AIAA.
4. *Proceedings of the 2nd International Conference on Software Engineering* (San Francisco), October 1976, IEEE Catalog No. 76CH1125-4C.
5. Wolverton, R. W., "The Cost of Developing Large-Scale Software," *IEEE Transactions on Computers,* Vol. C-23, No. 6, June 1974, pp. 615–636.
6. *Proceedings of the International Conference on Reliable Software* (Los Angeles), April 1975, IEEE Catalog No. 75CH0940-7CSR (see especially pp. 51–71, 221–245).
7. Shooman, M. L., "Software Reliability: Measurement and Models," *Proceedings of the 1975 Annual Reliability and Maintainability Symposium* (Washington), January 1975, pp. 485–489.

3-11 PERSISTENT SOFTWARE ERRORS*

Robert L. Glass

3-11-1 INTRODUCTION

It is well known that software errors vary in expense. That is, software errors which are found quickly and easily, such as syntactic errors and blatantly catastrophic errors, are detected and corrected at little cost (see Figure 3-11-1). On the other hand, those errors which elude normal software review and debug practices, and persist into the software operation–maintenance phase, may be quite expensive.

The expense connected with such errors lies partly in the cost to detect, partly in the cost to correct, and partly in the cost of an inoperable or unsafe software product. Although the first two costs are important, the third is far and away the most significant. Especially in embedded computer systems, such as those controlling aircraft in flight, or a rapid transit vehicle, or a spacecraft, software error cost may be measurable in lives as well as dollars.

Little has appeared in the literature distinguishing between errors by cost. Tools and methodologies for the detection and correction of software errors are proposed and advocated independent of their value in identifying high-expense versus low-expense errors. Software reliability practices and software reliability research which focus on this dichotomy would appear to have large payoff. This paper reports on a study which is an initial effort in that direction.

This study seeks to better understand "persistent" software errors. An error is defined to be persistent if it eludes early detection efforts and does not surface until the software is operational.

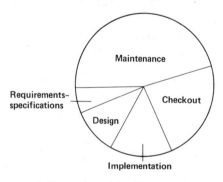

Figure 3-11-1 Error fix cost per life cycle phase.

*From *Software Soliloquies,* Computing Trends, 1981. A similar paper was published in IEEE Transactions on Software Engineering, March, 1981, Vol. SE-7, No. 2.

3-11-2 THE STUDY

In order to study those kinds of errors, two significant and mature software products were analyzed. Both are operational real-time software systems for military aircraft use. Project A involved 150 programmers at the peak person-load, and contains about a half million instructions in the operational software alone. Project B involved thirty programmers and about 100,000 instructions. Thus these software products may be considered to be typical of the state-of-the-art in large embedded computer system software.

The size of these software products is important. The point has frequently been made in the literature that large software systems and small software systems are entirely different, and that research "in the small" (using small programs or data–people populations) cannot be extrapolated to be equivalent to research "in the large" (BROO75), (BROW77), (DERE76), (GLAS79), (HORO75). This study is an example of research in the large; no other approach is likely to be meaningful in the world of large, significant software products.

The method of approach in this study was to examine project-specific software error reports. State-of-the-art methodology in embedded computer systems calls for the filing of a Software Problem Report (SPR) for each software error detected. The report provides spaces for three categories of information—(1) a symptomatic description of the problem from a user point of view, (2) a description of the problem from an internal software point of view, and (3) a description of the software correction.

Typically, large software efforts spawn hundreds or even thousands of such reports. SPRs are filed because of real software errors; because of problems which turn out to be errors not caused by software (for example, computer hardware errors); and for changes which are desired by the user but are not errors. Only the first category of problems—real software errors—was examined in this study.

The SPRs were studied in "raw" (handwritten report) form. Every attempt was made to utilize the information as the programmer reported it, in order to eliminate deletions or transcription errors which result from clerical encoding of the information, such as for a computerized database.

The thrust of the study was to divide these SPRs into categories, in order to identify the type of errors which are most prevalent. Here, an unusual approach was taken. Although error categories are well-known in the literature—TRW developed a pioneering software error category system (SUKE77)—those categories were not used in this study. Instead, the errors were allowed to "self-categorize." That is, as each SPR was reviewed, either it was assigned to (1) a category which described its own nature, or (2) a category self-generated by some previous error.

There is some controversy attached to the use of raw SPRs and the use of self-categorization.

Regarding raw SPRs, the best approach—that is, the one closest to complete knowledge of the error—would appear to be actual review of the erroneous code and the correction. This has been used by Howden in his error data studies (HOWD79). Use of raw SPRs, however, is an accurate and reproducible approach, since the SPR form is filled out by those most knowledgeable in the problem and its solution, and since SPR repositories are typically subject to configuration management practices. The decision to use raw SPRs in this case was purely pragmatic—a large number of errors can be reviewed rapidly with minimal loss of authenticity.

Regarding self-categorization, the study was built on the premise of exploring new ground. That is, to the author's knowledge, no one has studied persistent software errors per se before. To avoid the possibility that traditional error categories were not appropriate to persistent errors, the traditional categories were deliberately avoided. Self-categorization, of course, has the flaw that the judgment of the individual researcher will have some impact on the final results. However, the traditional categories discussed in SUKE77 are ambiguous enough that they share this problem.

In any case, 100 software errors from each of two projects were subjected to review at the raw SPR level via self-categorization techniques. The errors were considered to be persistent on the basis that they were the most recent errors detected on those production-status projects. In most cases, this proved to be a sufficiently valid basis. In some cases, however, the errors were spawned by the correction of other persistent errors (these are commonly called "regression errors"). Errors of this class were included in the study on the grounds that such regression errors are just as costly as nonregression persistent errors; however, these errors were allowed to self-categorize a category for themselves.

An error was allowed to tally in more than one category. No attempt was made to provide mutually exclusive categories; the emphasis was on creating a realistic summary of the data as it was analyzed, and not to force it to fit an externally applied artifice.

The process of analysis, then, was simply this: (1) project-specific, configuration-managed SPR forms, filed in chronological sequence, were examined one at a time; (2) using the "problem," "analysis," and "correction" information the nature of the error was ascertained; (3) that error was categorized into its own and/or a previously-selected category; (4) a tally was added to those categories. At the conclusion of analysis of a set of project-specific SPRs, tallies for the (variable number of) categories were summed. The categories for one project overlapped partially but not entirely with those of the other project (for example, in Table 3–11–1 note that project A had no patching or commentary errors. Presumably project A did not allow patches and did not file SPRs on commentary errors).

3-11-3 THE FINDINGS

The findings of this study appear to be significant. That is, the categorized persistent SPRs show a consistent and definite pattern. Not only is that pattern well-defined, but it is different from any predictions which might have been made in advance based on a study of the literature (see Table 3-11-1).

The major finding of the study is that a large percentage of persistent software errors are instances of the software not being sufficiently complex to match the problem being solved. It is as if the programmer's mind is straining to handle the complex interrelationships of a problem solution, and has failed. For example, a large number of such errors are the result of a predicate not having enough conditions—some flag or piece of data was not taken into account when it should have been—or of a variable not being reset to some baseline value after a major functional logic segment had finished dealing with it.

TABLE 3-11-1   Persistent Software Errors by Frequency of Occurrence (200 Errors Examined, 100 on Each Project)

Category:	Project A	Project B	Total:
1. Omitted logic (existing code too simple)	36	24	60
2. Failure to reset data	17	6	23
3. Regression error	5	12	17
4. Documentation in error (software correct)	10	6	16
5. Requirements inadequate	10	1	11
6. Patch in error	0	11	11
7. Commentary in error	0	11	11
8. IF statement too simple	9	2	11
9. Referenced wrong data variable	6	4	10
10. Data alignment error (e.g., leftmost vs. rightmost bits)	4	3	7
11. Timing error causes data loss	3	3	6
12. Failure to initialize data	4	1	5

13. Other categories of lesser importance (total four or less)—Logic too complex, compiler error, data storage overflow, expression incorrectly coded, pointer one off, dynamic allocation failure, data not included in checkpoint, microcode error, data boundary problem, macroerror, multitasking synchronizing error, erroneous initialization, naming conventions violated, logic order incorrect, interface mismatch, data reset in error, parameter mismatch, inefficient code, data declaration wrong, bad overlay, statement label at wrong place, data clobbered.

NOTE: An error was allowed to tally in more than one category. "Failure to reset data", for example, is almost always a specific instance of "omitted logic." So are "if statement too simple" and "failure to initialize data." Any error could also be a "regression error."

NOTE ALSO: "Interface mismatch" and "parameter mismatch" errors are infrequent.

Here again, it is important to distinguish between the large problem and the small problem environment. Intuitively, it is easily seen that this kind of error is much more likely to emerge in the large rather than the small problem. The interrelationships between data and logic are much more entwined and complex in the large problem environment. It has even been said that "a 25 percent increase in problem complexity leads to a 100 percent increase in program complexity" (WOOD79). And in fact, most professional programmers have built software which they then realized was, in some areas, beyond their ability to comprehend (in the sense that its results were not predictable prior to its execution).

Thus the major finding of the study is not contrary to experienced intuition. It is, however, contrary to some current directions in software research. There is an underlying presumption in many of the research-defined methodologies, such as structured programming, that simplification of the software methodologies is the solution to the problems of complex software. That presumption, based on the findings of this study and those of WOOD79, appears to be naive.

That is not to say, of course, that simplified logic is undesirable. Simplification is highly desirable, both because of its logical elegance and because it enhances such software quality attributes as reliability and maintainability. What *is* naive is the belief that, given the proper application of brilliant thought, all problem solutions may be made simple.[1] The fact of the matter is that real-world problems are anomaly-ridden and complex; and so, all too often, are their solutions. (This should never be taken, of course, as an excuse to avoid the search for problem and solution simplification).

3-11-4 WHAT TO DO ABOUT THE FINDINGS

The findings of this study are unsettling. They are unsettling not because they are a major redirection of our understandings of software problem solutions. They are unsettling because it is not at all clear what we should do about them.

Philosophically, what is needed is obvious. We need a human mind extender, one which makes it possible for the human mind to conceive problems and solutions beyond its current capacity.

That, of course, is as naive as the view that all problem solutions can be made simple. And yet, such a solution can at least be considered.

How could the mind be extended in these specific directions?

Perhaps by Very High Order Languages, which remove solution details from the domain of the programmer into the domain of the compiler (analogous to computer hardware register management being moved into the High Order Language compiler).

---

[1] See also "Structured Programming is Reductionistic!," Charles Crowley, ACM SIGPLAN Notices, May 1980, which identifies this same naiveté.

Perhaps by a design aid which manages and analyzes design details which the human mind cannot.

Perhaps by a maintenance tool which extracts from existing software its underlying design elements, and subjects them to (human-assisted?) consistency analysis.

Those answers are not very satisfying, for they are beyond the state-of-the-computer art. And yet they are promising, because they represent a level of computer application breakthrough which, if achieved, obviously transcends the software engineering problem which spawned it.

Of course, there are mundane but useful answers. If the designer, the implementer, and the tester employ a deep level of concentration and rigor, the omitted logic error is preventable or detectable. In-depth technical peer design review and peer code review can, for example, detect these errors before they become "persistent." Rigorous test case definition, especially where the test cases are driven by comprehensive specifications, can also detect most "persis-

TABLE 3-11-2 Error Category Definition

Category	Definition, Example
1. Omitted logic	Code is lacking which should be present. Variable A is assigned a new value in logic path X but is not reset to the value required prior to entering path Y.
2. Failure to reset data	Reassignment of needed value to a variable omitted. See example for "omitted logic."
3. Regression error	Attempt to correct one error causes another.
4. Documentation in error	Software and documentation conflict; software is correct. User manual says to input a value in inches, but program consistently assumes the value is in centimeters.
5. Requirements inadequate	Specification of the problem insufficient to define the desired solution.
6. Patch in error	Temporary machine code change contains an error. Source code is correct, but "jump to 14000" should have been "jump to 14004."
7. Commentary in error	Source code comment is incorrect. Program says DO I = 1, 5 while comment says "loop 4 times."
8. IF statement too simple	Not all conditions necessary for an IF statement are present. IF A < B should be IF A < B AND B < C.
9. Referenced wrong data variable	Self-explanatory
10. Data alignment error	Data accessed is not the same as data desired due to using wrong set of bits. Leftmost instead of rightmost substring of bits used from a data structure.
11. Timing error causes data loss	Shared data changed by a process at an unexpected time. Parallel task B changes XYZ just before task A uses it.
12. Failure to initialize data	Nonpreset data is referenced before a value is assigned.

Lesser categories are not defined here.

tent" errors early. Simple traditional deck checking, if properly applied, can also do the job.

The problem with these mundane but useful solutions is that, in the complex problems being solved by today's professional programmer, the necessary concentration and rigor is difficult to achieve. Still, given proper application they can be viable solutions.

3-11-5 CONCLUSION

Persistent software errors are seen to be dominated by a class of error which can be categorized as 'the failure of the problem solution to match the complexity of the problem to be solved.' Examples of such errors are predicates with insufficient conditions, and failure to reset data to some baseline value after its use in a functional logic segment.

The solution to this class of problems is difficult. Somehow, the programmer's mind must be extended to encompass complexity beyond its current capability. This is obviously a solution beyond the current state-of-the-art.

Solutions which can be effective for today's large software system producer are maintaining awareness of the problem, and spending more time analyzing complex interrelationships via peer review, program desk checking, and rigorous testing. As is already well-known, identifying those (persistent) problems early in the software life cycle can have major positive cost impact on total system cost.

3-11-6 ACKNOWLEDGMENTS

The ideas and support of Dave Feinberg, Lee MacLaren, Ron Noiseux, and Ed Presson have been important in the development of this research.

3-11-7 REFERENCES

[BROO75] *The Mythical Man-Month,* Addison-Wesley, 1975; Brooks.

Describes the experiences of and insights resulting from the development of the operating system for the IBM 360. Recommends small teams organized in specific ways, project workbooks, change-oriented organizations, effective tool usage, and a plans and controls group among other methodologies for assisting the large project manager.

[BROW77] "Impact of MPP on System Development," RADC-TR-77-121, 1977; Brown.

Describes the modern programming practices (MPP) used on a huge (up to 400 people) software development project (an anti-ballistic-missile system) at TRW. Evaluates those practices by polling technically knowledgeable participants. Finds they improve quality but have a less obvious impact on costs and schedules.

[DERE76]   "Programming-in-the-Large Versus Programming-in-the-Small," IEEE Transactions of Software Engineering, June, 1976; DeRemer and Kron.

Defines the need for a "module interconnection language" (MIL) for the large project environment. Sees the MIL as enhancing reliability through improved project management, technological communication, design support, and design documentation. Shows examples of use.

[ENDR75]   "An Analysis of Errors and Their Causes In System Programs," IEEE Transactions on Software Engineering, June, 1975; Endres.

Reviews errors detected in a large assembler-coded operating system. Studies causes of errors, and detection and prevention methodologies. States "almost half of all errors (46 percent) are found in the area of understanding the problem..."

[GLAS79]   "Small Versus Large Projects," *Software Reliability Guidebook,* Prentice-Hall, 1979; Glass.

Makes the distinction that reliability techniques for large projects should be different from those for small projects. Defines "large" and "small," and suggests value judgments for technologies to use on each.

[HORO75]   Practical Strategies for Developing Large Software Systems, Addison-Wesley, 1975; Horowitz.

A collection of papers with the common theme of solutions to large system problems. Two papers on each phase of the life cycle (except maintenance) and on the management of large projects. Well-chosen authors (Boehm, Schwartz, Royce, Wolverton, Brown, Stucki, Bratman).

[HOWD79]   "An Analysis of Software Validation Techniques for Scientific Programs," University of Victoria report DM-171-1R, 1979; Howden.

Evaluates software reliability methodologies by judging their value to identify a base of known errors. The errors are studied by reading and understanding the programs containing them.

[STAN77]   Software Acquisition Management Guidebook, Software Maintenance Volume, System Development Corp., TM-5772/004/02, Nov., 1977; Stanfield and Skrukrud.

Discusses techniques for improving the maintenance traits of acquired software. Provides ideas and checklists for maintenance-oriented review.

[SCHN79]   "An Experiment in Software Error Data Collection and Analysis," Transactions on Software Engineering, May, 1979; Schneidewind and Hoffman.

Analyzes errors and complexity measures. Concludes that program structure, measurable by complexity techniques, has a significant impact on the existence, detection, and correction of errors.

[SUKE77]   "A Multiproject Comparison of Software Reliability Models," Proceedings of the AIAA Conference on Computers in Aerospace, 1977; Sukert.

Discusses error modeling using data from a large number of projects. Evaluates different modeling techniques. Describes the Rome Air Development Center error data bank.

[WOOD79] "An Experiment on Unit Increase in Program Complexity," IEEE Transactions on Software Engineering, March, 1979; Woodfield.

Finds that software complexity increases far more rapidly than the complexity of the problem being solved.

~~~~~~

3-12   SOFTWARE VERSUS HARDWARE ERRORS*

ROBERT L. GLASS

~~~~~~

Software is the "new kid on the block" in the systems world.

Whereas engineering, accounting, and other older disciplines are firmly established, software is a new consideration and an unknown to many of those responsible for large systems development.

The result is that a mysticism and, sometimes, a resentment has grown up around the role of software in the overall project. Mature project leaders, comfortable and confident in their knowledge of established disciplines, wonder why a whole new learning experience has been thrust upon them.

To complicate matters, software is an intangible. Whereas one can see and feel a space vehicle, or an accounts receivable ledger, or even a computer, software is a mysterious concept which has no weight and occupies no volume. People who do not understand software grasp at straws to try to conceptualize it—the myths that software is "just ones and zeroes," or a magnetic tape, die hard when no more visual image of software is presented.

Finally, software people do not communicate well with people from more established disciplines. We have our noses too close to the software grindstone to have begun to understand our importance in the broader world. Worse yet, we are still pretty bad about estimating how long it takes to do a software job. When we do manage to communicate, all too often it is cryptic or bad information.

The result of this "new kid on the block problem" is that software has a bad reputation in the overall system world. Technical papers say things like "Software is that part of a computer system that is always late, always over budget, and never works" (ROON77) with an almost gleeful tone, as if to say

---

*From *Software Soliloquies,* Computing Trends, 1981. A similar paper was published in IEEE Computer, Dec., 1980. Reprinted with permission.

either "There, we hung another one on the new kid," or (if it's said by a software person) "There, I'll get more credibility (and research money) if I play the self-deprecation game."[1]

Well, then: Is software always late, over budget, and unable to work? There are lots of opinions with which to answer those questions, but is there any hard data?

This paper reports on some hard data which pertains to part of one of those questions. It is the result of an investigation of the relative frequency of computer software and hardware errors. The paper provides one answer to the question, "Is it fair to say that software never works?"

3-12-1 THE STUDY

Gathering the data which underlies the findings of this paper was surprisingly difficult. Intuition says that in a world with formal hardware and software configuration management practices, it would be easy to find configuration management records of hardware and software errors. Experience, however, confounds intuition in this matter. Within some companies, apparently not all hardware errors are logged on formal error reports. Worse yet, almost no software errors are [logged]. The only configuration-managed software errors in the early findings of this study were "Unable to load software tape into computer." Clearly, this was the wrong data!

The data dilemma, it turns out, was part of the "new kid on the block" syndrome. Only a configuration manager who understands software is able to isolate software errors properly. Too few such software-knowledgeable people are around.

Further and more innovative probing into the record-keeping of system errors finally began to produce results. Some data was gleaned from the notebooks kept on the consoles of computers by technical specialists. Other data was obtained from more formal reports on projects where the importance of software was clearly understood.

In the final analysis, the data in this report is not totally conclusive, but there are some clear supportable trends. Those findings are discussed in the next section. They stand in marked contrast to the earlier findings cited by (SHOO77), that software errors were 48 percent of a total of fifty-six real-time data acquisition system errors. But then, those findings were contradicted by another study cited by (AMST75) which showed software errors as only 12 per-

---

[1](FOST78) says software is of "poor quality"; (RAMA75) says most software is "unsuccessful;" and (WALL77) says "The authors estimate that approximately half of the flight failures of some of the major space and weapons systems have been attributable to software; and it appears that with the introduction of highly integrated (and reliable) electronics, in the future as many as 90 percent of the failures during the development of a complex system will be induced by software." These quotations should be reviewed by the reader at the end of this paper.

cent of the critical failures on a telephone electronics switching system, and still another performed by (YOUR72) which showed hardware errors clearly dominant in three separate studies.

Because of the early difficulties of gathering data, and the substantial ignorance encountered in that pursuit, it was decided to also conduct a programmer poll. The goal here was for the study not only to answer the question "Is it fair to say that software never works?", but to answer the auxiliary question "Do software people themselves know the answer to that question?" The results of that poll are, perhaps, more surprising than the "never works" findings themselves.

3-12-2 THE FINDINGS

The bottom line of this report is software has been getting a bad reliability rap. The fact of the matter is, as we can see in Table 3–12–1, for a mature system, where both computer software and hardware are at comparable levels of development, hardware appears to be three times as likely as software to fail. And, as times goes by, the ratio increases. Look at the E–3A data (these projects are explained in Table 3–12–3)—in 1978, with 1200 hardware-software errors, the ratio was 2.6 to 1 hardware. In 1979, with 2800, it was 3.3 to 1. In 1980, with 200 so far, it is 3.6 to 1.

The situation is even more dramatic—although with much less supporting data—on the MPRT project. Here, with commercial hardware and specially developed software (grown mature from high operational usage), hardware errors dominate by 13 to 1.

The CAD–CAM data tells a somewhat different story. On this project, with commercial hardware and software undergoing modification, the failure rate is dominated by software, roughly 1.6 to 1. But in the IUS data, under similar circumstances, once again hardware errors dominate, 5 to 1.

The data above should not be thought of as an attempt to shift software's

TABLE 3–12–1 Software vs. Hardware Errors

Project:	Phase		Errors		Period of Time:
	Software	Hardware	Software	Hardware	
MPRT	Production	Commercial	6	87	5 Months
E–3A	Production	Military, Production 1978	347	908	3 Months
		1979	658	2190	12 Months
		1980	46	167	2 Months
		TOTAL:	1051	3265	17 Months
CAD/CAM	Revision	Commercial	89	56	2 Years
IUS	Test	Commercial	11	60	2 Weeks

"bad reliability" image to hardware. There are good reasons for hardware's higher error rate. For one thing, many hardware errors are relatively trivial, like a bad connection or a missing element. For another, and more importantly, hardware deteriorates with age. It is inevitable—and not [due to] bad engineering—that hardware will break or wear out. Software cannot do either one.

You may be wondering what was considered a hardware error or a software error. The answer is, anything noticed and logged as such by the computer operator. In general, that means an error was something which took at least that component of the system down. No attempt is made to distinguish between "good" errors which had little system impact, and "bad errors" which took the system down for extended periods.

There's another bottom line to this report. Programmers appear to be surprisingly out of touch with the realities of hardware–software reliability (see Table 3-12-2). For example:

a. The error data tends to show that in stable production computer systems, hardware errors dominate software errors by 3 to 1. The programmers tended to believe the opposite—that in those circumstances hardware errors would be only 27 percent of the total.

b. The data implies that as the software matures, its relative error rate decreases. The programmers perceived no such trend.

These were wide variances in programmer opinions. Apparently this was a question the participating programmers simply had not really dealt with.

3-12-3 SOME CONCERNS

The data in this study seems superficially straightforward. Looked at in-depth, however, there is another story to tell.

First of all, there is the question of the meaning of comparing software and hardware errors. If there ever was an "apples and oranges" comparison, this is it. The nature of software and hardware errors is fundamentally different.

Additionally, there is the issue of multiple installations. If a software-hardware system is replicated twenty times, is it fair to say that this impacts

TABLE 3-12-2 Programmer Opinions

(From a Survey of 23 Experienced Aerospace Programmers)

"During checkout, hardware errors represent 25 percent of all errors."

"During qualification test, hardware errors represent 28 percent of all errors."

"During production, hardware errors represent 27 percent of all errors."

TABLE 3–12–3 Project Descriptions

Project:	Product:	Software Scope:	
MPRT	Experimental Rapid-Transit System	Medium-sized	27 programmers
E–3A	Radar Early-Warning Aircraft	Large:	150 programmers
CAD/CAM	Automated Aircraft Design/Manufacturing System (revision)	Small:	3 programmers
IUS	Space Vehicle (Software Simulator portion only)	Medium:	6 programmers

software error rates as much as hardware error rates? (YOUR72), for example, appears to average both hardware and software errors by dividing each by the number of installations. But twenty replications of software are not twenty times as likely to fail as one replication. (However, the proper answer is not that there is the same likelihood of failure, either, since different usage profiles will flush out different software errors.)

These questions impact this study particularly in the E–3A data. The number of computer installations in the study averaged sixteen, and varied from twelve at the beginning of the study to twenty at the end. However, there was rarely an occasion on which more than two of the computers operated simultaneously, and when there was simultaneous operation nonidentical sets of input data were processed. Thus the multiple installation issue is badly muddied for this data.

Simplistic answers to these questions were used in this study. All errors were treated alike, for one. Both total hardware and total software errors were tallied independent of the multiple installation question, for another. This approach is not entirely satisfying, but it appears to be consistent with previous studies of this kind (for example, [YOUR72]).

3-12-4 CONCLUSIONS

The findings of this study are fairly conclusive. Software, the new kid on the block, is doing all right—at least in the reliability realm. Statements that software "does not work" appear to be grossly exaggerated. However, surprisingly enough, programmers are apparently as unaware of this finding as everyone else.

This paper should not be used to support any other conclusions. It does not, for example, support the conclusion that hardware engineers must charge out and do better. There are some rational reasons why hardware could be expected to fail more frequently than software.

Nor, for example, does it support the conclusion that either software or hardware reliability people may rest on their oars. The literature is rich with recent ideas on how the reliability job can be done better (for example, (GILL80), (GLAS79), (MYER76), (RAND78), and (WULF75)).

This is, rather, a credibility study, performed to investigate the "poor software" claims of an all-too-large segment of the literature. As we have seen, the apparently prevailing opinion that software "never works," is of "poor quality," is "unsuccessful," or is responsible for "half of the . . . failures" is just plain wrong.

It is important to note that this is but one study in a series of needed studies. For one, more studies similar to this and the one cited by SHOO77 are needed. Do commercial computer vendors, for example, track this kind of data? Do their findings differ from these essentially aerospace ones?

For another, we need some data on the rest of the software bad rap. Is software really always late? Is it really always over budget? What is software's actually measured performance against older and more established disciplines?

The problem no longer is "shall we use software in this problem solution?" Software is the way of the digital-computer-controlled future. The problem is "how can we come to better understand what software is and is not?" This study has been an attempt to answer a small part of that very important question.

3-12-5 ACKNOWLEDGMENTS

The motivation to explore this area came from preliminary findings by Larry Broad. The bulk of the data was provided by Dave Webber. The opinions were provided by a collection of programmers for whom I have the highest respect.

3-12-6 REFERENCES

[AMST75] "Software Reliability: An Overview," *Reliability and Fault Tree Analysis,* SIAM, 1975; Amster and Shooman

[FOST78] "It's Time to Get Tough About Computer Software," Quality Progress, Aug. 1978; Foster

[GILL80] "A Unified Test Harness System for Avionics Software Development," Proceedings of NAECON '80; Gill and Thompson

[GLAS79] *Software Reliability Guidebook,* Prentice-Hall, 1979; Glass

[MYER76] *Software Reliability,* Wiley-Interscience, 1976; Myers

[RAMA75] "Testing Large Software with Automated Software Evaluation Systems," IEEE Transactions on Software Engineering, March 1975; Ramamoorthy and Ho

[RAND78] "Reliability Issues in Computing System Design," Computing Surveys, June 1978; Randell, Lee and Treleaven

[ROON77] "Currently Available Microprocessor Software," Proceedings of International Microcomputers/Minicomputers/Microprocessors '77, 1977; Rooney

[SHOO77] Comments in the Introduction to *Software Reliability,* an Infotech State-of-the-Art Report, 1977; Shooman

[YOUR72] "Reliability Measurements for Third Generation Computer Systems," Proceedings of the 1972 Annual Reliability and Maintainability Symposium; Yourdon

[WALL77] "Pragmatic Software Reliability Prediction," Proceedings of the 1977 Annual Reliability and Maintainability Symposium; Wall and Ferguson

[WULF75] "Reliable Hardware–Software Architecture," IEEE Transactions on Software Engineering, June 1975; Wulf

∼∼

3-13 INDEPENDENT VERIFICATION AND VALIDATION*

DONALD REIFER

∼∼

Independent Verification and Validation activities are aimed at providing systematic assurance that software will do what it is supposed to do and nothing more. This is accomplished by having an independent agency objectively critique the developer's products. IV and V concentrates on identifying requirements and design errors early in the life cycle and verifies, through independent test and evaluation, that the software is mechanized properly later on. Its benefits include:

(1) Early identification of ambiguous, ill-defined, and inadequate software requirements.
(2) Early and continued emphasis on test planning.
(3) Detection and correction of improperly mechanized designs and code.
(4) Improved visibility into the detailed status of the software development activity as it progresses.

---

*From Airborne Systems Software Acquisition Engineering Guidebook for Verification, Validation and Certification, Sept. 1978, ASD/ENAIA, Wright-Patterson AFB OH 45433.

(5) Reduced incidences of software errors once the system is operational.

(6) Ease of maintenance once the system is operational.

The potential benefits of IV and V are not free. Experience indicates that IV and V activities cost from 20 to 60 percent of that expended for software development. Because of the cost, an IV and V activity should be initiated only when it is economically justified in terms of life cycle benefits. Examples of candidate systems for IV and V are as follows:

> Software with a high cost of failure (for example, space systems).
>
> Software for which the cost of error detection through operational use is greater than the cost of IV and V (for example, aircraft operational flight programs).
>
> Real-time software which must work under all scenarios (for example, range or nuclear safety programs).

3-13-1 PERFORMER ORGANIZATION OPTIONS

The Verification and Validation function can be performed by any or all of the following:

> An independent group.
>
> The government organically.
>
> An independent contractor team.

All three of these options have been used successfully on avionics projects. A chart summarizing the advantages and disadvantages as well as the scope of the effort supported is included as Table 3-13-1. Each of the options is discussed in more detail in the following paragraphs.

3-13-1-1 Independent Test Group

The first performer option to be examined is the Independent Test Group (ITG). Basically, an ITG is an organizational entity created as part of the development contractor's team to be responsible for independently testing and evaluating the software development group's products. ITG characteristics are as follows:

(1) The ITG typically reports to the test or integration manager, while the development group reports to the engineering manager. This preserves objectivity.

TABLE 3-13-1 IV and V Performer Alternatives

Alternative	V and V Scope Realized	Comments
Independent Test Group	• Independent Testing	• Available technical capabilities limited: best people usually assigned to development effort • Tool independency not maintained • Visibility limited • Lowest cost • Questionable objectivity
Government Organic	• Independent Testing • Limited Systems Analysis and Audit Roles • Critical Element Analysis	• Available government resources limited • Tool independence maintained • Facilitates training and transition to operational role • Improved management span of control

Independent Contractor Team	• Broad IV and V Capability
	  • Systems Engineering Support
	  • Independent Testing
	  • Audit Role
	  • Independent Analysis
		• Contractual commitment to do good job
		• Tool independence maintained
		• Provides second source for development
		• Highest cost
		• Objective and proven approach

(2) The ITG can be staffed internally or subcontracted. Either arrangement has proven satisfactory as long as the reporting independence is preserved.

(3) The ITG's job is test-oriented. It does not purport to accomplish a full IV and V. . . .

(4) The development contractor's program or facility manager is the final authority for settling disputes between the ITG and the development group.

(5) The ITG tends to use the same tools and facilities that the development group uses [on its] job. These could introduce the same errors and should be avoided.

Advantages and disadvantages of using an ITG are summarized in Table 3-13-2. As seen in the table, the main advantage of an ITG, its test orientation, is also a major disadvantage. The ITG is brought aboard specifically to test the developed software. [The group] analyzes the front-end products for testability, not correctness. Their primary goal is to find errors and to bring them to the attention of the developer for correction. The ITG assumes errors exist in the

TABLE 3-13-2   Independent Test Group Evaluation

Advantages	Disadvantages
• Test process oriented	• Available technical capabilities limited
• Assures early test planning	• Best people assigned to development effort
• Clearly defined test objectives	• Tool independency not maintained
• Greater comprehensiveness in testing	• External visibility limited
• Experience continuity	• Objectivity questionable
• Builds on accumulated test experience	• Lack of concentration on front-end
• Familiarity with use of test tools	
• Least cost	

software and uses every trick of the trade to identify them during testing. Unfortunately, front-end analysis is sacrificed in this arrangement. Another major disadvantage of this approach is the questionable objectivity of the results. When development and testing are under the control of one contractor, pressures can be exerted to dilute or eliminate embarassing discoveries.

Guidelines for use of an ITG are provided in Table 3-13-3. Projects which are characterized by low to medium cost and risk seem to benefit most from an ITG approach.

3-13-1-2 Government Organic

The second performer option to be examined is Government Organic (GO). In this option, the government assumes the responsibility for conducting IV and V during either the early stages or during the operation and maintenance phase of the project. In either case, government personnel review the developer's products and provide feedback as to its correctness.

The GO approach offers the government many advantages. When properly conducted, it gets the user and supporting commands involved early. This early involvement fosters a team atmosphere. It also assists in providing essential user and supporter feedback to the developer for incorporation into his trade studies and requirements specifications. The GO approach can be characterized as follows:

- A government team of civil servants and military personnel assumes the responsibility for IV and V either during development or at the start of operations and maintenance. . . .
- The government team accomplishes the IV and V tasks . . . according to agreed upon schedules using its own or a mix of government and contractor resources.
- The government team maintains facilities and tools that are independent of the development contractors. The tools are either developed by the

TABLE 3-13-3 Performer Selection Guidelines

Factor	Independent Test Group	Government Organic	Independent Contractor Team
Type of Project	Consider for any avionics project.	Consider for large projects or small projects which are upgrades of current capabilities.	Consider for any avionics project.
Technical Risk	Consider when limited risk in requirements and limited exploitation of new technology.	Consider when there is large risk in requirements or schedules.	Consider when there is large risk in requirements and in implementation mistakes.
Criticality	Use when there is an identifiable critical function.	Use when identified critical functions and/or maintenance requirements justify IV and V.	Use for full range of criticality as justified by cost–benefit analysis.
Developer's Experience	Consider whenever developer has extensive experience in technical application area.	Consider whenever developer has limited experience in the user and supporter applications areas and these areas are essential for mission success.	Consider whenever developer lacks experience or is using new methods.
Available Dollars	Consider when there is a requirement for IV and V but limited funds.	Consider after agreement is reached as to which agency will do what task and contribute what resources (dollars and people). Maintain reserves as contingency for contracting the IV and V in case of emergency.	Allocate sufficient funds to accomplish the tasks. . . .
Available Personnel	Use when there are severe limitations in the number of personnel available.	Consider if the appropriate number of qualified and trained personnel can be made available.	Use if only a limited number of personnel available. Have them manage effort.

government or transitioned for their use from an independent contractor source.

Advantages and disadvantages of using a GO approach are summarized in Table 3-13-4. The major advantage of this approach is the government's improved span of control. By conducting IV and V themselves, the government reduces the number of contracts it has to manage and the related administrative burden. It creates a larger and more talented team of technical and managerial specialists who will work with their contractors to ensure the technical adequacy of their products. Such teams are synergistic when adequately staffed. Unfortunately, acquiring the people to staff such teams is difficult. This is the major disadvantage of the approach.

Guidelines for use of a GO approach are provided in Table 3-13-3. Projects which are characterized by long life and frequent changes seem to benefit the most from a GO approach. . . .

3-13-1-3 Independent Contractor Team

The final performer option to be examined is the Independent Contractor Team (ICT). This option assumes that the government contracts with a contractor or contractor team to perform an IV and V of the development contractor's products.

The ICT is the most commonly used approach for IV and V. Its wide use is predicated on the fact that most Project Offices (POs) find it easier to get money allocated than people. The ICT approach can be characterized as follows:

A contractor or contractor team is selected competitively to perform IV and V. A source election is held and a contract is negotiated and signed.

The ICT accomplishes the IV and V tasks called out in their contract according to an agreed upon schedule and an agreed to budget. The contractual IV and V tasks reflect those contained in the VVMP. . . .

TABLE 3-13-4 Government Organic Evaluation

Advantages	Disadvantages
• All of those for ITG (except cost)	• Available government resources limited
• Improved management span of control	• Hard to get slots and good people to fill them
• Fewer contracts to manage	
• Improved communications	• People continuity difficult to maintain
• Facilitates training and transition to [operational] role	• Lead times for equipment acquisition can be prohibitive
• Objectivity least questionable	• Additional cost
• Tool independence maintained	
• Excellent visibility into critical areas	

TABLE 3-13-5 Independent Contractor Team Evaluation

Advantages	Disadvantages

• All of those for ITG (except cost)
• Contractual commitment to do a good job
  • Ensures resource availability
  • Provides performance incentives
• Provides second source for development
• Objective and proven approach on large systems
• Tool independence maintained
• Excellent visibility into critical areas
	• Additional resources needed
	  • Source selection must be held
	  • Another contract must be managed
	• Potential communications problems and organizational conflicts
	• Large additional cost

The ICT is systems engineering-oriented. They concentrate on front-end analysis activities in hopes of identifying errors early in the development. The ICT develops and maintains facilities and tools that are independent of the development contractors. The tools can be transitioned to a GO team at the start of the maintenance phase, if desired.

Advantages and disadvantages of using an ICT approach are summarized in Table 3-13-5. The ICT represents a compromise which can help solve manpower problems. The major benefits of the GO approach can be captured at the cost of money and a limited number of personnel using the ICT approach. In addition, the ICT approach can set the stage for orderly transition to GO maintenance and provides a second source for development. The major disadvantage of the approach is its cost. However, this can be justified in many instances in terms of return on investment.

Guidelines for use of an ICT approach are provided in Table 3-13-3. Projects which are characterized by high technology and high cost of failure seem to benefit the most from the ICT approach. . . .

3-13-2 TASKS

A list of representative IV and V tasks, major subtasks, and appropriate organization(s) to perform them is illustrated in Table 3-13-6. Each task is briefly discussed in the following sub-paragraphs.

3-13-2-1 System Specification Verification

System specification verification is the Verification and Validation activity conducted . . . to ensure that the system–system segment being considered will fulfill its mission goals and objectives. The IV and V agency is typically brought

TABLE 3-13-6   Typical IV&V Tasks

Task	Subtasks	Performer
System Specification Verification	• V and V planning • Requirements analysis • Documentation review	• Government Organic (GO) • Independent Contractor Team (ICT)
Tool Development and Maintenance	• Tool evaluation • Tool development • Installation and demonstration • Training • Tool maintenance	• GO • ICT • Independent Test Group (ITG)
Software Requirements Verification	• Requirements analysis • Critical requirements identification • Documentation review	• GO • ICT
Software Design Verification	• Design analysis • Performance analysis • Documentation review	• GO • ICT
Program Verification	• Code analysis • Machine level testing • Documentation review	• GO • ICT • ITG
Software Validation	• Formal testing • DT and E review • Documentation review	• GO • ICT • ITG
Meeting Support	• Working groups • Reviews and audits • Management	• GO • ICT • ITG
Special Studies	• Quick turnaround studies • Design analysis trades	• ICT
Configuration and Data Management Support	• Configuration management • Data management	• ICT • GO

on contract just after [approval of the system requirements.] They prepare a Verification and Validation Master Plan and initiate their tool development activity during this period. They review the validation phase products and actively participate in the design reviews. . . .

3-13-2-2 Tool Development and Maintenance

As part of the verification and validation planning activity, the IV and V agency will identify an integrated set of tools for use throughout the life cycle. Some tools can be used as is or with minor adaptations. Others will have to be developed. . . . If delivered, the completed tools should be installed and demonstrated prior to being accepted. User-oriented training should be provided to facilitate both the government's understanding of the tool's capabilities and or the transfer of IV and V responsibility from a contractor to a government organization. Tool maintenance is provided as required. . . .

3-13-2-3 Software Requirements Verification

Software requirements verification is the Verification and Validation activity conducted prior to the end of the Validation Phase which ensures that the software requirements are an adequate translation of the system requirements allocated to software and that implementation is feasible. The IV and V agency evaluates the developer's products to ensure their technical adequacy and to identify those critical requirements for which . . . IV and V is economically justified. Requirements are analyzed and are sometimes independently derived in order to verify their viability. . . .

3-13-2-4 Software Design Verification

Software design verification is the Verification and Validation activity conducted to ensure that . . . the software design represents a clear, consistent, and accurate translation of the software requirements, and that the key algorithms perform with the required precision and accuracy. The IV and V agency evaluates the developer's products to ensure their technical adequacy and to contribute to the design refinement process. Key algorithms may either be simulated or rederived in order to demonstrate their technical viability. Timing and sizing budgets are monitored. . . .

3-13-2-5 Program Verification

Program verification is the Verification and Validation activity conducted . . . to independently assure that the actual code developed is compliant with the approved design specification. The IV and V agency's responsibilities are to independently test and evaluate the developer's products using separate facilities and tools. . . .

3-13-2-6 Software Validation

Software validation is the Verification and Validation activity conducted . . .
to ensure that every requirement is adequately tested and that the software has
been adequately shaken down from a system perspective. The IV and V agency
tests and evaluates the code that was identified as critical in parallel with both
its program verification and the developer's test activities. . . .

3-13-2-7 Meeting Support

As part of mainstream Verification and Validation activities, the IV and V
agency will participate in a number of meetings. These meetings include working groups established to get the IV and V and development agencies working
together, formal and informal (for example, design inspections, code walkthroughs, and so on) reviews and audits, and a variety of project management
meetings.

3-13-2-8 Special Studies

If desired, the IV and V agency can contractually support either quick turnaround or design analysis trade studies. Quick-turnaround studies are typically
conducted to work a specific problem area and recommend solutions. Design
analysis trade studies are normally conducted to document the results of an important trade that impacts the software.

3-13-2-9 Configuration and Data Management Support

In a number of instances, noncritical configuration and data management tasks
can be off-loaded to the IV and V agency. These activities would be in addition
to those normally considered a part of the IV and V job. . . .

3-13-3 CONTRACTUAL PROVISIONS

Typical contracting approaches are summarized in Table 3-13-7 for an IV and
V effort performed by an ICT. Because of the degree of cost risk and the need
for flexibility, a cost type contract with provisions for incentives (either incentive or award fee) seems the most advantageous. This type of contractual relationship allows the government and the IV and V contractor to share the
risk. . . .

TABLE 3-13-7 Generally Accepted Rules for Selecting Contract Types

Cost-Plus-Fixed-Fee. Appropriate where "level of effort" is required or where high technical and cost uncertainties exist.

Cost-Plus-Award-Fee. Appropriate where conditions for use of a CPFE are presented but where improved performance is also desired and where performance cannot be measured objectively.

Cost-Plus-Incentive-Fee (Cost Incentive Only). Appropriate where a given level of performance is desired and confidence in achieving that performance level is reasonably good but where technical and cost uncertainties are excessive for use of a fixed-price incentive.

Cost-Plus-Incentive-Fee (Multiple Incentives). Appropriate where expectation of achieving an acceptable performance is good but improvement over that level is desired and where technical and cost uncertainties are excessive for use of FPI.

Fixed-Price-Incentive (Cost Incentive Only). Appropriate where confidence in achieving performance is high but cost and technical uncertainties can be reasonably identified.

Fixed-Price-Incentive (Multiple Incentives). Appropriate where improved performance is desired and technical and cost uncertainties are reasonably identifiable.

Firm-Fixed-Price. Appropriate where performance has already been demonstrated and technical and cost uncertainties are low.

Firm-Fixed-Price (With Incentives Added). Appropriate where improved performance or schedule is desired and technical and cost uncertainties are low.

3-13-4 TAILORED COMPLIANCE LEVELS

Verification and Validation should be tailored to the unique . . . overall system requirements. There is no single approach that can be universally applied across the board to structuring the effort. Rather, human judgment is needed to adapt the concepts and methods to the specifics of the job. This section defines three levels of Verification and Validation that can be used in constructing a responsive IV and V program. Each level is briefly summarized as follows:

(1) Level 1: Critical Function Identification–Consultant. The IV and V agency directs its efforts toward identifying and monitoring the critical functions. Consultation is provided to work specific problems as they occur and to constructively critique the developer's products. The effort is characterized by review and has limited tool development and testing associated with it.

(2) Level 2: Design Review–Selected Item Evaluation. The IV and V agency does selected testing in addition to Level 1 activities. The testing is accomplished to independently verify and validate that the critical functions identified during specification verification have been properly mechanized in the code. The IV and V agency may also be tasked to perform additional surveillance in the test area.

(3) Level 3: System-Level Verification and Validation. The IV and V agency does a complete Verification and Validation of the developer's products.

TABLE 3-13-8   Comparison of V and V Levels

Level 1	• Constructively critique developer's documentation
	• Participate actively in milestone reviews
	• Identify critical requirements and design problems and recommend solutions
	• Provide selected technical consultants
	• Monitor development
Level 2	• Level 1, and
	• Analyze selected critical functions using available tools
	• Spot check design performance
	• Evaluate alternate approaches
	• Conduct limited testing
	• Evaluate critical development test results
	• Perform selected audits
	• Develop selected tools
Level 3	• Levels 1 and 2, and
	• Independently analyze requirements and design
	• Rederive key algorithms
	• Confirm technical adequacy
	• Independently test and evaluate operational software
	• Conduct nominal and stress tests
	• Identify discrepancies
	• Develop additional tools
	• Provide additional support functions
	• Special studies
	• Meetings
	• Configuration and Data Management

These three levels of Verification and Validation are compared in Table 3-13-8.

Selection of the appropriate level is governed by many parameters. Several of the more important of these include: applicable local policy, available resources, impact of an operational error, and criticality of application. Selection guidelines based upon these four parameters are offered in Table 3-13-9. The selected level should be applied to:

All software development phases
All change requests
All deliverable products

An IV and V program can apply different levels to deliverable products if deemed appropriate.

TABLE 3-13-9 IV and V Level Selection Guidelines

Level 1	Level 2	Level 3
• Consider for all applications	• Consider for potentially critical applications	• Consider for all critical applications • Use for nuclear or safety critical applications
• Consider when PO has severe budget limitations	• Consider when PO has staff and budget limitations	• Consider when PO has serious staff limitations
	• Consider when developer has limitations in a specific technical area	• Consider when developer is new to application area and has recognizable limitations
• Consider when cost of error is moderate, but IV&V can be justified	• Consider when error could jeopardize mission success, but cost is hard to quantify	• Consider when impact of error is serious enough to justify cost
• Consider for moderately critical applications	• Consider when there are potential critical requirements that need crystallization	• Consider only when criticality of application is high enough to justify costs

3-13-5 COST ESTIMATING

Guidelines for estimating the total cost in terms of percentage of the software development cost for the three levels of Verification and Validation . . . are presented in Table 3-13-10. The guidelines assume that the developer's effort has been appropriately scoped in terms of the following nine factors per deliverable software product:

(1) Number of instructions
(2) Programming language
(3) Type and criticality of software
(4) Requirements volatility
(5) Difficulty
(6) Personnel experience and mix
(7) Programming practices
(8) Documentation requirements
(9) Security level

Variation in any of these factors during the course of software development can significantly impact the projected cost of the effort. Therefore, it pays to understand the application thoroughly before venturing an estimate.

TABLE 3-13-10   IV and V Cost Estimation Guidelines

Level	Cost Relationships	Comments
3	30 to 60 Percent of Development Cost	• Cost Significantly Impacted by: • Hardware Constraints • Software Size and Difficulty • Schedule Inflexibility
2	20 to 40 Percent of Development Cost	• Cost Significantly Impacted by: • Documentation Requirements • Tool Development Needs
1	10 to 30 Percent of Development Cost	• Cost Significantly Impacted by: • Schedule Delays

Cost of all options is impacted by:
  • Developer's Knowledge and Approach
  • IV and V Agency's Experience and Personnel
  • Security Level

A typical allocation of resources to the different IV and V activities is shown in Figure 3–13–1. This distribution will vary depending upon the nature of the work to be performed. . . .

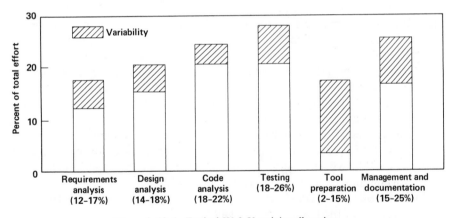

Figure 3–13–1 Typical IV & V activity allocation.

3-13-6 INTERFACE CONTROL

No matter which contractual option is selected, there will be interface problems between the various agencies involved. People resent the fact that other people are checking their work. Team spirit must be built and "ruffled feathers" smoothed. . . . The consequences of inaction are dire. Both teams will fight each other instead of working together during the critical front-end phases of the development cycle. The following four approaches have been used effectively to reduce the potential problem:

Working Groups
Informal Information Channels
Third-Party Arbitration
Management Agreement

Each approach is explained in subsequent paragraphs.

Working groups are formally chartered collections of key personnel who periodically meet to work common problems. The purpose of working groups is to get the working level personnel collaborating with each other in a complementary manner. . . . As the effort progresses, the group should meet more frequently. Using the group to prescreen and reach agreement on discrepancies has proved [to be] a successful means of reducing organizational friction. Joint action items calling for a combined recommended solution to a problem area is a useful approach to team building.

Another approach used to get the players working together is the establishment of informal information channels. All too often the Project Office acts as the only interface between agencies. This frequently creates an information bottleneck. Allowing for contractor-to-contractor information exchanges through established and controlled channels allows for effective supervision and timely contractor action. . . .

The third-party arbitration approach should be used only when there is a major technical disagreement between agencies. . . . This has been employed to get a decision made in a manner that doesn't reduce team effectiveness. All parties [are] usually more ready to accept the opinion of an outside expert than that of another team member.

The management agreement approach is one where management representatives of the organizations involved mutually agree as to how and when the interfaces will be worked. Agreements are made (both verbal and written) and joint working procedures are published. Typically, these agreements are made at the start of the IV and V effort. This helps establish what the roles and responsibilities of the team members will be.

3-13-7 ORGANIZATION STRUCTURE

A typical functional organizational structure for an IV and V agency is illustrated in Figure 3-13-2. The function of each of the four groups and how it changes as the project transitions from development to operations and maintenance is explained in the following text.

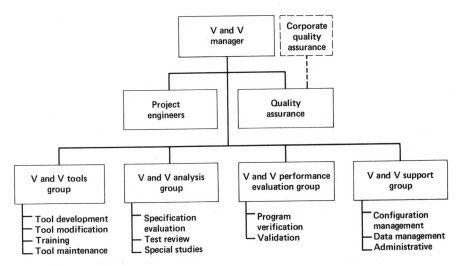

Figure 3-13-2 Typical IV & V organizational structure.

The V and V Tools Group is responsible for the following functions:

- Tool Development
- Tool Modification
- Training
- Tool Maintenance

Because tools should be user-oriented, each of the other three groups provide requirements to the Tools Group and participate in acceptance testing and training. The Tools Group is used throughout the life cycle to provide a level of support.

The V and V Analysis Group is responsible for the following functions:

- Specification Evaluation
- Test Review
- Special Studies

Again, they are active throughout the life cycle. Some of the key personnel from this group become the nucleus of the Performance Evaluation Group. In this way, knowledge gained can be used–applied during code evaluation efforts. As transition to operations and maintenance nears, they become actively involved in the analysis of change requests. They provide an independent assessment of the impact of the change and evaluate whether or not IV and V is warranted.

The Verification and Validation Performance Evaluation Group is responsible for accomplishing program verification and software validation. They work with the developer and independently test and evaluate the code. During operations and maintenance, they reverify and revalidate the program as changes are introduced and as circumstances require.

The V and V Support Group is responsible for providing configuration management, data management, and administrative support as required. Administrative support includes financial management functions of the IV and V contract.

Because quality assurance like IV and V requires an independent reporting channel, it is broken out as a separate organizational entity reporting to the V and V Manager. The quality assurance manager should also report on a dotted line to some higher level quality assurance authority so that leverage can be exerted on the V and V Manager.

In the case where there are multiple packages being verified and validated, a project engineer should be assigned the responsibility of ensuring that tasks are completed on time and within budget. Project engineers should report to the V and V Manager. Because there are different discipline mix requirements during the project lifetime, the nature of this staff will change over time. . . .

REAL-TIME TOOLS
AND EXECUTIVES

Earlier chapters of this book have shown that real-time software is beginning to appear all around us in our daily lives, real-time applications software is amazingly diverse, and underlying real-time methodologies are far less diverse and are even predictable.

In fact, as James Martin showed us in Chapter 2, real-time software almost always consists of the application software, the supervisory system, and the support programs. As we have seen, that breakdown of function is *very* predictably true of real-time software.

Chapter 4 discusses the latter two elements of Martin's breakdown. Supervisory systems, frequently called "executives," are discussed by the first two authors. The third paper talks about the general class of support software, and in the last two we look at some specifics of one type of support software—the high-order language compiler.

Earlier in this book Niklaus Wirth characterized real-time as the most complex of all software. In the first paper of this chapter, James Martin focuses on what is probably the most complicated part of this complex genre, the executive, and with amazing verbal dexterity reduces that complexity to simplicity. Martin's work is well over ten years old and is still amazingly appropriate as an easy-to-read introduction to real-time executives. Martin concentrates on the scheduling aspects of the executive and leads us through the options open to the designer of a scheduler for some typical real-time executive systems, complete with sample flowcharts.

In marked contrast to Martin's simplicity, the next paper, by Lee MacLaren, is a thorough analysis—from the point of view of an experienced designer of real-time executives—of the problems and solutions introduced by the new Department of Defense programming language, Ada. Ada is a language designed not only to interface well with operating systems and executives but to provide facilities for their *creation* as well. This presents a dilemma to the experienced designer of traditional executives, because the traditional ways appear, at first, to be incompatible with the Ada methods. MacLaren describes the design elements of several levels of traditional executives, then shows how the facilities of Ada may provide evolutionary support

249

to creating those executives in some new and improved ways. The paper identifies some levels of executives which are not compatible with the new Ada mechanisms.

The problem of squeezing all the needed horsepower out of a time-constrained real-time system is often complex and uncomfortable. In section 4–3, Dennis Leinbaugh looks at the scheduling algorithms which an executive might employ to solve this problem. In this case, the problem is a so-called "hard" real-time system, where failure to complete a task, once started, is a failure of the system. The theory of scheduling is surveyed, and an algorithm is developed for determining the response times that can be guaranteed.

Section 4–4 by Chris Gill and Bill Garrison scopes the contents of a good set of support software for a real-time application. Their system, designed to support assembler-language coding, supplies a cross assembler, a generalized linker, a global cross-reference lister, and a source file comparator. But the authors present these tools in the context of a portable system which can quickly be transported from one project's host computer to that of another. They say the portable system is needed because (1) their company works on several different real-time projects, and (2) there is seldom sufficient lead time on a new project to allow for creating a support system from scratch. Their solution is the creation of an abstract machine for which all support software is written, and the construction of a simulator for that machine on the actual host machine. (The University of California at San Diego Pascal P-Code system is probably the most famous user of this approach.) The authors confront the major problem of this approach—loss of efficiency—and point out that the 3 to 1 slowdown factor is usually tolerable for *support* software. This would not, of course, be acceptable for real-time *application* software.

The most important tool in the support software world is generally considered to be the language processor. In sections 4–5 and 4–6, we deal with a specific kind of language processor—the compiler for a high-order language (HOL)—and with a specific aspect of that compiler—efficiency of generated object code. In the timing- and sizing-constrained real-time software world, compiler code generation efficiency is so important that frequently high-order languages are avoided because their efficiency penalty is too high. These two papers confront that issue head-on.

The first paper, by R. E. Walters, offers what I believe is the most important insight yet provided into the penalties of high-order language. Written in England and presented at a conference in Finland, this paper is not in the mainstream of computing literature. Yet it presents an analysis which I believe is more accurate than the typical mainstream article on the same subject. According to Walters, HOL efficiency is enormously variable, and that variability is dependent on three things: (1) the computer for which code is being generated, (2) the application, and (3) the compiler quality. Using four benchmark programs written in both assembler and CORAL 66 (an English real-time standard language), Walters found inefficiency of storage varying from 20 percent to 80 percent worse than assembler, and inefficiency of timing ranging from 30 percent to 340 percent. This is in considerable disagreement with the frequently expressed 15 to 20 percent degradation of HOL code in the mainstream literature. Walters says his findings "emphasize the dangers of quoting a single expansion ratio." The conclusion here is *not* that HOL is inappropriate for real-time software. Many case studies, including that in section 4-6, demonstrate that to be false. The conclusion is that care must be used in the choice of computers and compilers, and in the breakdown of HOL versus assembler application code in order to avoid serious problems.

Section 4-6 contrasts dramatically with Walters' study. In this paper, by Fred Martin, a 15 percent maximum degradation for HOL code is already a contractual fact, and the problem is to measure whether it has been achieved. A friendly competition evolves between a team of assembly program experts and a team of HOL experts to write the benchmark programs via which the conformance to the 15 percent maximum will be measured. The ground rules are essentially that (1) the assembly programmers must conform to compiler-defined interfaces, such as subroutines calls and database layout, and (2) the competitors may take as long as they like to refine their code. The outcome showed the measured inefficiencies to be: sizing 11 to 13 percent, timing 9 to 11 percent. Why are these figures so dramatically different from Walters'? The answer lies partially in the ground rules. For example, it was easy for the HOL programmers to tweak and retweak their code to get improvements, whereas the assembly people were reluctant to revise their sequences once coded. Thus we see that the two apparently contradictory papers may not conflict at all. On an average, and with much work (facilitated by the ease of changing HOL code), 15 percent HOL degradation is achievable. But specific sections of code, or code from mediocre compilers, may not come anywhere near that figure. (It is interesting to note that programmer experience had a 17 to 25 percent impact on code timing and sizing, according to an aside in the Martin study.)

In this book a clear distinction is made between language processors (compilers) and languages. The quality of the language processor, discussed as a tool in this chapter, can make or break system performance, and therefore it assumes a particularly dramatic role in real-time work. The quality of the language, discussed in Chapter 5, is also important but in an entirely different way. In real-time software, a top-notch compiler for a mediocre language may be preferable to a mediocre compiler for a top-notch language.

4-1   THE TOP EXECUTIVE*

JAMES MARTIN

In the real-time world it is not possible to plan ahead with exactitude. Except in the simplest scientific systems in which instruments are scanned cyclically, events occur in an unscheduled manner. The demands on the system will vary from moment to moment in an unpredictable fashion.

At the center of most real-time systems there is, therefore, a scheduling routine which looks periodically at the current demands on the system and decides what program will operate next. Control returns to this central scheduling routine frequently enough to ensure that the demands on the system are met.

The sets of rules that are used for scheduling the work differ considerably from one system to another, depending upon its needs. The scheduling routine scans the current status of messages or system functions and, according to its rules, transfers control to the required program. All the programs are in a sense subroutines of this top executive.

This section discusses the needs of the central scheduling routine and gives examples from different types of systems.

A scheduling routine is likely to be entered whenever an Application Program or segment of program ends its work, and the decision must be made what to do next. If the Application Program, for example a linear programming routine, takes a long time, interrupts may cause the scheduling routine to be entered. The interrupts could be caused by new transactions arriving, or they might be periodic interrupts caused by a clock.

A simple example of a central scheduling routine . . . might be the following: A routine which is entered very frequently scans the queues of items that may be waiting for processing. There is no priority differentiation between the messages, except that nonreal-time messages are only processed when there is enough time and core storage available to prevent the nonreal-time work from interfering with the real-time work. If there are no items currently requiring the central processor and if the queues are empty, the scheduling routine cycles in a closed loop waiting for new additions.

In this example, items in the Work-in-Progress Queue requiring work are attended to before the items in the New Input Queue. The reason for this is that partially processed items normally tie up more core storage than new messages. It is desirable to release this storage as soon as possible; otherwise an emergency situation may arise when the system becomes short of available core blocks. Furthermore, if part of the system fails, for example one of the random-access

---

*From James Martin, *Programming Real-Time Computer Systems,* © 1965, pp. 61–67. Reprinted by permission of Prentice-Hall, Inc., Englewood Cliffs, N.J.

files, or if the system becomes similarly degraded, it is preferable to complete half-processed messages rather than to start on new ones.

A reason for examining new inputs first could exist, however. For example, some of the new messages might require a very quick response, and it would be desirable to preempt existing work. It may be necessary to preempt other running items in order to obtain equipment to execute this high-priority work.

Priority considerations are likely to differ from one type of application to another. The sequence in which processing is done may differ on priority grounds in two ways. First, different messages may be of different importance and may have different priorities. In an airline reservations system, for example, all messages may have the same priority, but in a banking system it may be desirable to give customer enquiries from the bank counter priority over transaction processing in order to ensure a fast response time. In some systems there may be many different message priorities. Second, different functions of the system may have different priorities. For example, high speed output to data displays is likely to have priority over teletype output; vital calculations may have priority over data logging or other types of processing. A vital message or a vital function may have to jump the queues, either those waiting for the central processing unit or those waiting for an input–output unit or file.

Any difference in the priority of processing means a difference in the main scheduling routine. The simpler the priority structure, the simpler will be this routine. If, as in some airline applications, the Supervisory Programs recognize no difference in message priority and no difference in priorities of functions, then the central scanning loop will be a simple routine of ten or so instructions as above. If there are a number of different priorities between functions and messages, the scanning loop will need more elaborate logic, such as the testing of a priority table.

Although some large real-time systems give a fast response to all their messages (for example, most airline booking systems reply in three seconds or less), there are many applications in which only a portion of the messages require such fast reaction. This would be a reason for building a priority structure into the main scheduling routine.

On a small computer a program priority structure may be used when restricting the degree of multiprogramming in the system. Suppose that a maximum of three messages may be processeed in parallel. Messages may be assigned priorities one, two, and three. Only messages of a higher priority may take control of the central processing unit when the program for the current message gives a WAIT macroinstruction.

Figure 4–1–1 illustrates such a scheduling routine. Here there are three priorities of program in the system, distinguished from one another by the degree to which they may interrupt each other:

(a) High-Priority Real-Time Programs (HRT). During a WAIT given by these programs, no other Application Programs may be entered.

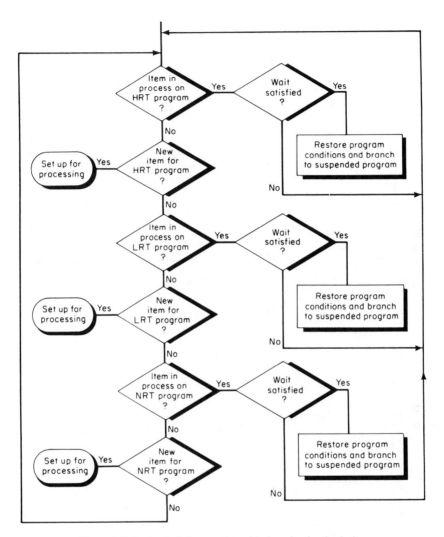

Figure 4-1-1 A scheduling routine with three levels of priority.

(b) Low-Priority Real-Time Programs (LRT). During a WAIT given by these programs, only an HRT program may be entered. The processing of the LRT program is thus suppressed until no High Priority messages are waiting for processing.

(c) Nonreal-Time Programs (NRT). During a WAIT given by these programs, HRT or LRT programs may be entered. The processing of the NRT program is thus suppressed until no real-time messages are in the system.

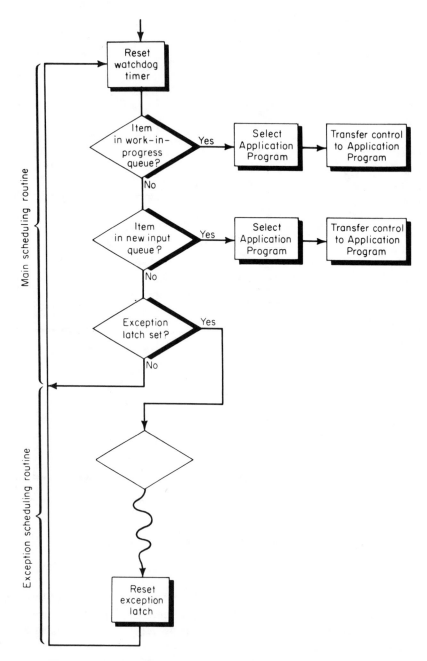

Figure 4-1-2 An exception scheduling routine separate from the main scheduling routine. Messages or situations requiring exception action cause the exception latch to be set.

In a system with a high throughput the main scheduling routine is entered many times per second. It is therefore desirable that it should be tightly programmed to be as short as possible.

Certain infrequently occurring events or messages in the system may need more complex analysis than that above. It is sometimes desirable, therefore, to have an *exception* scheduling routine separate from the loop that is entered many times per second. This is illustrated in Figure 4-1-2.

Some real-time systems execute their Application Programs in a *preset sequence* rather than selecting them at random. For example, read a group of plant instruments, perform calculations, print instruction to operator if required, read instruments again, and so on. Deviations from the preset cycle would occur only when exception conditions arise. In a system like this a latch may be set by any conditions needing exception scheduling. This would be tested between Application Programs and then, if necessary, a scheduling routine might be executed.

Most real-time systems will overlap their input–output operations with processing. In this case the scheduling of input–output and file operations is normally separate from the scheduling of Application Programs. The input–output scheduling routines may be entered when an interrupt signifies that such an operation is complete, so that another one can be started on that channel and unit. On a slower or less sophisticated machine, however, there may not be such an interrupt. The main scheduling routine may then incorporate input–output scheduling also, testing first to see whether any input–output channel is not busy. This is illustrated in Figure 4-1-3.

The decision as to which Application Program to execute next, or what message to process next, can, indeed, become involved with the availability of equipment. In systems using more than one computer and different memory units, channels, and so on, the scheduling routine may have a dynamic record of how equipment is assigned, and it may check that the required equipment is available before allowing work to begin on a particular operation. This could become very complex, especially if multithread programming is in use.

Just as a Supervisory Program might check the availability of equipment, so also might it check the availability of other programs, and this could be a criterion in deciding which job is to be done next.

Consider a system with a large core storage in which all the Application Programs are in core, with the exception of those very infrequently used such as error routines. Of the messages entering the system some may be processed quickly, but others take a relatively long time. Some of the messages are urgent and need a quick response, and these must interrupt the processing of others. A program may thus be left partially completed for some time. Control will return to it when higher priority work has been done. But meanwhile it cannot be used by other messages, and for reasons of logic other associated programs or subroutines may have to be made unavailable to other messages.

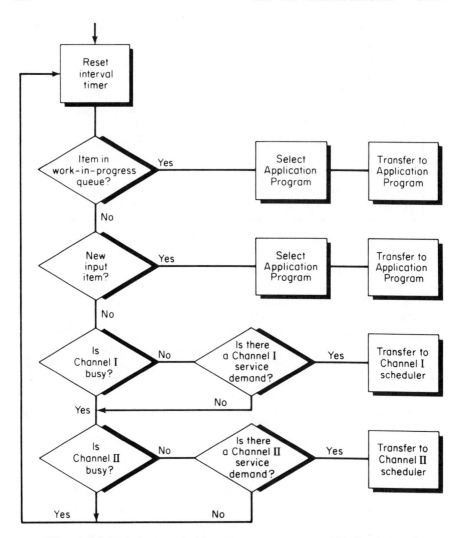

Figure 4-1-3 Main loop test for channel status on a system with a low degree of multiprogramming.

Figure 4-1-4 illustrates the scheduling routine for such a system. This illustration is taken from the computer programs used for Project Mercury in which duplexed IBM 7090s were used to monitor the first manned space flights from Cape Kennedy.

In this system, there is a relatively small number of Application Programs (Ordinary Processors). A table, called the Priority Table, contains one word for each Application Program in the system. In that word one bit is used for various indicators—A, B, C, D, and so on—for that program. Indicator A is on

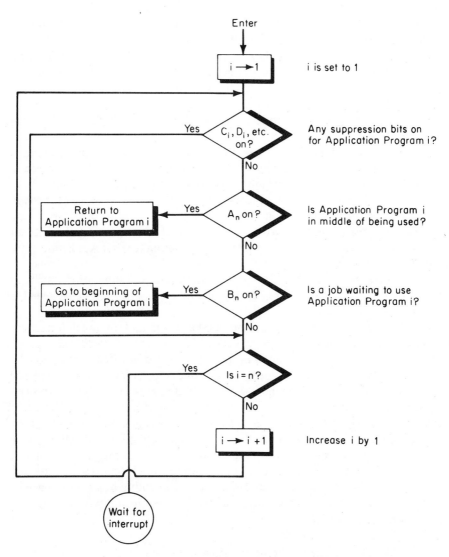

Figure 4-1-4   The priority routine of Project Mercury. Items in the priority table are arranged so that those with high priority have a low value of i.

when that Application Program is in the middle of being used and has been interrupted. Indicator B is on when a job is waiting to use that Application Program. Indicators C, D, and so on, are suppression indicators. When a suppression bit is on for some reason or other, a transfer may not be made to that Application Program.

Immediately upon entry to a routine, it switches on its A indicator, and thus records the fact that it is active. If it is interrupted the A indicator remains on. When a routine is completed it switches its A indicator off.

Each routine has as many suppression indicators (C, D, and so on) as there are reasons for its being suppressed. Every condition which requires the suppression of a given routine is associated with a suppression indicator of that routine. For example, a low-priority routine may have some special relationship with a high-priority routine which requires that the latter should not be entered for a period of time.

As is shown in Figure 4–1–4, the scheduling routine scans through the Operational Programs in sequence 1, 2, 3—up to n, the high priority programs being the first. On each program it looks first at the suppression indicators.

If any of these are on, it ignores that program. Next it looks at the A indicator to see whether a job is in the middle of being processed by that program. If this is the case, then control is returned to that program. Otherwise the scheduling routine tests whether there is a job waiting for that Application Program.

If there is no item for this Application Program, it looks at the next Application Program in the priority sequence, and so on, until it has checked all of them.

It will be seen that this procedure makes the main loop much longer and needs a computer with fast logic capacity. Such a scheme could only be used where there is a reasonably small number of Application Programs, though a variation of it could check all programs of one priority level with one instruction, rather than checking each program individually. A procedure of this type is of value only where priority considerations are of importance. The use of suppression indicators introduces a form of logical interaction between different Application Programs which could become complex—and perhaps unmanageably complex—where there are many such programs.

As will be seen, the main scheduling routine is likely to differ considerably from one application to another. Basically, a scheduling algorithm is needed for each application. This algorithm can be simple or it can become very complex. It is a function of factors such as:

1. The priority structure between different tasks.
2. The precedence rules. Can one task interrupt another? Can one message preempt another?
3. How is the available equipment allocated? Are the input–output schedulers separate from the main scheduler?
4. What response times or deadlines must be met?
5. Are real-time work and nonreal-time work combined?

In general, when designing a real-time system, every attempt should be made to simplify the way work is scheduled. Too complex a mechanism for scheduling gives rise to many difficulties in the implementation of the systems, especially in program and system testing.

4-2 EVOLVING TOWARD ADA IN REAL-TIME SYSTEMS*

Lee MacLaren

Boeing Military Airplane Company

4-2-1 ABSTRACT

The Ada view of multitasking represents a radical departure from the traditional "cyclic executive" approach to real-time operating systems. Since system designers must by necessity be conservative, it would be unrealistic to expect an abrupt change of this magnitude in engineering practice. Instead, this paper outlines a sequence of intermediate steps designed so that the advantages and familiar structures of cyclic systems may be retained, while the capabilities of Ada multitasking are gradually incorporated. A scale of increasing scheduling complexity provides the justification for this sequence. The discussion of each step then briefly mentions some of the related benefits and costs. The paper draws some conclusions about the use of Ada in real-time systems.

4-2-2 INTRODUCTION

The designers of certain classes of embedded computer systems, especially in the field of vehicle guidance and control, have evolved a characteristic approach to real-time operating systems that is quite different from, and seemingly incompatible with, the Ada view of multitasking. Given the usual project constraints of cost, schedule, reliability, and performance, it would be unreasonable to ask these designers to make an abrupt change in their approach. Instead, this paper presents a sequence of intermediate steps by which designers may retain the advantages and familiar structures of their current systems while gradually incorporating the capabilities of Ada multitasking. For

*From the Proceedings of the ACM SIGPLAN Symposium on the Ada Language, Boston, Dec. 1980. Copyright 1980, Association for Computing Machinery, Inc., reprinted by permission.

each step, a brief discussion of the benefits, costs, and domain of applicability is also given.

4-2-2-1 The End Points

The designer of a control or navigation system naturally thinks in cycles, since the digital realization of the design consists almost entirely of periodic sensor sampling and filter computations. For example, a very simple flight control system might have the following structure:

```
LOOP
    − −SAMPLE SENSORS AND UPLINK COMMANDS
    − −EXECUTE FILTER COMPUTATIONS
    − −OUTPUT TO CONTROL SURFACE ACTUATORS
    FOR I IN 1..COUNT  − −IDLE LOOP
    LOOP NULL; END LOOP;
END LOOP;
```

Since filter computations do not always take the same amount of time (due, for example, to changes in flight regime), and since guidance equations may require better timing accuracy than the idle loop provides, a more common approach is to employ a timer interrupt to trigger the periodic processing.

As the system being controlled grows more complex, so does the number of quasi-independent functions to be performed. Furthermore, the functions require processing at different frequencies. This gives rise to an elaborate method for allocating computer time explicitly. A "minor frame" is defined as the basic timing interval triggered by the timer interrupt. The higher frequency functions are assigned segments in each minor frame. The next longer timing interval may be called a "major frame" and will consist of a fixed number of minor frames. Each function executing at this lower frequency is assigned a portion of one of the minor frames in a major frame. If a function is too large to fit in an available slot, it is broken into subfunctions and distributed over several minor frames. In some systems, a still longer timing cycle composed of a number of major frames may be employed.

Since this time allocation can be quite complex, it is usually centralized in a "scheduler." A unit of computation (function or subfunction) is called a "task," and the scheduler may employ precompiled tables of task names to determine which tasks will be invoked in each minor frame, as well as the order in which they will be invoked. Each task is run to completion, and has exclusive access to all global data. The order in which the tasks are executed is used to synchronize data transmission among them. This approach to real-time operating systems is sometimes called a "cyclic executive" approach.

The Ada view of multitasking is diametrically opposed to that of a cyclic executive. Ada tasks are asynchronous and concurrent, whereas cyclic tasks are synchronous and sequential. Data shared among Ada tasks must be explicitly protected, but cyclic tasks are assumed to have exclusive access to all global data. If an Ada task requires periodic execution, it must include explicit loop and delay statements and a record of its most recent execution point, whereas a cyclic task is periodic by definition.

An even more profound difference is in the role that time plays. Ada multitasking seems to assume that a calling task requesting a resource can wait until that resource is available. But cyclic tasks cannot be delayed under normal circumstances. Rather, the manual scheduling process must ensure that resources will always be available when they are needed. This is partly for efficiency, and partly due to the treatment of time as an implicit parameter in digital filters and control loops. The algorithms assume that sensor samples and control outputs will occur at known frequencies, with constraints on timing variation ("jitter"), delay, and drift. While it may be possible to deal with time explicitly, it is expensive to do so in terms of both complexity and computation.

4-2-2-2 Benefits and Costs

The cyclic executive approach has survived as long as it has in the aerospace industry because it is eminently well-suited to many of the applications found there. If designers are to be persuaded to use the Ada multitasking facilities, they must also be persuaded that they will not lose the benefits of cyclic executives, and that any additional benefits will outweigh the costs of obtaining them. The perceived risk associated with the conceptual distance between the two approaches must also be considered.

The benefits and costs of multitasking approaches depend heavily on the nature of the applications, especially the degree to which they are dominated by cyclic processing requirements. It will be useful to distinguish three levels, in order of increasing scheduling complexity:

> Level 1—purely cyclic, no asynchronous events or variations in computing requirements. Very simple control systems, such as those for small missiles and target drones, often satisfy these conditions.
>
> Level 2—mostly cyclic, with some asynchronous events and "burst" computing loads, such as fault recovery, external commands, or operator interfaces. "Natural" processing frequencies for the different functions may not be convenient multiples of each other. This level is typical of modern avionics and space systems.
>
> Level 3—asynchronous, or event-driven. Cyclic processing does not dominate. Examples of such applications would include communications, radar tracking, and most general purpose operating systems.

For Level 1 applications, the cyclic executive approach is clearly beneficial in terms of efficiency, simplicity, and predictability. The efficiency and simplicity of a cyclic executive at this level cannot be improved upon, since there is really no executive at all. The predictability follows from the invariant execution order and facilitates reconstructing the sequence of events leading to a failure.

When faced with a Level 2 problem, it is common practice to transform it into a Level 1 problem. This may be done, for example, by buffering asynchronous events in hardware, and adapting cyclic algorithms to a convenient frequency that is higher than the minimum required. Burst computing loads are accommodated by allocating space in the timing cycle for worst case situations.

Under the right conditions, a cyclic executive will still retain the efficiency advantage in the following sense: the number of scheduling decisions and context switches is the minimum possible given the (adjusted) cyclic processing requirements. This efficiency can turn out to be illusory, however. If a cyclic algorithm has been adapted to a much higher frequency than required, the additional processing should be counted as executive overhead. Likewise, the dead space left to accommodate worst case timing situations could be partially eliminated if a more flexible executive were employed.

When a cyclic executive is imposed on a Level 2 or 3 application, the simplicity advantage is completely lost. The resulting scheduling tables become quite complex. Because they are usually built by hand, they are also difficult to maintain. In addition, the use of scheduling order to control data sharing among tasks results in a very complex network of potential intertask dependencies.

The benefits of Ada multitasking first appear in Level 2 applications, and become almost essential for solving the problems of Level 3. Ada multitasking supports cyclic processing at arbitrary frequencies, easily absorbs asynchronous events and burst computing loads, and provides simple and explicit documentation of intertask dependencies. Against these benefits must be weighed several obvious costs, including: queue manipulation and semaphore processing; clock queue maintenance and computation of delays; extra data contention resolution; and task state vectors. Ada also sacrifices the predictability of a cyclic executive and would have to make up for it by keeping a record of scheduling operations.

It would seem then, that the designer of a Level 2 control system might be tempted to use Ada multitasking if:

1. there is no net loss of efficiency,
2. the solutions to Level 2 problems appear simpler, or
3. a satisfactory test instrumentation capability can be provided (the cost of which counts against efficiency).

In addition, the temptation will be much stronger if the conceptual distance between the two approaches can be made to appear small.

4-2-2-3 A Basic Bridge

The first and most important step will be to reconcile the seemingly separate concepts of cyclic task and Ada task. Two observations may help in making this step. First, the cyclic tasks within a minor cycle are executed in a group and in a fixed order. In fact, a simple cyclic executive can be implemented as a series of procedure calls triggered by a timer interrupt. The second observation is that there is no concept of parallelism in a cyclic executive. Each cyclic task runs to completion, and has exclusive access to all global data during its execution.

These observations suggest that a cyclic system could be implemented as a single Ada task that is executed once every minor cycle and contains all data used by the cyclic tasks. For a Level 1 application, this Ada task would be the handler for the timer interrupt, and there would be no other tasks in the system. Theoretically, none of the costs of Ada tasking would be incurred, although it is unlikely that a compiler would recognize this. Thus, this first step is strictly a conceptual aid. (See Exhibit 1.)

A profitable second step would be to simplify some of the scheduling difficulties associated with burst computing loads and with cyclic tasks of different frequencies. Instead of explicitly budgeting all of the time in each minor cycle, the concept of a "background" (that is, lower priority) task may be introduced as a way of utilizing "leftover" time. Of course, this background task must be written so as to be interruptible, since it is likely to be preempted at any time by the cyclic foreground processing. The idea may be extended to several background tasks, scheduled on a preemptive priority basis. In this way, processing which is noncyclic or of relatively low frequency can be allocated to background tasks, thereby simplifying the cyclic executive and potentially making better use of available time. The implementation in Ada involves one task for the foreground plus one task for each separate background function.

Even a traditional cyclic system usually has a computer self-check program running in the background, and some systems have employed the extension to multiple tasks. What is often missing from current systems with background tasks is a safe, uniform approach to data sharing between background and foreground and among background tasks. Here, Ada multitasking can contribute a great deal by way of its explicit support for controlled task interactions.

(A self-check task appears in Exhibit 1. Some data sharing techniques are described in Exhibit 2 and used in foreground–background cooperation in Exhibit 3.)

4-2-2-4 Evaluation of the Basic Bridge

By noting that the cyclic tasks and their scheduler can be combined into a single Ada task, it is possible to think about implementations as being single-task or multitask in Ada terms. Since Level 1 applications are simply and efficiently expressible as single-task systems, there seems little point in asking a designer to make use of Ada's multitasking facilities in these cases.

There comes a point in a Level 2 application where it is both simpler and more efficient to use a multitask implementation. It is at this point that the Ada facilities become attractive, particularly because of their explicit support for task interactions.

Simplicity is served because those functions for which it would be difficult to allocate time explicitly may be assigned to separate Ada tasks and scheduled automatically. Thus the simple cyclic aspects of the system are retained in the single Ada task which implements the cyclic executive, while the more complex processing is done whenever it is needed during the remaining available time. In some current systems where this approach has been tried, the methods for sharing data among tasks have been ad hoc and error prone. Ada's explicit support for controlled task interactions promises to reduce this kind of complexity as well.

The efficiency of a cyclic executive derives from its minimal scheduling property, and from the very small implementation cost. However, in a purely cyclic system time must be allocated for all processing which could conceivably be simultaneously pending, even though such a burst load would be infrequent. When such a load does occur, it may be possible to postpone certain functions, such as operator display updates, until the time-critical backlog is worked off. In such cases, the implementation cost of using a multitask approach may be more than offset by the improved time utilization. In the basic bridge outlined in the previous section, flexible scheduling may be applied where it is cost effective, while otherwise retaining the efficiency of the cyclic executive.

Predictability is retained for that portion of the system which remains cyclic. Otherwise, the costs and benefits of instrumentation must figure in the decision to allocate a function to a separate Ada task. Since much of the need for predictability comes when analyzing problems with shared data, the Ada facilities for task interaction should help make it less necessary.

The conceptual distance between two technologies can be a barrier to change. In the discussion thus far, two conceptual steps have been required. The first was a recognition that all the cyclic tasks in a system correspond to a single Ada task, which also contains the cyclic executive. Since this single task can be written as an interrupt handler, the Ada implementation can be made to look very much like a traditional cyclic executive. The second step involves separate background tasks and the concept of concurrency. This is indeed a large step for those who are seeing it for the first time, although an explanation in terms of a simple priority scheduling algorithm seems to help. It is significant that this second step is already being taken in some current control systems, even though the languages being used provide no support for multitasking.

4-2-2-5 Gradual Evolution toward "Advanced" Techniques

Previous sections have concentrated on the transition point at which Ada multitasking becomes an attractive alternative to traditional cyclic executives. Once that transition is made, many more sophisticated capabilities become accessible. This section describes how some of these capabilities may be achieved by means of a gradual evolution in programming style. At each stage in the evolution, a decision to continue may be based on whether the additional benefits outweigh the costs.

Two basic restructuring activities will be illustrated here. First, noncyclic processing is removed from the cyclic executive. Provided there is adequate buffering and time for response, this allows at least some tasks to wait for resources when they are temporarily unavailable, thus permitting the simpler "academic" approaches to synchronization and data sharing. The second restructuring activity involves modifying the cyclic processing so that it can recover from temporary overloads and short delays. This makes it possible to employ arbitrary cycle rates, and to allow some high priority asynchronous processing.

BUFFERING EVENTS AND DATA.   A real-time system must often respond to asynchronous events, such as external communications or operator requests. Under a cyclic executive, the strategy would be to provide a hardware buffer to record the event and its associated data, plus a cyclic task to poll the buffer sufficiently often so that no data would be lost. This strategy becomes unattractive if bursts of events can occur faster than they can be processed, or if hardware buffering is overly expensive (as it would be in a small missile or target drone).

An alternative approach is to connect an interrupt to the event, and to employ an interrupt handler to buffer the event record in the computer. The event processor is then assigned to a separate Ada task to execute whenever there is time available and there are events to be processed. (Exhibit 4 illustrates the technique.)

The costs of this approach include the additional task control blocks and the context saving and restoring by the interrupt handler. The benefits are the decreased average frequency of the event polling operation (it is done only when needed) and the improved ability to handle bursts of events without loss of data.

RECOVERING FROM CYCLE OVERFLOWS.   In some cyclic systems it is possible for unscheduled loads, such as fault recovery or extra input–output activity, to prevent a minor cycle from completing before the next timer interrupt. One solution is to treat the cyclic executive task as an event processor, as in the above example, and to have the timer-interrupt handler serve as a buffer for the timer events and the time-critical input operations. The costs of this additional flexibility are the additional task, the buffer space, and the additional scheduling operations.

TIME TAGGING. If, because of flexibility requirements, a system becomes heavily interrupt driven, it can become impossible to guarantee that a particular interrupt will be serviced immediately. While many control algorithms can tolerate substantial jitter in their sampling intervals, "integrating" tasks, such as inertial navigation, cannot. If other design constraints warrant it, it is usually possible to rewrite the equations to include the time of the sample explicitly. Then the interrupt handler may be easily modified to include the real-time clock as one of the values it samples. While this approach is very expensive in terms of both complexity and computation, it is available if needed.

SKIPPING CYCLES. Just as control loops can often tolerate timing jitter, they can also accommodate occasional, modest (up to a few cycles) gaps in processing. Of course, the frequency and length of these gaps must be carefully negotiated with the control system analysts. This property may be exploited to help recover from temporary overloads as follows. Divide the cyclic tasks into those which cannot tolerate skipped cycles and those which can and assign an Ada task to each of the two classes. Let the timer-interrupt handler similarly keep two buffers, one of sufficient length never to lose the data of the intolerant functions, and the other to hold only the most recent data of the functions that can tolerate skipped cycles. Each of the two processing tasks will then acquire inputs from the corresponding buffers and the desired effect will be achieved. The cost, of course, is yet another task and its scheduling operations. (Exhibit 5 offers an illustration.)

ARBITRARY CYCLE RATES. One of the potential advantages of Ada multitasking over traditional cyclic executives is that it permits cyclic algorithms to be run at their minimum required rate, rather than at some higher rate selected for scheduling convenience. This may be achieved either by providing a separate timer-interrupt for each desired frequency or by using the delay statement and real-time clock facilities provided by Ada (as illustrated in Exhibit 6).

In either case there will be the costs of additional tasks and their scheduling operations, plus additional scheduling as required to synchronize the uses of shared data. If delay statements are used, there will also be the costs of maintaining a clock queue and computing the delay periods. An additional cost is the loss of timing accuracy, since the time between a timer interrupt and the start of a periodic task can be quite variable. These costs may be justified if the total processing load is reduced.

By now the need for the several approaches to scheduling flexibility discussed above should be clear—a system with arbitrary cycle rates is almost guaranteed to have periodic overloads as the cycles move in and out of phase with each other. A designer would be ill-advised to allow arbitrary cycle rates without first providing the facilities and structures needed to accommodate these overloads.

DATA SHARING AND SYNCHRONIZATION.   Some examples of rather specialized data sharing schemes have already been mentioned. The more general-purpose techniques are of course also available, including semaphores, readers–writers, resource managers, and several variations on bounded buffers. (These algorithms are quite easy to code in Ada, and can serve as highly edifying introductory exercises.)

The most important point with respect to the theme of this paper is that these general-purpose techniques usually assume that a task requesting access to a resource can wait until the resource is available. In a traditional cyclic executive such delays cannot be tolerated. It is only after the system has been restructured to provide flexible scheduling that the "textbook" data-sharing techniques may be employed.

4-2-2-6 Summary

There is a large gap between the traditional "cyclic executive" approach to real-time operating systems and the Ada view of multitasking. This paper has shown that the gap can be bridged by a sequence of intermediate steps, each of which may be added when the nature of the application justifies it.

Applications may be classified according to the degree to which they are dominated by cyclic activity. While a purely cyclic system might be composed of several "cyclic tasks," it would actually be implemented as a single Ada task, and would therefore not benefit from the Ada facilities. As the timing requirements of an application become more complex, the need for more flexible scheduling eventually outweighs the cost of providing it. At first, some of the processing may be allocated to a few "background" tasks in order to make better use of the gaps in the cyclic schedule. This marks the transition to a multitasking system in the Ada sense. Later, various techniques may be employed to allow recovery from temporary overloads without loss of important data. Finally, once this level of flexibility has been achieved, the full range of capabilities for concurrent processing may be introduced.

This paper makes three fairly strong statements about the use of Ada multitasking in real-time operating systems:

1. There is definitely a category of applications for which a multitasking approach (in the Ada sense) is inappropriate.
2. Applications with an intermediate level of timing complexity may profitably employ a limited set of multitasking techniques, even though a fully general multitasking system is not warranted.

3. In Ada it is possible to retain the simplicity and efficiency of a cyclic executive where appropriate, while gradually incorporating those multitasking facilities required by the application.

4-2-3 EXHIBIT 1. CYCLIC EXECUTIVE

Cyclic tasks are visible procedures from the corresponding packages. Communication is through visible data blocks.

```
PACKAGE EVENTPROCESSOR IS
    TYPE EVENTOUTTYPE IS . . .;
    EVENTOUT:  EVENTOUTTYPE;
      --OUTPUTS FOR OTHER COMPONENTS
    PROCEDURE EPROC;
      --POLL DEVICE AND PROCESS NEW DATA (IF ANY).
      --EVENT RATE <= EVERY OTHER FRAME.
END;

PACKAGE BODY EVENTPROCESSOR IS

    . . .
END;

PACKAGE INTEGRATOR IS
    TYPE INTOUTTYPE IS . . .;
    INTOUT:  INTOUTTYPE;
      --OUTPUTS FOR OTHER COMPONENTS
    PROCEDURE INTF;
      --SAMPLE AND INTEGRATE. AVERAGE SAMPLING
      --RATE REQUIREMENT FIXES MINOR FRAME RATE.
    PROCEDURE INTB1;
      --UPDATE AND FILTER.
      --THIS STAGE SPANS SEVERAL FRAMES.
    PROCEDURE INTB2;
    PROCEDURE INTB3;
END;

WITH EVENTPROCESSOR;
WITH CYCLICEXEC;
PACKAGE BODY INTEGRATOR IS
    TYPE INTSTATE IS . . .;
    STATE:  INTSTATE;
    PROCEDURE INTF IS

    . . .

END INTEGRATOR;
```

```
PACKAGE CONTROLLER IS
  PROCEDURE CTRL;
    — —SAMPLE, FILTER, AND OUTPUT.
    — —IDEAL RATE ABOUT 2/3 MINOR FRAME RATE.
END;

WITH INTEGRATOR;
WITH EVENTPROCESSOR;
PACKAGE BODY CONTROLLER IS
  PROCEDURE CTRL IS
    — —GAINS AND MODE SELECTION IMPORTED
    — —FROM OTHER PACKAGES.
    . . .
END CONTROLLER;


PACKAGE CYCLICEXEC IS
  SUBTYPE FRAMENUMBER IS
    INTEGER RANGE 1 . . 4;
    — —FOUR MINOR FRAMES PER MAJOR FRAME
  FRAME: FRAMENUMBER := 1;
END;

WITH INTEGRATOR; USE INTEGRATOR;
WITH CONTROLLER; USE CONTROLLER;
WITH EVENTPROCESSOR; USE EVENTPROCESSOR;

— — — — — — — — — — — —
PACKAGE BODY CYCLICEXEC IS
— — — — — — — — — — — —

  TASK EXEC IS
    ENTRY DING;
      — —TIMER INTERRUPT
    FOR DING USE AT . . .;
    PRAGMA PRIORITY (10);
  END;

  TASK SELFTEST IS
    PRAGMA PRIORITY (0);
  END;

  TASK BODY EXEC IS
  BEGIN
    LOOP
      ACCEPT DING;
      CASE FRAME IS
      WHEN 1 = >
        INTF;
        INTB1;
        CTRL;
```

```
        WHEN 2 => 
          INTF;
          EPROC;
          CTRL;
        WHEN 3 =>
          INTF;
          INTB2;
          CTRL;
        WHEN 4 =>
          INTF;
          EPROC;
          INTB3;
          CTRL;
        END CASE;
        FRAME := FRAME + 1;
        IF FRAME > FRAMENUMBER'LAST THEN
          FRAME := FRAMENUMBER'FIRST;
        END IF;
      END LOOP;
    END EXEC;

      TASK BODY SELFTEST IS
        . . .
      END;

    BEGIN
    END CYCLICEXEC;
```

4-2-4 EXHIBIT 2. NONDELAYING BUFFERS

Buffering techniques are illustrated that never delay the foreground more than a few microseconds. As is often the case, the buffers are assumed too large to allow any unnecessary copying.

4-2-4-1 Fresh Data

Data is passed from foreground to background. Data not read in time is lost, but if the reader gets ahead, it waits for fresh data. Data read is most recent available.

```
        GENERIC
          TYPE T IS PRIVATE; — — BUFFER TYPE
          TYPE AT IS ACCESS T;
        PACKAGE FRESHDATA IS
          PROCEDURE STARTWRITE (BP: OUT AT);
```

```
        PROCEDURE STOPWRITE;
        PROCEDURE FRESH (BP: OUT AT);
        PRAGMA INLINE (STARTWRITE, STOPWRITE, FRESH);
    END;


    PACKAGE BODY FRESHDATA IS
        TASK FD IS
          ENTRY STARTW (BP: OUT AT);
          ENTRY STOPW;
          ENTRY FDATA (BP: OUT AT AT);
        END;


        PROCEDURE STARTWRITE (BP: OUT AT) IS
        BEGIN
          FD.STARTW (BP);
        END;
        . . .


        TASK BODY FD IS SEPARATE;


    BEGIN END FRESHDATA;


    SEPARATE (FRESHDATA)
    TASK BODY FD IS
        — —APPROACH USES THREE BUFFERS WHOSE NAMES
        — —(POINTERS) ARE MOVED BETWEEN BOXES TO MONI-
        — —TOR STATUS. THE BOX NAMES ARE FILLING,
        — —FULL, AND READ. A BOOLEAN VARIABLE NEWD
        — —RECORDS WHETHER THE BUFFER WHOSE NAME IS IN
        — —THE FULL BOX CONTAINS FRESH (UNEXAMINED)
        — —DATA.


        NEWD: BOOLEAN := FALSE;
        FILLING: AT := NEW T;
        FULL:    AT := NEW T;
        READ:    AT := NEW T;


        PROCEDURE WREXCHANGE IS
          TMP: AT;
        BEGIN
          TMP := FILLING;
          FILLING := FULL;
          FULL := TMP;
        END;
        PROCEDURE RDEXCHANGE IS
          TMP: AT;
```

```
BEGIN
  TMP := READ;
  READ := FULL;
  FULL := TMP;
END;
PRAGMA INLINE (WREXCHANGE, RDEXCHANGE);

BEGIN — — TASK BODY FD
  LOOP
    SELECT
      ACCEPT STARTW (BP: OUT AT) DO
        BP := FILLING;
      END;
    OR
      ACCEPT STOPW DO
        WREXCHANGE;
        NEWD := TRUE;
      END;
    OR
      WHEN NEWD =>
      ACCEPT FDATA (BP: OUT AT) DO
        RDEXCHANGE;
        BP := READ;
        NEWD := FALSE;
      END;
    END SELECT;
  END LOOP;
END FD;
```

4-2-4-2 Current Data

Same as FreshData except that the currently most recent buffer may be read
repeatedly. Thus the foreground may be the consumer.

```
GENERIC
  TYPE T IS PRIVATE; — — BUFFER TYPE
  TYPE AT IS ACCESS T;
PACKAGE CURRENTDATA IS
  PROCEDURE STARTWRITE (BP: OUT AT);
  PROCEDURE STOPWRITE;
  PROCEDURE CURRENT (BP: OUT AT);
  PRAGMA INLINE (STARTWRITE, STOPWRITE, CURRENT);
END;

PACKAGE BODY CURRENTDATA IS
  — —SAME AS FRESHDATA EXCEPT THAT INITIAL
  — —WRITE CYCLE IS REQUIRED TO PROVIDE VALID
```

```
— —DATA, AND READ BRANCH LOOKS LIKE:
  ACCEPT CDATA (BP: OUT AT) DO
    IF NEWD THEN
      RDEXCHANGE;
      NEWD := FALSE;
    END IF;
    BP := READ;
  END;
END CURRENTDATA;
```

4-2-4-3 Bounded Pool

This is just a standard bounded buffer except that 1) a fixed size pool of buffers is managed and passed by reference, and 2) an exception is raised if no buffers are available for a write request. (An overflow is a fatal design error, but it should be reported for later correction.)

```
GENERIC
  COUNT: INTEGER;   — —NUMBER OF BUFFERS
  TYPE T IS PRIVATE;— —BUFFER TYPE
  TYPE AT IS ACCESS T;
PACKAGE BOUNDEDPOOL IS
  PROCEDURE STARTWRITE (BP: OUT AT);
  PROCEDURE STOPWRITE;
  PROCEDURE STARTREAD (BP: OUT AT);
  PROCEDURE STOPREAD;
  NOMOREBUFFERS: EXCEPTION;
  PRAGMA INLINE (STARTWRITE, STOPWRITE,
    STARTREAD, STOPREAD);
END BOUNDEDPOOL;

PACKAGE BODY BOUNDEDPOOL IS
  . . .
END;
```

4-2-5 EXHIBIT 3. FOREGROUND PLUS BACKGROUND

The Integrator is split between "foreground" and "background" to simplify scheduling. Filtered samples are passed down via a Bounded Pool buffer. The background task maintains state information in a Current Data buffer for use by the foreground.

```
PACKAGE INTEGRATOR IS
  TYPE·INTOUTTYPE IS . . .;
  INTOUT: INTOUTTYPE;
  PROCEDURE INTF;
END;
```

```
WITH EVENTPROCESSOR;
PACKAGE BODY INTEGRATOR IS
  TYPE INTSTATE IS . . .;
  TYPE INTSTATEPTR IS ACCESS INTSTATE;
  TYPE FILTEREDSAMPLE IS . . .;
  TYPE FILTSAMPPTR IS ACCESS FILTEREDSAMPLE;
  CFS: FILTSAMPPTR;
      − −CURRENT FILTERED SAMPLE BEING BUILT
      − −BY THE FOREGROUND PROCEDURE.
  PACKAGE FSBUFFER IS NEW BOUNDEDPOOL (
    COUNT => 3,
    T => FILTEREDSAMPLE,
    AT => FILTSAMPPTR);
  PACKAGE STATEBUFFER IS NEW CURRENTDATA (
    T => INTSTATE, AT => INTSTATEPTR);

  TASK INTB IS − − BACKGROUND PROCESSING
    PRAGMA PRIORITY (9);
  END;


  PROCEDURE INTF IS− −FOREGROUND "CYCLIC TASK"
                     − −CALLED BY CYCLIC EXEC
    STATEPTR: INTSTATEPTR;
  BEGIN
      − −CFS IS INITIALIZED AT PACKAGE STARTUP.
    STATEBUFFER.CURRENT (STATEPTR);
      − −SAMPLE AND INTEGRATE BASED ON CURRENT
      − −STATE AND EVENT DATA. ADD TO CURRENT
      − −FILTERED SAMPLE.
    IF FILTEREDSAMPLEREADY THEN
        − −TRANSMIT FILTERED SAMPLE TO BACKGROUND
        FSBUFFER.STOPWRITE;
        − −GET A NEW SAMPLE BUFFER
        FSBUFFER.STARTWRITE (CFS);
        CFS.ALL := . . .;
    END IF;
  EXCEPTION
    WHEN FSBUFFER.NOMOREBUFFERS =
        − −REPORT TO COCKPIT RECORDER
      . . .
  END INTF;
  TASK BODY INTB IS
    FSAMP: FILTSAMPPTR;
    OLDSTATE, NEWSTATE: INTSTATEPTR;
  BEGIN
      − −BUILD AN INITIAL STATE (IN OLDSTATE.ALL)
      . . .
```

```
        LOOP
          — —GET NEXT FILTERED SAMPLE
          FSBUFFER.STARTREAD (FSAMP);
          — —OPEN A NEW STATE BUFFER
          STATEBUFFER.STARTWRITE (NEWSTATE);
          — —COMPUTE NEW STATE AND REMEMBER IT
          . . .
          OLDSTATE := NEWSTATE;
          — —TRANSMIT NEW STATE TO FOREGROUND
          STATEBUFFER.STOPWRITE;
          — —RELEASE FILTERED SAMPLE BUFFER
          FSBUFFER.STOPREAD;
        END LOOP;
      END INTB;
    BEGIN — — PACKAGE BODY INTEGRATOR
      — —INITIALIZE CURRENT FILTERED SAMPLE BUFFER
      FSBUFFER.STARTWRITE (CFS)
      CFS.ALL := . . .;
    END INTEGRATOR;
```

4-2-6 EXHIBIT 4. EVENT BUFFER

The event processing (which is basically asynchronous) is removed from the cyclic exec by connecting a buffer directly to an event interrupt. A small cyclic task remains to update visible event outputs.

```
    PACKAGE EVENTPROCESSOR IS
      TYPE EVENTOUTTYPE IS . . .;
      EVENTOUT: EVENTOUTTYPE . . .;
      PROCEDURE EUPDATE; — —FOREGROUND "CYCLIC TASK"
                          — —TO UPDATE EVENTOUT
    END;

    PACKAGE BODY EVENTPROCESSOR IS
      TYPE EVENTTYPE IS . . .;
      NULLEVENT: CONSTANT EVENTTYPE
        := . . .;

      TASK EVENTBUFFER IS
        ENTRY INCOMING; — — EVENT INTERRUPT
        ENTRY NEWEVENT (NE: OUT EVENTTYPE);
        FOR INCOMING USE AT . . .;
      END;
```

```
TASK PROCESSOR IS
  --TAKES NEW EVENTS FROM EVENTBUFFER AND
  --PROCESSES THEM, PLACING NEW INFORMATION
  --INTO OUTBUFFER.
  PRAGMA PRIORITY (9);
END;

TASK OUTBUFFER IS
  ENTRY UPDATE (EO: IN OUT EVENTOUTTYPE);
    --CALLED BY EUPDATE.
    --UPDATES EO IF THERE IS NEW DATA.
  ENTRY WRITE (EI: IN EVENTOUTTYPE);
END;

TASK BODY EVENTBUFFER IS
  TYPE EBUFPTR IS ACCESS;
  TYPE EBUF IS
    RECORD
      NEXT: EBUFPTR;
      VAL:  EVENTTYPE;
    END RECORD;
  TYPE EBUFPTR IS ACCESS EBUF;

  MAX: CONSTANT := 10;  --NUMBER OF BUFFERS
  COUNT: INTEGER RANGE 0 .. MAX := 0;

  DEPOSIT,
  WITHDRAW: EBUFPTR;

  PROCEDURE EREAD IS
  BEGIN
    --INLINE MACHINE CODE TO READ FROM THE
    --EVENT DEVICE INTO DEPOSIT.VAL.
  END;
  PRAGMA INLINE (EREAD);
BEGIN
  --BUILD A RING OF BUFFERS
  DEPOSIT := NEW EBUF (NULL, NULLEVENT);
  DEPOSIT.NEXT := DEPOSIT;
  FOR I IN 2 .. MAX
  LOOP
    DEPOSIT.NEXT := NEW EBUFF (
      NEXT  => DEPOSIT.NEXT;
      VAL  => NULLEVENT);
  END LOOP;
  WITHDRAW := DEPOSIT;

  --STANDARD BOUNDED BUFFER LOOP
```

```
LOOP
  SELECT
    WHEN COUNT < MAX = >
    ACCEPT INCOMING DO
      EREAD;
      DEPOSIT := DEPOSIT.NEXT;
      COUNT := COUNT + 1;
    END;
  OR
    WHEN COUNT > 0 = >
      ACCEPT NEWEVENT (NE: OUT EVENTTYPE) DO
        NE := WITHDRAW.VAL;
        WITHDRAW := WITHDRAW.NEXT;
        COUNT := COUNT - 1;
      END;
    END SELECT;
  END LOOP;
END EVENTBUFFER;

TASK BODY PROCESSOR IS
  X: EVENTTYPE;
  Y: EVENTOUTTYPE;
  . . .
BEGIN
  . . .
  LOOP
    EVENTBUFFER.NEWEVENT (X);
    MUNCH;
    OUTBUFFER.WRITE (Y);
  END LOOP;
  END PROCESSOR;
  . . .
BEGIN END EVENTPROCESSOR;
```

4-2-7 EXHIBIT 5. SKIPPING CYCLES

The controller is split into a data sampling part and a filter-and-output part so that the filter can skip cycles if necessary. The two parts are joined by a FreshData buffer. The Integrator foreground procedure is also split into separate sample and integrate parts, joined by a Bounded Pool to prevent loss of data. At this point it is no longer possible to have any unprotected data sharing.

```
PACKAGE CONTROLLER IS
  PROCEDURE CTRLSAMPLE;
    — —THE FOREGROUND SAMPLING "TASK"
  END;
```

```
PACKAGE INTEGRATOR IS
  TYPE INTOUTTYPE IS . . .;
  PROCEDURE IUPDATE (IO: IN OUT INTOUTTYPE);
    ——FOR LOCAL COPIES OF INTOUT DATA
  PROCEDURE INTSAMPLE;
    ——THE FOREGROUND SAMPLING "TASK"
END;

PACKAGE EVENTPROCESSOR IS
  TYPE EVENTOUTTYPE IS . . .;
  PROCEDURE EUPDATE (EO: IN OUT EVENTOUTTYPE);
    ——FOR LOCAL COPIES OF EVENTOUT DATA
END;

PACKAGE CYCLICEXEC;
  ——REDUCED TO ALMOST NOTHING

WITH INTEGRATOR; USE INTEGRATOR;
WITH CONTROLLER; USE CONTROLLER;
PACKAGE BODY CYCLICEXEC IS
  TASK EXEC IS
    ENTRY DING;
    FOR DING USE AT . . .;
    PRAGMA PRIORITY (10);
  END;

  TASK SELFTEST IS
    PRAGMA PRIORITY (0);
  END;

  TASK BODY EXEC IS
  BEGIN
    LOOP
      ACCEPT DING;
      INTSAMPLE;
      CTRLSAMPLE;
    END LOOP;
  END;

  TASK BODY SELFTEST IS
  BEGIN
    LOOP
      RUMINATE;
    END LOOP;
  END;

BEGIN END CYCLICEXEC;
```

```
WITH INTEGRATOR; USE INTEGRATOR;
WITH EVENTPROCESSOR; USE EVENTPROCESSOR;
PACKAGE BODY CONTROLLER IS
  TYPE CSAMPTYPE IS . . .;
  TYPE CSAMPPTR IS ACCESS CSAMPTYPE;
  PACKAGE CSAMPBUF IS NEW FRESHDATA (
    T => CSAMPTYPE, AT => CSAMPPTR);

  TASK CTRLPROCESS IS
    PRAGMA PRIORITY (9);
  END;

  PROCEDURE CTRLSAMPLE IS
    CSP: CSAMPPTR;
  BEGIN
    CSAMPBUF.STARTWRITE (CSP);
    --SAMPLE DATA INTO CSP.ALL
  . . .
    CSAMPBUF.STOPWRITE;
  END;

  TASK BODY CTRLPROCESS IS
    CSP: CSAMPPTR;
    INTOUT: INTOUTTYPE;
    EVENTOUT: EVENTOUTTYPE;
  BEGIN
    LOOP
      IUPDATE (INTOUT);
      EUPDATE (EVENTOUT);
      CSAMPBUF.FRESH (CSP);
      --FILTER AND OUTPUT
      . . .
    END LOOP;
  END;


BEGIN END CONTROLLER;


WITH EVENTPROCESSOR;
PACKAGE BODY INTEGRATOR IS
  . . .
END;


PACKAGE BODY EVENTPROCESSOR IS
  . . .
END;
```

4-2-8 EXHIBIT 6. ARBITRARY CYCLE RATE

The Controller is removed entirely from the cyclic exec so that it may cycle at its own rate. A nondrifting loop-delay is illustrated.

```
PACKAGE CALENDAR IS
  TYPE TIME IS
    RECORD
      YEAR: INTEGER RANGE 1901 . . 2099;
      MONTH: INTEGER RANGE 1 . . 12;
      DAY: INTEGER RANGE 1 . . 31;
      SEC: DURATION;  — —A FIXED POINT TYPE
    END RECORD;

  FUNCTION CLOCK RETURN TIME;

  FUNCTION "+" (A: TIME; B: DURATION) RETURN TIME;
  FUNCTION "+" (A: DURATION; B: TIME) RETURN TIME;
  FUNCTION "−" (A: TIME; B: DURATION) RETURN TIME;
  FUNCTION "−" (A: TIME; B: TIME) RETURN DURATION;

  FOR TIME USE . . .
    — —PACKING SPECIFICATIONS
    END RECORD;

END CALENDAR;

PACKAGE CONTROLLER;

WITH CALENDAR; USE CALENDAR;
WITH INTEGRATOR; USE INTEGRATOR;
WITH EVENTPROCESSOR; USE EVENTPROCESSOR;
PACKAGE BODY CONTROLLER IS

  TASK CTRL IS
    PRAGMA PRIORITY (9);
  END;

  TASK BODY CTRL IS
    INTOUT: INTOUTTYPE;
    EVENTOUT: EVENTOUTTYPE;
    . . .
    INTERVAL: CONSTANT DURATION := 0.1;
      — —10 CYCLES PER SECOND
    NEXTDATE: TIME := CLOCK + INTERVAL;
  BEGIN
    . . .
```

```
LOOP
   IUPDATE (INTOUT);
   EUPDATE (EVENTOUT);
   — —SAMPLE, FILTER, AND OUTPUT

   . . .

   WHILE (NEXTDATE — CLOCK) < 0
   LOOP — — ALLOW CYCLE SKIPPING
      NEXTDATE := NEXTDATE + INTERVAL;
   END LOOP;
   DELAY NEXTDATE — CLOCK;
   END LOOP;
 END CTRL;

BEGIN END CONTROLLER;
```

~~~~~~

4-3   GUARANTEED RESPONSE TIMES IN A HARD REAL-TIME ENVIRONMENT*

Dennis W. Leinbaugh
Computer Science Department
University of Nebraska

~~~~~~

This paper describes a scheduling algorithm for a set of tasks that guarantees the time within which a task, once started, will complete. A task is started upon receipt of an external signal or the completion of other tasks. Each task has a fixed set of requirements in processor time, resources, and device operations needed for completion of its various segments. A worst case analysis of task performance is carried out. An algorithm is developed for determining the response times that can be guaranteed for a set of tasks. Operating system overhead is also accounted for.

*© 1978 IEEE. Reprinted, with permission, from IEEE Transactions on Software Engineering, Vol. SE-6, No. 1, pp. 85-91, January 1980.

4-3-1 INTRODUCTION

In a hard real-time processing or control environment each task must be completed within a specified period of time after being requested. If any task fails to complete in time, the entire system has failed. Real-time can refer either to hard real-time or to those systems in which response times need only approximate externally specified times.

Many real-time systems fall into this second category. This paper is not concerned with these soft real-time systems. It instead examines what response times can be guaranteed for fixed sets of tasks run on a single dedicated processor.

Most of the previous work on hard real-time scheduling has dealt with processor scheduling only.

Early work by Manacher used a "task list" to control the assignment of tasks with precedence relations to processors.[13]

Muntz and Coffman find an efficient algorithm to find the minimal-length preemptive schedule for tree-structured computations on multiprocessor systems.[14]

Liu and Layland consider scheduling periodic tasks on a single processor.[12]

Johnson and Maddison examine single and multiple processor systems executing real-time jobs.[10] They develop a measure of free time to determine whether new jobs can be admitted and still meet every job's response specification.

Sahni studied several task scheduling problems and, because many of them are NP-complete, presented a dynamic programming type approach to obtain optimal schedules.[15]

Given a set of tasks, their deadlines, and precedence constraints, Garey and Johnson determine if a two processor schedule exists to complete all tasks before their deadline.[6] They also present an efficient algorithm for finding the schedule.

Gonzalez, Ibarra, and Sahni analyze the performance of a largest-processing-time-first heuristic algorithm for obtaining a near minimal finish time nonpreemptive schedule.[7]

Gonzalez and Sahni present an $O(n)$ time algorithm to find the minimal finish time preemptive schedule for independent tasks on uniform processors.[8]

A practical weakness shared by all of the above models is that they include only central processor requirements and do not allow for input–output or for competition among tasks needing the same devices or data (critical sections or resources).

Sorenson and Hamacher describe an entire real-time system design methodology.[16] Their processor allocation model is developed for a single processor. They do mention that device wait periods and process switching overhead times can be included in the model but don't allow device sharing and indicate that overhead would be included only on an averaged basis.

Easton eliminates critical sections by re-doing computations if the data being used is changed by other processes.[4] Sorenson and Hamacher define a real-time buffer which involves maintaining multiple copies of data and updating the copies when they are not being used.[16] If enough copies are used, processes don't have to wait upon one another. These techniques do prevent waiting for shared data, but have the disadvantage of extra processor overhead. Furthermore, these techniques cannot replace certain uses of critical sections.

When designers of actual real-time systems are forced to use critical sections, they keep these sections as short as possible and enter them as infrequently as possible. This is partially due to the lack of research on critical sections in real-time tasks.

Garey and Johnson describe a multiprocessing model consisting of a finite number of processors, resources, and tasks.[5] Each task needs zero or more resources to run and its start time may be restricted to follow the completion of other tasks. All tasks are to complete by a single deadline time.

Tasks competing for resources is a generalization of tasks using critical sections. If only one resource of each type exists, then requests for the same resource can replace all identical critical sections.

These authors found very quickly that one confronts NP-complete problems. For example, to decide whether the deadline can be met in a model consisting of two processors, one resource, unit-time processing, and each task restricted to directly follow at most one task is an NP-complete problem.

Kafura describes a multiprocessing model for running tasks. Tasks may contain critical sections which can be entered by a fixed number of tasks at one time.[11] He determines bounds upon worst case completion time of all tasks relative to the optimal under various scheduling algorithms.

A major difference between Garey and Johnson's and Kafura's models and the present model is that in their models each task is executed exactly once whereas in the model to be described each task can be executed any number of times. This necessitates limits upon the response time of each task rather than a single deadline time. This new model corresponds more closely to process control applications or any application where repetitive sensing and reacting is required.

The other major difference in the two models is that tasks in the new model can use devices.

Despite the computationally intractable questions described by Garey and Johnson, Sahni, and others, real-time problems need to be solved. Practitioners must settle for suboptimal schedules and affirmative answers for only some of the specific times which can actually be met.

Another practical weakness of the models described in the literature cited above is that zero system overhead is assumed. This paper specifies a system design and shows how to precisely account for the overhead time generated by that system.

4-3-2 WORST CASE ANALYSIS OF TASK PERFORMANCE

4-3-2-1 Real-Time Program Model

A hard real-time system consists of a known set of tasks with the following characteristics:

1. Each task consists of a series of segments which are run in order, one segment at a time.
2. Tasks may use devices.
3. A task may include critical sections to take exclusive use of data areas and/or devices for the duration of a segment.
4. A task may be started or restarted in response to external signals or by the termination of task(s).
5. Each task must complete within its guaranteed response time.

Devices may be used by any of the tasks, but a device will perform service for no more than one task at a time.

For flexibility in specifying critical sections each data area or device to be protected is given a symbolic resource name. These symbolic resources are allocated before the segment in which they are needed can start and are freed when that segment finishes. No critical section can extend across two or more segments.

Dijkstra's P and V operations on semaphores are used to regulate the starting of tasks.[3] A task may be prefixed with one or more P operations to control the circumstances under which it may start. If the task is to start in response to an external event, the handling of the event consists of performing the appropriate V operation. If the completion of one task is to signal the start of another task (or even itself) then the signaling task is suffixed with the appropriate V operation.

The time interval guaranteed for $task_i$ is that time from the successful start of the task (P operations satisfied) to the completion of the task, and is referred to as $task_i$'s *guaranteed response time,* or simply *guaranteed time* (GT_i). $Task_i$ is not allowed to restart any sooner than GT_i time units after its most recent previous starting time.

4-3-2-2 Determining Guaranteed Response Times

The information about the tasks needed to compute the collection of guaranteed response times is:

1. The maximum processor time needed by each segment
2. The maximum operating time of each device
3. The symbolic resources needed by each segment (that is, critical sections)
4. The placement of device requests within each segment and the placement of segments within each task

Figure 4-3-1 is an example of how this paper presents this needed information for a real-time program of two tasks. Task 1 consists of three segments and task 2 contains two segments. Task 2 has a resource segment needing 3 ms of processor time and has a nonresource segment needing 1 ms of processor time and an operation upon device D1 requiring 10 ms.

The rules that govern the treatment of tasks are:

1. Resource segments (that is, segments requiring symbolic resources) are run before other segments—they have priority.
2. If only nonresource segments are ready to use the processor, each is to run at a specified rate of processor progress.
3. Device requests are honored on a first-come-first-served (FCFS) basis.
4. All resources needed by a segment are allocated simultaneously. If more than one task has made the same requests, the earliest request is honored first.
5. No task may be restarted earlier than its guaranteed-response-time units after its most recent previous starting time.

In a multiprogramming environment, critical sections (that need exclusive use of resources) have priority over other sections to reduce the time during which resource conflicts can occur.[9] In this real-time model, resource segments have priority over other segments to prevent tasks' nonresource segments from competing excessively for the processor. This is explained in more detail at the end of this section.

Later, the time available to run task$_i$'s nonresource segments will be computed. Other nonresource segments will compete with task$_i$ for this processor

Figure 4-3-1 Example real-time system of two tasks.

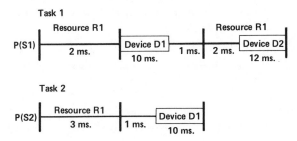

time. *Task$_i$'s nonresource running rate,* or simply *rate$_i$,* is defined as that fraction of the processor that task$_i$ must utilize to complete its nonresource segments within the available time. The sum of all tasks running rates must not exceed 1.

FCFS device scheduling is a simple method of avoiding indeterminate delays in satisfying a task's request for device service.

Resources needed by a segment are allocated as a block rather than one at a time and all are released at the end of the segment to avoid the possibility of deadlock.

Many sets of times will not work as the guaranteed response times for a given set of tasks. Rather than use a trial and error method to find times that work, the desired ratios (GT_i/GT_j) of guaranteed response times are selected. From these ratios, the actual guaranteed response times and running rates can be determined.

A worst case analysis is carried out separately for each task to determine the worst case blockage or slowdown it can suffer from all the other tasks.

The worst case time it takes task$_i$ to run is:

$$\text{Task}_i \text{ time} = \text{TOTR}_i + \text{TOTD}_i + \text{TOTN}_i/\text{rate}_i + \text{B}_i$$

where TOTR_i is task$_i$'s total processor requirement (processor time at 100 percent usage) for resource segments.

TOTD_i is the total time task$_i$ spends performing device operations.

TOTN_i is task$_i$'s total processor requirement (processor time at 100 percent usage) for nonresource segments.

B_i is the worst-case amount of time that task$_i$ is blocked or slowed down by other tasks.

Although rate$_i$ is yet to be determined, $\text{TOTN}_i/\text{rate}_i$ is the time to run task$_i$'s nonresource segments at rate$_i$.

Task$_i$ may be blocked in the following ways:

1. Task$_i$ in a nonresource segment and another task uses the processor while in a resource segment—since resource segments have priority (Figure 4-3-2 point c).
2. Task$_i$ needs a device already in use (Figure 4-3-2 point b).
3. Task$_i$ ready to start a segment needing a resource or resources already in use (Figure 4-3-2 points a & d).

Task$_i$ can be slowed down when:

4. Task$_i$ and other tasks are processing resource segments and share the processor.

Blockage because of (1) and (2) are straightforward. The amount of time task$_i$ is blocked because of (3) includes not only the time that a segment holding

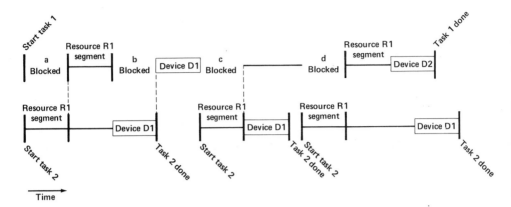

Figure 4-3-2 Worst case blockage of task 1 (of Fig. 1) is task 2's guaranteed time is 1/2 that of task 1. Note that portions of task 2 run 3 times for one run of task 1.

the needed resources uses the processor, but also the device time. This device time includes both the time the segment actually uses the devices as well as the time it must wait for other tasks to finish using them. If the segment in $task_i$ needs only one resource then each other $task_j$ can block the segment at most once. If, however, the segment in $task_i$ needs multiple resources, it can be blocked by more than one segment in $task_j$. The slowdown caused by (4) can be as much as the total processor requirement of those other resource segments.

Potentially, $task_j$ can execute $\lceil GT_i/GT_j \rceil + 1$ times during a given execution of $task_i$. The starting times of $task_i$ and $task_j$ are not synchronized and $task_j$ may begin late within its guaranteed time, GT_j, due to blockage and slowdown; or $task_j$ may complete early if it is not blocked or slowed down. The worst-case time that $task_i$ is blocked or slowed down is therefore:

$$B_i = \sum_{j \neq i} TOTR_j \cdot (\lceil GT_i/GT_j \rceil + 1) + BD_i$$

where $j \neq i$ if $j \neq i$ and $task_j$ can potentially interfere with $task_i$ (any task not synchronized to run before or after $task_i$) and where BD_i is the type of device blockage described under (3) above. For the examples given in this paper, BD_i is computed by hand but for larger problems the determination of BD_i should be automated.

The simplest algorithm to determine the upper bound of the blockage experienced by $task_i$, positions device requests and resource segments of other tasks to block $task_i$. An improved algorithm maintains the execution order of the device and resource requests within the tasks. A further refinement of the algorithm takes into account the duration of each segment.

The response time that can be guaranteed for $task_i$ is therefore:

$$GT_i = TOTR_i + TOTD_i + TOTN_i/rate_i + B_i \tag{1}$$

If the relative lengths of the guaranteed response times are to be maintained, then y can be chosen to select any set of times:

$$
\begin{bmatrix} GT_1 \\ \cdot \\ \cdot \\ \cdot \\ GT_n \end{bmatrix} = y \cdot \begin{bmatrix} GT_1/GTMIN \\ \cdot \\ \cdot \\ \cdot \\ GT_n/GTMIN \end{bmatrix} \tag{2}
$$

where GTMIN = min $\{GT_i\}$. Equation (1) rearranged to determine $rate_i$ in terms of y is then:

$$
rate_i = \frac{TOTN_i}{y \cdot GT_i/GTMIN - TOTR_i - TOTD_i - B_i} \tag{3}
$$

To be a proper solution, the sum of the running rates must not exceed unity ($\Sigma rate_i \leq 1$). This sum is a monotonically decreasing function of y, therefore y is easily used as an iteration parameter to achieve a set of running rates which sum sufficiently close to, but not exceeding, unity. Relationships (2) are then used to derive the response times that can be guaranteed.

An alternative solution technique is to set the sum of the rates to unity, express the relationships between the GT_i's, and then solve equations (1) as a set of simultaneous equations.

If priority were not given to resource segments, the above analysis of an upper bound for the response time of $task_i$ would have to include the effect of $\lceil GT_i/GT_j \rceil + 1$ times the nonresource time of each $task_j$. With the present policy, nonresource time can be ignored except for allowing enough time in the response time of $task_i$ to run $task_i$'s nonresource segments once at their specified rate. It must be cautioned that the above analysis is for an upper bound to the response time of each task—not necessarily the least upper bound.

4-3-2-3 Examples

The following examples illustrate the determination of guaranteed response times for the example shown in Figure 4-3-3. This example is similar to the classical reader-writer problem.[2]

Tasks 1 and 2 read information from device D1 and take action on devices D2 and D3, respectively. Task 3 must not be in the process of updating device D1 (in second segment) at the same time that task 1 and/or task 2 are examining device D1. This exclusion is accomplished with symbolic resources R1 and R2. Tasks 4, 5, and 6 are the same as tasks 1, 2, and 3, except they work with different data areas and devices. Each task is activated by an external signal that results in a V operation upon the appropriate semaphore (P operations shown in Figure 4-3-3).

In this example $TOTR_i = 1$ ms., $TOTD_i = 25$ ms., and $TOTN_i = 10$ ms. for $i = 1, \ldots, 6$.

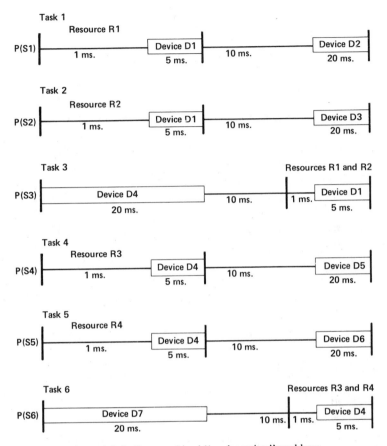

Figure 4-3-3 Two combined "reader-writer" problems.

Guaranteed times will first be found when all tasks have the same guaranteed response times.

Tasks 1, 2, 4, and 5 are all similar with $B_i = 2 \times 5 + 10$ ms. for $i = 1, 2, 4$, and 5. Blockage caused by devices in other paths is only 10 ms. because task 1, for example, can have its device D1 slowed down once by D1 in task 2 and once by D1 in task 3.

Tasks 3 and 6 are similar with $B_i = 2 \times 5 + 10$ ms. for $i = 3$ and 6. Note that task 3, for example, is not blocked twice by task 1 or task 2, as can sometimes occur when a segment needs more than one resource. The last segment of task 3 can be blocked once by the first segment of both tasks 1 and 2. It can also be slowed down by 1 ms. each if tasks 4, 5, and 6 at that time use the processor in their resource segments. This is a total of 15 ms. that task 3 is delayed, but tasks 1 and 2 take at least 30 ms. to get back to the point where they could reblock task 3.

Equation (3) becomes:

$$\text{rate}_i = \frac{10}{y \cdot 1 - 1 - 25 - 20} \qquad \text{for } i = 1,2,\ldots,6$$

When $y = 106$, the rates equal $1/6$ (.167) which sums to unity.

The guaranteed response times are 106 ms. If tasks are actually restarted that often, then the total processor usage is 62.3 percent rather than 30.6 percent when each is run separately.

The same example is now redone but this time let tasks 1, 2, and 3 complete twice as fast as tasks 4, 5, and 6.

This time $B_i = 2 \times 5 + 10$ for $i = 1,2,$ and 3. Each task can still interfere no more than twice with task 1, 2, or 3. Tasks 4, 5, and 6 can interfere with the other tasks no more than twice, but tasks 1, 2, and 3 can now interfere up to 3 times with tasks 4, 5, and 6. Therefore $B_i = 2 \times 2 + 3 \times 3 + 10$ for $i = 4, 5,$ and 6.

The guaranteed response times are determined as follows:

$$\begin{bmatrix} GT_1 \\ GT_2 \\ GT_3 \\ GT_4 \\ GT_5 \\ GT_6 \end{bmatrix} = y \cdot \begin{bmatrix} 1 \\ 1 \\ 1 \\ 2 \\ 2 \\ 2 \end{bmatrix}$$

$$\text{rate}_i = \frac{10}{y \cdot 1 - 1 - 25 - 20} \qquad \text{for } i = 1, 2, \text{ and } 3$$

$$\text{rate}_i = \frac{10}{y \cdot 2 - 1 - 25 - 23} \qquad \text{for } i = 4, 5, \text{ and } 6$$

The rates sum to nearly unity with $y = 85.8$. This yields rate .251 and guaranteed response time of 85.8 ms. for tasks 1, 2, and 3, and rate .0816 and response time of 171.6 ms. for tasks 4, 5, and 6.

4-3-3 IMPLEMENTATION

4-3-3-1 The Operating System

The operating system is controlled by a high precision interval timer. The timer must reset itself when its time interval expires. It must be possible for the machine to mask out all interrupts and only device interrupts.

The external events to which the operating system must respond are timer interrupt, device interrupt, and task-start signal. The internal events that must be handled are device request, P and V request, next segment request (which includes resource allocate and free), and task restart.

Ready resource segments are run before ready nonresource segments. The upper bound algorithm for response time does not specify any particular scheduling order for resource segments. If there are no ready resource segments, a ready nonresource segment is run.

Nonresource segments are not actually run at the rates derived for them. At best, they could be run at rates which only approximate their derived rates—at great task-switching overhead. The running rates function is to reserve enough time to run each task's nonresource segments prior to the expiration of its guaranteed response time. It can be observed that each task will complete its nonresource segments in time if ready nonresource segments are run in order of guaranteed task completion times (deadline scheduling of nonresource segments). A running nonresource segment must be preempted if another nonresource segment with an earlier completion time becomes ready or if any resource segment becomes ready.

Other features of the operating system are standard and will not be described here although flow charts for the entire system are given in appendix A. These features include queuing and assigning device requests in FCFS order, queuing and assigning resource requests, and doing P and V operations.

There are timing inaccuracies built into the way the operating system restarts tasks, but this introduces only a limited amount of error. Real-time tasks may not start on time. Depending upon how the test is done, tasks may start as much as a half time interval late or early, or they may start up to one interval late. If the guaranteed response time is much longer than one time interval, this is a minor error.

4-3-3-2 Operating System Overhead

Most services of the operating system are evoked by explicit requests from the tasks. The overhead time used by these services is assigned to the requesting task at the point of request. The explicit requests are: start task, start next segment, request device, handle device interrupt, and P and V synchronization.

The overhead time of a device interrupt is assigned to the task that requested the device at the point where the task resumes.

Appendix B shows at what points, and from which sources overhead is to be added to the tasks. This system overhead time is treated the same as resource segment time because once the system is evoked, it keeps control until the service is completed.

Usually operating system services do not interfere with device interrupts. However, several routines (including the timer routine) do disable device interrupts which delay their recognition. This has the effect of extending device times.

Timer interrupt handling is the only service whose overhead cannot be assigned to fixed points in each task. Timer interrupts are also a large source of system overhead. For this reason it is important to process timer interrupts efficiently, and even more important to accurately determine the upper bound on the time taken by timer interrupts.

Occasionally the timer may be ready to interrupt when interruptions are masked. Timer interruptions are never masked as long as a time interval so the only effect is for one time interval to be longer and the next one to be correspondingly shorter.

The timer overhead cannot be added directly to the processing time of the segments as can the overhead time of the other system services but is added separately.

Equation (3), when overhead is included, becomes:

$$\text{rate}_i = \frac{TOTN_i}{y \cdot GT_i/GTMIN - TOTR\&O_i - TOTD\&M_i - B\&O_i - TO_i}$$

where

$TOTR\&O_i$ is resource time in $task_i$, $TOTR_i$, plus the overhead costs that are assigned to fixed points in $task_i$,

$TOTD\&M_i$ is the device time in $task_i$, $TOTD_i$, plus the maximum time device interrupts are continuously masked times the number of device operations in $task_i$,

$B\&O_i$ is $\sum\limits_{j \neq i} TOTR\&O_j \cdot (\lceil GT_i/GT_j \rceil + 1) + BD\&O_i$ which is the blockage and slowdown that $task_i$ may suffer from other tasks (B_i adjusted to include overhead),

$BD\&O_i$ is BD_i but including the maximum length of time device interrupts are continuously masked times number of device operations included in BD_i,

TO_i is

$$\frac{\sum\limits_{j \neq i} TOTR\&O_i \cdot (\lceil GT_i/GT_j \rceil + 1) + TOTR\&O_i + TOTN_i}{T} \cdot TIO$$

which is the amount of time that can be spent handling timer interuptions during the duration of $task_i$.

T   is time interval, the time between
timer interrupts, and

TIO   is the overhead in handling a
timer interrupt.

4-3-4 IMPROVEMENTS AND EXTENSIONS

A more detailed analysis of the tasks in a dedicated real-time system will reveal even shorter guaranteed response times. The length and placement of each segment of each task is important. An automated search of the possible permutations of segment orderings will, however, be necessary.

With the current low price of microprocessors it is not unreasonable to allow the machine to be relatively lightly loaded (40 percent to 70 percent processor bound). If that is unacceptable, the remaining processor time can be used by background tasks which are independent of the real-time tasks. The available processor time can be used to process a second set of tasks in guaranteed time. This set of tasks has to be independent of the first set and have guaranteed response times which are several times longer than response times of the first set.

Three extensions to the model will make it more accurately reflect real-time programming.

First, the behavior of tasks in some applications depends to a great degree upon internal tests. An analysis can be done for each task to determine the chain of branches in the other tasks which will produce the most blockage.

Second, in some applications a task may create one or more other tasks. These synchronized tasks may compete with each other for devices and critical sections. Job shop scheduling can be used to determine the optimal schedule for each set of synchronized tasks.[1] The entire collection of tasks is run as described earlier with the constraint that each synchronized set follows the job shop optimal ordering.

Third, additional processors can be incorporated by modifying the operating system into a homogeneous (or symmetric) system. Locks will be [necessary] to permit orderly modifications of common information. The time that a processor is locked out by another must be included as overhead.

4-3-5 CONCLUDING COMMENTS

Hard real-time tasks which use critical sections and devices can run in guaranteed time.

The real-time task model presented is simple but adequate for many applications. Several extensions have also been suggested. The determination of guaranteed response times is uncomplicated but tedious for a large number of segments. The procedure can easily be automated.

The operating system which enforces the completion of tasks within their guaranteed response time is not complex. The operating system routines accomplishing this are quite short and do not use multiplication or division operations. These features and the low cost of small machines make a minicomputer or microcomputer attractive as the host machine.

The author is implementing the system defined in Appendix A on a small machine to determine worst case overhead values and to better decide the practicality of the model and its extensions.

The author wishes to thank one of the referees for some penetrating questions and helpful suggestions.

4-3-6 APPENDIX A SYSTEM FLOWCHARTS

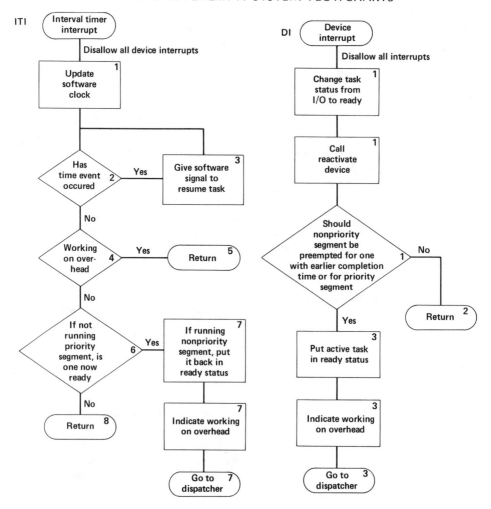

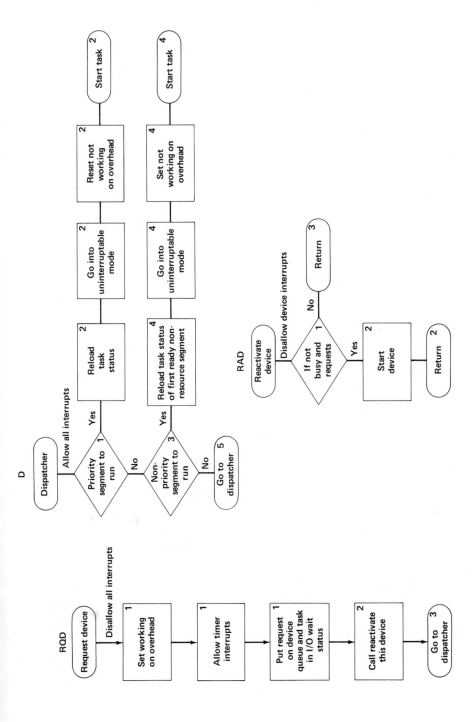

D

Dispatcher

Allow all interrupts

Priority segment to run 1
— Yes → Reload task status 2 → Go into uninterruptable mode 2 → Reset not working on overhead 2 → Start task 2

— No ↓

Non-priority segment to run 3
— Yes → Reload task status of first ready non-resource segment 4 → Go into uninterruptable mode 4 → Set not working on overhead 4 → Start task 4

— No ↓

Go to dispatcher 5

RAD

Reactivate device

Disallow device interrupts

If not busy and requests 1
— No → Return 3
— Yes → Start device 2 → Return 2

RQD

Request device

Disallow all interrupts

Set working on overhead 1 → Allow timer interrupts 1 → Put request on device queue and task in I/O wait status 1 → Call reactivate this device 2 → Go to dispatcher 3

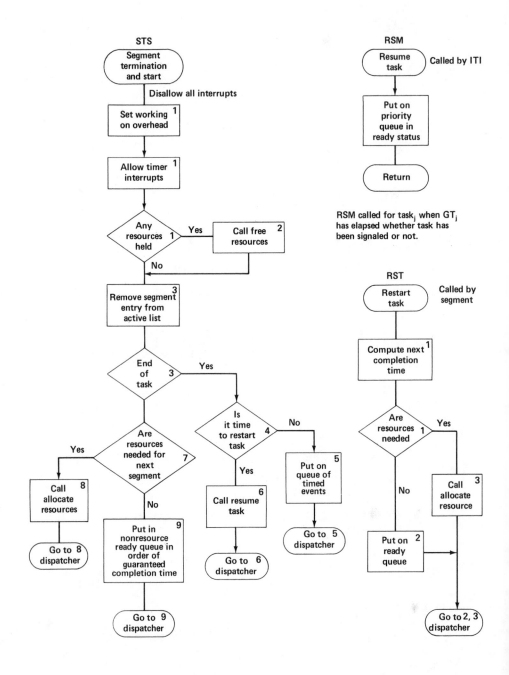

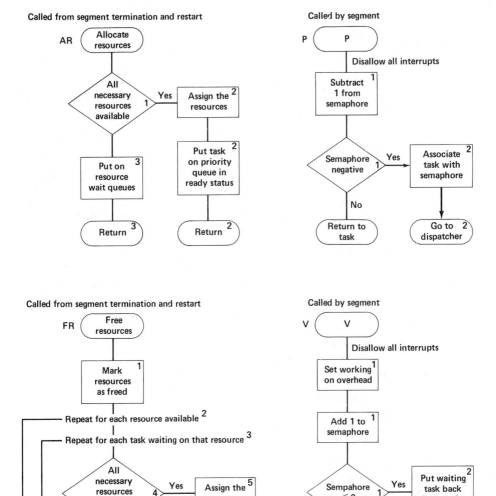

Note: there are much more efficient free algorithms, but this one is used for simplicity of design and bounded overhead.

4-3-7 APPENDIX B SYSTEM OVERHEAD

Example Task Code for Task 2 of Figure 4-3-1 With Overhead Placement Shown

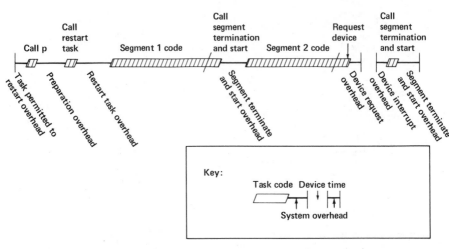

Correspondence Between Operating System Flowchart (Appendix A) and Overhead of its Services

Abbreviations of operating system module names:

AR	Allocate Resources
D	Dispatcher
DI	Device Interrupt Handler
FR	Free Resources
ITI	Interval Timer Interrupt Handler
P	P operation
RAD	Reactivate Device
RST	Restart Task
RSM	Resume Task
RQD	Request Device
STS	Section Terminate and Start
V	V operation

Service	*Components of system used*
	(*D 1,2 indicates boxes labeled 1 & 2 in dispatcher, for example*)
Task permitted to restart	ITI 2,3; RSM, ITI 7
Do P operation & proceed	P 1,2; D 1; MAX {D2, D3}; V2

Service	Components of system used
	(*D 1,2 indicates boxes labeled 1 & 2 in dispatcher, for example*)

Service	Components of system used
Do V operation	V 1,2,3
Restart task (nonresource)	RST 1,2
Restart task (resource)	RST 1,3; AR 1,3; FR 2,3,4,5,6
Segment termination and start (nonresource to nonresource)	STS 1,3,7,9; D 1,2
Segment termination and start (nonresource to resource)	STS 1,3,7,8; AR 1,3; FR 2,3,4,5,6; D 1,3
Segment termination and start (resource to resource)	STS 1,2; FR 1; k*(FR 2,3,4): STS 3,7,8; AR 1,3; FR 2,3,4,5,6; D 1,3
Segment termination and start (last segment-nonresource)	STS 1,3,4,5; D 1; MAX {D2, D3}
Segment termination and start (last segment-resource)	STS 1,2; FR 1; k*(FR 2,3,4); STS 3,4,5; D 1; MAX (D2,D3)
Request device	RQD 1,2; RAD 1,3; D 1; MAX {D2, D3}; RAD 2
Process device interrupt	DI 1,2; RAD 1,3 (When nonresource segment add DI 3; D 1,3,4) (When resource segment add DI 3; D 1,2)
Time overhead (TIO)	ITI 1,2,4,6,8
	k is not derived here but is bounded by (number of resources)*(number of tasks − 1)

4-3-8 REFERENCES

[1] Coffman, E. G., Jr. *Computer and Job Shop Scheduling Theory.* Wiley & Sons, New York, NY, 1976.

[2] Courtois, P. J., Henmans, F., and Parnas, D. L. Concurrent Control with "Readers" and "Writers." *Comm. ACM 14,* 10 (October 1971), pp. 667–668.

[3] Dijkstra, W. E. Hierarchical Ordering of Sequential Processes. Acta *Informatica 1,* (1971), 115–138.

[4] Easton, William B. Process Synchronization Without Long-term Interlock, *ACM SIGOPS* 6, 1 & 2, (June 1972), 95–100.

[5] Garey, M. R. and Johnson, D. S. Complexity Results for Multiprocessor Scheduling under Resource Constraints. *SIAM J. Comput. 4,* (1975), 397–411.

[6] Garey, M. R. and Johnson, D. S. Scheduling Tasks with Nonuniform Deadlines on Two Processors. *J. ACM 23,* 3, (July 1976), 461–467.

[7] Gonzalez, T., Ibarra, O. H., and Sahni, S. Bounds for LPT Schedules on Uniform Processors. *SIAM J. Comput. 5,* 1, (1977), 155–166.

[8] Gonzalez, Teofilo, and Sahni, Sartaj. Preemptive scheduling of Uniform Processor Systems. *J. ACM 25,* 1, (Jan. 1978), 92–101.

[9] Habermann, A. N. A New Approach to Avoidance of System Deadlocks. *Lecture Notes in Computer Science #16: Operating Systems,* Proceedings of an International Symposium held at Rocquencourt, April 23-25, 1974, 163–170.

[10] Johnson, H. H. and Maddison, M. S. Deadline Scheduling for a Real Time Multiprocessor. May, 1974, NTIS (N76–15843) Springfield, VA, 10p.

[11] Kafura, D. Scheduling Tasks With Critical Sections, Proceedings of the Annual Conference of the ACM (at Seattle), Oct., 1977.

[12] Lui, C. L. and Layland, James W. Scheduling Algorithms for Multiprocessing in a Hard-Real-Time Environment. *J. ACM 20,* 1, (Jan. 1973), 46–61.

[13] Manacher, G. K. Production and Stabilization of Real-Time Task Schedules. *J. ACM 14,* 3, (July 1967), 439–465.

[14] Muntz, R. R. and Coffman, E. G. Jr. Preemptive Scheduling of Real-Time Tasks on Multiprocessor Systems. *J. ACM 17,* 2, (April 1970), 324–338.

[15] Sahni, Sartaj K. Algorithms for Scheduling Independent Tasks. *J. ACM 23,* 1, (Jan. 1976), 116–127.

[16] Sorenson, P. G. and Hamachen, V. C. A Real-Time System Design Methodology. *INFOR 13,* 1, (Feb. 1975), 1–18.

~~~~~~

4-4 CREATION OF A PORTABLE SUPPORT SOFTWARE SYSTEM UTILIZING AN ABSTRACT MACHINE*

C. F. GILL AND W. F. GARRISON
The Boeing Company

~~~~~~

4-4-1 ABSTRACT

A technique for the implementation of a portable support software system is being successfully used at Boeing. The technique involves the creation of an abstract machine, that is, an imaginary computer specifically designed for the representation of software development tools. All tools in the system are coded expressly for the abstract machine; the system is then implemented on a specific host computing system by emulating the abstract machine on the actual com-

*From the Proceedings of the AIAA Conference, Oct. 1979. Reprinted with permission.

puter with a small interpreter. The desired portability is thus attained since it is much simpler to redo the interpreter for a new host than it is to rewrite an entire support software system. The interpretive execution approach for abstract machine implementation promised the best compromise among ease of portability, compactness of tool representation, and power of expression. Design details, execution analyses, and portability data are presented in a discussion of the success of that compromise.

4-4-2 THE PROBLEM OF SOFTWARE TOOL AVAILABILITY

The problem addressed by this paper is the rapid, low cost provision of software tools for projects that elect to use smaller computing systems for software development. The aerospace industry makes extensive use of complex electronic systems containing one or more computers as components. These "embedded" computers are frequently unsuitable for software development because of their special processing characteristics, insufficient memory, or limited peripherals. Software development for embedded computers is, therefore, often performed on a separate computing system, a "host" more suitable for the production of software systems. The software constructed on the host is subsequently transferred to the embedded "target" computer for test, integration, and eventual use. Although adequate tools usually exist for developing software to be executed on the host, "cross-tools" for developing software to be executed on a specific target computer are rarely available on an arbitrary host. Experience has repeatedly demonstrated the importance of adequate cross-tools for the development of embedded computer software, regardless of the host–target configuration used.

The provision of software development tools for use in the production of software for embedded computing systems is plagued by two major problems: availability and cost. Most software development tools are needed early in the development process, often immediately after the host and target computers have been selected. This allows little time for the development of the tools themselves. In addition, many users perceive the costs associated with the development of an adequate set of support tools to be excessive. This is partially a problem of user perception, but lowering both the development and utilization costs for support tools remains a desirable goal.

One technique that provides a partial solution to both the cost and availability problems is the reuse of previously developed support tools. Over the past ten years Boeing has demonstrated the validity of constructing a flexible, extendible support software system and reusing the tools in this system on a variety of software development efforts.[1,2] This system was designed to be hosted on a large scale computer, such as an IBM/370, and it has been used primarily by projects employing large numbers of operational programmers, with the associated number of configuration control and software test personnel also using the system. The system has proven to be extremely valuable for embedded computer software development and has been heavily used throughout its existence. However, it was not designed for projects wishing to utilize smaller computer systems for software development.

The rapid proliferation of small- to medium-scale computing systems throughout the aerospace industry, coupled with the expanded peripheral and processing capabilities available with many of these systems, has begun to transform such systems into attractive hosts for software development tools. Many smaller software development efforts would not require the utilization of a large central computing facility if an integrated, adaptive set of support tools, similar to the current Boeing support software system, were available on these smaller machines. The existence of such a compact system would allow smaller projects to make cost-effective use of software development tools on computing systems collocated with both their personnel and software integration laboratories. This capability would also permit projects with special security requirements the option of isolating a cheaper, stand-alone software development facility rather than periodically securing a more expensive and vulnerable large scale computing system.

4-4-3 THE PORTABILITY APPROACH

4-4-3-1 Alternatives

A basic approach utilized to obtain a reusable software development system for smaller projects is the construction of a portable system, one which can readily be hosted on a wide range of small- to medium-scale computing systems. A properly designed software development system can be rehosted with less cost and time than that required for the reimplementation of the system. In addition, projects may then utilize already purchased computers for software development, or maintain compatibility with their simulation, test, or even operational computers. In general, projects may select the computing system or systems that best fulfill their overall requirements and not be forced to obtain a particular computing system solely to acquire the software development tools available on that system.

Consideration was initially given to three techniques that were believed capable of providing the desired portability: machine independent Fortran, abstract machine modeling using macroprocessors, and abstract machine modeling using interpretive execution. A portable Fortran approach, similar to PFortran,[3] was attractive because of the near-universal availability of Fortran compilers on the potential systems hosts. However, the unsuitability of the language for software tool development and the extreme variability in the Fortran compilers surveyed eliminated this option from our review. The technique of defining an abstract machine model for the construction of software development tools and then implementing the machine using a macrotranslator such as STAGE2[4] was also considered attractive. In this case, however, the inefficient use of storage encountered with such a scheme, the complexity of the macros required to implement a reasonably powerful abstract machine, and the unreadable syntax used for the macrobody definition combined to dissuade us from utilizing this approach. The technique selected, abstract machine modeling using interpretive execution, promised the best compromise among ease of portability, compactness of tool representation, and power of expression for the implementation of software development tools. This technique has been widely used, most notably by the Pascal P compilers,[5,6] and has proved to be successful in providing the desired portability.

4-4-3-2 Abstract Machines

Abstract machine modeling has been succinctly described by Newey, Poole, and Waite:

> *Abstract machine modeling is based on the concept that the fundamental operations and data types required to solve a particular problem define a special purpose computer which is ideally suited to that problem. The algorithm for producing the solution can then be encoded as a program for this abstract machine model. In order to obtain a running version, the abstract machine model is realized on an existing computer by implementing its basic operations and data types.[7]*

An abstract machine (AM) may be defined as, in effect, a "higher-order language machine" for the construction of software development tools. The fundamental operations required to implement software tools become the machine operations for the AM; the data structures required become the basic data types of the AM. Programming an individual support tool is accomplished by specifying a sequence of fundamental operations acting on the associated basic data types. The operation sequence represents the actions to be performed during execution of the support tool. Figure 4-4-1 presents an example of such a sequence. This abstraction greatly facilitates the construction of support tools since the AM operations are designed specifically for this task. Note also that a compiler is no longer required for tool implementation; the use of higher-order machine operations means an assembler for the AM can provide the equivalent power of a typical HOL compiler.

A further benefit of AM use is the compact size of the tool representation afforded by the power of the fundamental operations. Since each AM operation represents a comprehensive, often complex, series of actions, a smaller number of these operations is required to specify a given support tool. As il-

Example: An abstract machine for character manipulation

Basic data types are character strings and pointers to character strings:

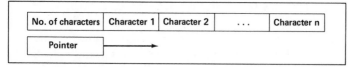

Sample operation sequence might be:

Fetch next character from input stream
concatenate character to string 1
if string 1 not equal to string 2 then
    allocate free storage area and copy string 1 into it
endif

Abstract machine operations are:

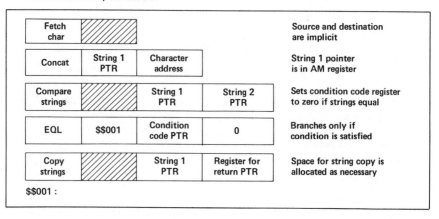

Figure 4–4–1 Abstract machine example.

lustrated in Figure 4–4–2, each AM operator represents a lengthy sequence of machine operations on a typical host computer. This compactness further enhances the portability of the AM by permitting the use of small computing systems as hosts, computing systems that usually would be considered too small to host a support software system without the extensive use of overlays.

4-4-3-3 Interpretive Execution

The AM representation, with all its compactness and power of expression, is of slight value unless the tools expressed in this representation can be executed on an actual host computing system. It is desired that software written for one machine (in this case, the AM) be executed on another machine (the selected host). The emulation of one machine on another is not a particularly novel technique, but one that can provide great portability. Software expressed as a

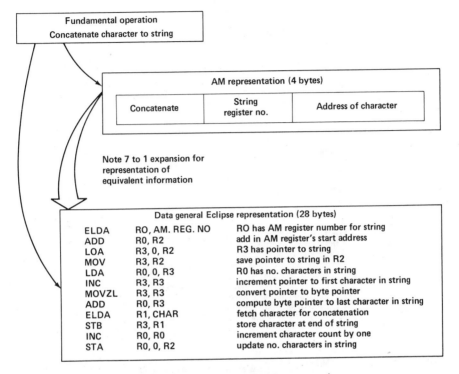

Figure 4-4-2 Compactness of AM representation.

sequence of AM operations does not need to be rewritten for transferal to a new host, only the implementation of an AM emulator is required. For each new host, an interpreter may be constructed that acts as an emulator for the AM by taking each AM instruction in turn, decoding it, and invoking the code on the host computer required to implement the specified operation. Figure 4-4-3 outlines the design of an AM interpreter.

With the use of interpretive execution, the proper construction of the AM interpreter becomes essential to the efficient execution of software development tools expressed in the AM operations. The operation decode and operand address computations are of special importance since they are performed every time an AM operation is executed, including loop executions. The basic operation decode function is therefore typically coded in the host assembly language and carefully optimized for execution speed. In addition, because of the speed considerations and the small size of the interpreter (usually less than 10K bytes), all the AM operation functions are coded in the host assembly language. Additional techniques for speed optimization, such as a direct mapping of the AM address space onto the host address space for rapid operand address calculation, may also be used.

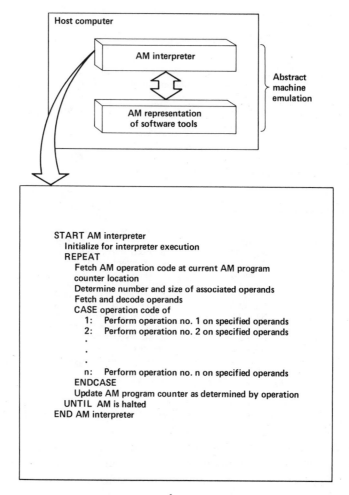

Figure 4–4–3 S³ AM interpreter.

4–4–3–4 The S³ Abstract Machine

The selection process for the actual AM operations used by the Boeing portable Support Software System (S³) was one of compromise. The dual goals of power of expression for the implementation of software tools and ease of implementation on a selected host (ease of portability) contain contradictory requirements. An AM with a large set of very specific, powerful operations could provide for a succinct and elegant representation of the software tools being implemented. However, the quick, reliable construction of the AM interpreter would then be hampered because of the number and complexity of the functions required for implementation on the selected host. A small set of low-level operations could be utilized to form a notably portable system, but an AM so defined would be ill-suited for the task of building software development tools.

Great care was taken to ensure that the basic S^3 AM architecture was amenable to efficient execution on the potential system hosts. As illustrated in Figure 4-4-4, the AM used is an 8-bit byte oriented machine, with the operations and data types being contained in multiples of 16 bits. This orientation was considered compatible with the majority of the potential S^3 hosts, permitting the AM operation fetch and decode cycle to be performed in an efficient manner. Encoding schemes with a higher information density are possible but the relative slowness of most computer shift operations required to decode the operations negates any advantages associated with the compactness of the representation.

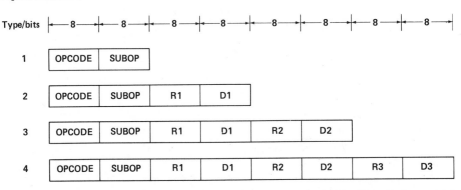

An effective operand address is formed by adding the contents of the specified register (Rx) with the associated displacement (Dx). All quantities are consigned positive integers.

Figure 4-4-4 S^3 AM operation format.

The use of 8-bit bytes influenced the AM design to incorporate 256 general purpose 16-bit registers, with all operands being specified in a register-displacement (0 to 255) format. Several of the AM registers are reserved for specific functions; for example, R0 contains the AM program counter, R1 points to the start of the AM registers, R3 contains a pointer to the procedure linkage stack frame, and R8 contains a condition code set by certain operations. As shown in Figure 4-4-5, the AM orientation around 8-bit bytes also influenced the selection of the AM data types.

The current S^3 AM operation set is summarized in the appendix.

4-4-3-5 Implementation

The current S^3 comprises a basic set of tools for use in the development of embedded computer software, including a retargetable cross assembler, a

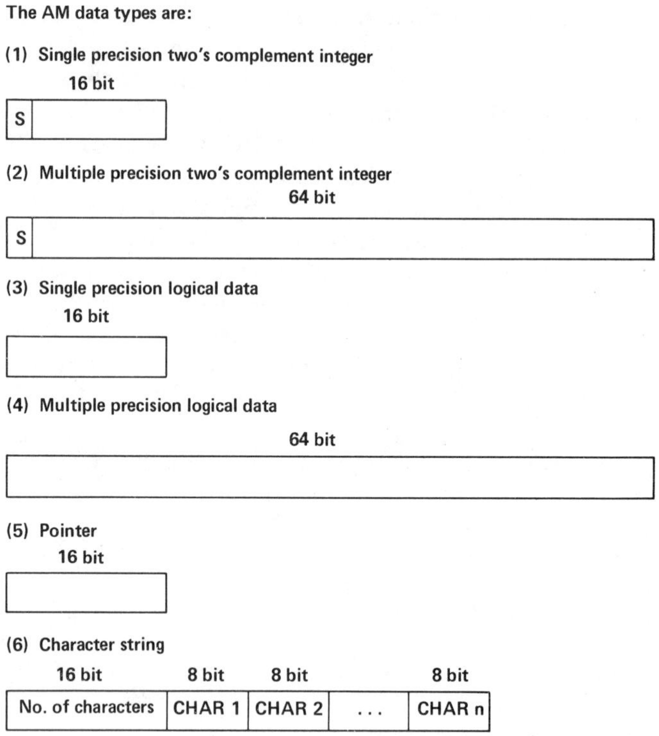

The AM data types are:

(1) Single precision two's complement integer

16 bit

S	

(2) Multiple precision two's complement integer

64 bit

S	

(3) Single precision logical data

16 bit

(4) Multiple precision logical data

64 bit

(5) Pointer

16 bit

(6) Character string

16 bit	8 bit	8 bit		8 bit
No. of characters	CHAR 1	CHAR 2	. . .	CHAR n

Figure 4-4-5 S^3 AM data types.

target-independent link editor, a global cross-reference processor, a symbolic file comparison processor, and the associated utilities and operating system interface. The implementation of such a set of software development tools using interpretive execution of an abstract machine is a two step process: the expression of the tools in AM operations and the construction of an AM interpreter on the selected host. As illustrated in Figure 4-4-6, the production of an AM load module for use on the host computer is equivalent to the usual language translation process. For the Boeing S^3, the design of a particular software development tool is first expressed in the S^3 problem-oriented language (POL). Since the S^3 AM was designed specifically for the representation of these tools, the POL is basically the S^3 AM assembly language augmented to include structured programming control statements and a procedure linkage convention. Therefore, only a simple preprocessor is required to translate a POL module into the equivalent AM assembly language module. This assembly language module may then be assembled and subsequently linked with the other modules constituting the support software system. After the AM absolute module is processed into the proper host computer format, this AM load module may be transferred to the selected host computer system via some suitable medium, or

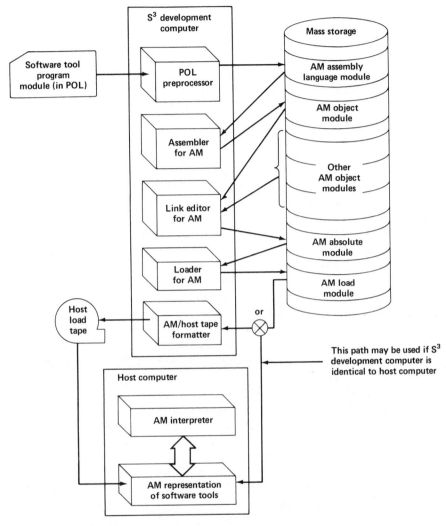

Figure 4-4-6   S³ construction process.

merely made available to the system if the translation processors described above are already present on the host.

The tools that constitute S³ are also the same basic tools required to construct S³. In order to permit the construction process to be portable, all the S³ developmental tools illustrated in Figure 4-4-6 have been implemented with the S³ AM. The step of transferring the AM load module from the S³ development computer to the selected host thus becomes unnecessary. In addition, this implementation of S³ in itself allows all tools developed as part of S³ to be used in the production of subsequent tools.

4-4-4 S³ EXPERIENCE

4-4-4-1 Expressiveness and Portability

Boeing personnel had previously implemented several translator systems utilizing an abstract machine approach, and this experience was employed in selecting the actual AM used in S³. Our subsequent utilization has demonstrated that the S³ AM is a suitable compromise among expressiveness, compactness, and ease of portability.

The power of the AM has become evident as we have implemented several software development tools, including a retargettable cross assembler and a target-independent linkage editor, with a level of effort roughly equivalent to that required if a systems programming language were used. The expressiveness of the AM for the software tool construction task is also evidenced by the compactness of software tools implemented in S³. We have produced two different target cross-assembler systems, one requiring only 20K bytes, the other 27K bytes of storage for the AM load module. A target-independent linkage editor required 18K bytes. The AM interpreters have required between 8 and 11K additional bytes, depending on the host machine used and the debugging options provided. Thus, since each software tool processor is essentially an overlay leg on a small S³ base leg, entire software development systems may execute in less than 40K bytes of main memory. The AM tools use the remaining available memory area as a dynamic free storage pool. Figure 4-4-7 provides an example of the S³ AM memory utilization.

The portability of the S³ AM has been demonstrated by the ease with which S³ has been rehosted. The AM was originally hosted on a Varian V77 system with less than four person-months of effort and then on a Data General Eclipse with slightly over four person-months. Both AM interpreters were coded in the host machine assembly language, and both were coded by personnel initially unfamiliar with the particular host being used. The AM was also implemented on an IBM/360, using a higher order language to code the interpreter, with only one person-month of effort. The entire S³, including all implemented tools, may thus be rapidly rehosted with each AM implementation on a new host. In fact, our most troublesome portability problems have been in the traditional, and often overlooked, areas of source file transferal (because of tape format and character set discrepancies) and consistent database access (because of differing file structures and file management systems).

We thus feel the feasibility of constructing a portable set of software development tools utilizing an abstract machine modeling technique has been demonstrated. S³ implementations are being successfully used within Boeing for the production of contracted software, and the original set of tools has been augmented in response to the needs of these users. This is not to imply, however, that all issues concerning this approach have been resolved; two of the primary issues are execution speed and memory usage.

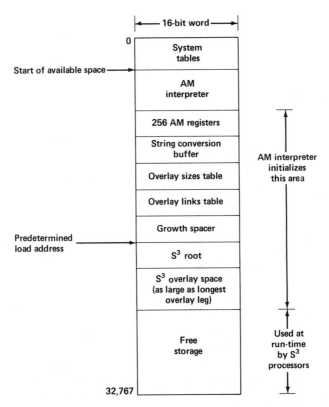

Figure 4-4-7 S³ AM on data general eclipse.

4-4-4-2 Execution Speed

Execution speed requirements for software development tools are somewhat nebulous, particularly when utilizing a small-scale host computer system in an interactive mode. The primary requirement for this type of usage is that the users not be unduly slowed in their interaction with the system by long waits for system responses to their commands. The system response speed may be influenced by several factors, including host machine execution speed, operating system efficiency, host system peripheral configuration, number of users concurrently accessing the system, and efficiency of the processing functions being performed.

Although efficiency is one factor of many, it becomes an issue because functions performed by interpreting an AM model are inherently slower in execution speed than equivalent functions coded directly for implementation on a given host system. As each AM operator is executed, there is an associated overhead of execution time involved in fetching and decoding the operation and any associated operands. For example, the S³ interpreter implemented on the

Data General Eclipse uses 23.5 microseconds for the AM operation decode and an additional 8 microseconds for each explicit operand address computation. The execution time for the function specified by the operation can often be significantly less than the execution time required to fetch and decode the operation, particularly for the simpler operations like integer assignment or incrementation. A preliminary analysis, with the average AM operation time being weighted by the AM operation frequency of usage for a typical software development tool, shows the average S^3 AM operation requires slightly less than half the time needed for the operation decode and operand address resolution. This implies that a comparable system, coded expressly for a selected host, could execute three times as fast as the S^3 implementation.

Several options have been considered for improving the execution time for S^3, including:

1. performing the AM emulation with hardware microprogramming rather than software interpretation;
2. restructuring of the AM to a stack-oriented architecture with implicit operands, although this approach involves a trade-off between the decrease in overhead because fewer operands need to be decoded and the decrease in speed because of the poor mapping between a stack-oriented machine and most of the potential host computers for S^3; and
3. selecting a small subset of S^3 (that is, those portions most often executed) for direct host machine implementation, thus having the bulk of S^3 in the AM representation for compactness but allowing for an increase in the execution speed of the entire system.

The concept that only certain portions of any given system need be considered for optimization is well known and the mixture of direct and interpretive code could provide sizable execution speed advantages.[8,9] However, we have had little impetus to pursue any enhancement techniques to date; initial experience with S^3 in an interactive mode, both in single- and multiple-user configurations, has shown no significant effects attributable to this execution slowdown. The use of S^3 for larger software development projects, its use on more fully-loaded computer systems, or the inclusion of more complex software tools may cause the execution speed effects to be more evident.

4-4-4-3 Memory Usage

Certain aspects of memory usage by software development tools on small-scale systems have proved disconcerting. Despite the extreme compactness of representation afforded by the AM concept, S^3 user projects have encountered memory limitations. Typical small system hosts allow maximum user regions of only 64K bytes and the S^3 AM address space is limited to this size. Assembling very large programs or linking a large number of modules can cause the S^3 assembler or link editor to use all the available storage in a region. The techniques currently used to alleviate these memory limitations include advising the user to restructure the task, redesigning the particular S^3 tool to utilize auxiliary storage for certain data structures, or segmenting the tool with a more fragmented overlay structure. Since all three options have the disadvantage of increasing the total execution time required to perform a task, the restructure of the S^3 AM for more compactness [10,11] is being investigated.

4-4-4-4 Improvements

In addition to the potential enhancements for speed and compactness mentioned previously, several other S^3 improvements are being investigated:

1. Implementation of an interactive debug package in the AM operations. The initial S^3 interpreter was designed with a modest set of interactive debug aids for use during the development of an S^3 processor. This capability was quite useful but subsequent hosts have not included it, primarily because of insufficient time during the interpreter implementation. The use of the AM to perform the debug functions will advance the portability of this capability.

2. Elimination of rarely used operations. The execution of S^3 has been instrumented to determine AM operation utilization frequency and several operations (for example, binary number to ASCII string conversion, ASCII string to hexadecimal conversion) were found to be virtually unused during the performance of some representative S^3 tasks. This infrequent use implies that these functions may be deleted as AM operations and instead, without significant speed penalties, coded as sequences of other AM operations. Decreasing the number of operations in the AM enhances its portability since fewer operations need be implemented in the AM interpreter.

3. Optimization of high-use operations. For instance, frequency utilization analysis for the S^3 AM operations has shown integer assignment and incrementation to be frequently executed functions. The modification of the AM to include a specific integer assignment operation (rather than a subcase of COPY) and an add literal operation (rather than ADD with the address of an integer constant) would increase the S^3 execution speed.

4. Revision of the S^3 linkage convention. An elegant, recursive linkage mechanism is currently used for S^3, with a dynamic stack frame being allocated from free storage for each procedure invocation. Unfortunately, this mechanism is slow, a significant factor in light of the highly-modular structure of S^3. A faster, static stack linkage mechanism could be efficiently implemented with the addition of a procedure entry and a pro-

cedure return operation to the AM; recursion would then be provided only on programmer option.

4-4-5 CONCLUSIONS

The utilization of an abstract machine modeling technique to provide a portable set of software development tools has proved to be effective. Production software for embedded computer systems has been successfully developed using S^3 and its utilization is continuing. Further use of S^3 on software production projects and the addition of more tools to the current set available are anticipated. In addition, we are currently performing research on the AM structure and operation set to determine improvements that will enhance the execution speed, compactness, and portability of S^3. The long-term feasibility of this approach is apparent; its utilization will depend on the availability of more effective techniques.

4-4-6 ACKNOWLEDGMENTS

We wish to acknowledge the contributions of R. L. Wilson, who championed the abstract machine approach throughout our initial skepticism. We also wish to thank Maretta Holden, Elmer Reed, and John Thompson for helpful critiques on the initial drafts of this paper.

4-4-7 REFERENCES

[1] Gill, C. F., and Holden, M. T., "On the Evolution of an Adaptive Support Software System," 1977, Computers in Aerospace Conference.

[2] Holden, M. T., "The B-1 Support Software System for Development and Maintenance of Operational Flight Software," NAECON '76.

[3] Whitten, D. I., and deMaine, P. A. D., "A Machine and Configuration Independent Fortran: Portable Fortran (PFortran)," *IEEE Transactions on Software Engineering,* Vol. SE-1, No. 1, March 1975.

[4] Waite, W. M., "Building a Mobile Programming System," *The Computer Journal,* Vol. 13, No. 1, February 1970.

[5] Nori, K. V., Annann, V., Jensen, K., and Nageli, H. H., "The PASCAL (P) Compiler: Implementation Notes," December 1974.

[6] Shillington, K. A., and Ackland, G. M. (editors), "USCD PASCAL Version 1.5," Institute for Information Systems, University of California, San Diego, 1978.

[7] Newey, M. C., Poole, P. C., and Waite, W. M., "Abstract Machine Modeling to Produce Portable Software—A Review and Evaluation," *Software-Practice and Experience,* Vol. 2, 1972.

[8] Dakin, R. J., and Poole, P. C., "A Mixed Code Approach," *The Computer Journal,* Vol. 16, No. 3, August 1973.

⁹ Dawson, J. L., "Combining Interpretive Code with Machine Code," *The Computer Journal,* Vol. 16, No. 3, August 1973.

¹⁰ Helps, K. A., "Compact Interpreters—Their Implications on Software and Hardware Design," AGARD-CP-149, Real Time Computer Based Systems Symposium, 1974.

¹¹ Hoevel, L. W., and Flynn, M. J., "The Structure of Directly Executed Languages: A New Theory of Interpretive System Design," Stanford Electronics Laboratories, Stanford University, Stanford, CA, March, 1977.

4-4-8   APPENDIX

Mnemonic	Name	Type	Description
ADD	Add	4	16-bit add of operand 2 to operand 3, sum is placed in operand 1
ADDM	Add, multiple precision	3	64-bit add of operand 2 to operand 1, sum is placed in operand 1
ANDM	Logical and, multiple precision	3	64-bit logical product of operand 2 with operand 1, result is placed in operand 1
BAL	Branch and link	2 (modified)	Save current program counter and branch to effective address (full 16-bit address is used rather than register/displacement)
BALI	Branch and link, indirect	2	Save current program counter and branch to contents of effective address
BINTOS	Binary to string	3	Convert operand 1 into an ASCII string of binary characters at operand 2
CATC	Concatenate character to string	2	Concatenate character at operand 1 to string pointed to by register in subop field
CATS	Concatenate substring to string	4	Concatenate substring starting at operand 2 and of length specified by operand 3 onto string at operand 1
CHAR	Character	1	Fetch next character from input stream and place in standard buffer
CHARNB	Character nonblank	1	Fetch next nonblank character from input stream and place in standard buffer
CLOSE	Close file	2	Close file whose description is at operand 1
COMPS	Compare strings	3	Compare string at operand 1 with string at operand 2 and set condition code accordingly
COPY	Copy (assignment)	3	Copy number of words specified by subop field from operand 2 into operand 1
COPYS	Copy string	3	Allocate string of required size from free storage, set contents of operand 1 to point to it, and copy string at operand 2 into it
CVD	Covered divide	4	16-bit covered division of operand 2 by operand 3, result is placed in operand 1
DECTOS	Decimal to string	3	Convert operand 1 into an ASCII string of decimal characters at operand 2
DIV	Divide	4	16-bit division of operand 2 by operand 3, quotient is placed in operand 1
EQL	Equality comparison	3	If operand 1 is equal to operand 2 then proceed to next operation, otherwise increment program counter by subop field

Figure 4-4-8a S^3 AM operations.

Mnemonic	Name	Type	Description
GEQ	Greater than or equal to comparison	3	If operand 1 is greater than or equal to operand 2 then proceed to next operation, otherwise increment program counter by subop field
GET	Get data block from file	4	Input block of length specified by operand 3 from file whose description is at operand 1 and store into operand 2
GETC	Get character from string	3	Fetch character at position specified by operand 1 in string pointed to by register in subop field and store into operand 2
GIVE	Give back free storage	2	Return block of free storage of size specified by operand 1 and pointed to by register in subop field
GIVES	Give back string to free storage	1	Return string pointed to by register in subop field to free storage
GOTO	GOTO	1	Increment program counter by subop field
GOTOI	GOTO, indirect	2	Replace program counter by operand 1
GRT	Greater than comparison	3	If operand 1 is greater than operand 2 then proceed to next operation, otherwise increment program counter by subop field
HEXTOS	Hexadecimal to string	3	Convert operand 1 into an ASCII string of hexadecimal characters at operand 2
LDIF	Logical difference	4	16-bit exclusive or of operand 2 and operand 3, result is placed in operand 1
LEFTM	Left logical shift, multiple precision	3	64-bit left logical shift of operand 1 by count specified in operand 2
LEQ	Less than or equal to comparison	3	If operand 1 is less than or equal to operand 2 then proceed to next operation, otherwise increment program counter by subop field
LES	Less than comparison	3	If operand 1 is less than operand 2 then proceed to next operation, otherwise increment program counter by subop field
LPRO	Logical product	4	16-bit and of operand 2 and operand 3, result is placed in operand 1
LSUM	Logical sum	4	16-bit or of operand 2 and operand 3, result is placed in operand 1
MUL	Multiply	4	16-bit multiplication of operand 2 by operand 3, product is placed in operand 1
NEQ	Not equal comparison	3	If operand 1 is not equal to operand 2 then proceed to next operation, otherwise increment program counter by subop field
NOTE	Note current file position	3	Return the current position for the file whose description is at operand 1 in operand 2
OCTTOS	Octal to string	3	Convert operand 1 into an ASCII string of octal characters at operand 2
OPEN	Open file	2	Open file of type specified by subop field whose description is at operand 1
ORM	Logical or, multiple precision	3	64-bit logical sum of operand 2 and operand 1, result is placed in operand 1
POINT	Set pointer to file position	3	Set current position for file whose description is at operand 1 to operand 2
POP	Pop element from linked list stack	2	Remove bead from top of linked list pointed to by register in subop field, return pointer to bead in operand 1
POPG	Pop element from linked list stack and give back to free storage	2	Remove bead of size specified by operand 1 from top of linked list pointed to by register in subop field and return bead to free storage
PRINT	Output record to sequential file (e.g., print file)	3	Convert character string at operand 2 to a host dependent print record and output to the file whose description is at operand 1

Figure 4-4-8a (cont.).

Mnemonic	Name	Type	Description
PUSH	Push element onto linked list stack	2	Insert bead pointed to by operand 1 into front of linked list pointed to by register in subop field
PUSHT	Push element taken from free storage onto linked list stack	2	Allocate bead from free storage of size specified by operand 1 and insert into front of linked list pointed to by register in subop field
PUT	Put data block into file	4	Output block at operand 2 of length specified by operand 3 into file whose description is at operand 1
PUTC	Put character into string	3	Put character at operand 2 into position specified by operand 1 in string pointed to by subop field
READ	Read record from sequential file	3	Input next record from file whose description is at operand 1, store as character string at operand 2
RIGHTM	Right logical shift, multiple precision	3	64-bit right logical shift of operand 1 by count specified in operand 2
STOBIN	String to binary	3	Convert ASCII string of binary characters at operand 1 to 16-bit integer at operand 2
STODEC	String to decimal	3	Convert ASCII string of decimal characters at operand 1 to 16-bit integer at operand 2
STOHEX	String to hexadecimal	3	Convert ASCII string of hexadecimal characters at operand 1 to 16-bit integer at operand 2
STOOCT	String to octal	3	Convert ASCII string of octal characters at operand 1 to 16-bit integer at operand 2
SUB	Subtract	4	16-bit subtraction of operand 3 from operand 2, difference is placed in operand 1
SUBM	Subtract, multiple precision	3	64-bit subtract of operand 2 from operand 1, difference is placed in operand 1
SUPR	Supervisor call	3	Operating system interface, function depends on subop field (e.g., stop interpreter, initialize free storage)
TAKE	Take free storage	2	Allocate block of free storage of size specified by operand 1 and return pointer to it in register in subop field
TAKES	Take string from free storage	2	Allocate block of free storage of size required by number of characters specified by operand 1 and return pointer to it in register in subop field
USER	User function	4	Special user functions not included in basic operation set (e.g., value truncation, hash code calculation)
XORM	Exclusive or, multiple precision	3	64-bit logical difference of operand 2 and operand 1, result is placed in operand 1

Figure 4-4-8a   (cont.).

4-5 ESTIMATION OF COMPUTER RESOURCE OVERHEADS INCURRED BY USING A HIGH-LEVEL LANGUAGE*

R. E. WALTERS

Post Office Research Centre, UK

4-5-1 INTRODUCTION

This paper addresses the problem of measuring the efficiency of code generated by high-level language compilers. A simple tool, which has general uses in the estimation of computer resources, has been applied to various compilers and machines. The results obtained are of general interest since they not only compare the behavior of different compilers, but also indicate the variation of performance obtained for differing workloads. The tool used is the Standardized-Kernel Evaluation Technique (SKET) which will be briefly described in the paper. The high level language studied is CORAL (1), a language specifically designed for real-time applications.

4-5-2 SKET—BRIEF DESCRIPTION

SKET has been more generally described elsewhere (2) but a brief description is necessary here in order that its limitations and usefulness in the context of high-level language testing can be appreciated.

The technique is based on a set of kernels (fourteen in all, though five are not used here). The kernels define a set of tasks known to be useful in constructing telephone switching application programs. Two examples which are indicative of the level of kernel complexity are: search a table for a given item of data and, move a specified amount of data within the computer store.

Nearly all kernels have parameters (for example the amount of data to be moved) and all have a variable weighting. Thus by selection of appropriate kernels, parameter values, and weightings a representative approximation to a given telephonic function can be assembled.

The kernels are rigorously and unambiguously defined in English. They can therefore be coded either in assembly language or a high-level language and parameterized values for their execution times and store occupancy so obtained. These values can be combined with the representative approximation of

*Originally published in the Proceedings of the Conference on Software Engineering for Telecommunication Switching Systems (Third International) Helsinki, June 1978. Reprinted with permission.

a specified function (termed a kernel assembly) via a simple computer program to produce estimates to execution time and store requirement.

The entire procedure is similar to the production of a high-level program. However, rather than selecting a particular group of high level code statements to perform a task, a suitable kernel, or group of kernels, which, when parameterized, gives a good approximation to the task, is chosen. A high-level program is compiled to produce executable code, whereas a kernel assembly is compiled to produce estimated performance figures for a particular machine.

The important feature is that any kernel assembly can be processed for any machine which has a kernel compiler. The estimates produced, though approximate, are derived from identical applications.

SKET evolved initially as a benchmarking technique for comparing the power of different machines in a telephony environment. Later it was employed in the estimation of computer resource demands for specific machines and applications (3); that is, performance modeling. The use described here is somewhat parallel to those mentioned since compiler performance is basic to overall system performance.

The usefulness of the technique stems from its ability to give a quick and reasonably accurate estimate of the performance of a well-defined function, and its ability to provide that estimate for any machine which has a kernel compiler.

An assembly language version of a SKET compiler can be fairly readily produced for most machines since the kernels themselves are simple and well-defined. A high-level language version is even simpler since the kernels, once coded, can be applied directly, perhaps with a few small changes, to any machine which supports the particular high-level language (in this case CORAL).

4-5-3 COMPARISON PROCEDURE

We shall now show how SKET was employed in estimating the overhead incurred when using a high-level language instead of assembler. The procedure used is summarized in Figure 4-5-1 and described in detail below.

4-5-3-1 Preparation of Benchmarks

Fortunately, since SKET had already been used extensively for power comparison and performance modeling, a variety of benchmarks (or more accurately, kernel assemblies) already existed. This not only economized on the effort required for the study but also ensured that the benchmarks were truly independent and yet drawn from practical application designs. The benchmarks are representative of a telephony control environment, and are of specific interest since they demonstrate the variation in behavior of different functions within a specific application suite.

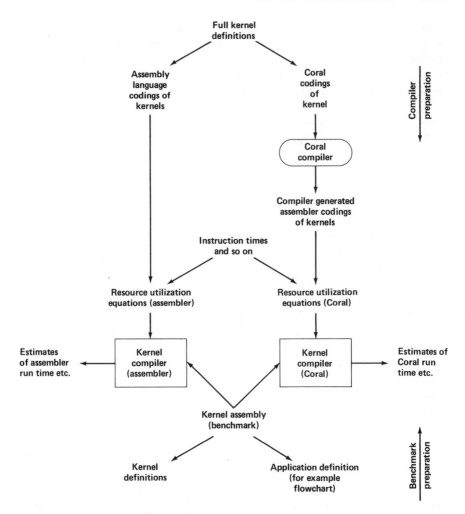

Figure 4-5-1 Comparison procedure.

4-5-3-2 Preparation of Kernel Compilers

The kernels used here are those necessary to estimate application program resource utilization. A full set contains five operating system kernels but these are rather specialized and have not been included in this study.

HIGH-LEVEL LANGUAGE VERSIONS.   Full definitions of the kernels are not included here, but extracts from codings produced for each of the nine kernels utilized are reproduced as Appendix 1 and should be viewed together with Appendix 2 which will be described below.

As previously noted the language used is CORAL; in fact a subset of the language has been found adequate for this purpose. Employing this subset the kernel code has been processed successfully by five distinct compilers with only minor modifications (none of which would seriously affect the validity of the comparisons made here). Thus the codings of Appendix 1 become the standard kernel definitions for this study.

To prepare a kernel compiler the codings are compiled and a listing of the assembly code generated is obtained. This code is then analyzed with the aid of relevant instruction formats and times such that a series of performance equations can be produced for each kernel. More specifically equations for execution time, store occupancy, instructions executed, and memory accesses are obtained. Each equation may be a function of the kernel parameters depending upon which variable is considered. The time equation for kernel 2, for example, will depend on the number of data items moved whereas the storage occupied is insensitive to this parameter (data storage is excluded from the equations).

In some cases more than one version of code is produced for a single kernel. This too depends on parameter values. In such instances the parameter performs a switching function to select the requisite version. Parameter values are, of course, defined by the benchmarks. Hence at the kernel compiler production stage all reasonable values must be catered for.

ASSEMBLER VERSIONS.   Similar equations are derived from assembly language code produced directly from the definitions—a very brief summary is included as Appendix 2. The standard here is the English definition of each kernel and it will be obvious that rigorous and unambiguous descriptions are mandatory if programmer variation is to be avoided. However the kernels are fairly simple so that the amount of code produced is small. The definitions have been in use for some time and subject to many revisions aimed at eradicating ambiguities; consequently, a high degree of confidence can be expressed in their ability to minimize programmer variation.

THE KERNEL COMPILERS.   The kernel compiler is a simple program which accepts an assembly of kernels, each with a specified weighting and defined parameter values, derives the resource utilization for each from the equations described above and calculates overall values of execution time and store occupancy for the complete assembly.

In this study four machines have been included, each of which can be considered to have two kernel compilers; a CORAL version and an assembler version.

4-5-4 STUDY SUBJECTS

It would not be appropriate to identify the particular machines tested and their respective compilers here. They are merely referenced as M1, M2, M3, and M4. This anonymity should not detract from the results presented, since it is the range and variation of efficiency ratios which are of more general interest.

All four machines are designed for, or used in, environments similar to that represented by the benchmarks (that is, telephone exchange control), and of course each machine has a CORAL compiler capable of processing the kernel code of Appendix 1.

Four distinct benchmarks are used. These will be referenced as B1, B2, B3, and B4. They represent a signaling subsystem process, a peripheral handler process, a digital switch control process, and a call handling process respectively. They are all reasonably large, B4 being the largest.

4-5-5 STUDY RESULTS

The ratio of CORAL execution time to assembler execution time and of CORAL store requirement to assembler requirement has been calculated for each benchmark when applied to each machine. The ratios are referred to as time and store expansion ratios.

The expansion ratios are presented as Tables 4-5-1 and 4-5-2 for time and store respectively. However bald figures are a little difficult to digest so the results of Table 4-4-1 are presented pictorially as Figure 4-5-2. Here the time expansion ratios are plotted for each benchmark. The ratios pertaining to each machine have been linked for ease of identity and to facilitate comparison.

TABLE 4-5-1   Time Expansion Ratios

Benchmark	Machine			
	M1	M2	M3	M4
B1	1.8	1.8	2.2	3.0
B2	2.2	1.6	2.4	4.4
B3	2.0	1.7	2.0	3.6
B4	1.6	1.3	1.5	2.5

TABLE 4-5-2   Store Expansion Ratios

Benchmark	Machine			
	M1	M2	M3	M4
B1	1.7	1.5	1.6	1.6
B2	1.8	1.2	1.7	1.5
B3	1.3	1.2	1.3	1.6
B4	1.6	1.3	1.3	1.6

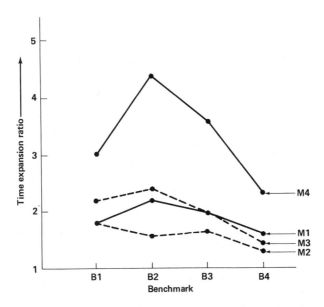

Figure 4-5-2   Variation of time expansion ratio with benchmark.

It is evident that considerable variation in expansion ratio is exhibited for differing benchmarks—especially for the particular machine which returns large expansion ratios. It is also evident that each machine exhibits a similar pattern of behavior, though machine M2 displays an ability to deal . . . better with benchmark B2 whereas the others behave decidedly worse.

The figure emphasizes the dangers of quoting a single expansion ratio for a given compiler. In the least spectacular case (M2), a variation in time overhead incurred in using CORAL over assembler of 30 percent to 80 percent is predicted for the four benchmarks. The least efficient machine exhibits a variation of 150 percent to 340 percent.

The behavior of store expansion ratios is not plotted since these are evidently not so greatly affected by choice of benchmark.

The disparity in time and store expansion ratio is interesting since they are often quoted as being much the same. At first this was thought to stem directly from program loops but, since the benchmarks applied are identical, loop counts for each machine must be identical; time and store ratios should therefore be the same. However, further investigation indicated that the disparity was indeed due to program loops. Detailed study of the code produced by some of the compilers indicated a very high expansion ratio within loops as compared with that in serially executed code. In fact manipulation of the benchmarks, such that all loop counts were reduced to unity, yielded very similar store and time expansion ratios. As the loop counts were increased then

TABLE 4-5-3 Reduction in expansion ratio with
loop count

Expansion Ratio	Normal Loop Counts	Unity Loop Counts
Time	2.00	1.12
Store	1.35	1.03

loop expansion ratios began to dominate execution time comparison, store expansion ratios are, of course, relatively unaffected.

Actual figures derived for machine M2 using an example benchmark yielded the expansion ratios quoted in Table 4-5-3. With normal loop counts (that is, those specified by the kernel parameters) expansion ratios were quite significant. Reducing all loop counts to unity reduces the expansion ratios to near unity. It is worth noting however that this was the most efficient compiler examined here.

The determining role of loop expansion ratios emphasizes the need for optimizing code generated by compilers from the "FOR" construct. But at the same time, it is perhaps worth noting that the technique used here does tend to produce "tight" loops, that is those without a great deal of executable code within them. Many of the loops contain array accesses whereas the serial code does not and this, together with the overhead normally produced by the loop control code generated by compilers, accounts for observed disparities in time and store expansion ratios.

4-5-6 LIMITATIONS OF THE STUDY

Using SKET to estimate high-level language expansion ratios is open to criticisms—some of which have already been mentioned in passing. By its very nature the test applied to each compiler is limited since the facilities used in programming the kernels are but a fraction of those available from the language.

Within this limitation the technique used has some advantages over the more conventional approach to the measurement of compiler efficiency. Normally comparisons are made between two programs, both supposedly performing identical tasks, one programmed in assembler, the other in a high-level language. This approach, though it allows full use of available language facilities, suffers other failings. First it is difficult to ensure that the two programs do in fact perform the same task. Second it is almost impossible to standardize the competence of programmers; where a program of any substance is to be written variations in the abilities of either assembler or high-level programmers are almost bound to distort results. Third, within the constraints of reasonable expenditure, it is . . . [almost] impossible to utilize a benchmark which is sufficiently large to be considered representative.

The technique used here goes some way towards overcoming these practical difficulties. We can be reasonably certain that programmer variation has been minimized, that both assembler and high-level programs are doing the same job, and that the jobs are reasonably representative (the largest benchmark, B4, has an estimated program store requirement of nearly 8000 words in assembly language).

The tendency for small loops to dominate time expansion ratios has been noted in the last section. Obviously in some cases this can lead to unexpectedly high estimates of CORAL run time over those obtained for assembler. However this in no way detracts from what is perhaps the most important facet of this study: comparing the efficiency of various compilers in performing identical tasks.

4-5-7 DISCUSSION

The results obtained here form a useful indicator of the widely varying code generation efficiencies of a specific selection of CORAL compilers. The variations are partly a reflection of target-machine architecture, and partly an indication of different compiler design philosophies.

Detailed comparison of assembly and CORAL generated code unearthed various reasons for the variations. Machine M4, for example, suffered heavy time penalties because the compiler utilized library procedures to perform certain functions in its generated code. Storage occupied by these procedures has, reasonably, been excluded from store occupancy estimates since in any large system this will be negligible. However, general procedures are inevitably less efficient than the alternative (in-line code) and this is aptly demonstrated by the results. This then is an example of inefficiency directly accountable to the particular compiler used.

High expansion ratios which can be directly traced to machine architecture arose in cases where specialized instructions were available to improve assembly program efficiency, but were barred to the CORAL programmer since they had no counterparts in the language definition. Obviously this is an area where assembly language inserts to the CORAL program will be useful.

Although it would be unrealistic to attempt to draw general conclusions from these observations, they do form a fertile source of specific comments pertaining to each compiler.

4-5-8 ACKNOWLEDGMENTS

Acknowledgment is made to the Director of Research of the Post Office for permission to publish this paper.

4-5-9 REFERENCES

1 H.M.S.O., *Official Definition of CORAL 66.*
2 Walters, R. E., 1976, *The Computer Journal,* 19, 50–55.
3 Key, M., and Tomlinson, P. N., *Software Engineering for Telecommunications Switching System.* IEE Conf. Pubn. No. 135, 117–120.

4-5-10 APPENDIX 1

4-5-10-1 Coral Code Produced from Kernel Definitions

NECESSARY DECLARATIONS

```
'COMMON' ('INTEGER' 'ARRAY' CA[0:5];
          'INTEGER' EXT;
          'PROCEDURE' PROC;)
'INTEGER' X, Y, Z, I, P2, LENGTH,FLAG;
'INTEGER' 'ARRAY' A, F[0:5];
'INTEGER' 'ARRAY' D [0:500] ;
'TABLE'  TABIN [1,10] [ENTRY1 'INTEGER' 0] ;
'TABLE'  TABOUT[1, 10] [ENTRY2 'INTEGER' 0];
'TABLE'  TABINL[1,1000] [ENTRY1L 'INTEGER' 0];
'TABLE'  TABOUTL[1,1000] [ENTRY2L 'INTEGER' 0];
'TABLE'  LIST  [4, 10] [VAR 'INTEGER' 0;
                        PTR 'INTEGER' 1;
                        VAR1 'INTEGER' 2;
                        VAR2 'INTEGER' 3];
```

CODE PRODUCED FOR KERNELS 2-10

KERNEL 2

(For P2 less than one word)

```
X: = Y;  (P3=0)
EXT: = Y;  (P3 = 1)
```

(For P2 greater than one word)

```
I: = 0;  (P3=0)
'FOR' I: = I+1 'WHILE' I<P2
'DO'  A [I]: = F [I];
```

KERNEL 3

(For P1 equal to 8 bits and word size equal to 16 bits)

```
'BITS' [8,8]X: = 'BITS' [8,0]Y;
```

KERNEL 4

```
'IF' X=Y 'THEN' 'GOTO' LABEL;
```

KERNEL 5

(For P1 small and P2 equal 0)

```
I:=0;
'FOR' I:=I+1 'WHILE' I<LENGTH
'BEGIN'
    'IF' ENTRY1[I]=X 'THEN'
    'BEGIN'
        X:=ENTRY2[I];
        I:=LENGTH+1;
    'END';
'END';
```

(For P1 large and P2 equal to 1)

```
'IF'X<LENGTH 'THEN' X:=ENTRY1L [X];
```

KERNEL 6

```
      INDEX:=1;
L1:   'IF' VAR[INDEX]<>X 'AND' PTR [INDEX]<>0
      'THEN'
      'BEGIN'
          INDEX:=PTR[INDEX];
          'GOTO' L1;
      'END';
```

KERNEL 7

(For P1 equal to 1)

```
Z:=((X+13) 'UNION'Y) *16;
```

KERNEL 8

```
'PROCEDURE' PROC;
'BEGIN'
'END';
```

KERNEL 9

(Not relevant for High Level Language)

KERNEL 10

(For P1 = 1)

```
'IF' 'BITS' [1,2]FLAG = 1 'THEN'
        'GOTO' LABEL;
'BITS' [1,2]FLAG: = 1;
```

4-5-11 APPENDIX 2

4-5-11-1 Brief Definitions of Kernels

KERNEL 2 — MOVE DATA

P1 DATA SIZE UNITS (P1 = $\emptyset$ BITS, P1 = 1 WORDS)

P2 NUMBER OF BITS/WORDS TO BE MOVED

P3 DESTINATION LOCATION (P3 = $\emptyset$-LOCAL,
     P3 = 1-EXTERNAL)

Move P2 items of data to a new location.

KERNEL 3 — PARTIAL WORD EXTRACT AND STORE

P1 ITEM SIZE (BITS)

Extract a P1 bit item from a location, then store the item in another location.

KERNEL 4 — DATA CHECK

P1 NUMBER OF CHECKS

Check the value of a data location, causing a program branch if the check is successful.

KERNEL 5 — TABLE SEARCH

P1 NUMBER OF TABLE ENTRIES (WORDS)

P2 SEARCH MODE (P2 = $\emptyset$-RANDOM, P2 = 1-INDEXED)

P3 MATCHING ENTRY NUMBER (e.g., P1/2 FOR
     NORMAL TABLES)

Search through a table, attempting to match a specified item of data. Random search is a conventional scan of the entries. Indexed search provides direct access to the matching item. If search is successful, extract corresponding item from output table (translation).

Kernel 6 — List Search

> P1   LIST SIZE (RECORDS)
>
> P2   MATCHING ENTRY NUMBER (e.g., P1/2 FOR
>   NORMAL LISTS)

Search through a one-way linked list of records, attempting to match a specified data item.

Kernel 7 — Compute

> P1   NUMBER OF COMPUTATIONS

Perform a simple three-operator, two-operand computation.

Kernel 8 — Subroutine Linkage

Call a subroutine and return immediately.

Kernel 9 — Environment Creation

> P1   NUMBER OF ENVIRONMENTS

Create the necessary addressing environment to allow access to store.

Kernel 10 — Flag Check and Set

> P1   SET SELECT (P1 = $\emptyset$-CHECK ONLY, P1 = 1-CHECK AND SET)

Check the value of a single bit flag and branch if set. Set the flag under the direction of P1.

(Where: P1 represents parameter number, and so on)

4-6 PERFORMANCE OF THE HAL/S FLIGHT COMPUTER COMPILER*

Fred H. Martin

Executive Officer, Software Systems Group
Intermetrics, Inc.

4-6-1 ABSTRACT

HAL/S is an advanced real-time higher order programming language specifically designed and implemented to meet stringent reliability and performance criteria. HAL/S was developed for NASA and is now operational and in use for Space Shuttle on-board software. A performance exercise is described which compares HAL/S to assembler language. Data was derived, under controlled conditions, by programming teams from two independent contractors. Detailed groundrules were agreed to by both parties, the key points being a common data base and the absolute requirement of verified execution. The results are presented in terms of several suggested measures which relate HAL/S size and speed performance to that achieved with assembler language. Shuttle requirements are factored in. In addition to size and speed performance the beneficial effects of compiler optimization are recorded along with the influence of programmer experience on achieving object code efficiency.

4-6-2 INTRODUCTION

Based upon the Apollo–Saturn experience, the National Aeronautics and Space Administration recognized the need for more effective programming methods. Programming language clarity, readability, enforced standards, and extensive automatic checking were needed to reduce costs and enhance reliability. With these motivations, NASA selected HAL/S, a new higher order language, for programming the Space Shuttle on-board software. HAL/S thus becomes the first such language to be employed on a manned space program.

HAL/S[1] is a linear algebraic language particularly suited for aerospace programming. Integer, scalar, vector, and matrix data types, together with appropriate operators and built-in functions (for example, a complete vector-matrix library) provide an extremely powerful tool for the implementation of mathematical (navigation, guidance, and control) algorithms. In addition, a wide range of commands for controlling real-time tasks is provided, including

*© 1976 IEEE. Reprinted, with permission, from IEEE 1976 NATIONAL AEROSPACE ELECTRONICS CONFERENCE NAECON 76, Dayton, OH, May 18–20, 1976, pp. 701–708.

one-shot and cyclic scheduling on time, priority, and hardware and/or software events.

The major goal of the HAL/S design is the production of reliable software. A standard formatted and annotated HAL/S listing enhances program production and maintenance. Effective isolation between separately compiled program blocks contributes to modularity while communication is supervised through centrally managed and highly visible common subroutines and data pools. Access to common resources may be granted or restricted centrally. HAL/S also includes a locking mechanism which can automatically protect shared data and code.

Within the Shuttle context three HAL/S compilers have been developed* for on-board software production and laboratory checkout: HAL/S-360 generates code for the IBM System 360/370; HAL/S-FC for the Shuttle flight computers—the IBM AP-101; and HAL/S NOVA. All compilers execute on a host IBM System 360/370.

While reliable code is of the utmost importance, efficiency may not be overlooked. The Shuttle on-board computers' size and speed requirements dictate a need for a high performance compiler. NASA accepted the HAL/S-FC compiler for the task based on its efficiency as demonstrated by a series of well-defined, controlled, and documented Acceptance Tests.

4-6-3 BACKGROUND

On July 16, 1975, NASA/JSC conducted the HAL/S Configuration Inspection (CI) at Intermetrics in Cambridge, MA. In a sense the CI was the culmination of five years of development in bringing HAL/S from a research concept to an operational language and compiler. The development of HAL/S had been carefully monitored by NASA from its inception and strictly controlled for the past two years.[2]

The performance objectives for the HAL/S compilers were established at the Preliminary Design Reviews and documented in the Compiler System Functional Specification documents.[3,4] Of particular interest here is the stated HAL/S-FC requirement of generated object code:

> *The object code produced will not exceed that produced via hand-coded assembler language methods by more than 15 percent in either memory requirements or execution time.*[4]

The effort to define and conduct compiler acceptance testing was formulated under NASA direction in January, 1975. The overall plan called for

---

*By Intermetrics, Inc., Cambridge, MA, under contract to NASA's Johnson Space Center, Houston, Texas.

establishing a representative set of benchmarks, coding them in both HAL/S and AP-101 assembler language and then comparing performance. It was recognized very early that the higher order language–assembler language comparisons would be influenced by many variables and may be subject to varying interpretations. In order for the exercise to have acknowledged validity it would have to be carefully designed and controlled, with all parties participating and cognizant of its progress.

Intermetrics, the compiler developer, and IBM–Houston, the compiler user, approached the task from different points of view. Intermetrics first suggested benchmarks that represented theoretical HAL/S usage. That is, the selected routines should contain a wide sample of HAL/S constructs designed to correspond to expected Shuttle applications. IBM was more interested in HAL/S performance as it related to actual Shuttle code. Many of their sizing and timing estimates for the Shuttle Approach and Landing Test (ALT) and Operational Flight Program (OFP) were based on a HAL/S performance of 15 percent in size and speed and they desired a true reading of the delivered product. The IBM approach was adopted and fourteen test routines were established as the acceptance set. Each routine was approved for suitability by both Intermetrics and IBM.

In order to insure an objective comparison, and also inject an element of competition, experienced personnel from IBM/OWEGO were selected to program the routines in AP-101 assembler language while Intermetrics would produce the HAL/S code.

4-6-4 ACCEPTANCE TEST PROCEDURES

Because of time and resource limitations, it was decided to use already existing HAL/S routines as the test specifications instead of generating abstract word representations. . . . [Having established] that these coded routines would properly execute, they formed the test baseline from which the HAL/S versus assembler language exercise could begin.

From the outset it was believed that both HAL/S and assembler language performance would be dependent to some extent on programmer skill. Nevertheless, in setting the ground rules for the performance exercise it was felt unfair to match "any" HAL/S code, written by an "average" programmer against the tightly written assembler code submitted by IBM personnel from the manufacturer's plant. Instead all parties agreed to a best-on-best contest. This was more easily defined. Intermetrics would try its best to produce the most favorable results for HAL/S while IBM/OWEGO would do the same for AP-101 assembler code. Cross-fertilization between the two groups served as a means to reduce the effect of programmer ingenuity or "tricks". The object was to test the compiler, not the cleverness of the programmers.

It was very important to establish from the beginning, a set of strict ground rules that would result in valid comparisons and stand up under scrutiny. Otherwise, there would be plenty of opportunity for misinterpretations due to run time, environments, different conventions, presumptions about data, and so on. The Acceptance Test ground rules were:

1. The original set of fourteen routines coded in HAL/S would serve as the test baseline.

2. Execution results would be based on initialization data for each routine. These data values would be established and held constant throughout the testing exercise.

3. Assembler language routines would be coded as total substitutes for corresponding HAL/S modules, that is,
   a) flight computer operating system interfaces would be maintained.
   b) the data base established for the HAL/S routines would be frozen and accessed by assembler language code.
   c) where assembler language routines needed and called library functions already existing in the HAL/S system, these same library routines were to be used with the same conventions as HAL/S.

4. While meeting the above requirements, the programmers, using either language, were free to improve the size and/or speed performance of their routines by such devices as
   a) in-line loops versus subroutines
   b) straight line code versus loops
   c) common subexpression elimination
   d) redesign of execution order
   e) elimination of redundant decision points, and so on

With respect to this last point (4), there was no doubt that both groups would be striving to compare "best" HAL/S against "best" assembler language. This was felt [to be] justified because of the iterative aspect of improvement. On many occasions Intermetrics would receive from IBM/OWEGO an assembler code version which out-performed, by far, the latest attempt using HAL/S. More often than not the HAL/S code could be further improved, sometimes exceeding assembler language performance. The reverse was also true. By the CI, both groups were convinced that each had benefitted from the designs and "clever" ideas of the other, and that for the most part the comparisons reflected compiler performance and not human ingenuity.

Figure 4-6-1 depicts the process described above. After selecting the examples (1), and establishing the data bases (2), each group attempted to run and improve their respective routines (3). At first, execution was stand-alone (4) in order to check out operation, interfaces, use of simulator, and so on. Eventually, the official database was used (5), results were compared, and the routines rewritten (6) to improve performance. Best against best, and the pressure of schedule, produced the final results (7).

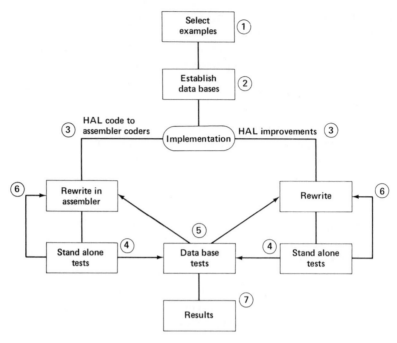

Figure 4-6-1 The testing process.

4-6-5 TEST ROUTINES

Fourteen routines were selected to form the baseline set. All routines were reviewed and approved by IBM and Intermetrics before being incorporated. A brief functional description of each routine follows:

> *Test No. 1:* SECOND_ORDER_FILTER implements a second order discrete linear recursive filter.
>
> *Test No. 2:* MEASINCORP implements an optimal filtering algorithm which incorporates external measurements into position and time components of the state vector. One compool is involved.
>
> *Test No. 3:* G_FILTER implements a recursive linear least squares filter which estimates gyro drift on the basis of differencing platform altitudes. One compool is involved.
>
> *Test No. 4:* GNC_TACAN_AZ calculates the TACAN azimuth from the state vector, the measurement residual, and the vector of azimuth partials; the routine also computes the variance of the azimuth measurement error.
>
> *Test No. 5:* ELCOM computes several Shuttle elevator commands.

Test No. 6: GCB_YR_CE represents the yaw/roll control element and performs aileron, rudder, and nosewheel processing for yaw/roll flight control modes.

Test No. 7: GRI_RGA_FDIR performs fault detection indication and recovery (FDIR) for the rate gyro assemblies.

Test No. 8: GRE_3ELEM performs the necessary three-element processing as determined by the FDIR status.

Test No. 9: GGJ_AL_FDCMD performs functions for the Approach and Landing (A/L) Flight Director Command Processor for roll and pitch.

Test No. 10: DMC_DISPLAY determines the starting location of one of four display format buffers. Six compools are involved.

Test No. 11: DMC_NEW_DISPLAY performs control data maintenance and logic in order to output format control words (FCW's) to the display electronics units (DEU's).

Test No. 12: DMC_FILL_BACK_GROUND_FCWS locates the background FCW's and issues appropriate SVC's to send the FCW's to the DEU's.

Test No. 13: SAS_ANALOG_SCALE converts parameters from pulse code modulation units to engineering units, and vice versa. Five compools are involved.

Test No. 14: SAS_POLYSOL performs several polynominal solutions as determined by SAS_ANALOG_SCALE.

Taken together the fourteen routines exercise most of the programming features available in HAL/S. These are summarized in matrix form in Figure 4-6-2.

4-6-6 DATA COLLECTION AND TEST RESULTS

The data collected for each test routine was recorded on a template, as shown in Figure 4-6-3 at the end of the paper. The percent measures shown were designed to answer the performance questions most often asked; that is, what percent improvement was achieved by a new compiler, or through programmer experience; and what percent inefficiency is HAL/S over assembler code. Note that only code size was measured, since both compiler and assembler language code utilized identical data areas. Also, speed data for original sources using FC-5 was "not available"; therefore, columns (1) and (3) do not contribute to the study.

The collection of a large amount of compiler performance data afforded the opportunity of reporting on several interesting characteristics of HAL/S development and usage. Since the baseline set of routines was compiled using

Language feature	Acceptance test number													
	1	2	3	4	5	6	7	8	9	10	11	12	13	14
Integer			✓			✓	✓	✓		✓	✓	✓	✓	✓
Scalar	✓	✓		✓	✓			✓	✓				✓	
Vector		✓	✓	✓										
Matrix		✓	✓	✓										
Bit Strings							✓	✓		✓	✓	✓		✓
Booleans	✓				✓				✓				✓	
Array	✓	✓	✓				✓	✓					✓	✓
Structure	✓				✓					✓	✓	✓	✓	✓
Subscript	✓	✓	✓	✓			✓	✓		✓	✓	✓	✓	✓
BUILT-IN FUNCTION				✓				✓	✓	✓		✓	✓	
IF_Then_ELSE	✓	✓	✓		✓	✓	✓	✓	✓	✓	✓	✓	✓	
DO CASE					✓		✓	✓				✓		
DO FOR		✓	✓				✓	✓		✓		✓		✓
DO WHILE										✓	✓	✓		
REPEAT/EXIT/RETURN										✓				
Procedure		✓		✓	✓	✓	✓			✓	✓	✓		
Function			✓		✓	✓			✓					
Compool		✓	✓							✓	✓	✓	✓	✓
REPLACE										✓	✓			
REENTRANT/AUTOMATIC													✓	
NAME Variables										✓		✓	✓	
TEMPORARY			✓	✓					✓	✓				

Figure 4-6-2   Language features exercised within test routines.

the preliminary release FC-5, an unoptimized compiler, and new data were to be collected using FC-8, the demonstrated benefit of the FC-8 optimization features could be measured directly. Also, in an effort to demonstrate "best" HAL/S performance, Intermetrics would improve the original sources. The differences in resulting performance between "old" and "new" sources, using the same compiler (FC-8), would then be a measure of the influence of programmer experience on size and speed.

The question of how to measure the execution time of a routine, and what is a proper comparison between HAL/S and assembler language caused a certain amount of difficulty in gathering and interpreting data. Two points of view were expressed:

1. the HAL/S compiler represented an integrated design of code generator and libraries and therefore timing data should be computed "end-to-end".

2. since the HAL/S libraries are themselves written in assembler language, the time spent in the libraries should be subtracted.

This second point of view was, in some cases, easier to state than to measure. No particular problem existed where both HAL/S and assembler

Test description

Test no.: _2_   Test name: _Measincorp_   Source: Intermetrics

Functional group: _GBC_

Functional description: Optimal filtering algorithm to incorporate external measurements into position and time components of the state vector.

Programming characteristics: n-dimensional vector/matrix, 1 compool

Size performance data:

(1)	(2)	(3)	(4)	(5)	(6)	(7)
Original HAL/S code size (HW)		Improvement $\frac{(1)-(2)}{(1)}$	Improved HAL/S code size (HW)	Improvement $\frac{(2)-(4)}{(2)}$	Independent assembler language size (HW)	HAL/S inefficiency $\frac{(4)-(6)}{(6)}$
FC–3	FC–8		FC–8			
550	450	18.2	316	29.8	268	17.9

Speed performance data:

(1)	(2)	(3)	(4)	(5)	(6)	(7)
Original HAL/S code (μsec)		Improvement $\frac{(1)-(2)}{(1)}$	Improved HAL/S code (μsec)	Improvement $\frac{(2)-(4)}{(2)}$	Independent assembler language (μsec)	HAL/S inefficiency $\frac{(4)-(6)}{(6)}$
FC–5	FC–8		FC–8			
N.A.	16327.8	N.A.	15507.6	5.0	14674.4	5.7

Figure 4-6-3   Test description template.

language routines used the same libraries. But when the assembler language design elected to compute a library function in-line, direct comparison became difficult. In such cases it was decided to subtract the library time from the HAL/S total, and the "functional library" time from the assembler language total. On occasion it became difficult to decide what belonged to the function and what did not.

For the most part Intermetrics subscribed to the first point of view, considering the HAL/S compiler product as an entity. IBM was inclined toward the second. In the final analysis, both types of data were collected and integrated before arriving at the final performance figures.

The results of the fourteen tests were first recorded individually; a single example of the template entries is shown in Figure 4-6-3. All data were then collected for convenience in the two summary tables, Figures 4-6-4 and 4-6-5. Note that the tests were grouped by applications characteristics, that is, GNC-

Group	Test #	HAL size	Assembly size	Percent	HAL time	(no-lib)	Assembly time	(no-lib)	Percent	(no-lib)
G N C	1**	77	64	20.3	234.5	(234.5)	213.5	(213.5)	9.8	(9.8)
					345.3	(345.3)	326.7	(326.7)	5.7	(5.7)
	2	316	268	17.9	15507.6	(1433.1)	14674.4	(1262.5)	5.7	(13.5)
	3	308	256	20.3	1917.3	(1722.7)	1857.9	(1856.9)	-2.2	(-7.3)
					976.3	(931.7)	874.1	(874.1)	11.7	(6.6)
	4	93	132	-29.5	872.2	(92.7)	735.4	(93.5)	18.6	(-0.9)
	5	166	138	20.3	446.0	(285.7)	422.6	(262.3)	5.5	(8.9)
					442.2	(281.9)	418.4	(258.1)	5.7	(9.2)
	6**	108	98	10.2	70.1	(70.1)	68.3	(68.3)	2.6	(2.6)
					116.3	(116.3)	113.9	(113.9)	2.1	(2.1)
	7**	165	137	20.4	443.9	(443.9)	453.3*	(453.3)*	-2.1	(-2.1)
	8	138	100	38.0	592.5	(592.5)	418.5	(418.5)	41.6	(41.6)
					836.3	(836.3)	772.3	(772.3)	8.3	(8.3)
	9	104	84	23.8	654.2	(221.9)	647.8	(215.5)	1.0	(3.0)
					146.3	(146.3)	131.9	(131.9)	10.9	(10.9)
	Sub-total	1475	1277	15.5*	23501.0	(7754.9)	22129.0	(7322.3)	6.2*	(5.9)*
U I	10**	166	214	-22.4	303.5	(303.5)	320.9	(320.9)	-5.4	(-5.4)
	11**	199	138	44.2	111.1	(111.1)	101.3	(101.3)	9.7	(9.7)
	12**	256	292	-12.3	884.7	(884.7)	730.8	(730.8)	21.1	(21.1)
	Sub-total	621	644	-3.6	1299.3	(1299.3)	1153.0	(1153.0)	12.7	(12.7)
S M	13**	238	208	14.4	268.7	(268.7)	206.8	(206.8)	29.9	(29.9)
					111.3	(111.3)	112.8	(112.8)	-1.3	(-1.3)
	14**	87	66	31.8	868.2	(868.2)	594.3	(594.3)	46.1	(46.1)
	Sub-total	325	274	18.6*	1248.2	(1248.2)	913.9	(913.9)	36.6*	(36.6)*
	TOTAL	2421	2195	10.3	26048.4	(10302.4)	24195.9	(9389.2)	7.7*	(9.7)*

*Aggregate % improvement   ● "Best" HAL/S vs. "Best" assembler language
**Routines using no HAL/S libraries at all

Figure 4-6-4 HAL/S–FC acceptance test raw data.

guidance, navigation, control; UI-user interface (keyboard, display, manual control); SM-systems management (data analysis). This was necessary in order to reflect and measure the utility of HAL/S for actual Shuttle on-board programming. Although each template did contain size comparisons between FC-5 and FC-8, showing the effect of compiler optimization, this raw data is not included in the summary tables. However, the data was analyzed and the results are presented below.

4-6-7 DATA ANALYSIS

In order to arrive at a performance characteristic for the HAL/S-FC compiler a number of candidate "averaging" measures were considered. The basic approaches were:

1. Performance based on the set of routines taken as an aggregate.

Group	Test #	Size			Time		
		Version		Percent Improved	Version		Percent Improved
		Original	Improved		Original	Improved	
	1	91	77	15.4%	249.7	234.5	6.1%
					356.3	345.3	3.1%
	2	450	316	29.8%	16327.8	15507.6	5.0%
	3	606	308	49.2%	4432.9	1817.3	58.1%
					2161.7	976.3	54.8%
G	4	100	93	7.0%	1050.2	872.2	16.9%
N	5	181	166	8.3%	459.6	446.0	3.0%
C					448.8	442.2	1.5%
	6	114	108	5.3%	70.1	70.1	0.0%
					122.1	116.3	4.8%
	7	267	165	38.2%	504.3	443.9	12.0%
	8	194	138	28.9%	578.7	592.5	−2.4%
					1103.9	836.3	24.2%
	9	134	104	22.4%	1169.7	654.2	44.1%
					221.9	146.3	34.1%
	Sub-total	2137	1475	31.0%*	29157.7	23501.0	19.4%*
U	10	365	145	60.3%	377.9	166.9	55.8%
I	11	206	199	3.4%	114.3	111.1	2.8%
	12	689	248	64.0%	907.7	802.5	11.6%
	Sub-total	1260	592	53.0%*	1399.9	1080.5	22.8%*
S	13	238	238	0.0%	268.7	268.7	0.0%
M					111.3	111.3	0.0%
	14	110	87	20.9%	921.6	868.2	3.8%
	Sub-total	348	325	6.6%	1301.6	1248.2	4.1%
	Total	3745	2392	36.1%*	31859.2	25829.7	18.9%*

*Aggregate % improvement

Figure 4-6-5 Size and speed of original and improved HAL/S source using FC-8.

$$T = \left(\frac{\sum\limits_{1}^{N} H_i}{\sum\limits_{1}^{N} A_i} - 1 \right) \times 100, \text{ IN } \%$$

where H_1 = size/speed of each HAL/S routine;

A_1 = size/speed of corresponding assembler language routine.

2. Performance defined as the average performance of the routines taken individually.

$$A = \frac{1}{N} \sum\limits_{1}^{N} \left(\frac{H_i}{A_i} - 1 \right) \times 100$$

3. Performance based on the expected applicability of HAL/S to Shuttle application programming.

$$WT = W_{GNC}\left(\frac{\Sigma H_j}{\Sigma A_j} - 1\right) \times 100 + W_{SM}\left(\frac{\Sigma H_k}{\Sigma A_k} - 1\right) \times 100 + W_{UI}\left(\frac{\Sigma H_l}{\Sigma A_l} - 1\right) \times 100$$

and

$$WA = W_{GNC}\frac{1}{N_{GNC}} \Sigma \left(\frac{H_j}{A_j} - 1\right) \times 100 + W_{SM}\frac{1}{N_{SM}} \Sigma \left(\frac{H_k}{A_k} - 1\right) \times 100$$

$$+ W_{UI}\frac{1}{N_{UI}} \Sigma \left(\frac{H_l}{A_l} - 1\right) \times 100$$

4. Speed performance evaluated with and without libraries.

The weighting factors W_{GNC}, W_{SM}, W_{UI} reflect the relative dominance of GNC, SM, UI routines in the Shuttle applications programming. At the time of the test exercise the estimated values were:

	W_{GNC}	W_{SM}	W_{UI}
Size	.672	.250	.077
Speed	.732	.190	.077

After giving careful consideration to these approaches it became apparent that the "correct one" was a matter of subjective judgment. In order to enhance objectivity and promote the credibility of the results, it was decided not to confine the analysis to a single approach, but instead to utilize [all of them.]

The size and speed results for the fourteen test routines summarized in Figure 4-6-4 were analyzed using the four measures above. The resulting compiler performance, expressed as percent inefficiency over assembler language is shown in Figure 4-6-6.

Measure	HAL/S size inefficiency	HAL/S speed inefficiency (end-to-end)
1) T	10.3%	7.7%
2) A	14.1%	10.7%
3) WT	10.9%	9.8%
4) WA	13.2%	8.6%

Figure 4-6-6 HAL/S-FC compiler performance.

The issue of "end-to-end" versus "no libraries" performance was previously mentioned. The "no-lib" data has been included in Figure 4-6-4 and was subjected to the same four measures. The resulting performance figures are shown in Figure 4-6-7, in addition to the end-to-end data.

Additional speed cases were created by the observation that the end-to-end aggregate timing data was subject to significant influence by the test routine No. 2. Taken as an aggregate this single routine consumed approximately 60 percent of the total execution time. Therefore in Figure 4-6-7, measures 9) and

Measure	HAL/S inefficiency	
1) T	7.7%	End-to-end
2) A	10.7%	
3) WT	9.8%	
4) WA	8.6%	
5) T	9.7%	"No lib"
6) A	10.1%	
7) WT	9.5%	
8) WA	9.0%	
9) T	10.7%	Routine #2 excluded
10) A	10.5%	

Figure 4-6-7 HAL/S design goals and capabilities.

10) represent compiler speed performance excluding the results of routine No. 2. (Only the aggregate speed measures apply.)

The test routines were originally coded with no particular attention paid to demonstrated performance. As discussed previously, numerous iterations of both HAL/S and assembler language code followed before the "best" results were achieved. A summary of improvements using each defined measure is shown in Figure 4-6-8 based on an analysis of the results presented in Figure 4-6-5. These values reflect the influence of programmer experience.

Measure	Description	Size reduction using FC-8	Speed reduction using FC-8
T	Straight aggregate	36.10%	18.9%
A	Average of percents	25.20%	16.3%
WT	Wtd. group average	36.90%	18.8%
WA	Wtd. average of percents	26.10%	17.6%

Figure 4-6-8 HAL/S summary of statements.

The HAL/S-FC compiler had been undergoing an optimization program prior to acceptance. The acceptance test activities permitted at least a tentative assessment of its progress. Only size comparison data was available and a summary is shown in Figure 4-6-9.

Figure 4-6-9 HAL/S real-time process control.

Measure	Description	Size reduction from FC-5 to FC-8
T	Straight aggregate	10.23%
A	Average of percents	9.51%
WT	Weighted group aggregates	10.28%
WA	Weighted average of percents	9.03%

4-6-8 CONCLUSIONS AND OBSERVATIONS

The HAL/S Acceptance Test exercise was characterized by the sincere efforts of all parties to derive compiler performance through carefully planned, controlled procedures, and objective criteria. Every effort was made to conduct the tests with a maximum of openness and communication. A number of important elements contributed to its success:

1. selection of independent programming teams for HAL/S and assembler language
2. establishment of comprehensive mutually acceptable ground rules
3. definition of representative benchmarks and common databases
4. requirement for successful execution, and full interchangeability, of HAL/S and assembler language routines
5. the sharing of design approaches between teams and the maintenance of a friendly spirit of competition
6. the reporting of all data without prejudice.

The resulting performance data was scrutinized thoroughly, discussed, and finally accepted by consensus, at the Configuration Inspection (CI) meeting. The following figures were stated for HAL/S-FC compiler performance:

HAL/S-FC Size Inefficiency:	approximately 11–13 percent over Assembler language
HAL/S-FC Speed Inefficiency:	approximately 9–11 percent over Assembler language

These values should be qualified as follows: only a sample of Shuttle routines was utilized in the testing, the Shuttle category weighting factors were based on preliminary design data, the programming was accomplished by experienced individuals (at Intermetrics and IBM/OWEGO) participating in a competition—not in the line production of flight code.

An interesting by-product in the struggle and competition to achieve better performance was the obvious benefit of a compiler in terms of increased productivity. Many new designs and source modifications were attempted by the HAL/S team because the compiler automatically attended to the details of addressing and instruction selection, and provided comprehensive diagnostics. The assembler language group was more cautious and less inclined to change a working routine because of the potential for programming error. The result was more tries at the problem for HAL/S and a better appreciation for design tradeoffs. As can be seen in Figure 4-6-4, some of the HAL/S results were, in fact, "better" than the corresponding assembler language. In these cases the assembler language team had stopped at some point, presuming that their routines had reached satisfactory performance. HAL/S work continued, sometimes achieving surprising results.

Conclusions were also drawn on the secondary objectives of compiler optimization and programmer experience. The following characteristics were noted:

FC-8 size optimization improvement over FC-5	~ 10 percent
Influence of programmer experience reduced the size of HAL/S routines by	~ 25 percent
Influence of programmer experience reduced the execution time of HAL/S routines by	~ 17 percent

Finally, as a result of the data and with the benefit of discussions among HAL/S and assembler language team members, a number of areas were identified for improvement in HAL/S code generator and compiler design. Most will contribute to time efficiency by substituting in-line code for the current library calls. The features to be improved are:

Structure moves

Vector–matrix moves

Zeroing of vector–matrices

Maintain vector of size three in a vector accumulator and perform simple computations in-line

Vector (size N) and matrix addition and subtraction done in-line

Loop streamlining

Common subexpression

All items have become part of a continuing HAL/S optimization program.

Recently a new HAL/S-FC compiler (FC-10) with enhanced optimization has been released and is now in the field. Most of the acceptance tests have been rerun showing improved performance. Of particular interest has been the reduction in the inefficiencies due to programmer inexperience. These have dropped in speed from 17 percent to 14 percent and in size from 25 percent to 23 percent. Although modest, this trend is encouraging and the current HAL/S design effort is attempting to further reduce this effect.

A significant programmatic cost savings will have been achieved when using a compiler which emits efficient object code produced by nonexpert personnel writing straightforward higher order language source statements.

4-6-9 APPENDIX: VERY BRIEF DESCRIPTION OF HAL/S

The HAL/S design goals and matching capabilities are shown in Figure 4–6–10. The single most important goal was to increase the reliability of the programming process. This has been approached by paying careful attention to the appearance of the language (for example, its clarity and readability), and through a system of enforced standards and extensive automatic checking.

Design goals	HAL/S capabilities
1. Increased readability, human comprehension	Output orientation annotated program listing
2. Increased reliability	Extensive automatic checking, program structure, controlled memory sharing
3. Guidance, navigation, control	Complete vector–matrix arithmetic
4. Data management	Organizations of data into arrays, structures and tables
5. Systems, communications and I/O	Bits and characters, extensions for systems programming
6. Command and control	Real–time control

Figure 4–6–10

The distinctive "output orientation" of HAL/S is its two-dimensional appearance which brings the language closer to being natural in expression and mathematical form. Aggregate data types (vector, matrix, bit, and character strings), and structure and array organizations are annotated for easy recognition. For example, an equation might take on the following form:

$$\overline{VDOT} = -\overline{G} + K_3^2 \, M \, \overline{C};$$

where VDOT, G and C are vectors; M is a matrix.

In this brief description of HAL/S, the various programming features of the language are best summarized by the two figures below (Figures 4–6–11 and 4–6–12).

4-6-10 ACKNOWLEDGMENT

The author wishes to acknowledge the many contributors to the HAL/S Acceptance Test Activity. Within Intermetrics, Ron Kole assumed principal responsibility for the definition, organization, and conduct of the test effort. Don Sakahara performed most of the tests and collected and organized the data.

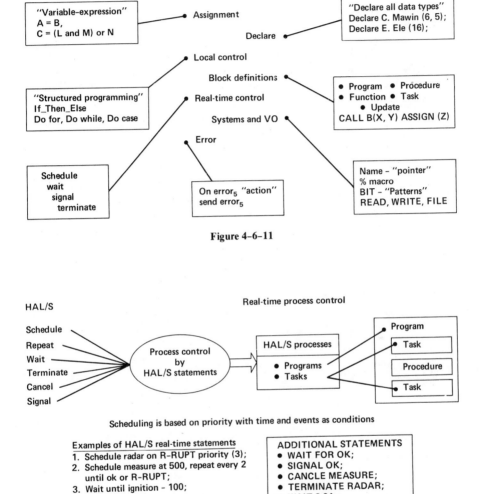

Figure 4-6-11

Figure 4-6-12

Dan Lickly and Arra Avakian helped to analyze the data and suggest iterations and new design methods.

The whole exercise could not have been a success without the cooperation of Al Mandelin and Gerry Pew of IBM/Houston, the dedicated efforts of Jim Marple and his associates from IBM/OWEGO, and the coordination provided by Jack Garman and Josephine Jue of NASA/JSC.

4-6-11 REFERENCES

[1.] HAL/S Language Specification, Intermetrics, Inc., IR–61–7, November 14, 1975.

[2.] On the Performance of the HAL/S-FC Compiler, Intermetrics, Inc., IR–162, October 22, 1975.

[3.] HAL/S-360 Compiler System Functional Specification, Intermetrics, Inc., PDR2 #IM004, July 13, 1973.

[4.] HAL/S-FC Compiler System Functional Specification, Intermetrics, Inc., IR–59–4, July 24, 1974.

5

REAL-TIME LANGUAGES

There is a great temptation in the world of computer science to propose a new and better language as the solution to current computing concerns. There are two problems with this approach—economic forces have stagnated the industrial computing language world, so that the constant stream of proposed new languages serves to further separate the pragmatists and the theorists; and the incremental value of new languages is probably overrated by those who propose them.

Real-time software is no different from other software in this regard. A great deal of the none-too-available real-time software literature deals with languages. Some of those proposed languages contain excellent new ideas; but I feel the issues of real-time software are far more complex than a simple language treatment will allow. Therefore, this chapter dealing with languages, although inevitably present, deliberately comes last among the covered material and contains a heavy pragmatic flavor.

The first paper, by Peter Elzer, acts as a bridge between the previous chapter and this one. Elzer says, "The main problem area in the design of programming languages for real-time applications is their interface to the operating system." He then discusses several approaches to this problem and does an interesting job of putting real-time languages into an international political perspective. The paper also adds perspective to the issue raised earlier by MacLaren regarding the Ada executive mechanisms and traditional executive design; Elzer clearly favors the integrated design of language and operating systems. This paper, like several others throughout the book, is of European origin and provides international insight into the topic of real-time languages.

A treasury of real-time language pragmatism is presented by Raymond Rubey in section 5-2. Perhaps this paper is best described by the following extracted relevant quotations:

On the value of languages and compilers:
It is relatively cheap and easy (and interesting) to develop a new higher-order language; it is expensive (and laborious) to develop a suitable compiler . . .

On the problem of compiler code inefficiency:
The capability when an HOL is used to easily make . . . efficiency improvements through software redesign will . . . more than compensate for the currently-reported 10 to 20 percent HOL inefficiencies.

On why software engineering advances have not impacted real-time solutions:
Avionics is done by engineers who have little knowledge or interest in the advances . . . taking place in programming methods and theory.

Rubey may be talking explicitly about the use of *avionics* high-order languages, but if you substitute "real-time" for "avionics" the paper remains about as accurate.

The subject of real-time languages is almost as old as computing, and as new as Ada. Section 5-3 takes us back to 1967 to read about "A Language for Real-Time Systems," which summarizes the *issues* in real-time languages. Based on those issues, the authors propose a variant of Algol 60 called RTL (for "Real-Time Language"). Special consideration is given to timing and interrupt control, multiprogramming, and applicable data structures.

We return to the present in section 5-4, where the Ada language is dealing with many of those same issues. The presence of Ada in the real-time scene is striking. Although it has not yet been used (at this writing) for any real-time application solutions, it is virtually certain to impact programmers and the style used by programmers.

Obviously Ada is going to force programmers to think in some new ways, and Ada advocates see these new ways as advancement of the field of computer science. "The proper use of Ada features was discovered partly through trial and error," they cry, and add, "A cookbook of Ada Methodology is needed," because of Ada's blend of traditional and "novel" features. The real-time application they describe is simple, but they tackle the use of Ada tasking and packaging as they find a solution. An objective list of Ada "helps and hindrances" is included in the article.

As previously mentioned, computer science is sometimes too intent on the "see a problem–invent a language" method of solution. The final paper in section 5.5, by John L. Hennessy and others, describes such a language—TOMAL. It is defined to solve the problem of using a limited-capacity microcomputer to address real-time applications. Goals of TOMAL are to support tasking, high-level input-output, restricted interrupts, a high level of abstraction in data and control structure, program verification, and efficiency. The language, the goals, and the approach are all laudable. This paper is a good illustration of the direction of computer science thinking on real-time software problems.

5-1 REAL-TIME LANGUAGES AND OPERATING SYSTEMS*

P. Elzer
R. Roessler
Physics Institute III
of the University of
Erlangen-Nuernberg, Federal Republic of Germany

5-1-1 ABSTRACT

In this paper a short survey on the "real-time language scene" is given first, as far as industrial applications are concerned. Ongoing standardization and cooperative efforts are mentioned. Then [we try] to formulate some specific functional requirements for real-time languages for industrial purposes. Special emphasis is [put] upon an investigation of interface problems between languages and operating systems, and the mutual influences are discussed. An attempt is made to identify some future trends, and a rather extensive bibliography [will] allow the reader to trace original information.

5-1-2 THE "REAL-TIME LANGUAGE SCENE"

5-1-2-1 Currently Used Programming Languages for Industrial Process Control

Until some years ago the control of industrial processes with computers was one of the areas of computer application which [was] under the nearly undisputed predominance of assembly coding. There were many reasons for this, but these need not be discussed here. But with growing size and complexity of problems, systems, and programs and with the dramatic reverse of the cost-ratio between hardware and software, the need for handier and more efficient programming tools was recognized.

Several methods were tried, like the design of modular program packages, problem-oriented languages, and so on. One of these approaches, which in addition was very attractive under the aspect of improved portabiliy of user-programs, was the use or design of a suitable middle-level language for in-

*Originally published in the Proceedings of the Fifth International Conference on Digital Computer Applications to Process Control, 1977. Eds. H. R. Nauta Lemke and M. B. Verbrugger. Reprinted with permission.

dustrial control purposes. Evidence for the feasibility and possible outcome of such a method had been given by the success of COBOL, FORTRAN, ALGOL 60 in the areas of commercial and scientific computing. It is this line of development which shall be dealt with in the following paragraphs.

One of the earliest attempts for a solution was the expansion of FORTRAN for process control purposes. This method has come to a certain stability in the meantime and is obviously very popular in the user industry, especially in the United States. Nevertheless the shortcomings of this approach were recognized very early, too, and several other proposals were made and partially implemented in the mid-sixties, for example, BCS-RTL,[1] "Gertler's RTL,"[2] "Case-RTL,"[3] PAS-1.[4] Development of CORAL 66[5] also started at this time, which proved very successful until now, but used a rather different approach, as will be demonstrated later. Early small systems like INDAC 8[6] demonstrated the feasibility of the high-level language approach also for minicomputers.

Then "all of a sudden" during 1970 and 1971 a number of languages were developed explicitly for the purposes of industrial real-time programming: for example, HAL/S,[7] L.A.I.,[8] LTR,[9] JOVIAL,[10] PEARL,[11] PROCOL,[12] RTL.[2,13] Most of them have been successfully implemented in the meantime and are widely available now. They mostly could build upon (good or bad) experience with earlier developments of their kind and on the new insights in possibilities and limitations of language design which became evident during the work on PL/I[14] and ALGOL 68.[15]

There already exist several surveys on the technical properties and attempts at an evaluation of the relative merits of these languages. Therefore it does not seem to be very useful to produce just another one, especially since from a technical point of view the situation has not changed drastically since the very detailed and exhaustive survey paper of Gertler and Sedlak in 1974.[16] A still more detailed synopsis of language elements—but without an evaluation—was produced by the LTPL (long-term-procedural-language) group of the "International Purdue Workshop on Industrial Computer Systems."[17,18,19,20] It could be edited and printed with the support of the European Community and the US Navy and is available from

Dr. O. Diettrich
Commission of the European Community
B-1040 Bruxelles
Rue de la Loi 200
DG III/D-1, JE4/29
Belgium

or

Prof. T. J. Williams
PLAIC
Purdue University
Michael Golden Labs.
West Lafayette, Indiana 47907
USA

It comprises the following languages. ALGOL 68,[15] CAMAC-IML,[21] CORAL 66,[5] PAS-1,[4] PEARL,[11] PL/I,[14] PROCOL,[12] and RTL.[2,13] A very extensive comparison has recently been undertaken by the US-DoD.[22,23] This comparison includes more than twenty languages and is available on the ARPA-net. Some specific aspects of several real-time languages are dealt with in a paper by Baumann and Schwald.[24] There are other comparisons but as they are mostly of rather small scale and difficult of access, they shall not be quoted here.

5-1-2-2 Recent Developments

What has happened, however, is a process of gradual improvement of some of the above-mentioned languages. Experiences gained during implementations could be incorporated. Important users could be convinced to adopt the "new" technology. Some hopes had to be buried, too. People no longer believe that a computer can do everything and a compiler a little more (but this is not only true for computers and their languages).

Theoretical work has continued and some languages, developed outside the industrial computer control scene proper, have helped to gain new insights, for example, SIMULA 67,[25] PASCAL[26] and MODULA.[27,28] Other languages originally designed to help people write compilers, such as BCPL[29] or general program systems like LIS[30] contain solutions to problems which are also encountered in industrial computer applications. On the other side new operating systems, such as HYDRA[31] or CHA-OS[32] utilize modern principles for the management of resources in computer systems which may allow us to . . . forget about old problems. The work on structured programming[33] has already had implications on practically oriented concepts for industrial real-time computing.[34,35]

A new understanding of the descriptive power of declarative statements has already influenced purely industrial developments, like ILIAD.[36] A part of these recent developments on the real-time software scene has already been described in a comprehensive paper by Pyle.[37] At the moment, perhaps the most detailed and extensive compilation of the current state-of-the-art in language design is the paper by Fisher,[38] produced in the context of an already mentioned effort of the US Department of Defense and usually known as the TINMAN-report.

If one should try to identify where recent theoretical work is likely to have an impact on the real-time-language scene of the near future it might seem reasonable to name the following areas, where progress has been made:

The structuring of programs
The possibilities and limitations of compile-time checking
The descriptive power of declarative statements
The protection of program entities
The understanding of interactions between parallel processes

5-1-2-3 Standardization and Cooperative Efforts

It is a fact that "language proliferation" or even "method proliferation" is especially bad as far as industrial real-time programming is concerned. Certainly there are many reasons for this. One may be that the people working in this field have on the average a relatively high level of professional skill, a high creativity, and are therefore especially prone to the "not-invented-here-complex." Another reason could be the lack of an overwhelmingly powerful market-leader. Partially it may also have been mere chance, that is, the already mentioned "language explosion" around 1970. There, a lot of similar development work was done by people who could not know of each other because usually work gets published only after it is already done. Afterwards a kind of "feedback-loop" started: Because some years ago none of the above-mentioned languages was *really* widely accepted in the sense that you could buy a compiler "off-the-shelf" for a reasonable number of computers, each organization which was (or felt) large and powerful enough for such an enterprise, started to develop and implement a language of its own. Afterwards the necessity of a "return-of-investment" required use of their own development. This situation now makes the decision a little bit difficult for potential users, and the usual remedy . . . is the establishment of standards. Therefore some of the ongoing standardization efforts in the field of the real-time languages will be presented.

The "Purdue Workshop." The group which has already tried to bring a little bit of order and structure into all this confusion at a very early point in time, is the "International Purdue Workshop on Industrial Computer Systems" (IPW).

It was founded in 1969 by Prof. T. J. Williams of the Purdue University, Lafayette, [Indiana] USA, originally as a purely . . . American effort. Soon afterwards—in 1970—a number of European participants joined the group, who were especially interested in the activities of the Workshop concerning real-time languages, other than Process-FORTRAN. This led to the foundation of a European branch of the LTPL (long-term-procedural-language) committee in 1971.

The need for broader based activities on the European side was recognized soon and respective efforts resulted in a reorganization of the Workshop in 1973 and the establishment of three "regional" branches in America, Japan, and Europe in 1974.[39] The IPW is now affiliated with a number of national and international organizations, namely the International Federation for Information Processing (IFIP), where it is embedded as Working Group 4 in TC 5, the International Federation of Automatic Control (IFAC), the Instrument Society of America (ISA) and the Purdue Laboratory of Applied Industrial Control of Purdue University.

In the bylaws of the IPW . . . its objectives are stated: "to make the definition, justification, hardware and software design, procurement, programming, installation, commissioning, operation, and maintenance of industrial computer systems more efficient and economical through education, the organization and interchange of information, and the development of standards and/or guidelines." More detailed information on the current work of the IPW is given in an information summary edited by Prof. Williams, which can be obtained from Purdue University.[17]

The work of the IPW is organized in nine technical committees, although there are regional differences as to the main activities:

TC 1 Real-Time FORTRAN

TC 2 Real-Time BASIC

TC 3 Long-term procedural language (LTPL)

TC 4 Problem-oriented (application-oriented) languages (POL)

TC 5 Interfaces and data transmission

TC 6 Man-Machine communication

TC 7 Safety and Security

TC 8 Operating systems

TC 9 Glossary

Especially interesting in the context of this paper is the work of TC 1, TC 2, and TC 3. The results of TC 1 have been the basis for ISA Standards on Process-FORTRAN[40] [which] have been submitted to ISO and are already widely used in American industry. TC 2 is making good progress in its attempt to identify standard real-time extensions to BASIC. "TC 3 is concerned with the development of a middle-level programming language for a wide range of automation and control fields with considerations on the necessary support of and on the interfaces to other components of a software system."[41] The functional capabilities of this language will exceed those of FORTRAN or BASIC.

The IPW does not understand itself as a "Standardization body," and therefore one has to look at the actions of official bodies. Here indeed work has also started on an international level.

THE ISO WORKING GROUP ON "PROGRAMMING LANGUAGES FOR THE CONTROL OF INDUSTRIAL PROCESSES (PLIP)." Following an initiative by DIN (Deutsches Institut fuer Normung), which was supported by several member institutions of TC 3 in the IPW, a working group (WG 1) on "Programming Languages for the Control of Industrial Processes (PLIP)" was founded within SC 5 (Subcommittee on Programming Languages) of TC 97 (Technical Committee on Computers and Information Processing) of the International Standards Organization (ISO), founded during 1976. The first meeting of this ISO/TC 97/SC 5/WG 1 took place in Washington, D.C., USA, from November 16 to 18, 1976.

The agreed scope of this working group is: "Standardization of one or more high-level computer programming languages and/or extensions to languages intended for general applicability in Industrial Real-Time (IRT) computer systems. . . ." (from ISO-Doc: 97⁵ 1 N 1 Rev.)

The secretariat is provided by the German Member Body: DIN Deutsches Institut fuer Normung e.V., Postfach 1107, D-1000 Berlin 30.

At this session the already mentioned Process-FORTRAN-Standards ISA-S 61.1 and 61.2 have been submitted to this working group by the US member organization. PEARL was presented as an example by DIN, and CORAL was proposed by BSI (British Standards Institute). The group decided to work out functional requirements for such languages and the drafting process for this purpose was started.

As any standardization group on one hand can only fix already existing things and on the other hand should not have much power to suppress one line of development in favor of another, one should not expect too much from this side concerning measures against language proliferation. But development never stops and every individual designer (or company or technically oriented institution) always knows how to replace the product which has just been finished by a better one. So one might try to use this tendency, which normally tends to increase proliferation, in order to reduce it. This might be achieved by "convincing" the interested parties that it is advantageous to input their resources which are necessary for such a replacement into a "cooperative effort." Two of these can be identified at the moment.

THE US-DoD-HIGH-ORDER LANGUAGE DEVELOPMENT PROJECT. The US Department of Defense, being one of the biggest software customers (and producers) in the world and spending more than three billion dollars per year for system analysis, design, and programming of software[42] obviously felt that something had to be done to reduce this figure or at least make more efficient use of this amount of money. So in 1975 a large-scale program was started as a cooperative effort of the three armed forces with the "aim of developing a common high-order language which will eventually supplant all languages in application for which there is currently no common language."[42] But the areas of application summarized under this term are very similar to what is usually called "industrial real-time programming."

But the European side this time has not been inactive.

The LTPL-Project of the European Community.   At a relatively early point in time, TC 3 (LTPL) of the IPW (and especially the European section of this group) discovered that the resources of a group, the members of which worked on a voluntary basis, were not sufficient to achieve its aim with the necessary speed. In 1973, they therefore approached the Commission of the European Community for support.... Soon good relations were developed between the responsible department and the "Purdue Europe"-Organization as a whole. In late Autumn 1974, concrete preparations for "European project" were started with the aim of developing a programming language for industrial real-time applications, which will eventually replace the existing languages in the eighties.[43,44]

Since a confrontation between the US–DoD—HOL project and any European project in this field would have been unwise, the possibilities for cooperation between these two efforts were investigated by the current chairman of the European LTPL-group, Mr. P. Elzer. Prof. Williams of Purdue University also helped very actively in this direction and the prospects are quite good that in the next generation of programming languages for industrial applications proliferation will not be as bad as it is now.

5-1-3 PROPERTIES OF LANGUAGES FOR REAL-TIME APPLICATIONS

5-1-3-1 General Considerations

Among language designers, salesmen, and even "professional" standardization people it is a ... common custom to discuss whether a particular language is a "real-time language" or not and usually a great difference of opinion arises. There is [really] no answer to the question [of] whether or not a "real-time language" has to contain tasking or I/O. Such a durable and emotional difference of opinion regarding an answer ... indicates that the question is asked in a wrong way.

One should ... ask instead for which class of problems a language has been designed and for which kind of users. It may happen that these questions do not even come to the mind of designers because they are rooted so deeply in their own tradition of work that they simply cannot imagine any other approach than their own [being] of more than marginal value.

One should ... ask whether a particular language has been designed for

"real-time applications" and for which ones! One should [also] ask whether it
is suitable to the purpose it has been designed for.

It turns out that obviously all the languages mentioned—and . . . more—
do their jobs well and that the differences lie in the way they are used and by
whom.

Yet there are some design guidelines which must be followed much more
carefully during the design of a language for real-time applications than in the
case of a language for conventional purposes. Some such principles are:

> Reliability of the resulting programs
>
> Safety aspects
>
> Efficiency of the resulting code
>
> Possibility of adapting to hardware requirements
>
> *Different* I/O Mechanisms
>
> Possibilities to react to external events (= synchronization with real-time)
>
> Influence on the management of resources
>
> Control of parallel processes

(This list may look a little different from what is usually contained in sales
papers for "real-time languages.")

But there is one basic aspect which turns out to be common for all
languages, which "do the job" for real-time applications, and that is . . . they
allow the programmer to control the behavior of the operating system in some
way. This makes them different from languages for "conventional" programming, . . . for example, COBOL,[45] ALGOL 60,[46] FORTRAN, ALGOL 68, or
PL/I. This fact makes the interrelations between a language for real-time applications and an operating system so interesting [that] they shall therefore be
investigated more closely in the rest of this paper.

Higher level languages for conventional applications do not impose any
time constraints on the reactions of an operating system. A program written in
one of these languages is compiled nearly entirely into sequential code, which
may be regarded as a one-to-one mapping of the source text onto machine code.
Although some higher level features [such as] standard functions result in an
"incorporation" of entire routines (or code pieces) out of a library, such
routines can be regarded as just a complicated "virtual instruction."

There are only a few exceptions. One of them is Input–Output instructions. . . . They may contain calls of . . . device drivers which usually are part of
an operating system. In simple implementations this need not even alter the
flow of purely sequential execution. In more complex environments it does, but
nothing is said about any time constraints. So a program may do its calculations
at noon and produce a lengthy output during the "idle time" of a computing
center after midnight. The logic of the program is not changed in any way by
such a behavior.

In the case of a language for real-time applications the situation is quite different. Here the underlying "virtual machine" is not of purely sequential character but at least capable of "quasi-parallelism" if not of real parallelism. Additionally in some cases the number of "virtual processors" which execute a given program can vary and is only known at run time. In order to ensure that such a virtual machine really works according to the requirements of a given real-time application one has to be able to control the functions of the individual (virtual) processors and their interrelations.

5-1-3-2 Some Different Approaches for the Interface Between Language and Operating System

Of course the new problems caused by this global requirement can only be solved gradually in the course of time, and thus at the moment one can identify several rather different approaches to a solution.

A first choice is to use the features of an operating system "as they are," that is, to include in a language a "normal" subroutine call, a modified subroutine call ("superviser-call" = SVC), or a piece of assembly code which allows the utilization of components of the operating system. The most prominent specimen of this class of languages is CORAL 66. Advantages of this method are: one does not have to worry about properties of operating systems when designing the language; the absence of interface problems makes implementations rather easy and cheap; and one can bypass the operating system if necessary. One is even able to extend or to write an operating system by means of the language.

The main disadvantage is that the user of such a language . . . has to know almost as much about the properties of an operating system as when using assembler. Portability of the resulting programs may be very poor too, because the methods of access to different operating systems may vary so drastically that application programs have to be redone to a very large extent.

A second approach is that used by "Process-FORTRAN" [40] or "Real-time BASIC." [47] At first glance it looks quite similar insofar as operating system features are accessed by calls in the language and their functional capabilities are handed through to the user nearly unchanged. But there is one significant difference: It has tried to standardize the semantics of the individual "calls," for example:

CALL TRNON (I,J,M)

for starting a program at a specified time or

CALL AOW (I,J,K,M)

for the execution of an analog output.

The parameters are mostly integer numbers and describe the details of the respective function.

Implementors of 'Process-FORTRAN' have to adapt their operating systems in order to comply with the requirements of the standard. So, when looking at it closely, the standardization of "Process-FORTRAN" is . . . a step on the way to standardized real-time operating systems rather than standardization of a "language." But with respect to language the interrelations between the "algorithmic" language elements and the "real-time elements" are still very weak.

This is no longer true for a class of languages designed around 1970 and implemented since then, like HAL/S,[7] LTR,[9] PEARL,[11] PROCOL[12] and others. Partially, development of these languages was started with the explicit intention of influencing the design of real-time operating systems. So for example, together with PROCOL an entire system was developed. But more important may be [the fact] that it was tried here for the first time to integrate . . . elements for the control of parallel processes into the language structure and to identify their interrelations with 'algorithmic' (or "conventional") language elements. Consequently a user programming in one of these languages in many cases no longer uses the operating systems elements in their original shape, but combinations and/or modifications of such elements. This method causes some development problems but on the other hand offers new advantages.

First let us look at the disadvantages. If such a language does not contain just a subset of the facilities of the actual operating system of the machine on which it is implemented, adaptation effort is necessary. This can be quite high if the principles of the "virtual machine" assumed for a particular language, are too different from those of the actual operating system. Of course, from a technical point of view the [best] solution would be the implementation of a special operating system modeling the "virtual machine" of the language. But this seems to be too expensive in most cases although we will see later that under certain aspects it will pay [off] or cost less than expected.

But the [following] advantages seem to be well worth the effort: The interactions between "conventional" and "real-time" language elements provide new means for improving the resulting programs. Such improvements occur mainly in the area of reliability of programs by elimination of sources of error or by . . . enforcing better solutions than an assembly programmer would voluntarily use. Some examples in the next paragraph will illustrate this.

A fourth approach, which has been made possible by advances in research on operating systems and languages and which seems to be a consequent extension of considerations on the interactions between language and operating system, is the integrated design of language and operating system. MODULA[27] and, under different prerequisites, MASCOT–MORAL,[48] may be regarded as representatives of this class.

The designers of MODULA have tried to keep the interface between language proper and operating system as small and simple as possible—but nevertheless have provided a rather comfortable and well-structured synchronization mechanism. This allowed them to manage with a small dispatcher.[28] ... More complex operating system features can be implemented in the language itself, which potentially makes the final solution very consistent. But as a consequence this means that the compiler cannot know anything about these "second-step" features and therefore is again not able to check the correct use of facilities, which go beyond the kernel mechanisms.

The MASCOT–MORAL approach is different insofar as it provides the user with a rather powerful set of applications-oriented elements with emphasis on safety and system integrity, which results in a somewhat bigger system. But this disadvantage may nearly be eliminated by the design principle of implementing the system by means of a higher level language (CORAL) into which user programs would [also] finally be translated.

5-1-3-3 Interrelation of "Conventional" with "Real-Time" Language Features

Real-time programming is often characterized by actions which have to take place at different points in time and at different locations (with respect to the source text) but nevertheless are in close connection with each other. Only in a middle- or high-level language, where such interdependencies can be recognized by the compiler (which is only feasible when they are on language level), is it—to a considerable extent—possible to detect or to prevent incorrect use or forbidden combinations of such features at translation time. The following examples shall illustrate this:

CRITICAL SECTIONS.   Program segments in which exclusive access to resources is claimed are usually called "critical sections."[49] To guarantee this exclusion it is necessary to perform synchronization operations at the beginning and at the end of the respective code sequences. These operations are separated both in time and space as mentioned above but nevertheless are a logical unit. Only a language which allows [description of] the problem (namely the exclusive access) explicitly enables the compiler to detect or to enforce the correct symmetry of the respective synchronization operations. In addition it is possible to implicitly provide the necessary release of a resource after a critical section has to be left in an "exceptional" situation.

AUTOMATIC INSTALLATION OF PROTECTION ENTITIES.   Resources (for example, data, devices) which are declared on a level that is accessible by different parallel processes, may automatically be handled by the compiler in a special way. It may be checked [as to] whether there is really a potential conflict situation or whether there is a possibility that references to these resources exist in different parallel processes. In this case it may be enforced to incorporate the respective access operations in special program segments for which protection entities are automatically installed. So the possibility of uncoordinated use of common resources is reduced to a minimum.

PARALLELISM THAT IS VISIBLE ON LANGUAGE LEVEL.   The fact that the compiler may already recognize parallel activities in many cases enables the static reservation of necessary workspace or space for control information at translation time, which can be important for small systems without dynamic storage management. This also stands for the possible provision of re-entrancy or copy of procedures which are shared by parallel processes. As a consequence the compiler may detect the overall space requirement of the translated program.

Parallelism in connection with block structure in addition enables the recognition of mutual dependencies and the provision of respective control mechanisms by the compiler—for example, the control of the lifetime of parallel processes in relation to that of superior ones in hierarchical systems.

EXCEPTION HANDLING.[50]   Reactions to exceptions should be subject to scope rules like those for declarations of program entities; that is, a certain reaction should only be valid on that program level where it has been declared. When the respective region is left, the provided reactions are cancelled. This compensates for the otherwise necessary reconciliations between different programmers of a (large) system because it draws strict border lines. As mentioned above, the occurrence of an exception situation, which as a consequence causes the flow of control to leave the current program level (block, critical section, procedure), may implicitly lead to an automatic performance of necessary "closing actions," like release of resources, termination of dependent parallel processes, or closing of files.

INPUT–OUTPUT AND PARALLELISM.   When activating a (slow) input or output operation it is (also in assembler systems) possible to continue with the subsequent instructions of a program while the I/O device is working in parallel, until a "wait-for-I/O" instruction is encountered. This raises the danger that the program is using data which are no longer (or not yet) in the expected state. This is exactly a problem of two parallel activities using shared data and hence may [be] dealt with by respective synchronization mechanisms in the same way as this is done for "normal" parallel processes, although this principle is obscured in most assembler implementations.

5–1–4 CONSEQUENCES ON THE OPERATING SYSTEM

5–1–4–1 Traditional Techniques

Several sophisticated and well-functioning real-time operating systems exist [today] which have either been implemented by different vendors (or software houses) for actual industrial applications—and hence mainly for assembler systems—or by computer scientists, whose main aim has been to apply recent findings of operating systems research. Because of this situation and [because] of the fact that the interfaces required by the various languages for real-time applications differ from each other to a large extent, it seems to be a rather natural consequence that it is somewhat difficult to adapt any language for real-time applications to an already existing system. Therefore in most cases it is necessary to provide specially tailored operating systems when implementing such a language on a new computer. This does not mean that people are always forced to build an entirely new O.S., especially if an already existing one partially fulfills the requirements. In some cases it is possible to merely incorporate some extensions or modifications. But since respective activities are performed mainly under the aspect of saving money and manpower, this often results in slight violations of the language's semantics and therefore spoils the compatibility of different implementations, too.

In the following some problems with the adaptation of an already existing real-time operating system [will] be discussed.

[Today] the development of real-time operating systems for assembler programs is often characterized by the following steps: The design phase is mainly influenced by people who know how to implement a well-structured, modular, and homogeneous system. . . . But since there is usually a lack of communication between implementors and users, this first release doesn't contain all the things which the applications programmers might wish. When using this release for first projects a huge torrent of [requests] for changes or updates follows. The bad conscience of the designers . . . causes them to comply with these wishes. So one release is followed by the other and finally this results in an unhomogeneous product with interrelations [among] all modules which originally were well separated, with "dead ends" and all those [negative] things which are the consequences of changes, and, last but not least, with bugs, which usually [adhere] to the "$1 + \epsilon$" rule.

Our personal experiences with an implementation of the language PEARL[11,51] confirm these (and other) observations. The already existing operating systems of the target computers were rather comfortable and [mostly] quite capabile [of fulfilling] the requirements of the language. Therefore we decided not to implement a new system but only to incorporate some necessary modifications. As pointed out before, this resulted in some slight violations of the original language's semantics, which could however be restricted to implementation dependent subsetting. One example is the use of only static priority numbers instead of the fully dynamic scheme of the original specification. But the real deficiency of this approach was the fact that large parts of the existing operating system were not needed anymore for applications programs written in PEARL but nevertheless remained resident in core. Neither did the memory management of the system allow [us] to use this space for user programs, nor was it possible to eliminate the respective routines with a reasonable amount of manpower.

5–1–4–2 Advantages of "Language-Oriented"
Operating Systems

The situation is different with operating systems for languages for real-time applications: Since here the users' wishes are necessarily addressed to the language designers, the implementor of the operating system is provided with a well-defined set of functional requirements (which are represented by the language's semantics), as soon as the language has reached a stable state. It shall not be claimed that "language-oriented" operating systems are necessarily better structured than others, but we believe [there is] evidence that the expenses for such a system are by far not as big as generally assumed. On the background of our experience with the adaptation of an existing operating system we have implemented a small model operating system the features of which are strictly an image of the requirements of a subset of the language. It is able to handle parallel processes and contains almost the full range of synchronization primitives and scheduling mechanisms. It also contains drivers for some of the existing peripherals in our installation. But since the system does not yet provide for storage management the loader has to do (static) space allocation. About 80 percent of the system is machine independent in the sense that it can be easily transferred to computers whose hardware structure is not too different. The most interesting experience has been that modules for certain tasks are smaller, faster, and match the requirements better than those of the original system, although the portable technique necessarily resulted in some overhead. Of course this has to a certain degree been a consequence of the fact that the facilities of the original system have partially exceeded the language requirements, whereas the new one has only been designed for this purpose. But even under the assumption of adequate capabilities it still seems to be feasible to keep some of the modules of operating systems under a higher level language still smaller than those designed to support assembler programs. This assumption is supported by the following reasons:

1. Safety mechanisms which are otherwise necessary may be left out where the compiler already checks for correctness.

    Examples:

    parameters of supervisor calls need not be checked for consistency as far as the compiler guarantees their correct use. This stands . . . for identifiers of parallel processes, synchronization variables, schedules, and so on.

    the correct use of peripherals need not be checked if the language provides a suitable device description mechanism.

    missing or wrong synchronization of access to shared resources cannot occur on the operating system level, if the language provides for adequate and safe mechanisms.

2. Since the programming philosophy is different when using a real-time

language, several complicated capabilities may be left out of the operating system, which otherwise substitute the missing comfort of assembler programming. In other words:
A "language-oriented" operating system may be simpler, because the set of used mechanisms is limited and well defined. A possible lack of 'flexibility' is compensated by increased safety.

3. Debugging software may be much simpler in a "language-oriented" operating system because a large amount of failures can already be eliminated by the compiler. In addition another large number of bugs may be detected by testing aids, which can be incorporated into the executable code by the compiler and so be performed, for example, on a big host computer before finally testing and using the program on the target machine.

5-1-5 POSSIBLE FUTURE ASPECTS

One issue seems to have become clear in this paper: The main problem area in the design of programming languages for real-time applications is their interface [with] the operating system. And one reason for the problems seems to be that according to the state-of-the-art the languages allow (or force) the user to interfere with the operating system in the sense that [the user] directs the operating system how to do a certain job instead of just prescribing *what* to do.

It now seems, too, that research both on languages and on operating systems [52,53,54,55,56] has reached a state, where, on one hand, language elements can be imagined which are closer to a user's problem and on the other hand the basic elements of operating systems can be defined much more clearly and unambiguously and thus leave less room for unnecessary differences. In those cases, where the systems still have to be different, it seems also feasible to map more "user-oriented" language elements in different ways on different systems without having to modify or to "adapt" the latter ones. So one would be able to gain the advantages of a more integrated design without having to pay too high a price in the form of adaptation effort.

What has been said until now sounds a bit like the description of elements of [today's] POLs (= Problem Oriented Languages). But there is one significant difference: A classical "POL" describes a problem in terms of the problem itself, for example, in the form of parameters of a control-loop of a certain type. But a user-oriented general-purpose language for real-time applications might describe the program to solve the problem in terms of program structure, for example, resource requirements, concepts of synchronization, response times of program actions. It seems that the requirements of computer networks will even enforce such a programming style.

As an example of what might be expected one can look at a resource-reservation. What does the programmer have to consider [today], if he, for example, writes a procedure in which he wants to print a protocol without being disturbed:

1. "I need the printer exclusively therefore I have to lock it for anybody else during my output."
2. "I have to use a semaphore to indicate the reservation."
3. "I must not forget to release this semaphore after the use of the printer."

In the case of a more elaborate and simpler to use language his thoughts would read as follows:

1. "I need the printer exclusively."
2. "I indicate this in the header of my procedure."

One might even think of doing a good part of deadlock-detection already at compile time if the language rigorously enforces an appropriate ordering of activations of parallel processes and their resource claims. There are limits to such a method which lie in the very nature of an industrial real-time environment, but at least certain cases could already be foreseen by the compiler and others could be detected at real-time and appropriate actions be taken by the programmer.

Individual work on such topics is going on in several places, but it can only be hoped that results of this will be incorporated in cooperative efforts which will have an impact in the future.

5-1-6 REFERENCES

[1] "RTL"—A Language for Real-time Systems; The Computer Bulletin, Dec. 1967, pp. 202–212

[2] J. Gertler; High-level Programming for Process Control; The Computer Journal, 13, No. 1, Feb. 1970, pp. 70–75

[3] J. D. Schoeffler; RTL—A Real Time Language for Computer Control Software; Systems Research Center, Case Western Reserve University, Cleveland, Ohio 44106

[4] G. Müller; Die Verwendung einer problemorientierten Sprache für Prozeßrechner, Aufbau and Funktionsweise der zugehörigen Compilers; Paper given at the 'Jahreskolloqium zur Rechentechnik' Feb. 1970, Techn.Universität Braunschweig

[5] B. Corman, P. R. Wetherall, P. M. Woodward; Official Definition of CORAL 66; Her Majesty's Stationary Office, London (1970)

[6] INDAC-8 Software; Digital Equipment Corporation, Maynard, Mass.

[7] P. Newbold et al.; HAL/S Language Specification; Intermetrics Inc., Report No. IR–61–5 (Nov. 1974)

[8] M. Donal et al.; Specifications techniques d'un langage de programmation et d'un moniteur pour les applications industrielles en temps réel; CERCI–SESA (1970)

9   P. Parayre, M. Trocello; LTR, un système de realisation pour l'informatique temps réel;

10 JOVIAL J73/1 Computer Programming Manual; Computer Sciences Corp., El Segundo, Cal. (1975)

11 K. H. Timmesfeld et al.; PEARL—A proposal for a process- and experiment automation realtime language; Gesellschaft f. Kernforschung mbH., Karlsruhe, Report KFK-PDV 1 (1973)

12 M. Ritout, P. Bonnard, P. Hugot; PROCOL: Process Control Language; 5th IFAC Congress, Paris, June 1972

13 RTL/2—Language Specification; Corporate Laboratory, ICI Ltd., (1974)

14 ECMA/ANSI; PL/I, Basis/1–12, July 1974

15 Wijngarden, Mailloux, Peck, Koster; Report on the Algorithmic Language ALGOL 68; Num.Math. 14 (1969), 79–218

16 J. Gertler, J. Sedlak; Software for Process Control, A Survey; 4th IFAC/IFIP International Conference on Digital Computer Applications to Process Control, Zürich, March 1974

17 T. J. Williams; The International Purdue Workshop on Industrial Computer Systems and its Work in Promoting Computer Control Guidelines and Standards; Report No. 77, Purdue University, West Lafayette, Indiana 47907

18 P. Elzer, R. Roessler; A language comparison as a basis for an international standard for a process control language; 1974 IFAC/IFIP Workshop on Real-Time Programming, Hungarian Academy of Science, Budapest

19 R. Roessler, K. Schenk (ed.); LTPL-E language comparison; LTPL-E-330 (Nov. 1975)

20 R. Roessler, K. Schenk (ed.); A Language Comparison Developed by the LTPL-E Committee TC-3 of PURDUE-Europe; Republished by PLAIC, Purdue University, West Lafayette, Indiana 47907

21 ESONE-Committee; The Definition of IML—a language for use in CAMAC-systems; ESONE/IML/01 (Esone secretariat, Dr. H. Meyer, CCR-BCMN, B-2440 Geel)

22 B. D. De Roze; The U.S. Defence Systems Software Management Program; Software Management Conference, London (March 1977)

23 R. Gauthier; Evaluation Criteria to Determine High Order Language for the USA Department of Defense; IFAC/IFIP workshop on real-time programming (June 1976), IRIA—Rocquencourt

24 A. Schwald, R. Baumann; PEARL im Vergleich mit anderen Echtzeit-sprachen; Proceedings of the 'Aussprachetag PEARL', March 1977, Gesellschaft f. Kernforschung mbH. Karlsruhe

25 O.-J. Dahl et al.; The SIMULA 67 common base language; Norwegian Comp. Center, Oslo 1968

26 N. Wirth; The programming language PASCAL; Acta Informatica 1, 35–63 (1971)

27 N. Wirth; MODULA: A language for modular multiprogramming; Eidgen. Techn. Hochschule Zürich, (March 1976)

28 N. Wirth; The use of MODULA and design and implementation of MODULA ETH Zürich, June 1976

29 M. Richards; The BCPL Reference Manual; The University Mathematical Laboratory, Cambridge (1969)

30 P. Cousot; The System Implementation Language LIS; Institut de Recherche d'Informatique et d'Automatique (June 1976), Rocquencourt

31 W. Wulf et al.; HYDRA, the kernel of a multiprocessor operating system; CACM, June 1974, Vol. 17, No. 6, pp. 337–345

32 Th. Lalive d'Epinay; Development of the new operating system "CHA-OS" at the Federal Institute of Technology, Zürich; 1st IFAC/IFIP Symposium on Software for Computer Control, Tallinn, (May 1976) p. 143

33 O.-J. Dahl, E. W. Dijkstra, C. A. R. Hoare; Structured Programming; Ac. Press, New York, 1972

34 A. Zeh; Reliability of Process Control Computer Languages; 1st IFAC/IFIP Symposium on Software for Computer Control, Tallinn, (May 1976) p. 245

35 P. Elzer; Ein Mechanismus zur Erstellung strukturierter Prozeßautomatisierungsprogramme; Paper given at 'Fachtagung Prozeßrechner' (1977) Augsburg, to be published in SPRINGER lecture notes.

36 M. S. Adix, H. A. Schutz; ILIAD: A High-Level Language for Industrial Control Applications; GM Corp., Warren, Mich. (Nov. 1975)

37 I. C. Pyle; Developments in Real Time Software; University of York, Department of Computer Science

38 D. A. Fisher; A Common Programming Language for the Department of Defense—Background and Technical Requirements; Institute for Defense Analysis, June 1976

39 R. Baumann; Purdue Europe, Europäische Regionale Organisation des International Purdue Workshop on Industrial Computer Systems; Regelungstechnik und Prozeß-Datenverarbeitung 22 (1974) 182–183

40 ISA; Standard, Industrial Computer System Fortran Procedures for Executive Functions, Process Input/Output, and BIT Manipulation; Feb. 1976

41 P. Elzer; PURDUE-EUROPE TC 3 LTPL-E Information Summary (Oct. 1976), International Purdue Workshop on Industrial Computer Systems

42 D. A. Fisher; Programming Language Commonality in the Department of Defense; Defense Management Journal, Oct. 1975, pp. 29–33

43 'Community Policy for Data-Processing'; Commission of the European Communities, Doc. COM (75) 467 final, Brussels, Sept. 1975

44 Ch. Layton; The EEC Project for a Real-Time Language for Industrial Applications; Software Management Conference, London (March 1977)

45 J. F. Cunningham; COBOL; CACM 6, No. 3 (March 1963) pp. 79–82

46 P. Naur; Revised Report on the Algorithmic Language ALGOL 60; Num. Math. 4 (1963) pp. 420–453

47 Purdue Europe Real-Time Basic Committee; Report on Real-Time Extensions and Implementations of Real-Time Basic; First Report (Oct. 1975)

48 H. F. Harte; A description of the progamming language MORAL; Rep. No. 22/1132, Software Sciences Ltd., Farnborough, Hampshire, UK (Feb. 1976)

49 E.W. Dijkstra; Hierarchical Ordering of Sequential Processes; Operating System Techniques, Ac. Press, London and New York, (1972) pp. 72–93

50 J.B. Goodenough; Exception Handling, Issues and a Proposed Notation; CACM, Vol. 18, No. 12 (Dec. 1975) pp. 683–696

51 P. Elzer et al.; The implementation of a subset of the real-time language "PEARL" and examples of its applications; SOCOCO 76, 1st IFAC/IFIP Symposium on Software for Computer Control, Tallinn, USSR (May 1976)

52 C. A. R. Hoare; Monitors: An operating system structuring concept; CACM 11, 549–557 (1974)

53 H. Wettstein; Prozeßumschaltungen in Betriebssystemen; Computing 12, pp. 363–382 (1974)

54 J. Nehmer; Dispatcher Primitives for the Construction of Operating System Kernels; Acta Informatica 5, 237–255 (1975)

55 J. Nehmer, O. Eggenberger; Hardwarenahe Elementarfunktionen der Ablaufsteuerung für Prozeßrechnerbetriebssysteme; KFK-PDV 49, Gesellschaft für Kernforschung, Karlsruhe

56 J. Ehrig et al.; COPF: Ein Satz von Programmbausteinen für Realzeitbetriebssysteme; KFK-PDV 40, Gesellschaft für Kernforschung, Karlsruhe

5-2 HIGHER ORDER LANGUAGES FOR AVIONICS SOFTWARE—A SURVEY, SUMMARY, AND CRITIQUE*

Raymond J. Rubey

SofTech, Inc.

5-2-1 ABSTRACT

This paper surveys the activities of the last ten years with regard to avionics Higher Order Languages (HOLs). It presents reasons why HOLs were late arriving in the avionics arena and why they have not been more widely used today. In particular, the published experiences with existing HOLs in avionics applications are summarized. Descriptions of important HOL evaluation criteria, such as "efficiency" and "programmer productivity" are presented and the reported measurements with respect to these criteria are discussed. The problems and deficiencies of past reporting with respect to these criteria are highlighted. In addition to this summary of the quantitative information regarding avionics HOL use, the need for improvements is discussed. This includes the relationship of the HOL to the total software development process, the improved software tools that can be employed, and the level of HOL documentation available.

5-2-2 INTRODUCTION

For the last ten years there has been a growing interest and experience in the use of Higher Order Languages (HOLs) for avionics applications. During this period there has been a considerable increase in the capability of on-board digital avionics computers and a corresponding increase in the size and complexity of on-board avionics computer programs.

By the mid 1960s the use of HOLs for most programming applications had become common; languages such as FORTRAN and COBOL were widely accepted and implemented. However, in real-time software applications, and in particular for avionics applications, HOLs were not used. What are some of the reasons for this divergence in programming practices between the general application area and avionics applications? First, the avionics computers available were very difficult to program. Although this might seem an argument for the use of HOLs, in truth the programming difficulties associated with the avionics computers made it almost impossible to develop effective compilers for an HOL. Secondly, the avionics computers were expensive and it was necessary to extract the maximum performance from the smallest processors and least memory that would suffice. This heavy emphasis on efficiency placed further demands on HOLs and their compilers that were nearly impossible to satisfy. Finally, most avionics software developments were done in an environment that could not afford the cost or time for development of a suitable compiler and were done by engineers who had little knowledge or interest in the advances then taking place in programming methods and theory.

There were several observers of this situation, both in the Air Force and industry, who believed that steps should be taken to promote the use of HOLs in avionics applications.[2] The actions of these individuals and their organizations gradually led to the acceptance of the idea that HOLs and other related programming techniques had application in the avionics area. There were four phases in injecting HOLs into the avionics software development process:

(1) Survey, study, and define suitable avionics HOLs

(2) Develop compilers for the avionics HOLs

(3) Use the avionics HOL and compiler in a major software development

(4) Extend use of the HOL to a majority of avionics software developments

We have proceeded through the first three phases with much effort and are now involved in the fourth phase.

5-2-3 AVIONICS HOL DEFINITION

The first phase in introducing HOLs to the avionics area was the survey or study phase. This phase occurred in the late 1960s and involved surveys of existing languages to determine their suitability for avionics applications. In almost every case it was determined that existing HOLs (for example, FORTRAN, COBOL, PL/I, and JOVIAL) failed to meet the needs of the avionics software environment. Among the most frequently cited deficiencies of the commonly available HOLs for avionics applications were:

Inadequate bit and byte operations

Inability to perform fixed point arithmetic operations in a small word size computer

No provision for control over hardware features such as interrupts

Inadequate control over memory allocation

Inability to lapse into assembly code

Inappropriate input–output statements

The lack of features that promote efficient code in the avionics computer

In addition to the above disadvantages, most studies also indicated that there were aspects of the avionics application that could be expressed in an HOL much better than current HOLs permitted. A common recommended extension was the addition of facilities for matrix and vector operations.[1,3,19,20,22,23]

After having found the languages then in common use unsuitable or nonoptimum for avionics applications, new languages were designed to overcome the cited disadvantages and to incorporate desirable new facilities. In the late 1960s and early 1970s a great many new languages were defined. The bibliography of this paper contains references to some of the more widely publicized [ones]. A listing of the names of a few will give some indication of the scope and variety of the work that was done. A few of the HOLs defined are SPL,[3,17] CLASP,[13,20] APOL,[12] METAPLAN,[24,25] JOVIAL J3B, JOVIAL J73, CMS-2, CS-4, HAL/S,[15] and PL/ATAC.[18]

Obviously, many people and organizations attempted to create an HOL suitable for avionics applications. Two major problems with these early efforts are now apparent. First, too many avionics HOLs were being defined. Second, the avionics HOLs were not being put to use on important Air Force avionics software developments as fast as they were being defined. The situation where no HOLs were felt suitable for avionics applications quickly changed to a situation in which there were more HOLs than applications. Some standardization was necessary and an effort in this regard was one objective of DoD Instruction 5000.31, *Interim List of DoD Approved Higher Order Programming Languages.*[27]

HOLs that were defined could be grouped into two categories, each reflecting the thoughts of the language designers. In one cateogry would be the simple, basic languages that contained only those features that were necessary for avionics applications; JOVIAL J3B, CLASP, APOL and METAPLAN would be representatives of this category. The designers of these languages believed that the requisite efficiency could only be achieved if the language was simple, enabling the development of a relatively low cost, optimizing compiler. In the second category would be the omnibus languages containing a wide range of features; JOVIAL J73 and SPL (Space Programming Language) are representatives of this category. The designers of these languages believed that the benefits of HOL use could be realized to the greatest extent if not only the avionics software itself was written in the HOL, but also all of the support and simulation software also were written in the HOL. Both JOVIAL J73 and SPL were originally designed in "levels" or "subsets" in which a portion of the language (for example, SPL Mark II and J73/I) would be used for avionics applications while the total language (for example, SPL Mark IV and J73/III) would be suitable for almost any application. It should be noted that the subsequent work with the omnibus HOLs was with the small avionics-oriented subsets. On the other hand subsequent work with the simple HOLs resulted in enhancements to those HOLs (for example, JOVIAL J3B Level 0 grew to become the compatible extension J3B Level 2) so that the differences in capability between the two categories have become much less.

5-2-4 AVIONICS HOL COMPILER DEVELOPMENT

An avionics HOL by itself does nothing to help avionics software development. The next phase in the introduction of HOLs into avionics is the development of suitable HOL compilers. The compiler is a computer program that translates programs written in the avionics HOL into the avionics computer's machine or assembly language. This phase represents an appreciable cost step. It is relatively cheap and easy (and interesting) to define a new HOL; it is expensive (and laborious) to develop and maintain a suitable compiler for that HOL. Avionics HOL compilers have been exclusively cross compilers. A cross compiler executes on a large general-purpose computer (called the host computer) and generates code for the smaller avionics computer (called the target computer). This is in contrast to the usual commercial compilers that generate code for the computer on which the compiler itself executes. One possibility exists in the avionics area that can be used to facilitate software development; this is to have a compiler (or compilers) that generate machine code both for the avionics computer and the general-purpose computer on which the compiler executes. This possibility has been exploited for both JOVIAL J3B (that is, compilers hosted on the IBM 360/370 generate code for the IBM 360/370 and the SKC–2070, MAGIC 362F and LC4516 avionics computers) and JOVIAL J73I (that is, compilers hosted on the DEC 10 generate code for the DEC 10 and the DAIS processor). This capability enables a programmer to do the initial debugging and testing of the avionics software on a general-purpose computer that is more accessible and can provide more debugging facilities than the avionics computer.[21]

A compiler, like any other program, is written in some programming language; the choice of the particular language is the subject of much thought and some disagreement. One can write the compiler in the same HOL that the compiler itself processes. For example, the DAIS JOVIAL J73 compiler is written in JOVIAL J73. This selection is intended to enhance compiler transportability since to obtain a compiler hosted on and targeted to a new computer, one must rewrite only the portion of the existing compiler that is dependent on the target computer and then recompile the existing compiler for the new host machine, in a "bootstrapping" manner. One problem with writing a compiler for an avionics HOL in the same HOL is that the avionics HOL might not be as suitable for compiler writing as it is for avionics software development. Another alternative is to write the compiler in a HOL that is both effective for compiler writing and is available on a number of potential host computers. This approach was taken, for example, with the JOVIAL J3B compilers written in AED.

Regardless of the approach taken, compiler development for an avionics HOL is both expensive and time consuming. One approach to this cost and schedule problem is the use of special compiler-building tools. For avionics applications, the work in this area started with the Space Programming Language Implementation Tool—SPLIT.[6]

5-2-5 AVIONICS HOL USE

The third phase in the application of HOL techniques into avionics applications is the actual use of the selected HOL and its compiler in a real avionics software development (not just the experimental use on a pilot test basis).

The first major Air Force avionics software development effort to use an HOL was the B-1 Offensive Avionics System. As late as 1975 an Air Force survey indicated that the B-1 was the only one of fourteen Aeronautical Systems Division projects that employed an HOL; the language used was JOVIAL J3B.[11] Later in 1975, JOVIAL J3B was also selected as the HOL for the F-16 Fire Control Subsystem. JOVIAL J73 was selected as the HOL for the DAIS mission software (and a major portion of the DAIS support software) and for the Electronically Agile Radar software.[14,16] A major impetus for the initial use of HOLs has been the Air Force's urging and pressure to do so. Many recent avionics software developments (for example, B-1 Offensive and Defensive Flight Software) have had contractual requirements that at least 80 percent of the flight software be written in an HOL.

Only by actually using an HOL can the promises of HOL suitability for avionics and of HOL superiority over assembly language be verified. Nearly every application of HOLs in avionics applications has involved some quantitative comparison of the new HOL technique with past assembly language practice. The most important question to be answered in all of these comparisons has been: What loss of computer hardware efficiency results from assembly language use? In spite of decreases in computer hardware costs, it is apparent that the inefficiency of code generated by HOLs is a major deciding factor in HOL use. This is an aspect of the avionics application area that has not changed despite many predictions to the contrary. Perhaps a major reason for the persistence of this fact has been the continued inability to accurately estimate computer time and memory requirements at the beginning of an avionics system's development. Whether or not an HOL is used, most avionics computer programs, at some time during their developments, exceed the available computer time and memory. If an HOL is used, it is often tempting to blame the HOL or its compiler for this situation. Hence, the great interest in the inefficiency associated with HOL use.

5-2-6 HOL EFFICIENCY

First, one must understand what is meant by HOL inefficiency. The usual definition of HOL inefficiency begins with the assumption that there is some determinable memory size and execution time for an assembly version of the program being evaluated. One then compares size and time of the HOL version of a program that performs the same as the assembly language version with the size and time of the assembly language version. Any increase in the size or time of the HOL version would be expressed as a percentage of the assembly language version. For example, if the HOL version required 120 words of memory, and the assembly language version 100 words, the inefficiency of the HOL (and its compiler) would be 20 percent.

There are several problems with this inefficiency definition, but there is, as yet, no better definition. One problem is that one needs a baseline assembly language version for comparison. This requires that an assembly language version of the program be written. To write an assembly language version of a complete avionics computer program would at least double software development costs and be prohibitively expensive in most situations. Therefore, only a few, small segments of a complete program are selected for comparison. Each selected segment is intended to be typical of a larger part of the program; it is hoped that conclusions made about the efficiency of these segments can be extended over the entire program. In practice, a very wide range of efficiencies is observed for the individual segments and an average of the efficiencies is made. The use of an assembly language version as a standard of comparison also introduces the uncertainty as to whether that assembly language version could not be made smaller or faster through additional effort or by a better programmer. Occasionally, the HOL version is smaller than the assembly language version (that is, the HOL inefficiency is negative) indicating that a better assembly language version could have been written. Usually one assumes that the version one has is typical of the product of an average programmer working in the normal programming environment.

In examining the literature regarding HOL inefficiency, much more quantitative data is found regarding memory inefficiency than execution time inefficiency. This is due to several reasons. First, it is much easier to measure the size of a program than to measure its execution time; the latter measurement may vary depending on input data. The total memory required by a program is the sum of the memory required by each of its segments. However, the total execution time is not the simple sum of the execution times of each segment because some segments may be executed more often than others in actual operation. Very often the situation exists where 90 percent of the time is spent executing segments that represent less than 10 percent of the program size (for example, a major and minor loop organization of the program). Thus the effective execution time HOL inefficiency is very dependent on the organization of the program. By carefully optimizing heavily used portions of a program, or even writing those portions in assembly language, the effective execution time inefficiency may be very low even though the inefficiency appears substantial when large infrequently executed segments are considered independently. In many reports where execution time inefficiencies are not explicitly reported, it is stated that these inefficiencies are estimated to be the same as the memory inefficiencies. With attention to the optimization of time critical segments, and even the limited selective use of assembly language, this is a conservative estimation.

The reported overall size inefficiency of HOLs in avionics applications has been between 10 and 20 percent in nearly all reports.[4,10,15,26] It is surprising that there is such general agreement over the achievable size inefficiency for avionics HOLs. Part of this agreement is probably related to the needs of the avionics environment and the procedures for acquiring avionics HOL compilers. Many avionics HOL compiler procurements have required, as an acceptance criterion, that a size and execution time inefficiency of less than 20 percent be achieved. Many of the reported size inefficiency data are obtained from these compiler acceptance tests; it would be surprising if any greater inefficiency was reported. The literature does report many factors that affect the avionics HOL size inefficiency that can be achieved. These factors include:

(1) Compiler Optimization
(2) Programmer Ability
(3) Computer Hardware Characteristics

Most avionics HOL compilers have optimization features that increase the efficiency of the code they generate. The better the optimization techniques, the more efficient the coding; comprehensive and effective optimization capabilities add to the cost and time of compiler development. Therefore, an avionics HOL is a compromise between acceptable efficiency and having a compiler available on schedule and within cost. The literature does not present any qualitative information on the cost and time involved to include specific optimization features. At least a 10 percent decrease in inefficiency due to op-timization enhancements of an already quite good compiler has been reported.[15]

The programmer using an avionics HOL has many choices concerning the specific language features he uses to implement a function. These choices have a major influence on the efficiency of the code that results from the compiler. The best programmers have the experience and knowledge to select the language features that result in the greatest efficiency. For example, the author was involved in a test in which a programmer, having no prior experience with the CLASP HOL, wrote a program that was 100 percent inefficient while an experienced programmer wrote a version of the same program that was 20 percent inefficient. Another study reported a 25 percent improvement in efficiency with greater programmer experience.[15] Clearly, the programmer's experience is a major factor in achieving high efficiency. The claim that an avionics HOL will allow less experienced programmers to be used than are required when assembly language is used, should not be believed without reservation.

One related aspect of avionics HOL use is that one must not let any HOL code that is written go unexamined by experienced programmers. In one reported case, 20 percent of the code could be eliminated by more efficient rewriting in the HOL or by assembly language substitution.[4] It is important during the initial use of an avionics HOL compiler that there is continuous cooperation and interaction between the compiler-developers and applications programmers. Only by examining actual applications code on a specific avionics computer, can the compiler-developer design and implement effective optimization features.[28]

There is little information available on the relationship between the architecture of the avionics computer and the efficiency of the avionics software. There are some computer hardware features (such as floating point arithmetic and stack manipulation instructions) that make the development of efficient compilers easier; other features (such as a multiplicity of addressing modes and instruction sizes) can make the development of efficient compilers harder. There is evidence that memory efficiency is more dependent on the hardware instructions available than the HOL. The same algorithms required between 20 and 45 percent less memory on one avionics computer than another.[4]

The efficiency picture is not completely negative with respect to avionics HOLs. An assembly language program is much more difficult to modify than an HOL program. As errors are found during software debugging and testing, an assembly language programmer tends to make the needed corrections via patches; using an HOL the programmer can change the original program in a more efficient manner. One report indicated a 2 to 5 percent improvement in the efficiency of the HOL version after all checkout was completed as compared with its efficiency after the original coding.[7]

Even if the HOL version of a program is between 10 and 20 percent inefficient, the greater ease of modifying the program sometimes makes it possible to incorporate design changes that greatly increase overall efficiency. An example from one of the early uses of an HOL for systems programming illustrates this point. One segment of a very large program was completed, but upon closer examination it was found that by removing some nonessential features the size could be reduced by over 50 percent and the speed increased by a factor of five to ten. The HOL enabled these changes to be made without breaking the budget or schedule.[5] In one avionics HOL application, it was found that the HOL version of the program exceeded available memory capacity and it was estimated that even a 20 percent smaller assembly-language version would also exceed the capacity. However, because an HOL was used, significant design changes were made that would not have been considered feasible if assembly language had been used, and the program was made to fit.[4] The capability when an HOL is used to easily make significant efficiency improvements through software redesign will, for large avionics programs, more than compensate for the currently reported 10 to 20 percent HOL inefficiencies.

5-2-7 PROGRAMMER PRODUCTIVITY

The expectation of an increase in programmer productivity is a major motivation for using an HOL. However, there is little qualitative data to indicate the increase in programmer productivity when an avionics HOL has been used. When avionics HOLs were first considered, it was often stated that the effort in writing one HOL statement was about the same as that involved in writing one assembly language instruction. Since an average HOL statement expands to at least three or four assembly language statements, a factor of three or four increase in programmer productivity should be realized. Although such a great increase has not been observed, a doubling of programmer productivity has been reported.[4] Unfortunately, there has been less quantitative discussion of productivity improvements than of HOL inefficiency. In every case where an HOL has been used, however, it has been felt that there was an increase in programmer productivity.

One reason for the relative lack of quantitative data is that there are many difficulties in defining and measuring programmer productivity. First, there is the scope of the programming effort. Avionics software development involves requirements definition, software design, coding, debugging, integration, formal testing, documentation, and maintenance. The direct effect of HOL usage on the coding effort could be assessed, but this is only a small part of the total effort. One evaluation estimated a 20 percent savings in coding, 5 percent in documentation, and no savings in the other software development phases.[9] Attempting to extrapolate productivity measurements obtained from the parallel development of HOL and assembly language versions, as was done for HOL inefficiency determination, is difficult because many of the time and resource consuming efforts, such as integration, formal testing, and maintenance, can only be accomplished with the total program. This problem is compounded by the fact that most avionics software developments do not proceed in a step-by-step manner through each phase. Instead there are many iterations as requirements or the interfacing hardware changes and as software problems are discovered.

Another major difficulty in measuring programmer productivity is the lack of comparable data from past, assembly language-oriented avionics software developments. Because we have not accurately and consistently recorded what we spent on past efforts, we will have difficulty in determining if our newer techniques require less.

A technique that has been claimed to have a significant and favorable impact on programmer productivity is structured programming. The basic principles of structured programming, such as the use of a few simple to understand control structures, are closely linked with the use of an HOL. Although the principles of structured programming can be applied to assembly language coding, especially when the basic control structures are implemented through macros, most applications of structured programming have used an HOL. It is probable that most advances in programmer productivity achieved in other application areas through technology improvements, such as structured programming, will be applicable to avionics applications only if an HOL is used.

5-2-8 EXTENDING HOL AVIONICS USE

When they have been tried, avionics HOLs have been found effective.[4,10,11,16,25,26] As already discussed, needed HOL standardization efforts have begun.[27] However, much more remains to be done if the many advantages of HOL use cited in the studies done ten years ago are to be realized.

In spite of the favorable experience to date with avionics HOLs, there remain many areas for further exploration and exploitation. Two studies that estimate the impact on life cycle costs of avionics HOL use have been made; these studies reached opposite conclusions. One study indicated that the savings resulting from reduced software development and maintenance costs could not overcome the cost of the increased memory needed because of HOL inefficiency.[8] The other study indicated that there would be a small savings.[9] The critical parameters in these evaluations are the memory cost per bit, the number of computers procured, the cost of each programmer man-hour expended on development and maintenance, and the increase in productivity (both during development and maintenance) when an HOL is used. As memory costs decrease and as each programmer man-hour becomes more expensive, the balance can be further shifted if additional improvements in programmer productivity are made.

Although avionics HOLs have been used to code avionics software, they have made little impact on other software development stages. It was claimed that the use of the same HOL in initial engineering studies and in developing flight software, would greatly reduce the reprogramming required in each development stage.[21] One report indicated that up to 43 percent of the software errors can be found by execution of the avionics software on the "host" computer.[4] Another report indicates that software integration was accomplished in half the time previously experienced through the extensive use of simulation on the "host" computer with the HOL.[25] In most cases the avionics HOL is only used for flight software coding; FORTRAN is still the most commonly used language for the engineering study phases. If the avionics HOL were more extensively used early in the engineering study phases, the task of developing the flight software could be made much easier. In the future a much closer link between the engineering study software and the flight software must be formed with the common use of the avionics HOL.

Even if a program is written in an avionics HOL, most avionics testing facilities, employing the actual avionics computer, require that debugging and checkout be accomplished in something close to assembly or machine language. The test tools and facilities have not been built that enable a programmer to think and operate in the HOL during testing just as during coding. More time and effort is devoted to testing than to coding; many HOL benefits will be lost if the necessary improvements to the test tools are not made. Such tools are expensive to implement; HOL standardization may allow their cost to be spread across several projects. Considerable work remains to be done in this area, but the payoff will be great.

One problem with which HOL programmers must often struggle, is the delay between when a change is made to the program being tested and when a compiled HOL version of the modified program is available for further testing. Testing is usually done on a dedicated test facility while compilations are done at a central computer facility. If a programmer must wait overnight to receive the results of a compilation from the central computer facility, he will most likely attempt to make the change by an assembly language patch. This enables him to continue testing but requires him to revert to assembly language so that many HOL advantages are lost. An effective software development facility will allow changes to be made in the HOL version of the program and almost instantly will provide a compiled output for execution on the test facility. The computer hardware for such a capability has been available for some time; the support software to provide this capability should be developed to take full advantage of HOL use.

One problem with many general purpose HOLs, such as FORTRAN, that was cited in early avionics HOL studies, is the lack of a formal definition of these HOLs. Considerable effort was expended in developing a formal syntactic definition of many avionics HOLs in response to this problem. Today, a major problem with avionics HOLs is that few avionics HOLs have adequate user documentation. Even though formal BNF-like definitions exist, these definitions are not suitable for the training of, and day-to-day use by, the average avionics HOL programmer. If avionics HOLs are to be more widely used, tutorial and reference documentation suitable for both programmer-engineers and engineer-programmers must be made available. Better methods for distributing this documentation are also needed to replace the current word-of-mouth and informal methods. HOLs represent a significant improvement in avionics software development methods; publicity and better documentation will ensure that this improvement is more widely used.

5-2-9 REFERENCES

The following are papers that have reported the events of the ten-year effort to develop and utilize HOLs for avionics applications:

1 L. J. Carey and W. E. Meyer, "Preliminary SDC Recommendations for a Common Spaceborne Programming Language," Proceedings of 1st Spaceborne Computer Software Workshop, Santa Monica, Calif. pp. 253–273, 1966

2 L. J. Carey and W. A. Sturm, "Space Software: At the Crossroads," Space/Aeronautics pp. 62–69, December 1968

3 L. J. Carey, "Space Software—Production Problems and a Programming Language," AIAA Paper No. 68–821, 1968

4 R. L. Coffin, "Avionics Application Software Using the AED Language—Some Results and Conclusions," National Aerospace Electronics Conference Record, pp. 709–715, 1976.

5 F. J. Corbato, "PL/I as a Tool for System Programming," Proceedings of PL/I Seminars ESD–TR–68–154, pp. 103–114, 1968.

6 B. C. Corn, "A Compiler Development System," Proceedings of the Aeronautical Systems Software Workshop, pp. 418–424, 1974

7 W. O. Felsman and A. F. Schmitt, "Cost Aspects of Utilizing a Higher Order Language (HOL) for Airborne Computers," National Aerospace Electronics Conference Record, pp. 31–38, 1970.

8 V. V. Griffith, "Can HOL Use in Avionics Pay for Itself," Proceedings of the Aeronautical Systems Software Workshop, pp. 407–412, 1974

9 G. G. Hays, "HOL vs. AL for Avionic Software," National Aerospace Electronics Conference Record, pp. 716–721, 1976.

10 M. T. Holden, "JOVIAL/J3B Compiler Optimization for Time Critical B-1 RFS/ECM Application," Boeing, 1977

11 M. T. Holden, "JOVIAL/J3B Implementation of B-1 Operational Flight Software: An Evaluation," National Aerospace Electronics Conference Record, pp. 700, 1976

12 G. L. Kreglow and H. J. Apalategui, "Design Philosophy for the Aerospace Program—Oriented Language," National Aerospace Electronics Conference Record, pp. 52–59, 1970.

13 Logicon, "Flight Computer and Language Processor Study," NASA CR–1520, 1969

14 K. Liples, B. Allen, and W. L. Trainor, "Choosing a Higher Order Programming Language for the Digital Avionics Information System (DAIS)," Proceedings of the Aeronautical Systems Software Workshop, pp. 413–417, 1974

[15] F. H. Martin, "Performance of the HAL/S Flight Computer Compiler," National Aerospace Electronics Conference Record, pp. 701–708, 1976

[16] T. E. Matysek, "HOL in Operational Software from a User's Point of View," National Aerospace Electronics Conference Record, pp. 494–501, 1977

[17] R. E. Nimensky, "Space Programming Language: Flight Software Comes of Age," National Aerospace Electronics Conference Record, pp. 39–45, 1970.

[18] E. J. Radkowski, W. A. Minnick, and D. Blondin, "New Compiler Techniques Simplify Development of Higher Order Languages," Proceedings of the Aeronautical Systems Software Workshop, pp. 425–429, 1974

[19] L. M. Richards and G. H. Wille, "An Aerospace Compiler and Its Role in Software Development," National Aerospace Electronics Conference Record, pp. 60–66, 1970

[20] R. J. Rubey and E. H. Bersoff, "CLASP, Computer Language for Aeronautics and Space Programming," AIAA Paper No. 69-957, 1969

[21] R. J. Rubey, "The Case for Higher Order Aerospace Languages," National Aerospace Electronics Conference Record, pp. 46–51, 1970

[22] R. J. Rubey, "What's Different About Tactical Military Languages and Compilers," National Computer Conference Record, pp. 807–809, 1973

[23] T. C. Spillman, "Considerations in Selecting a Spaceborne Programming Language," Proceedings of the First Spaceborne Computer Software Workshop, pp. 205–210, 1966

[24] A. J. Stone, "Phoenix Compiler Language and Software System," Proceedings of the First Spaceborne Computer Software Workshop, pp. 224–233, 1966

[25] A. J. Stone, "Use of METAPLAN in the F14A/AWG-9," Data Systems Division, Hughes Aircraft Company, 1976

[26] W. L. Trainor and M. Burlakoff, "JOVIAL-73 Versus Assembly Language—An Efficiency Comparison," National Aerospace Electronics Conference Record, pp. 502–507, 1977

[27] W. L. Trainor and H. M. Grove, "Higher Order Language Standardization for Avionics," National Aerospace Electronics Conference Record, pp. 487–493, 1977

[28] B. L. Wolman and I. R. Nassi, "Regarding Efficiency in Avionic Higher Order Language Utilization," SofTech Report TP003, 1976

5-3   A LANGUAGE FOR REAL-TIME SYSTEMS*

The working party has been asked to consider particular problems involved in the programming of computers which are to operate in a real-time environment, and to recommend developments in programming languages which

*From The Computer Bulletin, Dec. 1967. Reprinted with permission. The "working party" is defined in paragraph 5-3-7.

would allow these problems to be handled in an easier, and thus cheaper and more efficient way than is generally used now. This report recommends, in some detail, extensions to existing programming techniques which could be made use of in the near future and which, it is hoped, are sufficiently general and flexible to remain useful for some years.

The report consists mainly of detailed recommendations for extensions and some alterations to an existing high-level scientific programming language. These changes and additions should provide the essential facilities required in real-time systems, and also include other features, not specifically related to real-time systems, which are considered to be generally desirable and useful. The report also discusses more general problems of real-time system operation which are not covered by the formal language structure but for which a real-time language compiling system must make provision. It includes, in outline, a description of one method of implementation which, although in no sense necessarily the best method, indicates that the generation of suitable compilers will be practicable.

5-3-1 REAL-TIME SYSTEMS

For this report the real-time environment referred to above is defined as one in which the time scale of computer operation is critical, and is dictated by the requirements of an environment external to the computer. The more obvious examples include:

(1) Industrial process control systems
(2) Automatic radar tracking systems
(3) High speed data gathering systems
(4) Air and ground traffic control systems

In all these examples it is vital that the computer (which may be a single or multiprocessor device) is not delayed by more than some short, strictly defined, response time from recognizing the occurrence of relevant external events, and from acting on these. Some appropriate rescue action should normally be programmed if, owing to the occurrence of unusual external circumstances the computer may become overloaded and unable to respond to events sufficiently rapidly.

A second group of applications contains similar real-time problems which are equally severe: these include complex computer systems which, when viewed overall, may not appear to be real-time systems but which include peripheral devices and perhaps a number of processors, each of which, for efficient use, must operate on its own time scale. We have in mind peripheral devices such as magnetic tape or other backing store units, and the input-output devices on a multiuser system.

In addition to the above requirements, real-time systems generally must be of exceptional reliability but remain flexible in use. This imposes further conditions on their programs. They must be very carefully tested and must often include provision for automatic remedial action in the event of hardware or software faults. It may also be necessary for programs to be easily modified, frequently without recourse to an off-line machine for recompilation, and sometimes without stopping the operation of the major functions of the real-time program.

5-3-1-1 Languages

Real-time systems which are operational have normally been programmed in codes which are closely related to the machine languages involved. This procedure is tedious and subject to error, but can provide, in relatively simple systems, an object program which is nearly optimal with regard to hardware cost, that is, minimizing storage requirements and necessary processor speed. To achieve such a result many highly qualified programmers are needed over a long period.

We are basing our report on the assumption that this will not remain an effective way of implementing real-time systems. Suitable programmers will become increasingly hard to get, and expensive. As systems become more complex the work of producing machine-coded or assembly-language coded programs will become impossibly great. It is essential therefore that a high-level language should come into widespread use for real-time programs. As in nonreal-time systems this is likely to reduce programming complexities and costs by amounts which will more than offset the extra cost for hardware which a program coded in a high-level language might require. This will not only make the overall costs of systems cheaper, it may enable systems to be installed which would involve programs of prohibitive complexity if coded by hand.

A substantial amount of work has been undertaken by various manufacturers and other bodies to this end. This is resulting in a range of executive programming systems orientated towards particular machines. These supervisory systems can be parameterized to permit flexible on-line programming, however they do not provide a generally acceptable language for real-time algorithms.

The working party has chosen ALGOL 60 as the most suitable language on which to base the discussion. This has the normal facilities for scientific programming, essential for the type of on-line applications envisaged, and is a well-defined language by comparison with other languages in widespread use. In addition, a general real-time programming system must provide for flexible multiprogramming and, except under special conditions, dynamic allocation of storage space. These features demand a highly structured language and in particular render unsuitable even well-defined versions of well-loved older languages such as FORTRAN.

The report therefore assumes the features of ALGOL 60 except for certain modifications which appear desirable for real-time operation. These are described in section 2. The extended facilities, superimposed on those of ALGOL 60, fall into the following main groups:

a) real-time multiprogramming features

b) more extensive data structures for on-line systems

c) features for machine-dependent and peripheral device programming.

These facilities are described in subsequent sections. This report makes no conceptual distinction between the various forms of multiprogramming. The term parallel programming is used to include one or more programs sharing one or more processors. Particular implementations may, of course, make distinctions.

There are available certain languages (for example, SIMULA and SOL) which have been designed for the programming of computer simulations of the external world. The reader may notice similarities between these languages and the proposals in this report since many problems encountered in simulation systems are akin to real-time problems. However the two types of system are not the same—a simulation program writer always has overall control of program behavior in a way that a real-time program writer has not—and the simulation languages themselves, though a valuable source of ideas, are not adequate for real-time purposes.

The ALGOL based language proposed in this report is referred to below as RTL (real-time language).

5-3-1-2 Real-Time System Operation

Real-time programs must be designed for use in a computer system, probably of specialized configuration or design, which is linked through a variety of channels to its external environment. Such a system may be a small one—a single processor with a single level of memory—or may be much more complex; its computing power, in speed and storage space, may be almost wholly utilized by the required responses to the real-time environment, or there may be a substantial amount of computing power not involved on essential tasks under normal running conditions.

A satisfactory real-time programming system must be capable of use on a considerable variety of systems. Where the requirements are relatively simple, it may be appropriate to compile the real-time programs on a larger machine than the object machine on which they will eventually be run. However, if it is more convenient to compile on the object machine itself this may be done either by temporarily devoting the whole machine to compiling purposes, or by operating a compiler in a time-sharing mode so that the programs may be recompiled and retested in whole or in part during real-time operation. This latter type of operation need not necessarily imply a very large machine; compiling time is of little account in the types of system we are considering (since programs are run for long periods, once developed) so that a segmented compiler residing in a cheap second level memory device is a practical possibility.

In order to implement RTL on a variety of systems, considerable flexibility in compiler design is clearly necessary. The techniques used may not necessarily be appropriate for compilers in normal off-line scientific systems. The object program produced should, however, contain these distinctive features:

a) it will include a variety of test and environment simulation facilities while under development, which are later removed to produce a fully optimized final program, if necessary by a lengthy recompiling process

b) the real-time supervisory program will be generated automatically by the compiler to some extent, but RTL can provide a programmer with detailed control of the relative timing or priority of program execution, and partial control over the movement of program and data material between various levels of memory if more than one exists.

5-3-1-3 Summary

The aim of the report is the description of a language capable of being used for programming computers for operation in a real-time environment.

A real-time environment is defined as one in which the time scale of the computer operation is critical, and dictated by the requirements of the environment external to the computer.

It is accepted by the working group that a high-level language is economically desirable. This is justified, as with off-line machines, by software savings more than compensating for any additional hardware demands of a high level language.

In the applications envisaged, where a program may run unchanged for very long periods, the efficiency of the object program is of paramount importance. In consequence a slow, optimizing compiler is justified. This compiling may, but need not, be done on the object machine.

The discussion will be based on ALGOL.

5-3-2 THE STRUCTURE OF RTL

Although the language described in this report is based on ALGOL 60, the basic structure of ALGOL has been extended in order to provide for the parallel programming and other on-line facilities characteristic of real-time applications. In order to provide these facilities in a consistent practical manner certain restrictions on the ALGOL structure have also been found necessary. The structure of RTL is discussed with reference to ALGOL 60 in the following subsections.

5-3-2-1 The Classification of Statements and Blocks

A semantic distinction is made between all RTL statements which explicitly define their successor, and those that do not. Thus the conceptual difference between goto statements and assignment statements is generalized. Only those statements, termed program statements, which do not define their successor explicitly are permitted to have parallel "lives" of their own. Thus a program statement has a well-defined unique end as well as a beginning. This classification leads naturally to the notion of program blocks, compound program statements and program procedures.

For reasons of program security a distinction is made between the two fundamental classes of procedures by means of the specifier **program procedure**. These procedures must not contain goto statements leading outside the procedure, either directly or through a parameter, and any nonlocal procedures called by a program procedure must also be program procedures. Compiler checking is therefore relatively simple.

5-3-2-2 Kinds of Procedure Parameters

A procedure parameter may be called by value or by reference. Call by value is the same as in ALGOL 60. An actual parameter corresponding to a formal parameter called by reference must be a variable. The replacement of the ALGOL call by name by the more restricted call by reference is done for the following reasons:

a) the implementation of a suitable dynamic storage-allocating mechanism for providing the global environments of parallel activations is made more practical by the restriction on the use of expressions as actual parameters in procedure calls

b) the need for program security in real-time environments makes it desirable that procedure side effects be prevented; in a parallel programming environment side effects are likely to be less predictable.

The kind of a formal parameter is required to be explicitly specified.

5-3-2-3 Statements

A number of multiprogramming statements have been introduced for real-time applications. These are discussed in part 5-3-3. An explicit transfer statement has also been introduced for use primarily with variables of non-standard type (*cf* part 5-3-4-1). A statement may be written in machine code, assembly language, or any other available programming language through the use of the delimiter **code**. A statement written in this manner must have the syntactic form: **code**

<STRING>.

Thus with reference to ALGOL 60, Section 4.1.1:

<UNLABELLED BASIC STATEMENT> ::=
    <ASSIGNMENT STATEMENT> | <GOTO STATEMENT> |
    <DUMMY STATEMENT> | <PROCEDURE STATEMENT> |
    <MULTIPROGRAMMING STATEMENT> | <CODE STATEMENT> |
    <EXPLICIT TRANSFER STATEMENT>

5-3-2-4 Input-Output and Peripheral Control

A characteristic of on-line computer systems is the wide range of input-output devices used to transfer data and control signals between the computer and the system under control of human operators.

Two distinct levels of input-output programming are envisaged. For routine use of a peripheral it is expected that library procedures will be available. However more fundamental, real-time control of a peripheral is also intended to be programmed in the language with the help of declarations of nonstandard types. The associated type changes may be defined by means of a compiler directive (part 5-3-4-1) which syntactically may be regarded as a declaration.

Although machine code may be necessary to describe special machine operations in some applications, it is considered that it will normally be possible to restrict this use of code to the defining statement within compiler directives. By this means the ability to set up the peripheral control timing and interrupt structure in the language can be utilized. An example appears in part 5-3-4-1.

5-3-2-5 Data Structures

Variables of type **list, facility, binal, string,** and **scaled** have been introduced (the last two optional), and a facility for the definition of nonstandard types is provided to permit the passage of special forms of data, for instance, to peripherals. Owing to the possibility of an arbitrary number of parallel program activations the need for lists is more essential than in other forms of programming. Queue structures are also introduced to satisfy real-time requirements and a form of table is specified as a standardization of on-line techniques.

It is intended that variables may be initialized at declaration.

```
< TYPE  LIST > ::= < SIMPLE  VARIABLE > |
                  < SIMPLE  VARIABLE > := < VALUE > |
                  < SIMPLE  VARIABLE >, < TYPE  LIST > |
                  < SIMPLE  VARIABLE > := < VALUE >, < TYPE  LIST >
< VALUE > ::=     < NUMBER > | < LOGICAL  VALUE > |
                  < STRING  VALUE > | < BINAL  VALUE >
```

Only the one simple variable is initialized by a value appearing in the declaration. In the case of arrays, queues and lists a sequence of values separated by commas is permitted. A facility variable may be initialized to an integer.

5-3-2-6 Sundry Restrictions and Implementation Constraints

To be consistent with practical implementation requirements and the accepted fallibility of any . . . human design effort, the following restrictions are made:

a) own variables may not have dynamic bounds

b) integer labels are not permitted

c) global variables should be implemented in a manner which makes them available to separately compiled procedures declared in the outermost program block.[1]

5-3-3 TIMING AND INTERRUPT CONTROL

A real-time computing system must operate in response to the demands of an external environment. The normal hardware device by which this is achieved is a form of interrupting facility, whereby the execution of any program can be suspended temporarily or permanently when some external event occurs, to allow the machine to respond to that event in an appropriate way. Although the actual interrupting mechanism and the corresponding ways in which it can be used effectively vary from one machine to another, the basic concept of a response to an external event is unchanged. Programs must be timed and organized in such a way that the machine can respond within a suitable response time to the external demands. A certain amount of flexibility is normally possible. For example, a demand for analog input in a process control system may normally require to be serviced within a few milliseconds, so as to obtain a steady sampling rate upon which subsequent digital filtering depends. Under exceptional circumstances, however, the machine may be taking some emergency action on other parts of the process which delay the normal sampling procedure. There will, consequently, be inaccurate filtering, but this may well be of

---

[1] This is similar to the COMPOOL facility of JOVIAL and its derivatives.

minor importance compared to the emergency actions which are competing for computer time.

Response times, modifiable in some cases under abnormal conditions, form one of the basic items of information available to the designer of a real-time system. Other basic items will be estimates of the frequencies at which demands for given responses occur, and a specification of the response behavior to each demand. Ideally, it would be desirable to specify this basic information directly to a compiler, in RTL, and leave the compiler to organize the various programs in such a way that the response times can be met under normal conditions, or within a stated tolerance under abnormal conditions—or to inform the designer that what he is asking is impossible on the available real-time machine.

Language facilities could, doubtless, be devised which would enable these response times and so on, to be defined for given programs or procedures and to be altered as appropriate dynamically. Such facilities would, however, be very different from established language facilities and would certainly introduce major difficulties in compiler implementation. We have therefore kept to an alternative technique, similar to that used in current real-time applications, which is to work in terms of program priorities rather than response times. If the execution times of different programs are known such a system may be adjusted (assuming adequate computing speed in the real-time machine) to conform with the required response times under the various operating conditions.

5-3-3-1 Introduction to RTL Real-Time Multiprogramming Facilities

The ALGOL based structure introduced in part 5-3-2 makes it possible to provide the real-time multiprogramming facilities desired. These facilities are in the form of statements and are broadly divided into three categories: those for the servicing of interrupts, those for multiprogramming organization, and those for the mutual protection of parallel programs. The scheme is based on one of two possible alternatives which were examined. The one chosen intuitively provides the type of features likely to be used by the applications programmer. Its soundness rests on practical experience with similar schemes and apparent compatibility with the other event-based scheme.

Syntax.

```
<MULTIPROGRAMMING STATEMENT>::=
<ON-STATEMENT> | <ACTIVATION STATEMENT> | <PROTECTION STATEMENT>
```

For the correct operation of some of these statements it is essential that certain sections of the machine instructions involved must be indivisible, that is, they may not be affected by any other operation. Means of achieving this can only be worked out in detail for individual implementations, but the protection statements of part 5–3–3–4 are high-level language expressions of the concepts required.

5-3-3-2 On-Statements

Syntax.

```
< ON CLAUSE > :: = ON < RESERVED  VARIABLE > DO
< RESERVED  VARIABLE > :: = < VARIABLE >
< RESPONSE  STATEMENT > :: = < PROGRAM STATEMENT >
< ON-STATEMENT > :: = < ON  CLAUSE > < RESPONSE  STATEMENT >  |
< LABEL > :< ON-STATEMENT >
```

Use. The on-statement is a means of specifying the response of the machine to the interrupts it receives. The reserved variables available for use in on-statements will be peculiar to a given installation. Since the specified response statement must in fact be a program statement *(cf* part 5–3–2–1), it will have a distinct ending.

Indivisibility. On-statements are indivisible and uninterruptable operations. A program interruption must not occur while an on-statement is being executed or until all successively written on-statements have been executed. If the first statement of a response statement is an on-statement, this will be executed before any new interruption occurs.

Operation. An on-statement becomes operative once it has been executed (in the normal course of a program), and any other previously operative on-statement for the same reserved identifier is thereby rendered inoperative. While an on-statement is operative it produces an unconditional execution of its response statement whenever the interruption specified by the reserved variable occurs. The ultimate speed of response will be dependent on the particular implementation.

Examples.

```
ON CLOCK PULSE DO TIME: = TIME + 1
ON INTERRUPT[I] DO IF BOOLEAN THEN PROCEDURE SERVICE
ON PARITY CHECK DO
BEGIN
    ON PARITY ERROR DO REPEAT: = REPEAT + 1;
    IF REPEAT > 5 THEN ACTIVATE PARITY ERROR WITH PRIORITY 1;
    A: TRY AGAIN;
END
```

5-3-3-3 Activation Statements

Syntax.

```
<ACTIVATION STATEMENT>::= <ACTIVATE STATEMENT> | <DELAY STATEMENT>
<ACTIVATE STATEMENT>::= ACTIVATE <PROCEDURE STATEMENT>
                       WITH PRIORITY<ARITHMETIC EXPRESSION>
<DELAY STATEMENT>::= DELAY<ARITHMETIC EXPRESSION>
```

Use.   Activate statements are intended for use in a procedure-based parallel programming system. The execution of an activate statement causes a new activation or "life" of the procedure called by the procedure statement within the activate statement. Any given procedure activation may be in one of four states

running that is, being executed by a processor
ready   that is, required to run as soon as a dynamically variable priority structure in the system allows
held up that is, partially executed but now temporarily suspended for one of various possible reasons
dead   that is, this procedure activation has been completed.

On activation a procedure is put in the ready state. Any procedure which has no activation in any of the first three states may be termed inert.

Priorities.   The arithmetic expression in an activate statement is evaluated as an integer at the time when the activate statement is executed. Only positive integers are permitted as priorities, and the highest priority is priority one. By convention a program at its initial commencement is assumed to be the lowest possible priority, that is, the maximum positive integer.

Operation.   Given a choice a processor will proceed with the highest priority ready activation. A procedure activation in the "ready" state will commence execution as soon as its priority number becomes sufficiently low (the lowest in the case of a single processor) with respect to the priority of all other "ready" or "running" procedures. In cases where two or more procedure activations have the same priority it is not defined which is executed first. An activation may become "held up" if sufficient other procedures acquire higher priorities or if unable to proceed owing to the action of a delay or release statement in its text. (cf parts 5-3-3-3 and 5-3-3-4 below.) When a procedure becomes "running" after having been "held up," it is continued from the point of interruption.

Procedure Environments.   Parameters called by value by the procedure statement of an activate statement are evaluated at the time of execution of the activate statement. Parameters called by reference and nonlocal procedure variables constitute the run-time environment of a procedure. These variables must be retained as active data locations in the computer until an activated procedure has run, even though the block in which the variables were declared may have already completed execution.

DELAY STATEMENTS.　　A delay statement in the text of a "running" procedure transfers that procedure from a "running" to a "held up" state. It remains in that state for the integral number of standard time units given by the expression. It then becomes "ready" and subsequently "running" if or when its priority allows.

EXAMPLE.

```
PROGRAM PROCEDURE TEST RUN (DURATION);
INTEGER DURATION;
COMMENT PROCEDURE 'TEST RUN' PERMITS A SET OF INTERRUPTS TO
BE SERVICED FOR A FINITE DURATION. PROCEDURES 'INITIALIZE',
'SERVICE' AND 'ANALYZE' ARE NON-LOCAL;
BEGIN INTEGER I;
    PROGRAM PROCEDURE STOP;
    BEGIN INTEGER I;
        FOR I:= 1 STEP 1 UNTIL 8 DO
        ON INTERRUPT [I] DO NOTHING:;
    END
    INITIALIZE;
    ON INTERRUPT [I] DO ACTIVATE SERVICE (I) WITH PRIORITY 3+I;
    DELAY DURATION;
    ACTIVATE STOP WITH PRIORITY 3
    ANALYZE
END TEST RUN;
```

5-3-3-4 Protection Statements

SYNTAX.

```
<PROTECTION STATEMENT>::= <SECURE STATEMENT> | <RELEASE STATEMENT>
<SECURE STATEMENT>      ::=  SECURE    <FACILITY VARIABLE>
<RELEASE STATEMENT>     ::=  RELEASE   <FACILITY VARIABLE>
<FACILITY VARIABLE>     ::= <VARIABLE>
```

SECURE AND RELEASE OPERATORS.　　These operators perform the task of "P" and "V" operators of Dijkstra.[2] They perform indivisible operations on one

---

[2] Dijkstra, E. W. *Co-operating Sequential Processes,* Lectures presented at the NATO Summer School on Advanced Programming, Villard de Lans, Isere, France, 1966.

argument. The function of **release** is to increase the value of its operand by one if this can be done without exceeding the upper bound of the facility variable. If this cannot be done the program performing the release operation is delayed until a subsequent secure operation by another program makes the release operation possible.

The function of the **secure** operation is to decrease the value of its operand facility by one. If the resultant contents of the facility variable is a negative (integer) number the program performing the secure operation is held up until an equal (positive) number of subsequent release operations have been performed on the same variable.

EXAMPLES.   *a*) Consider two procedures P1 and P2, each of which modifies a variable GLOB by means of respective functions MOD1 and MOD2 with GLOB as parameter. If both procedures may be activated concurrently it is necessary to protect one modification from the other.

```
PROCEDURE P1 (F); FACILITY (1) F;
BEGIN ..
    SECURE F; GLOB:=MOD1 (GLOB);
    RELEASE F;...
END
PROGRAM PROCEDURE P2 (G); FACILITY (1) G;
BEGIN ...
    SECURE G; GLOB:=MOD2 (GLOB);
    RELEASE G; ...
END
```

We can now write;

```
BEGIN FACILITY (1) F:=1;
    ACTIVATE P1 (F) WITH PRIORITY 5;
    P2 (F);
        . . .
END
```

b) This is an RTL version of an example due to Dijkstra. Consider a computer providing data for an asynchronous peripheral by means of a first-in-first-out buffer. We assume that the peripheral interrupts the computer by a device described by the reserved identifier "data demand" in order to get passed one data word after conversion to a special form corresponding to the compiler-recognized location PERIF1.

The buffer described above is a queue in RTL. The facility in this case is the queue length.

```
                . . .
BEGIN FACILITY (N) QUEUE LENGTH: = 0;
    REAL QUEUE BUFFER;
    REAL NEW WORD, OUTPUT;
    TYPE 'PERIF1' PERIPHERAL;
    COMPILE REAL TO TYPE 'PERIF' AS CODE '. . . ';
    ON DATA DEMAND DO
    BEGIN SECURE QUEUE LENGTH;
        OUTPUT: = BUFFER;
        SEND OUTPUT TO PERIPHERAL
    END DATA TRANSMISSION;
    DATA PRODUCTION:
    COMPUTE DATA WORD (NEW WORD);
    BUFFER: = NEW WORD;
    RELEASE QUEUE LENGTH;
    GOTO DATA PRODUCTION
END;
```

c) It may be desired to secure either one facility or an alternative. Such operations may be achieved with the help of additional artificial facilities.

program procedure access (facility) free set: (availability)
interrogator: (check)
set size: (N) element: (J) action: (option):

integer N, J;
string option;
facility (1) **array** facility [1 : N], check [0 : N];
facility (N) availability;
comment Procedure access permits more comprehensive operations on facilities than the **secure** and **release** by employing the auxiliary facilities "availability" and "check." However, since all programs using the main facility must obey the same rules, access to the facility should only be made through this procedure. For system facilities this can be achieved by making procedure "access" the essence of a set of library procedures for the various options and facilities. The actual facilities can then be declared as own variables in a block local to the system library. The bounds on these system facilities will be parameters on the computer operating configuration;

```
        IF OPTION= 'RELEASE' THEN
        BEGIN RELEASE FACILITY [J];
            RELEASE AVAILABILITY
        END ELEMENT RELEASE;
        ELSE
        BEGIN SECURE CHECK [0];
        IF OPTION= 'SECURE IF AVAILABLE' ∧
        CONTENTS(AVAILABILITY) >0
        V OPTION= 'SECURE' THEN
```

```
BEGIN INTEGER I;
    SECURE AVAILABILITY;
    RELEASE CHECK [0];
    FOR I:=1 STEP 1 UNTIL N DO
    BEGIN SECURE CHECK [I];
        IF CONTENTS (FACILITY [I])>0 THEN
        BEGIN SECURE FACILITY [I];
        RELEASE CHECK [I];
        J:=I;
        GOTO DONE
        END;
        ELSE RELEASE CHECK [I]
    END;
    DONE:
END;
ELSE J:=0
END;
```

d) Facility variables may be used simply to delay or hold up programs. This device is used in the following example in which the procedure "fetchable" is activated with high priority before required, but maintained in a held-up state (perhaps in a fast access store).

```
. . .
BEGIN FACILITY (1) HOLD:=0, CHECK:=1;
    BOOLEAN GO:=FALSE;
    PROGRAM PROCEDURE FETCHABLE;
    BEGIN SECURE CHECK;
        IF > GO THEN
        BEGIN RELEASE CHECK;
            SECURE HOLD;
            RELEASE HOLD
        END;
        ELSE
        BEGIN RELEASE CHECK;
        MAIN BODY:
        END;
        ACTIVATE FETCHABLE WITH PRIORITY 1;
        . . .
        SECURE check;
        GO:=TRUE;
        RELEASE CHECK;
        ACTIVATE FETCHABLE WITH PRIORITY M;
        . . .
        ACTIVATE FETCHABLE WITH PRIORITY N;
        RELEASE HOLD;
    END;
```

5-3-4 VARIABLE TYPES AND STRUCTURES

The variable types and structures listed below are thought to be necessary in a language for real-time use; indeed it could be argued that they should be included in any high-level language. Although unification of these by adoption of a variable type with a structure providing all the facilities required would be desirable, we do not regard any such unifying types so far defined (for example, the record of Hoare[3]) as entirely suitable.

The reason for inclusion of type **scaled** arises from the need to shorten the execution times of arithmetic operations while retaining control of the precision of these operations. Scaled variables may be used in conjunction with the structure table to make more economic use of the store by packing.

The type **binal** is included to provide a more economic (again in time and store) method of manipulating patterns of binary bits. This provides a highly computer-oriented structure with the advantage of interchangeability of programs, already provided by the rest of the language.

New declarators may be introduced by means of the delimiter **type** to describe identifiers intended to refer to nonstandard devices, for instance an input-output peripheral. The use of variables declared in this manner is restricted to explicit transfer function statements, that is, there is no facility for defining operations on new types and it is intended that transfer functions implied by assignment statements or reference to such a variable should not be permitted.

Brief descriptions including the required declarations are given in the following sections.

$<$ type $>$ :: $=$ **real** $\mid$ **integer** $\mid$ **scaled** ($<$ qual $>$, $<$ qual $>$) $\mid$
     string $\mid$ **binal** ($<$ qual $>$) $\mid$ **facility** ($<$ qual $>$) $\mid$
     type $<$ string $>$ $\mid$ **list**

A qual is an arithmetic expression to be evaluated in the same way as a subscript expression.

$<$ structure declaration $>$ :: $=$ $<$ array declaration $>$ $\mid$
           $<$ queue declaration $>$ $\mid$
           $<$ table declaration $>$

5-3-4-1 Variable Types

ARITHMETIC TYPES.

integer as in ALGOL 60

real as in ALGOL 60

scaled ($<$ arithmetic expression $>$, $<$ arithmetic expression $>$)

Scaled variables have a fixed point representation similar to the JOVIAL type **item**. The specificator **unsigned** is applicable to variables of type scaled.

---

[3]Hoare, C. A. R. *File Processing* ALGOL BULLETIN No. 25, March 1967

The first arithmetic expression in the declaration of a scaled variable is the overall bit length of the variable (including any sign bit). The second expression is the number of fractional bits.

Arithmetic types may be combined in arithmetic expressions, unsigned variables being treated as positive.

Boolean as in ALGOL 60

list A list variable has as value an S-expression as defined by LISP[4] with head, tail, and prefix operators in procedural form. *N.B.* "prefix" is the same as "cons."

FACILITY VARIABLES.   Variables of type **facility** have associated values which are bounded nonnegative integers. The declarator for this type of variable is

facility (< arithmetic expression >)

where the integer expression is the upper bound on the set of values of the variable so declared. The expression is evaluated on entry to the block in which the variable is declared.

Two indivisible operations, **secure** and **release** (*cf* part 5-3-3-4) permit the value of a facility variable to be varied between zero and the upper bound. No operations for combining facilities in expressions of this type have been introduced into RTL. (Such a feature is more the province of a simulation language.) The aims of program and device protection can be achieved by means of the two operations above and made more convenient through the use of initialization.

The standard function *contents*(F) will give the current integer value associated with the facility variable.

string The value of a string variable (a string value) can be any sequence of characters contained within string quotes " ", except unmatched closing string quotes, including the empty string " ". The value of a string can also be **null** which is different from the empty string (*cf* appendix).

EXAMPLE.

string s

s: = "abc"

For a description of the operators by which strings can be manipulated see appendix.

Binal variables A binal variable contains a declared number of bits, each able to take the value 0 or 1. The declarator for a binal variable is of the form **binal** (< arithmetic expression >)

EXAMPLE.

binal (24) **array** word [0:4095]

The following logical operations can be performed on the bits of binals

---

[4]McCarthy, J. et al. *LISP 1.5 Programmer's Manual.* MIT Computation Centre, 1962.

and
or
not
exor (exclusive or)

The bits of a binal are numbered, from one to as many as are declared, from the right. Binal constants (binal values) are written as a sequence of ones and zeros preceded by a suitable symbol **b,** but in any implementation more convenient methods such as octal representation may be allowed. Segments or single bits of binals are also binals and are specified by the following binal expressions

bit < integer expression > **of** < binal expression > ;
bits < integer expression > **to** < integer expression >
of < binal expression > ;

EXAMPLE.
binal (24) **array** word [0:4095]
bits 1 to 4 of word [i]: = **bits 5 to 9 of** word [j] **and b**1100;
if bit k of word [j] = **b** 0 then **bit k of** word [1]: = **b**1;
bits p to q of word [i]: = not **bits p to q of** word [j] **or b**11110000;

binal expressions are treated as being right justified, that is truncated from the left if too long or zeros added on left if too short.

EXAMPLE.
bits 1 to 10 of word [4]: =
bits 7 to 12 of word [i] **or bit 24 of** word [6];

is equivalent to

bit 1 of word [4]: = **bit 7 of** word [i] **or bit 24 of** word [6];
bits 2 to 6 of word [4]: = **bits 8 to 12 of** word [i];
bits 7 to 10 of word [4]: = **b**0000;

The following library procedures should be available for type changing to and from binal expressions

intof (< binal expression >) binal to integer
realof (< binal expression >) binal to real
binalofint (< expression >) integer to binal
binalofreal (< expression >) real to binal.

In any implementation, each of the above procedures has a value equivalent to the expression with the same pattern of bits as the variable specified.

NONSTANDARD TYPES.   Three features are introduced into the language to permit the programming of input-output or other special devices (hardware or concept). These features are:

    a) The declarator for a nonstandard type. Syntactically this is of the form
       type < string >

b) The compiler directive (*cf* part 5-3-2-4) for specifying explicit transfer functions between types, syntactically:
compile < variable declarator > **to** < variable declarator >
as < statement >
< variable declarator > :: = < type > | < structure >
Note that the defining statement, following the delimiter **as**, may commonly be a code statement.

c) The explicit transfer statement.
send < expression > **to** < variable >

In the case where both variables are of standard types this explicit transfer statement is equivalent to simple assignment, wherever this would be permitted.

> EXAMPLE.
>
> **procedure** write tape (A);
> **array** A;
> **begin type** 'tape control' control; **type** 'tape file' file;
>   **compile binal (1) to type** 'tape control' **as code** '. . .';
>   **compile real array to type** 'tape file' **as code** '. . .';
>   **comment** It is assumed that the reserved identifier tape
>   interrupt is recognized;
>   **send b 1 to** control;
>   **delay .01;**
>   **send A to** file;
>   **on** tape interrupt **do send b** 0 **to** control;
> **end**

5-3-4-2 Variable Structures

< structure > :: = **array** | **queue** | **table** |
                < type > < structure >

Arrays as in ALGOL 60, but may be of any RTL type.

QUEUES.   A queue is a first-in first-out structure of one dimension. It may be of any type.
< queue declaration > :: = **queue** < type list > |
                < local or own type > **queue** < type list >
The current queue length should be available as a library procedure *length* (Q). A queue can have an element included, or removed from it as shown in the following example:
    real queue q [i];
    real a, b;
    q: = a;
    b: = q;

The statement **q: = a** adds the value of a to the queue and the statement **b: = q** sets b equal to the value first added to the queue and removes that value from the queue.

TABLES.   These are single dimensional multicomponent structures and are required for economic packing of variable and fixed data. The components can be of types **scaled** and **binal** and each component is addressed explicitly by its name. The **table** declaration has two parameters which may be dynamic, the bounds of entries in the table and the bounds in bit numbers of an entry. This declaration is followed by the description of the components of an entry, which may be overlapped.

EXAMPLE.
table a[1 : 100, 1 : 48];
unsigned scaled (10, 10) x[1 : 10], y[11 : 20], z[25 : 34];
scaled (13, 0) u[35: 48];
binal (1) b1[21: 21], b2[22: 22], b3[23: 23], b4[24: 24];

This declaration would pack the three ten bit unsigned fractions x, y, and z, the fourteen bit integer u and the four one bit binal variables b1, b2, b3 and b4 as follows into a forty-eight bit entry of **table a.**

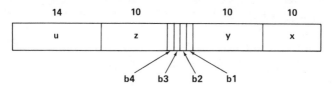

Tables can be manipulated as single dimensional arrays for the transfer of whole entries between tables. A table whose components are all of identical types, size, and scaling can be manipulated as a two dimensional array where the first suffix specifies the entry and the second suffix specifies the components in order of declaration starting from one. The declaration of this type differs from that of a table of mixed types of components in that the type declaration precedes the table declaration.

EXAMPLE.
binal (6) **table** texlist[1:100, 1:36]
cha [1:6],
chb [7:12],
chc [13:18],
chd [19:24],
che [25:30],
chf [31:36];
then texlist [i, 2] is the same 6 bit
binal as chb [i].

5-3-5 IMPLEMENTATION

While it is realized that no definitive statements can be made with regard to implementation, it is felt that some indication should be given of possible techniques, especially for some of the newer facilities presented.

5-3-5-1 Parallel Processing

Part 5-3-3 introduces the idea of a "program" procedure that can run conceptually in parallel with other programs according to a dynamic system of priorities. In practice the various activations of programs are usually run with a supervisor routine controlling the allocation of work. This supervisor is entered at intervals in the main routines from points known as "break-points." Whenever a program being currently obeyed can no longer continue or whenever an action occurs which might change the activation list (such as an interrupt or the obeying of an **activate** statement) then a break occurs to the supervisor.

ACTIVATION LIST.   This holds references to every activation of every program. Each reference includes the following data
   the link address (*cf* 5-3-5-1)
   the environment address (*cf* 5-3-5-2)
   the priority number
   the re-entry condition (*cf* 5-3-5-1)
   the procedure name, if the procedure is modifiable (*cf* 5-3-5-5)
and any other data relevant to the particular implementation.

SUPERVISOR.   At every break point the supervisor searches the activation list for the highest priority program that is able to run. The reentry condition specifies whether a program is able to run or not by giving the address of a short section of program that evaluates a boolean variable. Possible hold-up conditions are *a)* a **delay** statement that is not yet complete or *b)* a facility that is not yet available. As soon as a satisfactory program is found then the environment address of that program is set as the current environment and the program is entered at the point specified by the link address. A note is made of the program that is actually running so that at the next break point the appropriate address can be reset into the link address location, prior to a new search of the activation list.

5-3-5-2 Store Allocation

Because of the reentrant nature of the procedures and program procedures (*cf* part 5-3-3) it is essential to have some form of dynamic store allocation technique. The method of environments here described is a possible method of achieving re-entrance and at the same time allowing for all the normal store allocation facilities required.

An environment is an area of store used for data which is created at run times as and when required. In other words it is created

a) on entry to a procedure
b) at an activation of a program procedure
c) on declaring an array or table
d) on entry to a block in which an array or table is declared.

Each environment contains not only all the data for which it was created, but also a certain number of pointers to other environments. These pointers are used for a variety of reasons. They keep wanted environments alive, they enable references to be made to global data, and they allow reentry to the calling routine when required.

When a routine has finished with an environment, the environment cannot necessarily be returned to free storage—it may be required for global data of a subordinate program procedure that has been activated, but not yet run because of the priority structure. Therefore an environment that is no longer required by a routine is tagged as "terminated." A garbage collection routine later makes use of this tag in an algorithm for returning unused store to the free store area.

The general problem of garbage collection tends to be time consuming and care must be taken to implement it efficiently. It consists of marking all environments that are required and then moving all these environments so that they are contiguous, leaving all the free store in one consecutive area. The marking process starts with each environment mentioned in the activation list in turn. It makes extensive use of the various environment pointers mentioned above. These are illustrated symbolically in the diagram. All shaded boxes represent environments that have terminated. The arrowed lines represent the various pointers referred to earlier.

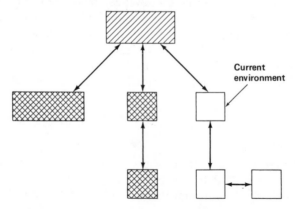

Current environment

If an environment and all its subordinate environments have terminated then they can be returned as free when garbage collection takes place. In the diagram the double shaded boxes are examples of such environments.

5-3-5-3 Two Level Storage Control

In any system there may only be room for a limited proportion of object program and data environments in the working store (for example, core store) of the system. Some program and data may have to be stored on a second level of storage (for example, magnetic disc, drum, and so on). Since the access times to the second level of storage may well be significantly long compared to the required system response to external interrupts, the movement of program or data between levels of storage is important to the on-line programmer.

The working party has considered means (such as exist in some languages) which give direct control over such movement. Such means suffer from the severe disadvantages that they reduce program security—the programmer's directives may conflict with the real-time operation of parallel processing and dynamic storage allocation.

We consider it important, therefore, that control over program and data environment movement should be automatic, under control of the portion of the real-time supervisor which is generated automatically by the compiler. The supervisor should operate on the basis that activation priorities for program material and associated data should govern the order of priority of fast storage allocation. For any piece of program coding, the relevant priority will therefore be the highest priority activation which that coding currently has (it may of course be simultaneously activated at several priorities) either directly, in the case of a program procedure, or indirectly, through procedure calls from an activated program procedure. For data environments, the relevant priority will be the highest current activation priority of any program procedure, or called procedure, which can, in principle, obtain access to that data.

Supervisor operation under these conditions is not simple. In the case of program, the implication is that at the instant of *activation* of a program procedure, the coding for that procedure, together with the coding of all procedures which it can in principle call—by virtue of their identifiers appearing in its text otherwise than in an activate statement—must be given the activation priority for storage allocation purposes, unless any of it already has a higher priority. This process must be extended to procedures which can in principle be called by called procedures to any necessary depth. At compiling time, the total coding which could in principle be required for the execution of a program procedure can be determined, and the compiler must provide the relevant information for the real-time supervisor. In the case of data, use must be made of the environment pointers set up as described in 5-3-5-2, to determine the highest priority at which that data could in principle be accessed—in general through procedure calls and activations to any depth. Global data must be permanently allocated the highest storage priority.

The automatic two level storage control system is thus complex in operation. It does produce a system, however, where program operation is secure (given an emergency procedure to come into action if available fast store reaches a dangerously low level) and where storage allocation priorities are related to activation priorities, that is to the required access times for various items of program and data. Note that the priorities only depend on activation, not on whether a program is running or held up. Material can therefore in effect be given a permanently high storage allocation priority by causing it to be permanently activated although it may only actually be running for short periods now and then.

This discussion of storage control is not intended to cover the use of other storage devices purely for data files. The control of the latter can be handled by the real-time programmer in the normal way, using the various language facilities provided.

Storage Allocation Example.

```
          BEGIN REAL . . . .
                    .
                    .
                    .
          PROGRAM PROCEDURE A(. . . .);
          BEGIN PROCEDURE B(. . . .);
              BEGIN .                                    (3), (7)
                    .
                    .
                    .
              END;
                    .                                    (2), (6)
                    .
                    .
                    .
              B (. . . .);
                    .
                    .
          END;
          PROGRAM PROCEDURE C(. . . .);
              BEGIN .
                    .
                    .
                    .
```

ACTIVATE A(. . . .) **WITH PRIORITY 2;**   (5)

.

.

.

.

.

END;
ACTIVATE A (. . . .) **WITH PRIORITY 4;**   (1)
ACTIVATE C (. . . .) **WITH PRIORITY 3;**   (4)
END;

In the example, stages in the execution of coding are shown in numerical order at the right hand side. Storage allocation priorities will be as follows

Stages	Allocation Priority	Material
1,2	0	Global data
	4	{ A and its environment { B
	lowest	Outer block, C
3	0	Global data
	4	{ A and environment { B and environment
	lowest	Outer block, C
4	0	Global data
	3	C and environment
	lowest	Outer block, A, B
5, 6	0	Global data
	2	{ A and environment { B { environment of C
	3	C
	lowest	Outer block
7	0	Global data
	2	{ A and environment { B and environment { environment of C
	3	C
	lowest	Outer block

N.B. In the example interrupts are not included; but the activations could equally well have occurred due to interrupts and the storage allocation process remains the same.

5-3-5-4 Program Checking Aids

An RTL compiler must obviously provide an extensive syntax check as do other high-level language compilers. It is important however that considerably more extensive tests of correct program construction and execution should be available, with related error tracing techniques, than are required on nonreal-time systems. This is because error patterns in a real-time system, where a variety of programs are sharing time and/or storage space, can be very complex, and because the consequences of any error in operation may be more serious than is usually the case in a nonreal-time system in which a faulty program may be rerun with no loss except of programming and computing time.

Program checking in a real-time system must clearly be carried out in at least two stages

off-line, in which individual procedures or groups of procedures are tested individually in a nonreal-time environment (whether on the object machine or not), and

on-line, in which all the processors and individual procedures are operating together in a partial or wholly real-time environment.

It is common experience that off-line checking alone will by no means reveal all types of faults.

Techniques for off-line checking are well established. For example, the compiler might arrange for the program material to be executed in an interpretive mode, with options for tracing the execution at specified points.

On-line program checking is more difficult. It is of course possible to execute a real-time program interpretively but only at the cost of a very fast processor and extensive storage for trace and checking information. This conflicts with the requirement for real-time programs to be efficient, and is in practice unacceptable. We can however provide a substantial degree of on-line security by providing

a) a syntax check (as is usual)

b) interpretive execution off-line

c) test compilation for execution on the object machine

d) final optimized compilation.

"Test compilation" is intended to produce a program which will run on the object machine at a speed not very much slower than that of the final program (as opposed to interpretive execution which would be many times slower). The object program would include software checks, generated automatically by the compiler, for likely run-time faults, for example, incorrect array bounds, memory-protection violation, data configurations which theoretically need not be catered for, and so on. A test-compiled program should also include some selective traces of a type which can be executed rapidly, for example, cyclic storage of the last fifty labels encountered, available if a fault arises. Some simulated input-output facilities might be required to protect the real-time environment from program faults.

In spite of extensive checking of this type some errors may still remain in the final compiled program. It is desirable to include some consistency checks permanently which will detect these and also check for correct hardware operation. Individual users must decide what facilities of this type are required, remembering that these will slow down the final program to some extent, but of course increase the reliability. Such facilities must be written directly in the high-level language.

We therefore recommend that the following directives at the head of a source program be recognized by the RTL compiler.

check syntax—syntax testing only (this should be very quick)

interpret—compile and execute in an interpretive mode

test compile—compile an object program with extensive check facilities

final compile—optimizing compilation.

5-3-5-5 Program Modification Facilities

Program material for real-time applications must be modified occasionally on all but the simplest systems, to incorporate changes which range from changes in values of constants to major changes in program specifications. In general, some of these changes at least will be in portions of program or data in which they were not initially envisaged.

Such changes are best accomplished, from the computer programmer's point of view, by complete recompilation and rechecking off-line, followed by substitution into the on-line machine and final checking. This is essential where major items or critical times of program material require to be changed. If security of program operation is of paramount importance it will in fact always be necessary. In many applications, however, it may well be appropriate, even highly desirable, to have a means of partial compilation or recompilation, followed by modification to the real-time program material with minimal interference to on-line operation.

Language Restrictions.   Due to the parallel processing and dynamic storage allocation features of a system programmed in RTL, there are inevitably considerable restrictions on ways in which programs may be modified while running. It is unlikely to be possible, in practical implementations, to allow modification except at the procedure level, except where special provision is built in from the start in the source code of a particular program. It will only be possible in fact to modify procedures which are declared in the outermost block of the system program, since modification at a deeper level would require an inordinate amount of source program data to reside in the object code. With modification permitted in the outermost block, the on-line system will have to retain the source coding of all identifiers declared in this block.

Procedures in the outer block which can be modified on-line will in practice always be program procedures (*cf* 5-3-2); other procedures in the outer block can be used in the outer block program only, and will in practice be part of the on-line supervisor and cannot be changed without full recompilation, in view of their fundamental role.

The process of modification must include

a) compilation of the replacement material, with the establishment of linkage to outer block identifiers;

b) loading of the new object material into available unused storage;

c) changing the supervisor linkage so that any new activations or calls to the modified procedure use the modified coding;

d) deletion of the original version of the affected procedure when all its associated data environments are terminated (*cf* section 5-3-2).

The possibility that the modified procedure may have several concurrent activations—and that the coding will always be in use on one or another—is catered to by this process, except for a procedure for which a particular activation never terminates. The latter cannot be modified.

The technique of introducing a modification into a system will be system-dependent as far as the method of calling the compiling and modification routine is concerned. It is suggested that compiler directives be available for use in the modification of coding.

Suitable directives might be

```
MOD BEGIN
MOD END
MODIFY IDENTIFIER        USED AS FOLLOWS
BEGIN MOD BEGIN
    PROGRAM PROCEDURE X(. . . .);
                    .
                    .
                    .
    PROGRAM PROCEDURE Y(. . . .);
                    .
                    .
                    .
    MOD END
    SECURE T;
    SECURE V;
    MODIFY X;
    RELEASE T;
    SECURE W;
    MODIFY Y;
    RELEASE V;
    RELEASE W;
END;
```

The directive **mod begin** precedes the new source version of the program procedure(s) to be changed. The directive **mod end** terminates the new source code. The directive **modify** denotes that the specified procedure is to be modified as outlined above, at this point in the operation of the modification process.

In the example various facility operations are included which might be required for the temporary protection of data and so on, during the changes. There need be no restriction on the language facilities used in this modification coding. The operation of the system could be that the whole text (**begin** to **end**) would be compiled in the spare time of the system—or if more convenient, off-line on another machine. The compiled code would contain supervisor directives (corresponding to **mod begin, mod end,** and **modify**) and would then be loaded and used as outlined above.

Applications.   In 5-3-5-5 a technique for on-line modification has been described which provides the ability to make unforeseen changes to a real-time system while it is running. A facility of this type may be necessary in cases where continuity of real-time operation is important. On-line modification is inevitably risky, where program security is concerned, but the risk of an interruption in on-line operation is in some cases preferable to the certainty of an interruption if complete recompilation and testing are to take place.

In many systems a facility of this complexity is not necessary or desirable. The possibility of partial compilation and modification may still be useful however. Systems where several jobs are undertaken by a computer which are wholly independent (for example, some multiaccess systems) will be of this type. In such cases it will be important to add and delete independent jobs. The process described in 5-3-5-5 allows this to occur, and may be simplified since it will not be necessary to allow for parallel processing of a job while it is being added or deleted. The same compiler directives can be used. A simplified system of this type, with a suitably adapted supervisor, will also allow partial compilation and subsequent assembly of a large system program.

5-3-6 APPENDIX

5-3-6-1   String Operators

The following operators can be used to manipulate strings in the ways specified. For the definition of the variable type string see section 5-3-4-1.
1 con Concatenate or addition of strings
eg s_1: = "abc"
    s_2: = "def" **con** s_1
assigns the value of "defabc" to s_2.
2 isin This forms a boolean variable true if the second string contains a substring equal to the first and false if not.

eg **if** "a" **isin s and** "b" **isin s**
then . . . . .

3 $=$ Two strings are equal if they contain exactly the same characters in the same order. The value of $s_1 = s_2$ is a boolean **true** or **false.**

4 leftof s_1 **leftof** s_2 takes the value of the substring of s_1 to the left of the leftmost substring equal to s_2 contained in s_1 or **null** if s_2 is not contained in s_1.

eg **if** $s_1 = $ "abacd"
then s_1 **leftof** "cd" $:= $ "aba"
and s_1 **leftof** "a" $= $ " " (the empty string).

5 rightof s_1 **rightof** s_2 takes the value of the substring of s_1 to the right of the leftmost substring equal to s_2 contained in s_1 or **null** if s_2 is not contained in s_1.

eg **if** $s_1 = $ "abacd"
then s_1 **rightof** a $:= $ "bacd"

6 firstof The value of **firstof** string is a string of length one character equal to the leftmost character of the string or **null** if the string is empty.

7 lastof The value of **lastof** string is a string of length one character equal to the rightmost character of the string or **null** if the string is empty.

The **null** string differs from the empty string in that the empty string is a defined string of no characters whereas the **null** string is an undefined string. The **null** string results from **leftof** and **rightof** if the specified substring is not contained in the mainstring. The empty string results from **leftof** if the substring has no characters to the left of it and from **rightof** if the leftmost substring has nothing to the right of it. Concatenation with the null string has no effect, that is, it is the same as concatenation with the empty string.

EXAMPLE OF THE USE OF STRING OPERATORS. s_1 and s_2 are strings not containing the character*

```
S₃:= S₁ CON "*" CON S₂;
IF S₃ = "*" THEN GOTO LABEL;
IF "A*B" ISIN S₃ THEN
BEGIN
    S₄:=S₃ LEFTOF "A*B";
    S₅:=S₃ RIGHTOF "A*B"
END;
ELSE
BEGIN
    S₄:=S₁;
    S₅:=S₂
END;
```

5-3-7 ACKNOWLEDGMENT

This report has been prepared by a working party formed out of the BCS specialist group on On-line Computing Systems and Their Languages.

Members responsible for this report are: D. Benson, R. J. Cunningham, I. F. Currie, M. Griffith, R. Kingslake, R. J. Long, and A. J. Southgate.

~~~~~~

5-4   USING PRELIMINARY ADA IN A PROCESS CONTROL APPLICATION*

M. E. GORDON and W. B. ROBINSON
The Foxboro Company

~~~~~~

5-4-1 INTRODUCTION

This section contains background information on the Ada language definition process, an introduction to features of Ada, and an overview of the Model Controller Operating System (MCOS), which was coded in Ada. More detailed information on Ada can be found in *The Ada Language Reference Manual,*[1] *The Ada Language Rationale,*[2] and *Programming with Ada.*[3]

An Ada Introduction

5-4-1-1 Background

Ada is the programming language being developed under the auspices of the Department of Defense. The language development has extended over a period of several years, from requirements specification (Strawman, Woodenman, Tinman, Ironman, Steelman) to language definition. Accompanying the language development is the specification of a language support environment (Sandman, Pebbleman, Stoneman), which is progressing closely after Ada itself.

Ada is being considered as a standard language for process control by the Long Term Programming Languages (LTPL) Committee of the Purdue Workshop and the European LTPL Committee. Both ANSI and ISO standardization efforts are being initiated.

Currently in a formative stage, Ada is undergoing revisions in response to a Test and Evaluation (T and E) of the language. The programming project

---

*By M. E. Gordon and W. B. Robinson, The Foxboro Co. Originally published in the Proceedings of the National Computer Conference, 1980.

described in this paper was undertaken as part of the T and E review, and is based on the preliminary Ada language definition of June 1979. Since there are, as yet, no Ada compilers available, the evaluation is static. However, the Ada features described below are intrinsic to the conceptual model of the language and are unlikely to change.

This section will discuss how Ada language features support the modern language concepts of: (1) data abstraction, (2) modularity, (3) encapsulation, (4) concurrent programming, (5) machine independence, and (6) orthogonality and extensibility.

In later sections, it will be shown how such language features may be applied to a typical programming problem in a process control systems application.

5-4-1-2 Data Abstraction

Data abstraction is supported in Ada by programmer-definable data types. Type declarations collect knowledge of common properties of objects in one place, thereby facilitating software maintenance. The principal advantage is greater software reliability, because the programmer's code is closer to the expression and solution of the applications problem.

Ada's strong typing is based on name equivalence, rather than structural equivalence. No implicit type conversions are allowed. Explicit conversions can be used in some cases, for instance, in converting numeric types. In other cases, Ada provides the UNSAFE CONVERSION function as an escape hatch.

For programmers accustomed to creating variables on-the-fly (as in FORTRAN), Ada's requirements for declaration of variables and types may seem overly restrictive at first. With proper use of Ada's data facilities, however, the benefits far outweigh the constraints.

5-4-1-3 Modularity and Program Structure

Modularity is supported not only by traditional subprograms (procedures and functions), but also by Ada modules (packages and tasks). Although the overall structure of an Ada program follows the conventional block structure of ALGOL 60, it differs in that modules may be separately compiled and arbitrarily included at various levels of the program hierarchy. Ada offers control over visibility and scope through *restricted* clauses, which may override inheritance rules of module nesting. Importing is done by program unit name, not by object name.

5-4-1-4 Encapsulation

Package modules are the cornerstone of the language. Through them, encapsulation of data with their associated operations is possible. Other uses of packages are grouping related procedures together and forming a collection of related types and data objects.

Packages consist of a specification part and an optional package body. The specification part of a package contains the logical interface (for example, type declarations, procedure specifications) which other modules and subprograms may access. The package body contains the implementation of the operations specified in the visible part. The package body is a mechanism for information-hiding, that is, concealing implementation details from the users of the package.

Ada's separate (but not independent) compilation reinforces the realization of encapsulation via modularization. Compilation checks between compilation units are the same as those within a unit. Therefore, it is not necessary to wait until link time to discover most interface errors. This checking will be accomplished through a library management system, which is a requirement of the Ada support environment.

5-4-1-5 Concurrent Programming

Tasks, similar to packages in format, are the means for implementing concurrent processes. Unique to the Ada tasking mechanism is the rendezvous concept, which serves the dual functions of synchronization and communication in a parallel processing environment. Three controversial features related to Ada's tasking are scheduling, interrupt handling, and access to shared data. They are likely to change in the final language definition.

5-4-1-6 Machine Independence

Machine independence is the ultimate goal of a high-level language such as Ada. Ada language features, as described above, allow the systems programmer and, later, the maintenance programmer to operate at a level which is closer to the system specification than is possible with older languages like FORTRAN (developed in 1954). Actual machine-dependent code may be kept to a minimum. The result is a more reliable, robust software system that is easier to develop and maintain, consistent with the conventional wisdom of software engineering.

5-4-1-7 Orthogonality and Extensibility

Ada offers language primitives and rules for combining them (orthogonality[4]) to build specialized structures and functions. This principle of orthogonality and the related principle of extensibility are demonstrated by the I/O packages, which are written in Ada. Although lacking some key features (for example, variable-length strings, bit types), Ada provides the tools to create them. This is a critical requirement for a systems implementation language.

Such freedom in a language exacts a price, that price being the responsibility for a programming discipline. When properly used, Ada can be a powerful tool for both systems and applications software development. However, without the appropriate programming methodology, the benefits of Ada are easily lost. For example, arbitrary use of the exit statement to create unstructured loop constructs would be a misuse of the language.

In the following sections, it will be shown how Ada may be applied properly to an embedded operating system for process control. In particular, the remaining discussion will illustrate how Ada influences all stages of the software development process, from initial design to final implementation.

THE MODEL CONTROLLER OPERATING SYSTEM.   The model controller is a system that allows digital implementation of multiloop control systems based on traditional (analog) control diagrams. It was conceived as a typical example of a small, real-time system providing these main features: (1) communications interface to host computers, (2) control algorithms and control database based on block diagrams, and (3) interface to process input/output components. Each of these is discussed in detail later.

The Model Controller Operating System (MCOS) supports these features with the multitasking facilities provided by Ada. Figure 5-4-1 shows a simplified sketch of the model controller.

One approach to reliability in digital control systems is redundancy. In the model controller, this is reflected in the dual-controller, dual-port, dual-link architecture. In the event of a failure of any main system component, the backup component is automatically activated. The process database is regularly (every control cycle) transferred to the backup, or tracking, controller via the shared data buffer. With appropriate checks against contaminating its database, the

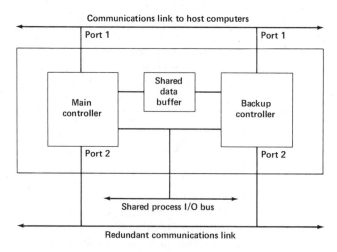

Figure 5-4-1 Model controller.

tracking controller is prepared to take control with a very recent database copy. The two controllers also share access to the process I/O bus. The hardware redundancy is complemented by a software redundancy; both controllers have their own copy of the MCOS software, which will be described in the following sections.

The communications link allows host computers to configure or to change the configuration of the control database, to read or write particular values in the database, and to monitor or change the status of each of the controllers.

The process I/O bus, which can be accessed by only one controller at a time, allows the controllers to read or write analog and digital input–output devices.

5-4-1-8 Overview of the Operation Sequence

At every quarter second clock interrupt, each controller begins by checking its mode. Typically one is on control, the other tracking. The lead controller processes all control blocks in the following manner: All process I/O components are read, conditioned, and stored in a table.

For each block: (1) appropriate parameters (such as measurement or set point) are updated; (2) the algorithm for each block is executed; (3) if needed, an output is sent from the block to the appropriate component.

After all blocks are processed, the database is written into the buffer.

The tracking controller copies the data buffer into its own database.

At any time, the system might receive an interrupt on the communications channel. Typical communications messages supported are: (1) secure–release, (2) read–write database, and (3) read–write controller status.

When neither the control processing nor the communications task is active, a security task executes, monitoring the health of the system.

5-4-2 SYSTEM DESIGN WITH ADA

This section contains discussions of some of the design decisions made and relates them to the facilities of Ada for modularization and for representation of data. The design issues are: (1) modularity and program structure, (2) data structures and representations, (3) exception handling, (4) scheduling, and (5) interrupt handling.

MODULARITY AND PROGRAM STRUCTURE. The overall program structure of the Model Controller Operating System (MCOS) is illustrated in Figure 5-4-2a. The main procedure contains the module specifications of the three primary tasks: communications, executive, and security. The function of the main pro-

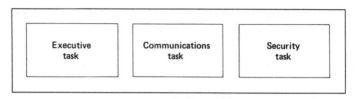

Figure 5-4-2a Main procedure contains specifications of the three primary tasks.

cedure is to initiate the three tasks. The code for the main procedure is straight forward, as shown in Figure 5-4-2b.

Each task body is a separate compilation unit. By separating the task body from its specification, implementation details may be changed without necessitating a recompilation of the main procedure (assuming the interface remains the same). Ada's separate compilation facility was used extensively in the design of MCOS, to take advantage of the logical interface—physical implementation separation. This facility supports top-down design in that the logical interfaces may be defined first, with the implementation stubs developed later. Another advantage of the separation principle is that it streamlines the code, improving the readability of Ada program units.

Within each task body, the specifications for its internal packages are local, while their bodies are separate. The tasks and their primary functions are: (1) communications task: handle port interrupts; (2) executive task: process control blocks (if main controller) or track the database (if backup controller); and (3) security task: perform various software checks during any idle time.

The communications and executive tasks are discussed more fully in later sections.

The final two main modules of MCOS are packages. The database package and status_manager package are separate compilation units in the

Figure 5-4-2b Main procedure of MCOS.

MCOS program library, and are independent of the overall block structure. The purpose of the status_manager package is to encapsulate global type and data declarations with their associated operations. The database package, on the other hand, contains related types and objects for global use and a synchronizing semaphore task. The two packages are self-sufficient in that they see no other units in the program library. Other program units which require access to the global data make it visible by including the package name in a visibility list. Therefore importing of global data is done on a module basis, rather than on a single variable basis. The global packages may be imported at any level of the block structure hierarchy.

As demonstrated in Figure 5-4-3c, good programming practice dictates explicit import lists of objects to be listed in comments. Without such information, the code is virtually unreadable, since it is not apparent which data objects are being referenced. Rather than burden the programmer (who may be inconsistent and/or error-prone), such information could be generated automatically by the compiler or text editor.

It must be noted that the MCOS program structure presented here was achieved through several iterations. Because of the novel interplay between traditional block structure and separately compiled modules, classic rules of thumb for structured design were not directly applicable. Ada is a language without a history and, consequently, without a refined programming methodology. Proper use of Ada features was discovered partly through trial and error. A good program structure for MCOS was achieved by following certain guidelines: (1) control visibility as much as possible by using traditional block structure; (2) within the general block structure of the program, textually include only the module specifications; use stubs for module bodies, which should be developed and compiled separately; (3) reserve use of separately compiled modules for global library packages; (4) whenever feasible, compile the specification part and the implementation part separately to reduce recompilation dependencies.

DATA STRUCTURES AND REPRESENTATIONS.   To quote Wirth,[5] "The choice of (abstract) representation of data is often a fairly difficult one, and it is not uniquely determined by the facilities available. It must always be taken in light of the operations to be performed on the data." In our model system, there are several instances where the choice of abstract representation was complicated by the fact that two different tasks required access to the same data objects. In another instance, to be described later, the strong type restraints of Ada had to be circumvented to allow a more flexible approach to handling raw data for input and output.

The largest data object, the array of control blocks, is considered in detail below. The design of data structures proceeded in parallel with the overall module design.

5-4-2-1 Shared Data

The critical issue here is the need to provide adequate protection of the database, which can be accessed by both the communications task and the control executive task.

In MCOS, total encapsulation of the database was rejected for two reasons: first and foremost, the number of transactions using the database is prohibitively large, and using specialized interfaces would degrade performance. In particular, the communications task has a ten millisecond timeout period and thus cannot be delayed too long by control processing. Second, a small dedicated system does not require the level of protection encapsulation offers. The communications task performs sufficient validity checks to protect the database in transactions with host computers.

Although encapsulation of the database was rejected, mutually exclusive access to the database must be provided so that consistent data is used by the tasks sharing access. The simplest solution, and the one finally used, employs Ada's generic semaphore task to create a critical region, during which only one task can access the database. It may be that this solution is too inefficient, in which case an equivalent solution would have to be implemented in machine code.

By way of contrast, the package status_manager, described below, is an example of the use of the package structure for encapsulating data objects and the operations performed on them. The brief duration of the exclusive read-write access to the status registers makes encapsulation feasible.

5-4-2-2 Physical Representations of Data Objects

Since the object machine for the Model Controller Operating System is predicated as having a small memory, space issues are important. Often a record has several components. To allow the compiler to assign the storage for these may use more storage than is desirable. Ada provides several representation facilities for records[1]. . .: One can specify the number of bits to be used representing objects of a given type, specify that the compiler is to use packing, or specify actual word and bit layouts for components of a record. All of these facilities were used in the MCOS exercise.

EXCEPTION HANDLING.   In any real-time system, security and robustness are essential. Exceptional conditions, such as overflow during a calculation, should not cause a system crash, but must be handled in a meaningful way so the system can recover and continue processing. Ada provides an exception handling facility which appears to be adequate, although sometimes cumbersome[1]. Examples of the use of exception handlers are given in later sections.

SCHEDULING.   The strategy for scheduling the tasks and procedures in a real-time system must be carefully thought out and ... implemented. In the MCOS, the communications task must execute immediately upon receipt of an interrupt. Other scheduling requirements are somewhat "softer." However, it is in the area of scheduling that Ada seems to have the greatest weakness. According to the LRM[1], "The language does not specify when a scheduling decision is made; for example, a round-robin time-sliced strategy is acceptable." There is a language-defined priority attribute for tasks which can be used in scheduling decisions. However, there seems to be little in the language to facilitate the design and implementation of a scheduling algorithm.

MCOS requires a scheduler with the following properties: (1) the scheduler is to be invoked when a new task enters the ready queue, in particular when an entry call or interrupt occurs; (2) when the scheduler is invoked, ready queues are examined and tasks with the higher priorities are executed first.

INTERRUPT HANDLING.   Interrupt handling is another area where Ada, as currently defined, falls far short of the mark. This is a critical area for real-time applications, such as process control, in which certain hardware interrupts demand immediate, and uninterrupted, service. In MCOS, for example, a communications interrupt requires that the message be processed and a reply sent within ten msec, otherwise a timeout occurs, putting the controller on standby. Unfortunately, there is no way to guarantee dedicated resources to a high-priority interrupt in Ada.

Ada does not distinguish between hardware interrupts and software signaling between tasks. An interrupt is mapped onto a rendezvous entry, via a representation specification. Yet, there is no way to indicate the urgency of an interrupt on the entry queue. Task priorities only determine which of several tasks waiting on the ready queue will be serviced next. However, entry queues are handled strictly on a first-in-first-out basis.

The Ada language design team has recognized the inadequacy of the current interrupt handling mechanism. It is expected that the problem will be rectified in the final language definition (June 1980). Therefore, in the MCOS programming exercise, the communications interrupt was coded in Ada for illustration purposes, with no assertion of correctness.

5-4-3 ADA IMPLEMENTATION OF MCOS

This section provides a more detailed view of some of the issues that were raised earlier. In particular, using Ada in the actual implementation of MCOS is discussed with regard to the database, control processing, and communications processing.

The database

5-4-3-1 Control Blocks

The primary function of the model controller is performed through the control blocks and their corresponding algorithms. In a typical process control application, several types of control algorithms, such as proportional-integral-derivative (pid), lead-lag (llag), and so on, would be used. MCOS has the pid, llag, nonlinear (nonl), and digital input (din) algorithms as a suitable cross section. Each system, however, can have up to thirty-two control blocks, of which an arbitrary number can be pid, an arbitrary number can be llag, and so on.

In a particular control scheme, blocks can be interconnected, can obtain inputs from process I/O devices, and can generate outputs for process I/O devices. A sample configuration is shown in Figure 5-4-3a. Because of this interconnectability, blocks are processed in sequence. In general, a block will obtain inputs only from blocks that have been processed before it. This ordering stems from the traditional digital implementation of continuous analog control.

A standard assembly language or FORTRAN implementation of such a system would have to treat the thirty-two blocks as a massive array of words of undifferentiated type, and the layout of parameters within different block types would be contained in an external document, presumably a system specification. Hence, the meaning of a particular word in the database would be obscured and opportunities for errors by both original writers and later maintainers is increased.

With the tools of Ada or any other sufficiently typed language, such a situation can be avoided, and the form and meaning of the database items can be given explicitly in the program itself. Variant records were chosen to represent the control blocks. (A variant record is a record with choice of alternative substructures based on the value of a discriminant component[1]). Two rules which affect the utility of variant records are: the discriminant can be changed

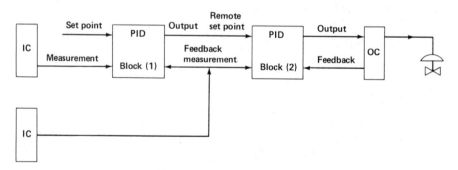

Figure 5-4-3a A sample control system.

only during a complete record assignment; and the same component name cannot be used in different variant parts. Both rules caused some difficulties, as will be discussed later.

An enumeration list of block types is the discriminant component for the variant record type. This has the declaration:

```
TYPE BLOCK_NAME IS (NULL_BLOCK, PID, NONL, DIN, LLAG);
```

The other components common to all blocks were the block status word, the name fields, the options word, and the block parameter. These required separate type declarations and representation specifications as well. In specifying the variants, it was necessary to identify common types that apply to the components of the different blocks. The four major types were value, logical, value-pointer, and logical-pointer. Each is a record in its own right, with a representation specifying one word of storage. For instance,

```
TYPE VALUE IS
  RECORD
    FROM_POINTER:BOOLEAN;
    VALUE_IS_BAD:BOOLEAN;
    COUNTS:NORMALIZED_COUNTS;
  END RECORD;
FOR VALUE USE
  RECORD
    FROM_POINTER: AT 0*WORD RANGE 0..0;
    VALUE_IS_BAD: AT 0*WORD RANGE 2..2;
    COUNTS: AT 0*WORD RANGE 3..15;
  END RECORD;
```

Examples of components in a pid block which are of type value are the measurement, set point, and output. On the other hand, in the din block, the measurement and output are of bit_pattern type, and there is no set point. Hence it was necessary to place these components in the variant part of the control block.

The final problem was to choose a naming scheme that allowed easy use of the control blocks in the algorithms. Separately named components would have led to tedious implementation of the algorithms. Instead, like parameters were grouped into arrays by type, with each array indexed by an appropriate enumeration type. For instance,

```
TYPE PIDLIST IS (MEAS, REMOTE_SP, FEEDBACK, HALIM, LALIM,
  HDLIM, LDLIM, HOLIM, LOLIM, BIAS, PBAND, RATE, INTEGRAL,
  SETPOINT, OUTPUT, ABSDB, DEVDB, OUTDB, KL,
  FILTERED_MEAS, INTEGRAL_BALANCE);
TYPE LLAGLIST IS (MEAS. DYNAMIC_GAIN, TIMEL, BIAS, OUTPUT);
```

Note that these lists overload literals, such as meas, and hence, when ambiguities arise, care must be taken in using them, for instance by writing "pid_list(meas)" explicitly.

Finally the data object *block* is declared in the database package by

```
BLOCK: ARRAY (1..32) OF CONTROL_BLOCK;
```

While the development of these types proceeded in top-down fashion, Ada has the unfortunate and annoying restriction that the type declarations must be presented in bottom-up order. This is a hindrance to both writers and readers of a program.

5-4-3-2 Status Manager Package

MCOS contains status registers to indicate certain conditions of the system hardware-software. The logical representation of the status flags and the specifications of the available operations are encapsulated in the visible part of the status_manager package. The physical representation of the registers (Boolean arrays), as well as the implementation of their corresponding access routines, are concealed in the package body. The status_manager package is global to MCOS. Its visible part provides a simple interface for accessing the status registers.

Within the package body, the implementation of the various access routines differs in the level of protection afforded to the status registers. Protection mechanisms are provided only as dictated by the functional requirements. For example, since writing to the controller status register is accomplished via hardware command registers, no extra protection is needed. On the other hand, since the unit status register is directly read-write accessible, a high degree of protection is desirable. A server task provides this protection. Here the rendezvous is used to prevent simultaneous access to the unit status register by parallel tasks:

```
PACKAGE BODY STATUS_MANAGER IS
  TASK BODY PROTECT_STATUS_REG IS
  BEGIN
    LOOP
      ACCEPT SET_STATUS (FLAG: UNIT_STAT_LIST_CHANGE;
      NEW_STAT: BOOLEAN) DO
        UNIT_STAT_REG (FLAG): = NEW_STAT;
      END SET_STATUS;
    END LOOP;
  END PROTECT_STATUS_REG;
BEGIN
  INITIATE PROTECT_STATUS_REG;
END STATUS_MANAGER;
```

Note that the initiate statement of the server task is placed in a begin block at the bottom of the package body. Task initiation occurs when the package body is elaborated at run-time.

Since Ada does not prevent simultaneous access to shared data by parallel tasks, it is the programmer's responsibility to ensure the proper level of protection by controlling access via the rendezvous or semaphore. Ada provides protective mechanisms, but does not enforce their use. For system reliability in a parallel processing environment, therefore, good programming discipline is required. Without it, system security is threatened.

Control processing

5-4-3-3 The Controller Executive

The controller executive is a task that executes in parallel with the communications task. The executive accepts a clock interrupt to begin the control cycle and determines the controller's current mode (for example, standby, control, and so on). A controller that is tracking reads the database buffer. A controller in standby simply exits. When the controller is in control mode or initializing mode, it runs a sample control algorithm and compares the output to a known result. If this checks, it proceeds to control block processing. Otherwise it takes itself off control and exits. The executive code is given in Figure 5-4-3b.

5-4-3-4 The Control Package

The procedure do_control_processing is in the module control_package and is called from the task executive. It handles block initialization and regular control processing in a uniform manner. Since blocks can be taken off control by a host computer, this must be checked by reading the appropriate block status bit. The control package is hierarchical in organization since no parallel processing occurs within it.

Two difficulties encountered in control processing involved type conversions and exception handling. We discuss these in detail below.

5-4-3-5 Process I/O Components

In the MCOS there are 100 input–output components, each of which can be one of several types. The first attempt at representing the components used an array of variant records. However, physical limitations required using the identification field (id) as a flag to indicate absence of an input. This is incompatible with the use of the id as a discriminant. Hence, the use of variant records was rejected.

```
RESTRICTED (MAIN, STATUS_MANAGER)
SEPARATE TASK BODY EXECUTIVE IS
USE MAIN, STATUS_MANAGER:
-- EXECUTIVE HAS THE FOLLOWING IMPORT LIST OF OBJECTS.
-- READ_BUFFER AND WRITE_BUFFER ARE IMPORTED FROM DATA_BUFFER_MANAGER
-- SET_STATUS AND THE LITERALS OK AND COMP_CHK_BAD ARE IMPORTED
-- FROM THE STATUS_MANAGER.

TYPE PROCESSOR_MODE IS (TRACKING_MODE, STANDBY_MODE, INIT_MODE,
                        CONTROL_MODE);
SUBTYPE ZERO_ONE_OR_TWO IS INTEGER RANGE 0. .2;

ENTRY CLOCK_INTERRUPT;

INIT_COUNT: ZERO_ONE_OR_TWO;
CONTROLLER_MODE: PROCESSOR_MODE: = STANDBY_MODE;

TASK DATA_BUFFER_MANAGER IS
-- THE TASK WHICH COORDINATES ACCESS TO THE DATA BUFFER,
-- WHICH IS USED TO TRANSFER THE DATA BASE FROM THE "ON"
-- CONTROLLER TO THE TRACKING CONTROLLER.
   ENTRY READ_GRANT, WRITE_GRANT; -- HARDWARE INTERRUPTS
   ENTRY READ_BUFFER; -- CALLED BY THE TRACKING CONTROLLER
   ENTRY WRITE_BUFFER; -- CALLED BY THE "ON" CONTROLLER
END DATA_BUFFER_MANAGER;

PACKAGE CONTROL_PACKAGE IS
   FUNCTION SAMPLE_PID_TEST_OK RETURN BOOLEAN;
   PROCEDURE DO_CONTROL_PROCESSING (INITIALIZATIONS_REQUIRED:
                       IN OUT ZERO_ONE_OR_TWO);
   PROCEDURE MODE_CHECK (MODE: IN OUT PROCESSOR_MODE;
                       INIT_COUNT: IN ZERO_ONE_OR_TWO);

-- THESE ARE THE THREE VISIBLE ENTRY POINTS INTO THE CONTROL
-- PROCESSING PACKAGE. THESE SUBROUTINES ARE CALLED FROM THE TASK
-- EXECUTIVE AND FROM NO OTHER.
END;

FOR HALF_SECOND_CLOCK USE AT 16:ffe;

PACKAGE BODY CONTROL_PACKAGE IS SEPARATE;

TASK BODY DATA_BUFFER_MANAGER IS SEPARATE;

BEGIN
   INIT_COUNT; =2; -- ALL BLOCKS ARE INITIALIZED TWICE
                   -- AT STARTUP

LOOP
            ACCEPT CLOCK_INTERRUPT;
            SET_WATCHDOG_TIMER; -- THIS REQUIRES ASSEMBLER LANGUAGE CODE
            MODE_CHECK (CONTROLLER_MODE, INIT_COUNT);
            CASE CONTROLLER_MODE OF
              WHEN TRACKING_MODE =>
                READ_BUFFER;
              WHEN STANDBY_MODE =>
                NULL;
              WHEN INIT_MODE:CONTROL_MODE =>
                   IF SAMPLE_PID_TEST_OK THEN
                      DO_CONTROL_PROCESSING (INIT_COUNT);
                      IF INIT_COUNT = 0 THEN
                         WRITE_BUFFER;
                      END IF;
                   ELSE SET_STATUS (OK, FALSE);
                         SET_STATUS (COMP_CHK_BAD, TRUE);
                   END IF;
              END CASE;
END LOOP;

EXCEPTION -- A GENERAL EXCEPTION HANDLER TO SET THE CONTROLLER
          -- TO STANDBY IF AN ERROR IS PROPAGATED FROM A
          -- LOWER LEVEL.
WHEN OTHERS =>
    SET_STATUS (OK, FALSE);
    CONTROLLER_MODE:=STANDBY_MODE;
END EXECUTIVE;
```

Figure 5–4–3b   Executive task body.

The solution adopted was to treat each I/O component as a (non-variant) record with two fields:

```
TYPE PIO_DATA IS
RECORD
   ID: PIO_TYPE:
   TWELVE_BITS: BOOLEAN_ARRAY (1..12);
END RECORD;
```

Now the id field can be revised independently of the twelve bit value. Moreover, in the case of the digital components, slice assignments can be used to get the information into the appropriate block components. But what happens when the twelve bits must be treated as an integer? Here the package UNSAFE_PROGRAMMING comes into play. It provides a generic facility for converting between otherwise incompatible types; for instance, for converting an object of type pio_data to an INTEGER occupying a sixteen-bit word.

The following representation ensures that each pio_data value occupies one word.

```
FOR TYPE PIO_DATA USE
RECORD
   ID: AT 0*WORD RANGE 0..3;
   TWELVE_BITS: AT 0*WORD RANGE 4..15;
END RECORD;
```

Now UNSAFE_CONVERSION can be used to translate the single word of pio_data type to a single word of INTEGER type. This requires the instantiations *function* data_to_int *is new* UNSAFE_CONVERSION (pio_data; INTEGER); temp_data: pio_data; followed by the conversion statements temp_data := (no_data, pio_data. twelve_bits); raw_count := data_to_int (temp_data);

5-4-3-6 Numeric Computation and Error Handling

During the processing of the control blocks, some of the algorithms require numeric computations. Because of the real-time nature of the controller, any error conditions that could arise must be handled in such a way that the system does not halt. This section contains a discussion of the error handlers used in designing the MCOS algorithm set.

Suppose we have three variables given by the declaration

```
X, Y, Z: INTEGER RANGE 0..4000;
```

followed by three assignment statements, where it is assumed that the expressions on the right-hand side yield INTEGER values:

```
BEGIN;
        X: = EXPRESSION_1;
        Y: = EXPRESSION_2;
F21     Z: = EXPRESSION_3;
END;
```

If one of the expressions has a valid INTEGER value outside the range 0..4000, the RANGE_ERROR condition is raised. At this point the program checks whether a handler has been included within the block. If so, the action specified in the handler is taken. If not, the search for a handler continues in the next outer scope. In the scope given even if we include an exception handler, the program will resume execution not at the next statement following the one raising the exception, but at the statement following the end of the block. Thus, in general, it is not possible to resume execution from the point of error.

In some problems, such as signal conditioning, one wishes to clamp the value that is out of range. In that case, the following seems cleanest for eliminating the RANGE_ERROR exception:

```
X: = MAX (MIN (EXPRESSION_1,4000), 0);
Y: = MAX (MIN (EXPRESSION_2,4000), 0);
Z: = MAX (MIN (EXPRESSION_3,4000), 0);
```

However, this will be valid only so long as the expressions on the right are valid INTEGER values. If one of them is not, an OVERFLOW or a DIVIDE_ERROR exception occurs in the expression evaluation. DIVIDE_ERROR can be avoided by testing the denominator beforehand. This leaves but two possibilities for OVERFLOW: (1) write the expression as a function within which error handlers are implemented; or (2) enclose each statement in a block with an exception handler, as in this block:

```
BEGIN
  X: = EXPRESSION_1;
  EXCEPTION
  — —NO MATTER WHAT GOES WRONG, CLAMP
  WHEN OVERFLOW = >
  X: = 4000;
END;
—ETC—
```

Both of the techniques were useful. In some circumstances it was possible to determine a priori that only RANGE_ERROR could occur and then the explicit clamping was used. In other cases, the special scope was inserted to localize the error handling.

COMMUNICATIONS PROCESSING. The model controller may receive communications interrupts at any time from either port. In MCOS, the communications task functions at the highest priority level to service such interrupts. As discussed in a previous section, the Ada mechanism for interrupt handling is inadequate, and is in the process of being revised by the language design team. By handling the communications interrupts in preliminary Ada, there is no way to guarantee that they will receive the immediate and dedicated attention that is demanded.

In addition to handling port interrupts, the communications task consists of the following units: (1) message_buffer_manager package encapsulates the input and output buffers together with the access routine, message_handler; (2) message_handler routine decodes the incoming message and calls the appropriate subroutine to process the message and send the reply; (3) error_counter_manager package contains the hardware registers (which record the occurrence of transmission errors), and corresponding software access routines.

5-4-3-7 Hardware Dependencies

The communications process is, perhaps, the most difficult to design and program because of the many direct connections between software and hardware. There are certain circumstances which require a machine code insertion in the Ada program to provide a high-level interface between the hardware and the rest of the software implementation. One advantage to Ada is that it permits such machine-dependent code to interface with the high-level code, isolating and minimizing the degree of machine dependencies. For example, a machine code routine is required to reset the watchdog timer to avoid a timeout.

5-4-3-8 Decoding Messages

The communications messages which are implemented in MCOS are grouped into three categories: station messages, task messages, and process I/O messages. MCOS responds to messages received from the host computer, but does not initiate them. Station messages involve retrieving status information about the controller, and getting–resetting transmission error counters. Task messages allow the host to switch the controller into tracking or standby modes. Process I/O messages get–set values in the database of control blocks.

Each message has a specific command code which indicates the content of the message. The command codes are implemented by a representation specification for elements of an enumeration type, where elements of the type are assigned internal codes corresponding to values of command codes, as shown in Figures 5-4-3c and 5-4-3d. Ada supports the principle of separation of logical properties from physical properties. However, in the case of an

TYPE COMMAND IS

          (GET_STATUS, GET_ERROR_CTRS, READ_DATA_STANDARD,
          RESET_ERROR_CTRS, STANDBY, STARTUP, SELECT,
          SECURE_RELEASE, SET_RESET_HOLD);

Figure 5–4–3c

FOR COMMAND USE

          (GET_STATUS => 16 : 030001,
          GET_ERROR_CTRS => 16 : 080002,
          READ_DATA_STANDARD => 16 : 080003,
          RESET_ERROR_CTRS => 16 : 180002,
          STANDBY => 16 : 190301,
          STARTUP => 16 : 190302,
          SELECT => 16 : 190303,
          SECURE_RELEASE => 16 : 190401,
          SET_RESET_HOLD => 16 : 190402);

Figure 5–4–3d Representation specification for command enumeration type (ascending order of internal codes determines ordering in Fig. 3a).

enumeration type, the ordering of elements in the logical specification must correspond to the ascending numerical values assigned in the representation specification. Yet, despite this dependency, Ada enforces a textual separation in that all associated representation specifications must follow the logical specifications in the declarative part.

The incoming message buffer is an array of bytes. The first part of the message containing the command code must be decoded before the rest of the message can be processed. The decoding was implemented in MCOS via UN-SAFE_CONVERSION of the appropriate bytes into the command code enumeration type. When a case is done on the command code, illegal codes are caught by the *when others* alternative.

5-4-3-9 Processing Messages

Legal commands are processed by their respective subroutines, whose stubs are internal to the message_handler procedure. The procedures themselves are separately compiled subunits (to disconnect the logical interface from the actual implementation). Except for the read_data_standard message, the message processing routines are relatively trivial. They perform their functions via the access routines provided in the status_manager package and the error_counter_manager package. Unsafe conversions are used, as necessary, to convert from Boolean arrays to the byte array of the out-going message buffer (and vice versa). A common routine, valid_reply, is used to set the appropriate return codes and transmit the reply by a hardware-implemented start_io routine.

The read_data_standard requests certain components from control blocks of the database. Rather than performing UNSAFE_CONVERSION on a record component basis (which would require a large case statement to distinguish variant record parts), the conversion is done on a block-by-block basis, accessing the requested components by relative physical location in the block. (A table-lookup provides the necessary information.) Bypassing the strong typing of the logical representation of the control block database greatly simplified the procedure code (a 75 percent reduction in the number of statements required). The protection afforded by Ada's strong typing is superfluous in response transmission, since the output buffer is simply an array of bytes.

5-4-4 SUMMARY AND CONCLUSIONS

As applied to a typical process control problem, the Model Controller Operating System, preliminary Ada sometimes helped and at other times hindered the program development process.

HINDRANCES.   The major deficiencies of preliminary Ada for real-time applications are the lack of a well-defined scheduler and the inadequacy of the mechanism for interrupt handling. The Ada language design team has acknowledged these problems, and, hopefully, will rectify them in the final language design. Otherwise, such functions will require a machine code implementation.

A related problem is synchronizing access to shared data in time-critical applications. Implementing mutual exclusion using the rendezvous construct is awkward and inefficient as compared to other synchronization primitives such as spin locks.[6]

Another hindrance to program development is the required bottom-up textual presentation of information. This is exhibited by the restriction of no forward referencing in specifications. Although easier for compiler implementation, linear elaboration of declarations is not easier for either writers or readers of Ada programs. A textual presentation reflecting the top-down design process would be preferable.

Also detracting from the readability of Ada programs is the lack of explicit import lists of objects. Import lists are not required, yet without them program maintenance is hampered. To avoid the excessive burden on program developers, the import lists could be automatically generated by compilers or text editors.

HELPS.   The major advantage of programming in Ada is the support provided by packages for encapsulation and information-hiding. The grouping of logically related data objects, types, and/or associated procedures greatly enhances the logical program structure. For instance, levels of protection of shared data objects may be implemented in the package body, concealing details from the users of the package.

Ada's separate compilation facility was used extensively to support modularization and enhance program structure. Separation of logical interface from physical implementation is a positive influence on program development.

Ada's strong typing is a definite plus. High-level data definitions improve the readability of the code. In this regard, enumeration types are particularly useful.

A necessary companion to strong typing is the ability to escape it when a different view of the object is required, such as in decoding a message buffer. This is neatly provided by Ada's UNSAFE_CONVERSION function. UN-SAFE_CONVERSION identifies those areas of the program where the safety checks of strong typing are temporarily suspended. Without this feature, a greater proportion of the program would have required machine code implementation. A related aid to systems programming in Ada is the coupling of logical to physical representations via the representation specification.

ISSUES IN PROGRAMMING METHODOLOGY.   During the design and coding of MCOS, some uncertainties about Ada were raised. They were eventually resolved as the authors gained experience with the language, and through consultations with various persons more closely connected with the Ada language development.*

Issues identified during the MCOS exercise were: (1) the interplay between traditional block structure and separately compiled modules, and how it affects program structure; (2) using visibility restrictions to advantage; (3) separate compilation of specification and implementation parts to reduce recompilation dependencies; (4) exception handling; and (5) dependency of logical representation on physical representation.

A programming methodology for Ada is required. A user's guide (an Ada cookbook) would facilitate program development. Due to the mixing of standard features with novel ones, the best Ada solution for a particular problem often cannot be ascertained. Current reference documentation [1,2] is inadequate.

5-4-5 CONCLUSION

Without a doubt, systems programming is facilitated by using Ada, as compared to a full assembly language implementation. As with any high-level language, a small proportion (5 to 10 percent) of the program will require assembly language, either to maximize efficiency or to interface with hardware. Ada provides an interface to assembly code. Yet, due to the power of the language, machine-dependent code may be kept to a minimum.

---

*In this regard, the authors would like to acknowledge John Barnes, Dennis Cornhill, Mark Davis, Robert Firth, John Goodenough, Oliver Roubine, and Peter Wegner.

5-4-6 REFERENCES

1   "Preliminary Ada Reference Manual," *SIGPLAN Notices,* Vol. 14 (6), June 1979, Part A.

2   "Rationale for the Design of the Ada Programming Language," *SIGPLAN Notices,* Vol. 14(6), June 1979, Part B.

3   Wegner, P., *Programming with Ada—An Introduction by Means of Graduated Examples,* New Jersey, Prentice-Hall, 1980.

4   Tannenbaum, A. S., "A Tutorial on ALGOL 68," *ACM Computing Surveys,* Vol. 8 (2), June 1978, pp. 155–190.

5   Wirth, N., *Algorithms & Data Structures = Programs,* New Jersey, Prentice-Hall, 1976.

6   Evans, A., Morgan, C., Roberts, E., and Clarke, E., "The Impact of Multiprocessor Technology on High-level Language Design," BBN Report No. 4188, September 1979.

5-5 TOMAL: A TASK-ORIENTED MICROPROCESSOR APPLICATIONS LANGUAGE*

JOHN L. HENNESSY
Student Member, IEEE,
RICHARD B. KIEBURTZ
Member, IEEE
DAVID R. SMITH
Member, IEEE †

5-5-1 ABSTRACT

The advent of the microprocessor to replace special purpose digital hardware in process control applications can result in greatly reduced hardware costs. However, in taking advantage of the modularity and reliability of program-

* © 1975 IEEE. Reprinted with permission from IEEE Transactions on Industrial Electronics and Control Instrumentation, Vol. IECI-22, No. 3, Aug. 1975, pp. 283–289.

† The research described in this paper was partially supported by the National Science Foundation under Grant J042203.

The authors are with the Department of Computer Science, State University of New York at Stony Brook, N.Y. 11794.

mable microprocessor chips, much of the burden of tailoring a control device to its application falls on the software. Because of the relatively primitive instruction set of the typical microprocessor, the cost and difficulty of software development can be troublesome if programming is done in machine language or with an assembler. These reasons provided motivation for the design of a higher level language for microprocessors.

In process control applications, microprocessors must exhibit capabilities including: 1) real time response; 2) flexible input-output; 3) multitasking. Taken in combination, these requirements often lead to complex programming problems. A high-level programming language, making special provision to implement these capabilities, offers a considerable advantage in rendering the problems manageable.

This processing capability centers around a task structure specifying task priorities and response times, and providing synchronization primitives to control task interaction. In addition, to remove the burden of complex input-output programming, the language provides a standard input-output interface. A user is only required to specify the data format and latency of the peripheral device. In a microcomputer system, no error recovery mechanism oversees the software execution; therefore, it is necessary to ensure absolute software reliability. A programming language tailored to process control applications is a powerful tool to use in achieving reliable software.

We have developed a language design to satisfy the above requirements, and test programmed some typical data acquisition problems. Implementation is now proceeding.

5-5-2 MOTIVATION AND DESIGN GOALS

The microprocessor has made possible the replacement of a large variety of special purpose hardware by modular programmable devices. This replacement has numerous incentives, a primary one being lower cost which can be attributed to a much smaller number of components and to component standardization. Increased versatility is also an important benefit. However, a great deal of the responsibility for an efficient and reliable system falls on the software designer.

In order to aid the software designer, it is imperative to understand the problems he faces and why a higher level language might be helpful in solving these problems. One of the foremost sources of difficulty usually associated with programming in a low-level language is that it does not provide much abstraction from the processor. This problem is more severe in programming a microprocessor because there is no operating system software to perform elementary program functions. With the use of a higher level language for programming complex applications, a substantial savings in cost may be realized since software development time can be expected to be drastically reduced. Many applications call for real-time processing capability and connected with this is the ability to multitask the processor. Many applications can be divided into tasks which may run concurrently or in arbitary sequences. Without a multitasking ability, the complexity of outside world problems is difficult to accommodate, and flexibility is limited. To add utility to multitasking capability, the programming language must provide mechanisms for specifying task interaction and synchronization. Also, the user should be given a capability to interface his task structure to an external environment to meet real time constraints.

The problems of input–output are formidable in several aspects. First, input–output is, in almost all microprocessor architectures, totally processor driven. Input–output transactions can easily tie up the processor. Secondly, the input–output instructions are primitive and the necessity of data conversion and handling multiple word lengths can be a cumbersome additional burden. Lastly, the input–output protocol must adapt to the device with which the processor is communicating, resulting in increased complexity in input–output programming. Such problems can be approached through the use of the interrupt. However, this sometimes provides a dangerous and inefficient solution. The main problems of an interrupt responding processor are due to the unpredictability of when an interrupt will occur. This unpredictability means that the entire state of the computation, that is, registers, accumulator, condition flags, program counter, and stack pointer must be saved. Secondly, problems arise when interrupts occur during the processing of a previous interrupt, and in a microprocessor system these problems are not easily or completely solvable. In addition, these problems are magnified in a real time system or any other configuration where interrupts are common or response time is critical. Hence, restricting the use of the interrupt mechanism can greatly enhance the reliability of the software and hence the system.

Software reliability is a stringent requirement in many microprocessor applications. When the processor is not a part of a general purpose computer system, there may be no easy way for a user to distinguish between software and hardware failure, and no way to recover, other than a cold restart. Therefore, it is important that an applications programming language should support program verification. This has led to the exclusion of pointer variables, recursion, variable sized data structures, and unrestricted control transfer from TOMAL.

In summary, a real-time higher level programming language for microprocessors would be very useful. This language should exhibit a wide range of capabilities among which are: 1) A multitasking ability with a synchronization mechanism; 2) A flexible high-level input–output scheme; 3) Restriction of interrupt usage; 4) A data and control structure giving a high level of abstraction; 5) A method of program verification; 6) Efficiency.

5-5-3 THE TASK STRUCTURE

The basic control element in our programming system is the task. A task is a module of declarations and sequentially executable statements to perform a single limited function. The task organization of a particular program is defined by the applications programmer to reflect the nature of the problem and the microprocessor environment.

The declaration of a task includes a task name and a number of attributes such as priority, response time, a semaphore for use in synchronizations and external request information. The priority of a task is a positive integer with one signifying the highest priority. Priority specifies a relative ordering among the tasks which is a factor in determining which task will be executed by the processor at any given time. Response time is also an important task characteristic which has a real number value with a time scale, microseconds, milliseconds, ... hours. The response time is an upper bound on the length of time that a task, once requested, may have to wait to become active. Priority and response time are determined by the constraints of the application.

Within each program, a task control monitor (TCM) is constructed and inserted into the program by the compiler to control the execution of tasks within the program. The TCM determines at any given time which task should be given control of the processor. The task control monitor itself obtains control of the processor periodically, by means of interleaving segments of the user's task with calls to the TCM. This technique, called codestripping, insures that the TCM can obtain control of the processor within a finite and bounded time limit. Each time the TCM obtains control, it determines which task is to be passed control next, in order to satisfy priority and response time requirements. This method has several effects:

1) It avoids the use of the interrupt.
2) It has easily controllable lengths between calls, that is, the length of the codestrip.
3) A compiler can place codestrips so that a maximum efficiency is obtained.

Avoiding the use of the interrupt also allows the system to implement noninterruptable operations. The length of codestrips, that is, the length of time it takes to execute the code between two successive calls to the TCM, is determined by the response time of the tasks. This response time gives an upper bound on how often the state of a task must be examined and hence an upper bound on the length of codestrips.

Functional responsibilities of the TCM are: 1) To monitor and keep track of the states of the tasks (requested, suspended, and so on); 2) To make scheduling decisions based on the states and status information including priority and response time; 3) To keep track of the synchronization activities of the tasks; 4) To handle I/O.

The database upon which the TCM operates in scheduling tasks is the system state vector. Each task must be in one of four possible states when control passes to the TCM:

1) requested—which indicates that a task has been requested to execute but execution has not yet begun on that task;
2) suspended—which indicates that a task was running, but its execution was temporarily delayed;
3) requested-suspended (R-S)—indicates that the task was running and was suspended and during a suspended state was requested again;
4) dormant—which indicates either that a task has terminated and has not been requested again at the current time or that the task was never requested.

Whenever the task control monitor is entered, the task that was running is suspended, but the knowledge of who was executing is known to the TCM. The following is the next state transition action for tasks.

Previous State Task	Action Affecting Task	Subsequent State of Task
dormant	request	requested
requested	request	requested
suspended	request	R-S
R-S	request	R-S
requested	termination	dormant
suspended	termination	dormant
R-S	termination	requested
suspended	suspension	suspended
R-S	suspension	R-S

The bookkeeping job of the TCM is relatively simple. When it receives control from an executing task, the completion status (termination or suspension) is passed, enabling the TCM to set appropriate bits in the task state vector. After updating the task state, the TCM then makes a new scheduling decision.

The scheduling policy of the task control monitor is basically to give processor control to the highest priority task ready for execution. The scheduling algorithm is indicated by the flow diagram of Figure 5-5-1. When a task whose state was suspended or requested-suspended is given control, the task is resumed at the point where it was last executing, otherwise, the task whose state was requested is started at its beginning.

Transition to and from the suspended or requested-suspended state is the most complicated case. A task which becomes suspended is either in the requested-suspended or suspended state. A task may become suspended through an action it specifies to the TCM or through an action the TCM decides

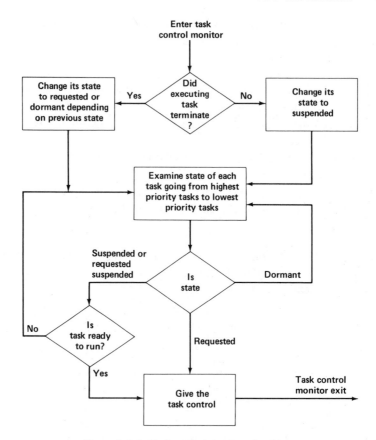

Figure 5-5-1 Task control monitor algorithm.

upon. The TCM suspends the task which was executing after every codestrip call, provided the task has not terminated. If no higher priority task which is ready for execution is found, then the task will be given processor control, otherwise, it will remain suspended while another higher priority task executes. If the originally executing task is not given control, then at some later time when it becomes the highest priority task ready for execution, it will resume execution. A task may also issue a request for service from the TCM, such as input–output or synchronization, which causes the TCM to suspend the task. These actions will be discussed at a later point as input–output and synchronization mechanisms.

To execute, a task must first be in the requested state, which can occur in two ways. First, the task may be specified to be initially requested. The second method is by execution of the scheduling instruction, *Request*. This instruction has format:

REQUEST(TASK1(PARAMETER LIST 1),
TASK2(PARAMETER LIST 2), $\cdots$).

Request specifies that the state of one or more tasks should be altered from dormant or suspended to requested or requested-suspended, respectively. The *Request* instruction may also optionally specify a parameter list for a task being requested if that task also has a parameter list. These parameters must match the parameters in the task declaration in number and data type. Parameters are passed by value, which means that the input variables of the task are initialized to the values of the parameters of the *Request* statement when it is executed. It is imperative to keep in mind that *Request* does not infer that a task is to be immediately executed but informs the TCM that sometime in the future the task whose state is now requested should begin execution. If a task in state requested or requested-suspended is again requested, the effect is to update the parameters to those appearing in the current request for the task.

Synchronization of tasks within a given microprocessor program is accomplished through the use of semaphores, testing of task states and the *Do when* instruction. A semaphore is a flag which in this system is associated with a specific task or tasks. These semaphores are declared as part of a task declaration and may be given a unique name, or may be bound to an existing task name. This allows a semaphore to be bound to one or more tasks.

There are three actions which occur on a semaphore. The first action is testing the state of the semaphores, *Free* or *Busy*. The second action permissible on a semaphore is a test and set operation, the *Acquire* operation. The *Acquire* operation takes as operands a list of one or more semaphores and has the form:

ACQUIRE (SEMAPHORE 1, SEMAPHORE 2, $\cdots$,
SEMAPHORE N).

The *Acquire* has the following effect: If the state of the semaphore is *Busy*, then return a false value for the *Acquire;* if the state of the semaphore is *Free*, then make the semaphore *Busy* and return a true value for the *Acquire*.

Thus, the *Acquire* is usually part of a logical expression since it returns a true or false value. The last action occurring on a semaphore is to free it. This action occurs automatically whenever all tasks to which a semaphore is bound have terminated. This guarantees that a semaphore which is *Busy* and has a task associated with it which is not in the dormant state will be released, that is made *Free*, at some time. Semaphores always have the initial value of *Free*.

In addition, if there is no semaphore using a given task name, then the task name may be tested with *Free* and *Busy*. A task is *Free* if it is dormant, and *Busy* otherwise.

Some synchronization can be accomplished with the iterative and conditional control structures provided in the language and operations on semaphores and states of tasks. Many typical synchronization problems must, however, be solved through the use of the *Do when* statement, if an efficient solution is desired. The *Do when* instruction provides for a usable time delay dependent on a logical condition. The form of the *Do when* instruction is:

DO WHEN (X)

where x is a logical expression. The semantics are that execution should be allowed to continue when x has the value true. Due to the constraint of efficient implementation, the components of the logical expression, x, are restricted to be either *Acquire* operations or comparisons to *Free*. This results in a general synchronization mechanism while permitting a highly effective implementation. Hence, the *Do when* statement can be used to detect the termination or current dormant state of a task and proceed with execution. Also, if there is a semaphore associated with the task, its state may be changed to *Busy*. The use of this construct will be further illustrated at a later point by example.

The wide variety of microprocessor applications led us to additionally allow the possible use of the interrupt mechanism, although in a highly structured manner. There were two important uses of the interrupt which led to the design of this mechanism. The first usage concerned the problem of the existence of a task which should be initiated from external sources. Under normal circumstances, the task structure supports a polling strategy. However, there were occasions where a task was requested in only rare circumstances and hence polling of an external register was not the best approach. One typical example of such a case is a task which handles rare exceptions such as an error mechanism. The other consideration was that many users may have clocks, of any type, available within the system. The clock is useful not only for scheduling within the task control monitor, but may also be a scheduling criteria for the user's tasks. Therefore, a structured interrupt handling mechanism was designed. The characteristics of this mechanism are:

1) An interrupt has a counter variable associated with it.
2) One counter may serve several interrupts; counters go from 0 to 255.
3) The interrupt handler may do one of three actions: a) increment the counter by one, b) decrement the counter by one, c) reset the counter to zero.
4) Alternatively, the interrupt handler can request a task.

This use of the interrupt in a structured and safe manner allows a variety of solutions to problems and versatility within the system while preserving the concept of the task structure and prohibiting undisciplined use of the interrupt.

A typical example of a microprocessor application[1] will now be con-

---

[1] We are indebted to Martin Rosenblum of the Brookhaven National Laboratory for the details of the application.

sidered to illustrate the use of the task structure. The example is a biomedical instrumentation application which involves device control, computation, and data output. The problem consists of controlling a scanner which moves an X-ray detector across a subject's arm or leg taking one hundred readings of X-ray intensity value. Data reduction involves computing the average of the $\log_2$ of the first sixteen points to calibrate background intensity, then to compute $\log_2$ of data point minus this average for the remaining eighty-four points. The average and eighty-four differences are to be output. In addition, to minimize memory requirements, the process will not use a vector but will execute on a point by point basis.

In illustrating the use of the task structure, the first decision which must be made is the number of tasks and their respective jobs. There are two devices in the bone scanner application, the X-ray scanner and the output device, which in this case will be a teletype. A task is dedicated to control each of these and a third task will be required to control the flow of execution between these two tasks and also to do the computation required. Hence, we have a program with three tasks.

Task Name	Task Job Description
1) Controller	Schedule the tasks reader and writer and do the arithmetic computation.
2) Reader	Read the next data point from the scanner.
3) Writer	Write one data point to the teletype.

First, consider the task characteristics of priority and response time. The main consideration for the setting of the response times is speed of the devices in the application. Both the scanner and the teletype are relatively slow having operations requiring about 100 milliseconds and ten milliseconds, respectively.

Since these two tasks serve only to drive the devices, the response times for reader and writer will be 100 and 10 ms. Since controller functions largely as a scheduler for these tasks and will always be active, it does not require a response time. The priorities are a more important characteristic in this application. First, since the writer task responds faster than the reader task, it will have the highest priority. The reader will have a higher priority than the controller. To make efficient use of the time during which the teletype and scanner are responding, computation should be available; the controller which does the arithmetic computation should have the lowest priority. In general, this scheme of giving the lowest priority to the computation bound task results in the most efficient execution if the I/O bound tasks have long device latency times. In this case, this priority setting together with the scheduling and synchronization scheme will provide a great deal of possible parallel execution making for efficient processor usage.

The scheduling of the tasks to be done by controller is fairly simple. First, the reader task is requested. Then computation is done. Then if the data point is the seventeenth to one hundredth, the writer task must be requested. The synchronization problem for these three tasks is slightly more complicated. Basically, there are two synchronization conditions. Reader and writer must complete the last execution before they are requested again. Second, there must always be exactly one data point available in any part of the computation. For example, reader cannot provide another data point until the computation is completed on the last one, nor may the computation proceed before reader has supplied the next point.

This application is implemented by allowing reader to use a single buffer variable to read into, while controller works on the previous point. Reader is requested before the loop begins to get one point in the system. Controller is initially requested to start the system and controller requests itself at its end to begin a new execution of the system.

This example appears fully coded in the Appendix.

5-5-4 THE DATA STRUCTURES, DEVICE SUPPORT, AND INPUT-OUTPUT

One of the primary motivations for providing a high-level language as a software development tool is to enable the programmer to use typed data structures and the operations provided with them. Suitable data structures support the capability to think about programs in terms of application-oriented concepts. Also of vital importance to the microprocessor programmer is a versatile method of external device description. Not only does this aid the programmer, it also makes possible the implementation of a general purpose I/O scheme allowing processor-I/O overlapping.

TOMAL provides a variety of data structures. The *integer* and *real* data types provide the ability to work with integer and floating-point numbers. Standard arithmetic and relational operators provide the necessary numeric capabilities required in microprocessor applications, while length specifications provide flexibility in integer size and floating-point precision. A *logical* data type is provided to formulate logical expressions used in program control statements. One-dimensional arrays of any of these types are allowed and are indexed by integers. There is also a type to represent character data. Other high-level data structures are provided to aid the programmer in composing correct programs.

Device declarations enable the programmer to communicate to the compiler the characteristics of his particular system configuration, enabling the compiler to generate suitable software device interfaces and I/O software. Information contained in a device declaration falls into three classes: the specific device connection address, information about control characteristics of the device, and the I/O formats.

The specific device connection is specified by the *Device* clause which has the form:

$$Device = \text{(list of integers)}$$

where the list of integers are the physical addresses by which to refer to an external device.

Control characteristics are given by the *Control* clause:

$$Control = \text{(list of control fields)}.$$

Control fields have two formats:

1) *status* (logical device expression);
2) *latency* (device name) $= x$ time scale.

The *status* field contains a logical device expression which is either a one-bit device or a device name followed by a relational operator followed by a constant. When the value of the expression is *true*, this indicates the device is ready. *Latency* is the time interval, x, between the last I/O operation to device name and the time when the processor may begin polling the status line of this device. If *status* is not declared, then after the latency interval the device should always be ready. If the device name is the same as the device being declared, the device name may be omitted.

The input–output formats are specified by the *input* or *output* clause of a device declaration:

Input (list of input data types or codes);
Output (list of output data types or codes).

The valid data types and codes specify how much information is to be input or output in a single I/O operation, and the form of the data. The possible data types and codes are:

1) *Logical*—single bit; $0 = $ *false*, $1 = $ *true*.
2) *Binary* (n)—n bits of uninterpreted binary data.
3) *Integer* (n)—an n bit integer including sign.
4) *Real* $(n.m$ optional scale factor): n—number of predecimal point bits including sign; m—number of post-decimal point bits; optional scale factor —if used has format $E(n1,n2):n1$—base of the exponent, $n2$—number of bits in dataword for exponent including sign.

5) BCD (*n*).

6) EBCDIC (*n*).

7) ASCII (*n*) (*n* bits of data in specific character codes 5–7).

8) *Null* (*n*)—the next *n* bits in the input–output word are not used.

Using these types the format of the input–output can be clearly and completely specified and any packing or unpacking of data which must be done can be indicated.

The device declaration has the form: *Declare* list of device names, list of device control, and input–output clauses · · · .

The system also supports the use of a special device, *clock*. This allows the integration of a clock into the system and is declared with an additional clause to specify its units. The system will support a real-time clock, external register count clock, or an interrupt clock through the use of the device declaration, the special units clause, and in the last case, the structured interrupt mechanism. However, a clock is not obligatory.

The highly descriptive device declarations allow the implementation of simple general input–output operations. The form of these instructions is: *Input* (device name, list of variables to be input into); *Output* (device name, list of expressions whose values are to be output).

Specifying latency of a device also informs the system that the task control monitor may schedule other tasks to run during the latent period following an I/O transaction to that device. This enables more efficient use of the processor since a great deal of idle time may be available between successive I/O operations.

The bone scanner application does not require sophisticated data structures but it makes good use of the device capabilities and I/O processor parallelism. The variables required in the program can be broken into two groups: global, those available for access by any task; and local, those available only to the task in which they are declared. The bone scanner requires the following data structures:

Variable Name	Type	Group	Use
Buffer	*integer*(16)	global	temporary input buffer
Data_pt	*integer*(16)	local, Controller	storage of an input point during computation
Sum	*real*(16)	local, Controller	running sum of data values
Value_computed	*real*(16)	local, Controller	holds result of a computation
Count	*integer*(8)	local, Controller	the number of points processed so far
Output_data	*real*(16)	local, Writer	an output buffer

There are two devices used in the bone scanner. The teletype, which has a ready line, has the following characteristics:

Description	Declaration of	Explanation
device name	Tty	the teletype
physical address	*device* = (1)	
control fields	*status* = (Tty_ready)	ready line
	latency = 10 *ms*	latency of the teletype
output format	*output* = (*ascii*(8))	ASCII teletype
device name	Tty_ready	ready line of teletype
physical address	*device* = (5)	
input format	*input* = (*null*(7), *logical*)	*true* if teletype is ready

The scanner is a little more complex as it has a sixteen bit input on two device numbers. Two control bits for the scanner are on another device, Scanner_control. They are for resetting and stepping the scanner to the next data point. Therefore, for Scanner and Scanner_control, the declarations are:

Description	Declaration of	Explanation
device name	Scanner	
physical address	*device* = (2,3)	data part of the scanning X-ray detector specifies two registers
control fields	*latency*(Scanner_control) = 100 *ms*	latent time from last I/O to Scanner_control
	status = (Scanner m = 0)	scanner ready condition
input format	*input* = (*integer*(16))	
device name	Scanner_control	the scanner control line
physical address	*device* = (4)	
output format	*output* = (*null*(6), *logical,logical*)	a two-bit control word to order positional reset or stepping of the scanning detector

5-5-5 STATEMENTS

TOMAL is a statement-oriented programming language. In addition to the task-scheduling (*request*) and synchronization (*do when*) statements and the input-output statements previously discussed, there is an assignment statement, procedure statement, and control statements.

Assignment has the syntax

VARIABLE : = EXPRESSION

or

(VARIABLE, VARIABLE, · · · , VARIABLE) : = EXPRESSION.

The symbol : = is used as the assignment operator to avoid syntactic confusion with the equality operator, = . In the second form, assignment to a parenthesized list of variables denotes simultaneous multiple assignment which is introduced for two reasons. It allows multiple values to be returned by a procedure without the need to pass variables through an argument list, and it allows a programmer to avoid unnecessary specification of temporary variables, as for instance, when values held by two program variables are to be interchanged.

The control structure of TOMAL is designed to facilitate the composition of well-structured programs. Control flow is specified by means of compound, conditional, iteration, and exit classes. A compound statement, or *do* group, consisting of a list of statements bracketed by *do;* · · · *end;* is treated as a single statement for control purposes. The enclosed statement list is executed sequentially. Direct transfer of control into the middle of a compound statement is not possible in TOMAL.

Conditional *if* and *case* clauses provide the capability to program alternative execution sequences. Iteration statements have the form *do* iteration clause; statement list *end;*. The iteration clauses are:

1) *do while* expression: In which execution of a following statement list is repeated until controlling logical-valued expression evaluates to *false*. If the expression evaluates to *false* upon the first try, the statement list will be bypassed.

2) *do for* variable : = expression *to* expression *by* expression: The semantics are similar to those of the *for* clause in PL/1 or ALGOL, except that the loop control expressions are evaluated only once, upon entry into the *for* clause, and these control values are stored for subsequent reference. Assignment to a loop control variable within the controlled statement list is prohibited. This injunction is enforced by the compiler.

3) *do repeat:* This clause calls for unlimited repetition of execution of a following statement list. Execution of a *repeat* loop is normally terminated by an exit statement.

There are two exit statements:

1) *return* causes a normal return from a procedure call. The keyword *return* may be followed by an expression whose value is to be returned, if the procedure is typed.

2) *break* causes an exit from a *do* group, transferring control to the statement immediately following the compound statement in which it is enclosed. If the keyword *break* is followed by a label name, exit will be from an enclosing compound group having the same label name following the *end*.

TOMAL provides three classes of procedures which have many common features but have a variety of capabilities. The general form of a procedure call is:

Procedure identifier (list of expressions);

where the list of expressions is the actual parameter list.

A procedure which does not return values is called a *proper* procedure. A proper procedure is a named program segment that may accept parameters, and may perform a transformation on global data. A procedure which returns a scalar value, but which has no side effects (does not modify values of global variables) is a *function* procedure. A function procedure may be used in an expression of its declared type. A procedure which returns a vector of values is called an *assignable* procedure. An assignable procedure may have its returned value assigned within a multiple assignment statement, but it may not appear as a component of an expression containing operators. A return from any procedure always transfers control to the instruction following the procedure call in the program text.

5-5-6 CONCLUSIONS

We have reported on TOMAL a new, high-level programming language designed to create software for microprocessor applications. Although TOMAL is a general purpose programming language, it includes special capabilities for multitasking, for meeting real time response requirements, and for specifying external world interfaces. A TOMAL compilation will also generate a task-control monitor program which performs task scheduling, and message-oriented I/O operations.

A TOMAL implementation is currently in progress. The initial implementation will be a cross compiler which runs on an IBM 370 and generates code for the INTEL 8080. Code generators for other commercially available microprocessors are planned. The compiler will include object code optimization and is expected to produce code which is comparable in run-time efficiency to hand coded programs.

5-5-7 APPENDIX

```
/* A TOMAL PROGRAM FOR CONTROL AND DATA ACQUISITION
   FROM A SCANNING X-RAY DETECTOR.*/
/* DEVICE DECLARATIONS*/
DECLARE TTY DEVICE = (1), CONTROL = (LATENCY = 10 MS,
            STATUS = (TTY_READY)), OUTPUT = (ASCII (8)),
            TTY_READY DEVICE = (5), INPUT = (NULL (7), LOGICAL),
            SCANNER DEVICE = (2,3), CONTROL = (STATUS =
            (SCANNER_ = 0), LATENCY (SCANNER_CONTROL) =
            100 MS), INPUT = (INTEGER (16)),
            SCANNER_CONTROL DEVICE = (4), OUTPUT = (NULL (6),
            LOGICAL, LOGICAL);
/* GLOBAL VARIABLE DECLARATION*/
DECLARE BUFFER INTEGER (16);
/* THE CONTROLLER TASK*/
CONTROLLER : TASK PRIORITY = 3;
  /* LOCAL VARIABLE DECLARATIONS*/
  DECLARE DATA_PT INTEGER (16),
            VALUE_COMPUTED REAL (16),
            SUM REAL (16),
            COUNT INTEGER (8);
  /* RESET SCANNER AND INITIALIZE BY ASKING FOR FIRST DATA
     POINT*/
  OUTPUT (SCANNER_CONTROL,TRUE,FALSE);
  IF ACQUIRE (READER) THEN REQUEST (READER);
  DO FOR COUNT := 1 TO 100;
    /* MAKE SURE READER HAS FINISHED */
    DO WHEN ACQUIRE (READER);
      DATA_PT := BUFFER;
      /* REQUEST NEXT DATA POINT */
      REQUEST (READER);
    END;
    /* DO THE NECESSARY COMPUTATION */
    IF COUNT = 16 THEN DO;
      SUM := SUM + LOG2 (DATA_PT);
      IF COUNT > = 16 THEN DO;
        SUM := SUM/16;
        VALUE_COMPUTED := SUM;
      END; /* OF COUNT = 16 */
    END; /* OF COUNT < = 16 */
    ELSE /* COUNT > 16 */
      /* SUBTRACT BACKGROUND INTENSITY */
      VALUE_COMPUTED := LOG2 (DATA_PT) − SUM;
    IF COUNT > = 16 THEN */ THERE IS OUTPUT TO BE DONE
    SO MAKE SURE WRITER HAS FINISHED */
    DO WHEN ACQUIRE (WRITER);
      REQUEST (WRITER (VALUE_COMPUTED));
    END; /* OF DO WHEN AND IF */
```

```
        END; /* OF 100 POINT LOOP */
        /* RESTART THE SYSTEM */
        SUM := 0;
        REQUEST (CONTROLLER);
    END CONTROLLER;
    /* READER TASK */
    READER : TASK PRIORITY = 2, RESPONSE = 100 MS, SEMAPHORE;
        /* INPUT ONE POINT */
        INPUT (SCANNER,BUFFER);
        /* STEP SCANNER TO GET NEXT POINT */
        OUTPUT (SCANNER_CONTROL,FALSE,TRUE);
    END READER;
    /* WRITER TASK */
    WRITER : TASK
        (OUTPUT_DATA) PRIORITY = 1, RESPONSE = 10 MS, SEMAPHORE;
        DECLARE OUTPUT_DATA REAL (16);
        OUTPUT (TTY,13,10); /* CARRIAGE RETURN, LINE FEED */
        OUTPUT (TTY,OUTPUT_DATA);
    END WRITER;
    /* SPECIFY TASK INITIALLY REQUESTED */
    REQUEST = (CONTROLLER).
```

CONCLUSIONS

Because this book is a collection of diverse papers by different authors, and because real-time software is still evolving, it is somewhat difficult to extract a common thread of conclusions.

In light of this, it is not an easy task to present a summary of this book. Yet it is essential that some attempt be made to tie up any loose ends if the material you have just read is to be of benefit to you. This is that attempt.

I will try to provide a set of conclusions that I would draw after applying my own experience to the information presented in this book. Therefore these conclusions are deeply subjective. You, the reader, are encouraged to develop your own.

1. Real-time software is influencing more and more everyday processes.
2. Efficiency is essential to real-time software.
3. Real-time applications are amazingly diverse.
4. Real-time methodologies are (almost as surprisingly) common.
5. The creation of real-time software, due to the constraints placed on it, is complex and may require incremental redesign or even throwaway prototypes.
6. Theory and practice are far apart in real-time software, and the attempts to bridge that gap are few but notable.
7. Requirements definition may well be the hardest real-time software problem. It is certainly the most important.
8. The interrelationship of real-time languages and real-time executives is still being explored.
9. High-order language, in spite of its (hard-to-measure) efficiency penalty, is probably preferable to assembler for real-time software. In addition to its obvious benefits, it facilitates checkout and redesign for increased efficiency where needed. After-the-fact assembler may later supplement it for efficiency.
10. Fault tolerance and/or independent verification and validation techniques may be necessary in supercritical systems.

11. The evolution to microcomputers is slow, so far, but undoubtedly sure.

12. The evolution to multiprocessing is equally slow, and less sure.

13. Source debugging techniques for the real-timer are gradually being made available.

14. Many problems remain in real-time executives. Interrupts, race conditions, data locks, and the evolution from cyclic to Ada-like scheduling are just a few.

15. Languages are not the ultimate solution to real-time software problems.

16. Real-time software is still an *engineering* activity, with all the inexactness and dogged determination that that implies.

There you are. How far apart are your conclusions from mine?

BIBLIOGRAPHY

The papers in this book were, in general, first published elsewhere. The citation for each is given on the first page of each paper.

A list of articles and books suggested for supplementary reading follows.

7-1 REQUIREMENTS

"The Evolution of Specification Techniques," Proceedings of the 1977 Annual Conference, Association for Computing Machinery; Wasserman.

Outlines the goals and trends in specification techniques. Identifies reliability and customer communication breakdown as the driving factors.

IEEE Transactions on Software Engineering, January, 1977.

Contains a collection of papers on requirements analysis. Covered concepts include SofTech's Structured Analysis and Design Technique (SADT), as described by Ross; the University of Michigan's Problem Statement Language–Problem Statement Analyzer (PSL/PSA), by Teichroew and Hershey; TRW's Requirements Standards Language and Requirements Engineering and Validation System (RSL/REVS), by Bell, Bixler, and Dyer; and others.

7-2 DESIGN

"Comparing Software Design Methodologies," Datamation, November 1977; Peters and Tripp.

Presents and analyzes five different design approaches. Evaluates the approaches based on trial usage. Concludes that no single approach is valid for all problems, and that "designers produce designs, methods do not."

Reliable Software Through Composite Design, Petrocelli/Charter, 1975; Myers.

Defines a design methodology and emphasizes its use in the creation of reliable software.

"Software Design Representation Schemes," Proceedings of the Symposium on Computer Software Engineering, 1976; Peters and Tripp.

Surveys contemporary design representations. Distinguishes between global (top level) and local (detail) representations. Analyzes possible future directions.

7-3 IMPLEMENTATION

Modern Programming Practices, Prentice-Hall, 1982; Glass.

Presents "modern" methodologies used in six industrial companies—Boeing Computer Services, Computer Sciences Corp., Martin-Marietta, Sperry-Univac, System Development Corp., TRW—in each company's own words.

ACM Computing Surveys, December 1976, is a special issue on fault-tolerant software. It contains these articles:

1. "Fault-Tolerant Operating Systems"; Denning.

   Stresses error confinement, and defines error confinement principles. Uses operating system methodology to illustrate the concepts. Discusses principles that should be used in operating system design and implementation.

2. "Fault-Tolerant Software for Real-Time Applications"; Hecht.

   Cites the need for software fault-tolerance methodologies in the real-time environment to match hardware fault tolerance. Stresses detection, recovery, and backup techniques. Shows examples in skeleton routines. Economics are discussed.

3. "Operating System Structures to Support Security and Reliable Software"; Linden.

   Focuses on security and its reliability implications, and the use of error confinement by small protection domains and extended-type objects (entities with a unique set of operations that can be performed on them). Access control on these objects is stressed. "The ideas discussed . . . involve a substantial amount of discontinuity with the past."

7-4 CHECKOUT

Software Reliability Principles and Practices, Wiley-Interscience, 1976; Myers.

Defines principles and practices that will lead to more reliable software; stresses testing and design.

The Art of Software Testing, Wiley-Interscience, 1979; Myers.

Focuses on proper testing methodology.

Software Reliability Guidebook, Prentice-Hall, 1979; Glass.

A "how-to" book on constructing more reliable software.

7-5 MANAGEMENT

The Mythical Man-Month, Addison-Wesley, 1975; Brooks.

A treasury of insights into software management, drawn from practical experience on the implementation of OS/360.

7-6 MAINTENANCE

Software Maintenance Guidebook, Prentice-Hall, 1981; Glass.

   A "how-to" book on constructing more maintainable software and on doing a better job of keeping it operating to the user's satisfaction.

INDEX